Yesterday There Was Glory

Yesterday There Was Glory

With the 4th Division, A.E.F., in World War I

By Gerald Andrew Howell
Edited by Jeffrey L. Patrick

Number 11 in the North Texas Military
Biography and Memoir Series

University of North Texas Press
Denton, Texas

10 9 8 7 6 5 4 3 2 1

Permissions:
University of North Texas Press
1155 Union Circle #311336
Denton, TX 76203-5017

The paper used in this book meets the minimum requirements of the American National Standard for Permanence of Paper for Printed Library Materials, z39.48.1984. Binding materials have been chosen for durability.

Library of Congress Cataloging-in-Publication Data
Howell, Gerald Andrew, 1889–1947.
Yesterday there was glory : with the 4th Division, A.E.F., in World War I / by Gerald Andrew Howell ; edited by Jeffrey L. Patrick.
pages cm.
Includes bibliographical references and index.
ISBN-13 978-1-57441-693-0 (cloth : alk. paper)
ISBN-13 978-1-57441-704-3 (ebook)
1. LCSH: Howell, Gerald Andrew, 1889–1947. 2. World War, 1914–1918—Personal narratives, American. 3. United States. Army. Division, 4th—History. 4. World War, 1914–1918—Regimental histories—United States. 5. World War, 1914–1918–Campaigns—Western Front. I. Title.

D570.33 4th .H69 2017
DDC 940.4/1273–dc23
2017020149

Yesterday There Was Glory: With the 4th Division, A.E.F., in World War I is Number 11 in the North Texas Military Biography and Memoir Series.

The electronic edition of this book was made possible by the support of the Vick Family Foundation. Typeset by vPrompt eServices.

Contents

List of Illustrations

Acknowledgments

First and foremost, my thanks to editor Ronald Chrisman of the University of North Texas Press for his support and encouragement throughout this project. Thanks are also due to World War I historian Mitchell Yockelson, who offered valuable suggestions and directed me to the records of the 39th Infantry in the National Archives.

Tom Burns of the Tompkins County Public Library generously located the one known photograph of young Gerald Howell and other important information relating to Howell's time in Ithaca.

Researchers Peggy Ann Brown, Lori Berdak Miller and Mike Constandy all did a superb job of finding and copying relevant information and photographs at the National Archives and National Personnel Records Center.

Finally, I'm grateful to my wife Tammy and children Joseph and Rebecca for understanding my need to fulfill an old soldier's wish to see his memories of the "Great War" appear in print.

Introduction

In October 1946, World War I combat veteran Gerald Howell submitted a manuscript entitled "Yesterday There Was Glory: Adventures & War Exploits of the First U.S. Troops on the Rhine, 1918" to the Barthold Fles Literary Agency in New York City to be considered for their "Rewrite Magazine Prize Book Award." Howell described his work as "an historical record that will become more valuable as the years pass by," of interest to the "general reader of history, biography, etc., written in a popular vein" and not "a dry regimental history."

Howell emphasized that his narrative was historically correct, as he had spent nearly a decade collecting and verifying its facts. Its chief interest for the general reader, he argued, "lies in the escapades of a squad of soldiers . . . speaking their own language, while you live with them moments of horror, tragedy, humor, amour, [and] promiscuity," while upholding the "traditional glory of U.S. Arms on foreign soil." This was "the old Army as it used to be." Howell even pointed out several "episodes" in the work that could be connected and turned into a film script.

Sadly, although Howell approached several other publishers as well, none showed an interest in his manuscript. In the aftermath of an even greater war, no one seemed to care about the long-past struggle of doughboys in France. Less than fifteen months after his project was rejected, Howell was dead from natural causes. Fortunately for historians, although he threatened to consign his manuscript "permanently to the ash barrel," Howell's saga of a company of hard-fighting and hard-living American infantrymen survived, waiting to be discovered for the centennial of the nation's entry into the war in Europe.[1]

"Yesterday There Was Glory" was certainly not a dry regimental history, but, as Howell explained, "a mixture of memoir and historical fact." His narrative was a study of a small group of American soldiers attempting to survive some of the most ferocious combat of the "Great War." He included information on the movements and activities of his 39th Infantry Regiment and the 4th Division, but Howell kept the focus of the story on his squad, a typical cross section of the A.E.F., of different nationalities and with varied backgrounds and occupations, including an Italian, a Jew, and a Midwesterner.

Apart from possible monetary gain, Howell, a self-described "'buck private in the rear rank,'" had a particular agenda in mind when he expended so much time and energy on "Yesterday There Was Glory." As he explained in his introduction, "most of the generals and pseudo captains" had written memoirs "telling us how they won the war by making themselves comfortable in ancient chateaus," and "attending dinner parties, riding . . . in high priced limousines, playing polo, inspecting recruits and ordering out military bands to salute them whenever they appeared in public and otherwise catering to their egos." Now was the time, Howell believed, "to take up the subject of the down-trodden doughboy."

1. In addition to *Rewrite*, Howell also submitted his manuscript to New York's John Day Company and Harper & Brothers, along with Houghton Mifflin Company in Boston. In his letter to the latter publisher, Howell explained that veterans of World War II would be interested in his book "because it parallels their experience before most of them were born," and since books about the 4th Division in World War II were likely to appear soon, Howell's book about the division in World War I would "make the final picture complete." He believed that his book would return the publisher's investment with "at least a reasonable profit (not spectacular)," and since Houghton Mifflin was "still fighting the U.S. Civil War," they should consider a World War I title as well. A copy of Howell's manuscript and his correspondence with potential publishers were purchased by the editor on an internet auction site in 2014.

Howell clearly wanted to write a gritty, unpretentious and honest account of men at war, similar to Thomas Boyd's *Through the Wheat*, published in 1923, and Hervey Allen's 1926 novel *Toward the Flame*. He wanted his readers to appreciate the difficult conditions experienced by ordinary doughboys at the front. "Shelling from the sides and even the rear. No shelter at night. Wet, dripping trees, gas burns and cooties. No warm food of any kind," he recalled. "The staccato of machine guns echoing through dark ravines and the acrid odor of chlorine and high explosive shell bursts floating on the air. It was a continuous performance, night and day. No rest, no sleep, no warm food, no shelter. Just holding on with our teeth." "At intervals between the attacks the men would lay in their wet holes and pray for relief," he continued. "But no relief came." He did not shrink from including graphic descriptions of the horrors of the battlefield: "Men with arms and legs missing, headless bodies, carcasses of dead horses, stench. . . hairy arms with hands only attached, in a death grip on a rifle, odd little pieces of brains. It was a sickening sight." He also did not spare his readers when describing how men died in battle: "Suddenly a shell would explode in front of them and they would drop and curl up like little brown earthworms, or fall like a bag of chaff. Some would squirm a little and that was the end."

Howell wished to expose readers to far more than the sights and sounds of the battlefield, however. He also wanted them to know that the American Expeditionary Forces was populated by a diverse collection of enlisted heroes, determined professional warriors, shirkers, braggarts, "chiselers" and "goldbricks." They were largely led by talented and conscientious officers, with a few of the pretentious and unskilled "Sears and Roebuck" type who "had a lot to learn—things that are never taught in training camps."

At times, Howell and his fellow soldiers exhibited all the characteristics of both "professional" and "citizen" soldiers. The young men of his squad were equally capable of longing for "a small injury of some kind, so as to be sent back to a hospital for a long rest and thus escape the incessant proximity of war," and capturing German machine-gun nests in vicious hand-to-hand combat. They were quite willing to poke fun at their fellow squad members and criticize their backgrounds and behavior, but at the same time were willing to share their last can of corned "willie" or, if necessary, give their lives for each other. They could endure a difficult march, pursue the "fräuleins" or "mademoiselles" they encountered, or participate in a "laydown strike" when they felt that they were being mistreated by their officers. They were as "ribald as any soldiery in any army," Howell admitted, but "underneath this veneer, they were really patriotic, steadfast and sincere."

For those interested in the social history of the American Army of this period, Howell endeavored to preserve the flavor of life in an infantry squad in the A.E.F. He reconstructed conversations and banter in typical soldier language (and in the accents and dialects he remembered), including the uncensored doughboy profanity so often heard but seldom recorded, and preserved details of how soldiers existed and survived behind and on the front lines.

Howell abhorred "stupid, insensate" war and the tragic loss of life he witnessed, particularly since he was forced to watch millions of fellow Americans return to Europe to give battle to the German Army again in 1941. Nevertheless, he confessed that war did possess some redeeming aspects. He clearly enjoyed the camaraderie fostered by his wartime experience. As has been the case throughout history, the soldiers of General Pershing's army acquired a unique bond. Howell was clearly not a member of the fabled "Lost Generation" of the World War I. He did not see himself as a bitter, disillusioned, shell-shocked veteran who had sacrificed much for a pointless cause. Howell was proud of the part played by his squad, the 39th Infantry and the 4th Division in the defeat of Imperial Germany. The 4th Division suffered appalling losses during the war, but performed magnificently in several key operations that contributed to Allied victory. "I am proud to have been a soldier in wartime. It was exciting, even with the hardships," he concluded, for they had stopped "the four long years of hell and carnage by sacrificing ourselves . . . in the cause of humanity." In the end, "the U.S. soldier did his duty nobly."

Every memoir is affected by the vagaries of memory. Howell obviously tried his best, however, to relate an accurate version of what he experienced in France. "Someone with a long, pointed nose may find gross inaccuracy due to misinformation and the meagre notes I made at the time," Howell admitted. "No one man could tell all as the show was too big. If this effort, therefore, chances to fall in other and more critical hands, I trust they will be tolerant."

Supply train of the 315th Field Artillery, 65th Brigade, 33rd Division, near Chattancourt, Meuse, France, making its way to the front with ammunition, the early morning fog is just lifting. September 26, 1918. U.S. Army Signal Corps Collection, National Archives, 34895 [383T8].

Now, nearly a century after Howell and his fellow soldiers boarded a troop transport to sail to Europe, his manuscript will help new generations understand what life was like for the doughboys who achieved victory "over there."

Gerald Andrew Howell

Gerald Andrew Howell remains something of an enigma. He was born on August 21, 1889, in Ithaca, New York, to James Philander and Harriet Jane Hazen Howell.[2] In the Ithaca city directory for 1907, he was listed as a student. In 1910, he was an assembler at a gun shop in Ithaca; in 1913, a gunsmith in Ithaca, and in 1915, an electrician in Ithaca.[3] By the time he registered for the draft

2. Tracy Elliot Hazen, *The Hazen Family in America* (New Haven, CT: The Tuttle, Morehouse & Taylor Company, 1947), 557.

3. Howell was likewise listed as a student in 1909. *Norton & Goodhue's Ithaca City Directory for 1909* (N.p.: M.P. Goodhue, 1909), 156; Thirteenth Census of the United States, 1910, City of Ithaca, Tompkins County, New York, Ward 3, E.D. 184, T624, Roll 1083,

in June 1917, Howell was working as an electrician in Waterbury, Connecticut, at the United Electric Light and Water Company.[4] On the morning of March 30, 1918, draftee Howell left his home at 23 Central Avenue in Waterbury and joined 107 other young men at Union Station to board a special train bound for Camp Devens, Massachusetts. With a Red Cross "comfort kit" in his hands and the song "Hanging the Kaiser to a Sour Apple Tree" ringing in his ears, Howell embarked on a sixteen-month odyssey that took him to France and back.[5] Following his discharge on August 6, 1919, as a private 1st class, Howell returned to Ithaca, New York, and worked as an electrician at the electrical company, living with his mother and sister. He moved to Rochester, New York, by 1921.[6]

By 1930 Howell was living alone in Rochester, employed as an engineer at a thermometer manufacturing company. In 1940, still alone in Rochester, he worked as a sales engineer in an electrical shop. By the time of his death, Howell was an inspector at an automobile equipment manufacturing business. He died in Rochester, New York, on January 2, 1948, at the age of fifty-eight, and was buried in the Howell family lot in the City Cemetery in Ithaca.[7]

National Archives and Records Administration; *Norton & Hanford's Ithaca City Directory for 1907* (N.p.: M.P. Goodhue, 1907), 174; *Norton & Goodhue's Ithaca City Directory for 1913–1914* (N.p.: M.P. Goodhue, 1913), 177; *Norton & Goodhue's Ithaca City Directory for 1915–1916* (N.p.: M.P. Goodhue, 1915), 174.

4. Ironically, Howell claimed "leak in breast" as a physical disability on his 1917 draft registration card, and claimed exemption from the draft due to the fact that his services at the electric company were necessary.

5. *The Waterbury* (CT) *Evening Democrat*, March 20, 28, 29, 30, 1918.

6. Nearly all of Howell's service record was destroyed in the 1973 fire at the National Personnel Records Center in St. Louis. Only his Veterans Administration index card and final payment voucher survive. Correspondence with Lori Berdak Miller, Redbird Research LLC, December 28, 2015; M.P. Goodhue, *Norton & Goodhue's Ithaca City Directory for 1919–20* (Ithaca, NY: Norton Printing Company, 1919), 163; Sampson & Murdock Co., *Rochester Directory* (Rochester, NY: Sampson & Murdock Co., Inc., 1921), 546; Fourteenth Census of the United States, 1920, City of Ithaca, Tompkins County, New York, Ward 3, E.D. 188, T625, Roll 1265, National Archives and Records Administration.

7. Fifteenth Census of the United States, 1930, City of Rochester, Monroe County, New York, Ward 6, E.D. 28–22, T626, Roll 1449, National Archives and Records Administration; Sixteenth Census of the United States, 1940, City of Rochester, Monroe County, New York, Ward 19, E.D. 65–285, T627, Roll 2850, National Archives and Records Administration. *The Ithaca* (NY) *Journal*, January 5, 1948; Death Certificate of Gerald A. Howell, Monroe County, New York, New York Department of Health.

Only known photograph of Gerald Andrew Howell, from the 1906 Ithaca High School yearbook (courtesy Tompkins County Public Library).

"Yesterday There Was Glory" may have been Howell's only book-length manuscript, but it was hardly his only creative effort. In 1912, he applied for a patent for a guard for hacksaws (subsequently approved in 1914), and received a copyright in 1919 for a "conundrum card" (a postcard printed on both sides).[8] In late 1921, he published "Ptoupaline, Cleopatra's Lucky Stone" in the *Sunday American*, and may have even written the music for the Otto Messmer song, "My Girl."[9]

8. United States Patent Office, Patent 1,100,305, accessed at http://patft.uspto.gov/netahtml/PTO/patimg.htm; United States Patent Office, *Annual Report of the Commissioner of Patents for the Year 1914* (Washington, D.C.: U.S. Government Printing Office, 1915), 279; Library of Congress, Copyright Office, *Catalog of Copyright Entries, Part 1, Group 2, 1919, New Series, Volume 16, No. 9* (Washington, D.C.: U.S. Government Printing Office, 1919), 1125.

9. Library of Congress, Copyright Office, *Catalogue of Copyright Entries, Part 1: Books, Group 2, New Series, Volume 18, Part 2* (Washington, D.C.: U.S. Government Printing Office, 1921), 1499; Library of Congress, Copyright Office, *Catalogue of Copyright Entries, Part 3: Musical Compositions, New Series, Volume 7, Part 1* (Washington, D.C.: U.S. Government Printing Office, 1912), 310.

The American Expeditionary Forces

The World War I officially began in late July 1914, when, in response to the murder of the heir to the Austrian throne by a Serbian nationalist, Austria-Hungary declared war on Serbia. The following month, other nations rushed to war in support of their respective allies, so that, in short order, Germany and Austria-Hungary were arrayed against France, Great Britain, Russia, Serbia, and Belgium.

Initially, most Americans wished to avoid participating in this European war. As the conflict intensified and German atrocities became more widespread, however, many Americans grew sympathetic to the Allied cause. In addition, American bankers provided massive loans to fund the Allied war effort, American factories and farms produced military supplies and foodstuffs to equip and feed their armies, and some Americans even volunteered for service in the ranks of the French and British forces.

Along with waging war in the trenches of the Western Front, the Germans launched an effective U-boat campaign on the high seas in February 1915. Believing that they could starve their enemies into submission, the Germans instituted unrestricted submarine warfare to sink merchant ships carrying supplies to the Allied nations. American outrage against this practice grew after the British passenger liner *Lusitania* was torpedoed three months later, killing 128 Americans. In response, the German government suspended their submarine campaign in April 1916. Nearly a year later, on February 1, 1917, the Germans reversed course and reinstituted their policy of attacking neutral ships. They gambled that they could force Britain and France to surrender long before the United States could declare war and enter the fighting in force.

In response to this German move, along with the discovery of an effort by German diplomats to draw Mexico into a war with the United States, President Woodrow Wilson appeared before a joint session of the U.S. Congress on April 2, 1917, to ask for a declaration of war against Germany. In his address, Wilson cited Germany's "warfare against mankind" and "war against all nations" and urged America "to exert all its power and employ all its resources to bring the Government of the German Empire to terms and end the war."

Two days later, the Senate voted in favor of war; the House did likewise on April 6.

Mobilizing, training, equipping, and transporting a force to fight in Europe proved to be a herculean task for the unprepared American army and navy. When war began, the Regular Army consisted of only about 137,000 men, with another 181,000 in the ranks of the National Guard. Nevertheless, thirty-two training camps were quickly established and filled with Regulars, National Guardsmen, volunteers, and draftees. Major General John J. Pershing, commander-in-chief of the American Expeditionary Forces, landed in France in mid-June to prepare for the arrival of a massive number of "doughboys" on the Western Front. By the end of 1917, nearly 200,000 Americans had been transported overseas. By the end of June 1918, nearly a million had arrived. By the time the fighting ended that November, more than two million Americans were in Europe. Most of the new soldiers of the American Expeditionary Forces spent the winter of 1917–18 manning quiet sections of the front line. The first major American battle and victory came when elements of the 1st Division seized the French village of Cantigny from the Germans on May 28, 1918.

Many more Americans were destined to play a critical role during the fighting in the summer of 1918. The day before Cantigny, the Germans launched an attack that broke through the French lines and drove to the Marne River, only about fifty miles from Paris. The 2nd and 3rd Divisions were placed at the disposal of the French and rushed to help stop the German attack. The U.S. Marines of the 2nd Division suffered heavy casualties driving the Germans from Belleau Wood. On July 15, when the Germans struck again, members of the 3rd Division earned the nickname "Rock of the Marne" for stubbornly holding the line near Château-Thierry. On July 18, the French launched the Aisne-Marne Campaign to eliminate the German salient in the line. Facing more than 270,000 doughboys (eight divisions attached to three French armies), the Germans carried out a gradual withdrawal from the salient, desperately defending each position before being forced to retreat. On August 6, the Allied offensive was halted at the Velse River. The Marne salient was eliminated, Paris was no longer threatened, and the American soldier had, according to General Pershing, delivered "a decisive blow" that dealt the Germans "a costly and disastrous defeat" and threw them "entirely to the defensive."[10]

A few weeks later, the First Army carried out the first American offensive operation under Pershing's independent command. The triangular German salient at St. Mihiel was the target of nine American and French divisions and a portion of a tenth in the main assault, with two divisions and part of a third in reserve. A combined force of more than 550,000 Americans and 110,000 French troops moved against the salient on September 12, and easily eliminated the German opposition by September 16. More than 200 square miles of French territory was liberated from German occupation in a campaign that cost 9,000 American casualties.

The Meuse-Argonne Offensive, a far more difficult operation and the largest American campaign of the war, began on September 26, 1918. Nine American divisions (five of which had seen service in "offensive combat" earlier in the war) assaulted German positions between the Meuse River and the Argonne Forest. Unlike the fighting at St. Mihiel, the Americans faced determined enemy troops emplaced in a series of excellent defensive lines. After furious and costly fighting, three spent divisions were replaced and the attack was renewed on October 4. The armistice on November 11 found the Americans overlooking Sedan, having driven the Germans back about thirty-five miles. More than 1.2 million soldiers, sailors, marines, and airmen participated in the forty-seven-day operation. The toll was enormous, with more than 26,000 dead and 95,000 wounded.

Despite significant internal limitations, external challenges, and heavy losses, the A.E.F. matured into a formidable and effective fighting force by the end of World War I. The doughboys who survived the bloodletting were justifiably proud of the fact that they had played an important role in defeating Imperial Germany, whether they fought through the Argonne Forest, moved supplies to the front lines, or maintained vital roads and bridges. Their commander, John Pershing, summed up their accomplishments this way: "With fortitude and perseverance he gave his every energy to the accomplishment of his task, whether it required him to charge the enemy's guns or play the less conspicuous role

10. John J. Pershing, *My Experiences in the World War*, 2 vols. (New York: Frederick A. Stokes Company, 1931), II: 211.

of forwarding supplies. In their devotion, their valor, and in the loyal fulfillment of their obligations, the officers and men of the American Expeditionary Forces have left a heritage of which those who follow may ever be proud."[11]

The 39th U.S. Infantry Regiment and the "Ivy" 4th Division

Officially organized at the State Fair Grounds in Syracuse, New York, on June 1, 1917, the 39th Infantry was an entirely new U.S. Regular Army regiment. The month before, Congress had authorized the recruitment of all Regular regiments in the U.S. Army to the maximum strength authorized by law. In order to do so, existing regiments were divided into three elements; one remained as the parent organization, while the other two became the nucleus of new regiments. In the case of the 39th, the existing 30th U.S. Infantry (a regiment that had seen service in the Philippine-American War and during the San Francisco earthquake) was divided, creating the 38th and 39th Infantry regiments.[12] Eager, raw recruits soon began to arrive in Syracuse, and rudimentary training began. Late that October, the new soldiers, about 1,300 men and fifty officers, left their comfortable barracks in Syracuse and moved to Camp Greene, near Charlotte, North Carolina.[13] Companies averaged only about sixty men, and some were without officers, but a small group of Regular Army non-commissioned officers formed "the real nucleus of the regiment."[14] At the end of the year, the

11. Pershing, *My Experiences in the World War*, II: 392–93.

12. The 39th U.S. Infantry was a cosmopolitan regiment. According to one undated document, of the 2,575 men in the unit, the greatest numbers were from Illinois (255), New York (188), Indiana (166), Michigan (160), and Pennsylvania (135), although representatives from all forty-eight states, the District of Columbia, the Regular Army, and Canada could be found in the regiment's ranks. Record Group 120, Records of the American Expeditionary Forces, World War I, Records of Combat Divisions 1917–1919, 4th Division, 4th Division Historical, Box 32, Folder: 39th Infantry, 4th Division, Consolidated Recapitulation Lists by States of Personnel of the 39th Infantry, Personnel, Historical Section, 204–65, National Archives and Records Administration, College Park, Maryland. Hereafter NARA.

13. *Charlotte* (NC) *Observer*, October 31, 1917.

14. Record Group 120, Records of the American Expeditionary Forces, World War I, Records of Combat Divisions 1917–1919, 4th Division, 4th Division Historical, Box 29, Folder: 39th Infantry, Histories, Commendations & Battle Participants, 4th Division, 204–11.4, Official History of the 39th Regiment of Infantry, 1917–1918, National Archives and Records Administration, College Park, Maryland. Hereafter cited as Record Group 120, 4th Division

regiment was assigned to the 7th Infantry Brigade of the new 4th Division. "Little did we realize then what an important part the Thirty-ninth Infantry was to play in the Great War," the regiment's historian recalled.[15]

The new members of the 39th, volunteers, draftees, and Regular Army veterans alike, faced challenges as soon as they arrived at Camp Greene. "Most of the men had gone south patting themselves on the back for their good fortune," wrote the 4th Division's historian, expecting warm sunshine and pleasant weather in the "Sunny South."[16] Instead, they found extreme cold, alternating rain and snow and abundant mud. In addition to the weather, the men had to contend with overcrowded pyramidal tents and green firewood for their stoves. The poor weather conditions and the need for men to cut and haul wood and work on nearly impassable roads severely curtailed outdoor training. A few practice marches and an occasional drill session were conducted, but mostly instructors did their best to teach the men in classrooms through "a heavy preponderance of tiresom [*sic*] lectures and pamphlet reading."[17]

Finally, in March 1918 the weather moderated, allowing the men to go outside to practice building field fortifications, throw hand grenades, drill with bayonets, and march on local roads. Even then the weather proved challenging. "We were out about a mile from the camp drilling when it began raining," reported Company C's John A. Barnwell on April 20, and "we waded water about shoemouth deep to get back to the camp. Then we had a job cleaning up our rifles to keep them from rusting."[18] Not every minute was devoted to training at Camp Greene, however. A vaudeville staged at the camp's Knights of Columbus Hall

---

Historical, Box 29, Folder: 39th Infantry, Histories, Commendations & Battle Participants, NARA.

15. Robert B. Cole and Barnard Eberlin, eds., *The History of the 39th U.S. Infantry During the World War* (New York: Press of J.D. McGuire, 1919), 12.

16. Christian A. Bach and Henry Noble Hall, *The Fourth Division: Its Services and Achievements in the World War* (Garden City, NY: Issued by the division, Country Life Press, 1920), 21.

17. Record Group 120, 4th Division Historical, Box 29, Folder: 39th Infantry, Histories, Commendations & Battle Participants, NARA.

18. John A. Barnwell to his sister, Camp Greene, Charlotte, North Carolina, April 20, 1918, World War I Service Questionnaires, U.S. Army Heritage and Education Center, Carlisle, Pennsylvania.

played to a packed house, and included clog dancing and singing by members of the 39th.[19]

Still understrength, the 39th Infantry received critical help in March 1918, when recruits from almost every National Army camp arrived for assignment to the regiment. With the inclusion of green soldiers such as Gerald Howell, men from every state in the nation filled the ranks of a truly national regiment. Further, "there was a new spirit of enthusiasm and energy in the training" with the arrival of Col. Frank C. Bolles, the regiment's new commanding officer, on April 9.[20]

In late April 1918, the enthusiastic doughboys left Camp Greene for Camp Mills, Long Island, New York, and soon boarded four troop transports for Europe. Two companies arrived at Bordeaux on May 18; Howell and the remainder of the regiment landed at Brest, France, on May 23.

The 39th moved to Calais, then to Samer, and on to Doudeauville on May 30, the regiment's training area. "The general state of apprehension in the Allied world" that the Germans would drive on Paris, and the likelihood that the regiment would be involved in stopping them, "keyed up the training," the author of the regiment's history recalled.[21] "We all feel the same way," soldier Kenneth C. Jarvis believed, "that the sooner we get at the Huns, the better we will like it."[22]

After only a few days of training with the British, the 39th moved closer to the front and were attached to the French 4th Division, Second Corps. Settling into the woods near Acy-en-Multien, about eighteen kilometers from Meaux, the Americans resumed intensive training. With no rifle range available, the men at first used "bully beef" and tomato cans as targets until a suitable range could be built. Nevertheless, the Americans "astonished" the French officers with their marksmanship, and their new allies "predicted great things of the regiment."[23] Officers and men went forward for

19. *History of the 7th Infantry Brigade During the World War, 1918* (Cologne, Germany: M. Dumont Schauberg, 1919), 6; *The Charlotte* (NC) *Observer*, January 14, 1918.

20. Record Group 120, 4th Division Historical, Box 29, Folder: 39th Infantry, Histories, Commendations & Battle Participants, NARA.

21. Cole and Eberlin, *The History of the 39th U.S. Infantry*, 19.

22. *Daily Kennebec Journal* (Augusta, ME), July 17, 1918.

23. Record Group 120, 4th Division Historical, Box 29, Folder: 39th Infantry, Histories, Commendations & Battle Participants, NARA.

short tours of the forward trenches with the French and members of the American Second Division. Periodic "alerts" required the doughboys to march twelve miles from their training area and take position in the French trenches near the front. Unlike other American units, however, the 39th was not assigned an extended tour of duty in a "quiet" section of the front line.

The men gradually became accustomed to life in the field. Eventually Sgt. William F. Krueger of Company B wrote home that he could "sleep [as well] on the ground with a few stumps and my rifle sticking me in the ribs, as I ever did in my bed at home."[24] A battalion of the regiment was even selected to participate in a Fourth of July military parade in Paris, where one participant thought that the 39th was "getting the same kind of name as the marines have," because of their performance, as every company marched in step, the men straight as a ruler, and in a perfect line.[25] It was "an impressive spectacle," according to one observer, and "not a drooping head or a heavy heart in Paris, only applause, cheering, gaiety."[26]

On the evening of July 15, the training and parades ended and the long awaited orders to move to the front finally arrived. Two nights later, the Americans completed the relief of two French regiments, taking over a 3,000-meter section of the front. Although the men were " 'keyed up' to a high pitch," extreme darkness and a blinding rain forced the Americans to hold on to each other as they stumbled slowly forward, struggling under heavy loads of packs, rations, and ammunition.[27] No sooner had the wet and tired troops settled in than orders arrived calling for an attack the next morning (July 18). The Allies planned a large counterattack that would eliminate a German salient in the line between Soissons and Reims and push the Germans back across the Vesle River.[28] The 39th, attached

24. *DuPage County* (IL) *Register*, August 16, 1918.

25. *The Alexandria* (IN) *Daily Times-Tribune*, August 20, 1918.

26. Record Group 120, 4th Division Historical, Box 29, Folder: 39th Infantry, Histories, Commendations & Battle Participants, NARA.

27. Henry Terrell, "The Attack of the 39th Infantry (U.S.) as part of the 33rd French Division South of Faverolles, July 18–19, 1918," The Infantry School, Advanced Officers' Course, 1923–1924, Maneuver Center of Excellence Libraries, Donovan Research Library, World War I Student Paper Collection, Fort Benning, Georgia, 6.

28. The Aisne-Marne Offensive is detailed in Edward G. Lengel's recent work, *Thunder and Flames: Americans in the Cruible of Combat, 1917–1918*, published in 2015 by the University of Kansas Press.

to the French 33rd Division, received the assignment of "mopping up" a forest known as the Buisson de Cresnes.

An early morning artillery barrage by an estimated seventy French batteries tested the nerves of the untried Americans. The "incessant whistling of the shells above their heads" was followed by a German counter-barrage "so severe that communication became difficult and several runners won citations for carrying messages."[29] Their next challenge before they could meet the enemy was the narrow but deep Savière River and an "immense bog" before it, but the undeterred doughboys either splashed across through mud and waist-deep water or walked over on fallen logs.[30] Fortunately for them, the Germans did not think that any force would be daring (or foolish) enough to cross the river, so the area was relatively lightly defended. By nightfall, Howell and the regiment's First Battalion had cleared their assigned portion of the dense forest and captured a number of Germans and several mortars and machine guns.[31]

The attack was resumed on the morning of July 19. At 4 a.m., the soldiers of the First Battalion left their foxholes in the Buisson de Cresnes and moved forward, making steady progress until they reached a wheat field that led to the crest of a ridge. The ground then fell away in a gradual slope, dotted with wooded thickets, to the village of Chouy. The Germans not only concealed machine guns in the wheat and thickets, but sited the area for their artillery. Initially halted by German machine gun and artillery fire, the Americans eventually silenced the machine guns and charged through cannon fire to enter the village late that afternoon. Relaxing that night, the

29. Record Group 120, 4th Division Historical, Box 29, Folder: 39th Infantry, Histories, Commendations & Battle Participants, NARA.

30. Terrell, "The Attack of the 39th Infantry (U.S.) as part of the 33rd French Division South of Faverolles, July 18–19, 1918," 13.

31. In two pages of handwritten notes, Captain Mathias W. Haney of the 39th recalled that his men crossed the river (which he incorrectly identified as the Ourcq) in a thin, single file line, at one point, over poles, although a few men waded. The stream had "lots of quick sand and soft mud," and "weeds up over your head." A German prisoner confirmed that their machine guns were positioned on the other side of the woods, as they thought the swampy ground would protect their flank. Later in the action, his men encountered a German machine gun nest positioned in a "little house" with "glass sides, sliding windows" in the top of a large oak tree. One of Haney's men shot the machine gunner out of the tree, who "fell like a man diving." Record Group 120, 4th Division Historical, Box 29, Folder: 39th Infantry, Histories, Commendations & Battle Participants, NARA.

men traded stories as "modesty and verity went by the boards," according to an eyewitness. The German strength and the number of captured enemy prisoners "increased in geometrical progression with each telling. Officers and men felt themselves veterans."[32] On the morning of July 20, the 39th was relieved and moved off the line for a brief rest, removed from French control and restored to the U.S. 4th Division's Seventh Infantry Brigade. Overall, regimental casualties had been heavy for such a brief action, with an estimated 2 officers and 54 enlisted men killed and 9 officers and 218 enlisted men wounded.[33]

Joseph Dilworth of the 39th took time to reflect on the regiment's baptism of fire in a letter to his postmaster. He reported that the German machine gun bullets that whistled around them produced "no grand and glorious feeling." He also admitted, "I always thought that when the time came to go under fire that a lot of us boys would not stand the test." It was like going into a football game, he explained, and the initial nervousness disappeared when the battle started. Dilworth was proud of what a "bunch of green troops" could do against "so-called crack German regiments." He promised to write again from Berlin, for they were "sure on our way."[34] Major Henry Terrell, Jr. was less enthusiastic about the performance of his troops, reflecting later that a number of mistakes were made in this first battle. Nevertheless, he admitted that "it must be borne in mind that the regiment was composed of men who had not more than six months service, and that the regiment as such had really functioned only since March." Further, more than six weeks of that time had been spent in transporting the unit from Camp Greene to France.[35] As American General Robert

32. Captain Walter B. Smith, "Operations of the 1st Battalion 39th Infantry (4th Division), in the Aisne-Marne Offensive, July 18–20, 1918," The Infantry School, Advanced Course, 1931–32, Maneuver Center of Excellence Libraries, Donovan Research Library, World War I Student Paper Collection, Fort Benning, Georgia, 20–21.

33. An unpublished regimental history gave the 39th's losses as 1 officer and 42 enlisted men killed and 282 wounded. Record Group 120, 4th Division Historical, Box 29, Folder: 39th Infantry, Histories, Commendations & Battle Participants, NARA.

34. *The Hartford* (CT) *Courant*, August 21, 1918. Dilworth did not live to see the end of the war. He was killed in action on September 26, 1918, while leading his men in an attack on German machine gun nests, and was awarded the Distinguished Service Cross for his heroism.

35. Terrell, "The Attack of the 39th Infantry (U.S.) as part of the 33rd French Division South of Faverolles, July 18–19, 1918," 22.

Lee Bullard later explained, the 39th Infantry, packed with "unfinished soldiers," was hurled against a veteran enemy in a "fiery baptism" and forced to fight "a grim sort of Indian warfare with modern equipment." "They were reckless, careless and brave," he concluded.[36] French General Albert Tanant, commanding the 33th Division, noted that the regiment "gave proof in receiving its baptism of fire, of admirable bravery."[37]

Although proud of their success, the 39th men realized that great challenges lay ahead that would expose them to all the grim realities of war. Moved back to the front line to act as a reserve force for the 42nd (Rainbow Division), the 39th took position on the northern edge of the Forêt de Fère. On the night of August 1 the regiment was being "re-arranged," taking up new positions in the forest, preparing for an advance the next day. "In the stillness of the night the movement had to be noiseless," explained one member of the 39th, "and all commands were in a very low voice." About midnight, just as the men were formed in a column of twos, ready to move to their new positions, a German bomber "glided quietly over them" and "almost exactly on a line with the column." The enemy plane dropped a string of bombs so quickly that individual explosions could not be heard. The aviator's success was accidental—he was searching for a battery of Allied heavy guns in the woods that had pounded the German lines that day.[38] "The resulting scene of death and horror was worse than battle," the regiment's historian recalled.[39] By the time the German flew off, twenty-seven men were dead and ninety-four were wounded.

Bloodied but undaunted, on the night of August 2–3 the 4th Division relieved the 42nd Division of their section of the front line. The Germans were withdrawing from the area to a prepared defensive line north of the Vesle River, and the Americans were ready to pursue. Any attempt to cross the Vesle was bound to be costly; no bridges were still standing in the sector assigned to the Americans,

36. Robert Lee Bullard, *American Soldiers Also Fought* (New York: Longmans, Green & Co., 1936), 64–68.

37. Record Group 120, 4th Division Historical, Box 29, Folder: 39th Infantry, Histories, Commendations & Battle Participants, NARA.

38. Record Group 120, 4th Division Historical, Box 29, Folder: 39th Infantry, Histories, Commendations & Battle Participants, NARA.

39. Cole and Eberlin, *The History of the 39th U.S. Infantry*, 35.

and the Germans had an excellent view of the approaches to the river and were strongly entrenched with machine guns, snipers, and artillery. The 39th began moving toward the river on the night of August 3, but a torrential downpour, combined with a lack of knowledge of the country and a German bombardment forced them to halt and wait for dawn.

The men of the 39th captured the village of St. Thibaut early the next morning, but were stopped again by German fire from across the Vesle. Patrols that managed to cross the chest-deep river returned with grim news. Barbed wire filled the steam and the opposite bank, and enemy machine gun nests were scattered through the area. Despite these obstacles, the regiment moved up to the river that afternoon.

After attempts to push across the Vesle failed on August 5, with only a small portion of the 39th able to gain a foothold, the frustrated Americans began an intense, several hours-long barrage of the area on August 6. Late that afternoon, a battalion of the 58th Infantry made it across the river, and although isolated, turned back several German counterattacks. That evening, Howell and the rest of the First Battalion of the 39th were ordered to force a crossing, but once more the American drive was stopped by "a destructive fire from guns of all calibres [*sic*]." Engineers cut telegraph poles, bound them together, and used them for a foot bridge across the river, but only a handful of 39th men could reach the other side of the Vesle, and even they were driven back by machine gun fire and hand grenades.[40] Fortunately, by the late afternoon of August 7, a portion of the 47th Infantry managed to make it across the river and made contact with the 58th Infantry Regiment.

Over the next few days, the Americans held on along the Vesle, while the 39th's companies, "exhausted by heavy losses, gas, marching and fighting," were withdrawn "for a well-earned rest."[41] The remainder of 4th Division was relieved on the night of

40. Record Group 120, Records of the American Expeditionary Forces, World War I, Records of Combat Divisions 1917–1919, 4th Division, 4th Division Historical, Box 29, Folder: 39th Infantry, History, [M.G., Supply, Hdrs, 1st, 2nd, 3rd Bn, and Co. A thru M], 4th Div., 204–11.4, Official History of the 39th Regiment of Infantry, 1917–1918, National Archives and Records Administration, College Park, Maryland.

41. Bach and Hall, *The Fourth Division*, 119. Even while relaxing in their reserve position in the Forêt de Dôle from August 7–11, however, they were subjected to heavy German

August 11–12. In total, the 39th suffered a staggering 827 casualties (130 killed, 646 wounded, and 51 died of wounds) between July 18 and August 15. They had "been subjected to the most grueling conditions of endurance, hardship and nerve racking strain," reported the 7th Brigade's historian.[42]

Despite their inability to score a dramatic victory on the Vesle, 4th Division commander Major General George Cameron issued general orders on August 14 in which he noted that his division, "baptized in full battle, has been christened a fighting unit. It has been tried out and has stood the test."[43] The men were now truly combat veterans. Fifteen-year-old Charles Fay Banks of the 39th's Headquarters Company wrote home to ask his mother to put double notches in the family's pump handle for the two Germans he had killed—one he shot or "knocked out" after the German killed his comrade, the other he bayoneted.[44] Claude A. Huff of Headquarters Company described the fighting as "some show," "beautiful, yet terrible," in which "our boys went over like wild men and fought like demons." "It was a wonderful experience," he concluded. "Our boys won barrels of honor for which America will be proud. We learned much and we are ready and anxious to get back now [into action]."[45] James Williams of Company M was finally able to sit in the woods on August 15 and write home about his participation in "two great battles," fully expecting orders to move forward again at any time. As he wrote, he noted that his shoes were off—the first time in a month he was able to be so comfortable. "I feel that the war cannot last much longer," he optimistically concluded. "It looks as if I might get back and eat Christmas dinner with you."[46]

The officers of the 39th were determined to learn from the bitter, intense fighting they had experienced along the Vesle. "But don't

---

artillery fire every evening, "especially with gas shells of assorted varieties." Record Group 120, Records of the American Expeditionary Forces, World War I, Records of Combat Divisions 1917–1919, 4th Division, 4th Division Historical, Box 29, Folder: 39th Infantry, Histories, Commendations & Battle Participants, 4th Division, 204–11.4, Official History of the 39th Regiment of Infantry, 1917–1918, National Archives and Records Administration, College Park, Maryland.

42. *History of the 7th Infantry Brigade*, 24.

43. Cole and Eberlin, *The History of the 39th U.S. Infantry*, 50.

44. *The Evening News* (Harrisburg, PA), September 3, 1918. Banks supposedly enlisted in January 1918 at the age of 14. *The Tyrone* (PA) *Daily Herald*, October 21, 1918.

45. *The Cedar Rapids* (IA) *Evening Gazette*, September 21, 1918.

46. *The Holt County* (MO) *Sentinel*, October 18, 1918.

you think by any means that it was a walk-over," confided an unidentified 39th lieutenant to his friends at home. "American blood flowed freely due to inexperience and rashness—we tried to rush them too much in order to get prisoners and see them run. They trapped us many times with machine gun bands of fire which actually wiped out platoons. But we had to learn. . . . We will do better in the next big drive."[47] After settling into billets near St. Blin, the regiment began training again, this time "with added interest."[48] Rifle ranges were in constant use to hone the men's marksmanship skills, and officers and NCOs emphasized the control of small units. The training progressed to the point where, on September 7, the regiment held a "highly instructive" exhibition demonstration, showing how a battalion should attack an enemy strong point using mortars, machine guns, and automatic rifles with live ammunition.[49]

Howell and his comrades were destined to play only a minor role in the A.E.F.'s next operation, the St. Mihiel Offensive, the first drive of the war that was planned, organized, and commanded by the Americans. St. Mihiel was another attempt to eliminate a salient in the front, in this case a triangular piece of land about twenty-five miles wide and fifteen miles deep that jutted into the Allied line. The 39th was assigned with the remainder of the 4th Division's 7th Brigade to the corps reserve on the salient's western face. That is not to suggest that the St. Mihiel Offensive was a restful event for the 39th. The 7th Brigade advanced a short distance late on the evening of September 12, completed the move early the next morning, and did not return to its position in reserve until the morning of September 14. Difficult marches in darkness through torrential rain and harassment by German shell fire was the lot of the men held in "reserve." Nevertheless, only one member of the regiment was killed and seven wounded during this period. Only a few days after the successful reduction of the St. Mihiel salient, the regiment was ordered north to take position for the Meuse-Argonne drive, the largest operation undertaken by Pershing's army.

The Meuse-Argonne Offensive (so named because the American First Army advanced through the area between the Aisne and

47. *The Charlotte* (NC) *News*, September 15, 1918.

48. Cole and Eberlin, *The History of the 39th U.S. Infantry*, 53.

49. *History of the 7th Infantry Brigade*, 34.

Meuse Rivers, including the Argonne Forest) was the bloodiest battle in American history to that time, with more than 120,000 U.S. casualties. The Allied goal was the critical Carignan-Sedan-Mézières rail line. If the Americans could advance fifty-three kilometers and capture Sedan, they would cut that vital lifeline, end the flow of supplies to the Germany Army, and greatly hamper the enemy's ability to escape. In order to capture Sedan, however, Pershing's troops would first need to overcome the front line and four German defensive lines: the Hagen Stellung, the Etzel-Giselher Stellung, the Kriemhilde Stellung, and the Freya Stellung. American success depended on surprising the German forces in the region, overwhelming them with superior numbers, and moving quickly toward their objectives before enemy reinforcements could arrive. The Germans were well prepared to meet the American offensive. They had carefully constructed a formidable array of defenses, bolstered by natural features. It was, in the words of French historian Hilaire Belloc, an area "ideally good for defense, and ideally bad for attack."[50]

The 4th Division was assigned to the American Third Corps, on the right flank of the First Army's approximately eighteen-mile-wide front. On the division's immediate left was the 79th Division of the Fifth Corps. The 4th's assigned sector was funnel shaped, about 2,500 yards wide at the jump off point and gradually widening to 5,000 yards.

At 2:30 a.m. on September 26, a massive artillery bombardment, which, according to one member of the 39th, was "amazing both for intensity and accuracy," "pounded beyond recognition the enemy positions which had been elaborated and strengthened for more than two years." Three hours later, the 39th Infantry moved forward through a heavy fog "with no trouble at all," through blasted enemy wire and trenches ruined by the shelling.[51] They trooped across Forges Brook on bridges of board and wire, and moved toward the German front line trenches. Enemy resistance was initially light, but stiffened somewhat as the doughboys approached the town of Cuisy.

50. Hilaire Belloc, "America in the Argonne," *The American Legion Monthly* 5, no. 5 (November 1928): 28–46.

51. Record Group 120, 4th Division Historical, Box 29, Folder: 39th Infantry, Histories, Commendations & Battle Participants, NARA.

The 39th men continued to press forward and reached the Third Corps objective about 12:30 that afternoon. There they dug in to wait for the divisions on their flanks to arrive on the same line. The 80th Division on their right reached the objective as well, but the 79th on their left was delayed by the Germans holding Montfaucon, a height that dominated the surrounding countryside. A precious five hours passed before orders finally arrived directing the 4th Division to keep pushing forward regardless of the progress of the units on their flanks. The Germans took full advantage of the lull to bring up reserves and reorganize their retreating units. When the Americans began to move forward again late that afternoon, their attack soon ground to a halt. With darkness approaching, the doughboys dug in at the corps objective.

The afternoon halt was not the only lost opportunity the 39th Infantry experienced that day. The regiment's 1st Battalion became lost in the early morning fog and veered to the left (west) out of the division's sector and in the direction of Montfaucon. Two platoons of Company A flanked the hill and captured more than 100 prisoners and a number of machine gun nests. The battalion commander, aware of Third Corps commander General Robert Bullard's strict orders to continue pushing north at all costs, ordered his men to abandon the assault on Montfaucon. In addition, that afternoon, the commander of the 4th Division's 8th Brigade, then being held in reserve, proposed that his troops flank Montfaucon, but Bullard denied his request. Had the 4th Division's soldiers been allowed to assist in the assault on the German stronghold, it is possible that a breakthrough might have been achieved that first day, shortening the war and saving countless American lives.

Early the following morning, September 27, the doughboys of the 39th pressed forward again. Crouching or crawling over open ground, "fighting for every foot" through heavy German artillery and machine gun fire that pummeled them from the front and both flanks, the 39th men made little headway.[52] The regiment's lieutenant colonel was killed, and eventually the enemy fire became so intense that most of two battalions of the regiment were forced into a disorganized retreat. Rallying, they dug in for the night, having

52. Record Group 120, 4th Division Historical, Box 29, Folder: 39th Infantry, Histories, Commendations & Battle Participants, NARA.

passed through "probably the most severe [day] in the history of the Regiment."[53] A cold rain set in as well, soaking the men and turning roads into quagmires, guaranteeing that rolling kitchens with hot food were unable to move forward.

Despite the "ill fortune of the day before," the 39th moved forward at 7 a.m. on September 28. The third day of the battle saw the 39th once again facing enemy machine gun and artillery fire as they slogged toward Nantillois. After its capture, they pushed into the Bois de Fays, where they found not only thick underbrush, but brush "literally alive with Minenwerfers [trench mortars], machine guns and snipers." Forced to withdraw to just south of the wood, the men endured yet another terrific artillery bombardment and saw their colonel evacuated to the rear, wounded.[54]

Finally, on the morning of September 29, the regiment was withdrawn to division reserve in the Bois de Septsarges. In three days of assaults, the 39th had advanced eleven kilometers, at the enormous cost of more than a hundred officers and men killed and more than 500 wounded. In the process, they claimed to have captured nearly 2,000 prisoners, thirty artillery pieces, and many machine guns and trench mortars.[55]

Sitting in the division reserve in the Bois de Septsarges offered no real relief for the battered doughboys, however. For ten "disagreeable" days, the "monotony" was broken when German artillery regularly threw shells into those woods, and German aircraft pounded the 39th there as well, causing many casualties. Both the 3rd Battalion's command post and the first aid station both suffered direct hits from German artillery.[56] A shell burst in Company I's kitchen, killing two cooks and blowing two mules into the branches

53. Cole and Eberlin, *The History of the 39th U.S. Infantry,* 65.

54. *History of the 7th Infantry Brigade*, 45. Captain Mathias W. Haney of the 39th claimed that American artillery from the 79th Division mistakenly shelled the 39th on the night of September 27 when they mistook them for Germans, and again on September 28 when their artillery barrage fell short. Record Group 120, 4th Division Historical, Box 29, Folder: 39th Infantry, Histories, Commendations & Battle Participants, NARA.

55. An unpublished regimental history claimed that in three days of combat (September 26–28), the 39th captured nearly a thousand prisoners, had advanced through "five kilos of barbed wire," and had "reclaimed for France a strip of territory one kilo wide and eleven kilos deep." Record Group 120, 4th Division Historical, Box 29, Folder: 39th Infantry, Histories, Commendations & Battle Participants, NARA.

56. Record Group 120, 4th Division Historical, Box 29, Folder: 39th Infantry, Histories, Commendations & Battle Participants, NARA.

of a tree. To add to their misery, rain fell every night "and the mud was a foot deep everywhere."[57]

For the second phase of the Meuse-Argonne assault, the 4th Division was given another difficult assignment--outflank the German positions near the Meuse River and the town of Brieulles by attacking through the Bois de Fays, Bois de Malaumont, and Bois de Forêt. Their capture would hopefully force the Germans to evacuate Brieulles, sparing the Americans a costly assault on the town. As the 39th attempted to recuperate in the Bois de Septsarges, the 4th Division's 8th Infantry Brigade pushed into the Bois de Fays. There they endured miserable conditions and made little progress. Rain, cold, mud, and the stench of the dead were ever present, and rations and ammunition began to grow scarce as the exhausted and dwindling brigade struggled to hold on against localized German counterattacks. Finally, the 39th and the rest of the 7th Brigade were ordered to relieve them and continue the attack.

On the night of October 9, the regiment began moving into the Bois de Fays. "A more ghastly sight never before had presented itself," recounted the unidentified author of a history of the regiment. "Only one path lead [*sic*] thru the Bois de Fay[s] to the front line position and it was strewn with the dead of both sides. In one spot over sixty men, both Germans and Americans lay; all showing up in the pale moonlight."[58]

The advance continued the next morning. 1st Lieutenant Henry O. Walters of Company B described the action on October 10th: "The order was given to advance. . . . The boch [*sic*] put over a very heavey [*sic*] barrage through which we advanced, had a number of men wounded and killed." A shell exploded in front of Lieutenant Walters, killing about eight men, with the lieutenant escaping unharmed, "I being the last man to go by after this shell hit."[59] On the eleventh, they pushed into the Bois de Forêt. There the Americans distinctly heard the cry, "Kamerad," above the din of machine gun fire and screaming shells, and saw their tormentors throw their hands into the air in surrender. "A yell of exultation

57. Record Group 120, 4th Division Historical, Box 29, Folder: 39th Infantry, Histories, Commendations & Battle Participants, NARA.

58. Record Group 120, 4th Division Historical, Box 29, Folder: 39th Infantry, Histories, Commendations & Battle Participants, NARA.

59. Record Group 120, 4th Division Historical, Box 29, Folder: 39th Infantry, Histories, Commendations & Battle Participants, NARA.

went up as the men hit the woods," according to an eyewitness, and many prisoners were taken to the rear. The American advance continued. By October 12, despite intense German opposition and heavy casualties, the 39th occupied a salient 400 yards wide and four kilometers deep in the German line. They were ordered to hold their position. "On all sides the machine guns [*sic*] nests poured in their fire to no avail," wrote one member of the 39th, because the men had "decided to stay" through "hellish artillery fire and the singing of the snipers [*sic*] bullet."[60] At night gas shells flooded the area with a dense, deadly fog. Each attempted enemy counterattack was broken by rifle and machine gun fire. Telephone lines were so frequently cut by artillery fire that communications could only be maintained by runner. Finally, on the morning of October 13, the regiment was relieved by the 3rd Division and withdrew once more to the Bois de Septsarges. In three days of fighting (October 10–12), the regiment again lost more than a hundred killed and five hundred wounded and missing. In total, the regiment spent seventeen days in the Meuse-Argonne Offensive, six of those in the front line, making assaults. They advanced eleven kilometers in September and three in October. In those six days on the front line, 292 men of the regiment were killed and 77 died of wounds, and 1,071 were wounded.[61] The 4th was the last American division involved in the initial attack of September 26 to be relieved.

Mercifully, the 39th was ordered out of the Bois de Septsarges to the Commercy area, their days of combat finally over. Lieutenant J.H. Gerdes of Company L sat down on October 14 to write a letter to his mother. He wrote that he had led his company through "some of the hardest fighting of all," was "pretty well worn out," and was hoping to be sent back for a rest. Even though he had suffered a slight wound, he was far more fortunate than his old

60. Record Group 120, 4th Division Historical, Box 29, Folder: 39th Infantry, Histories, Commendations & Battle Participants, NARA. One member of the regiment claimed that German artillery fire struck the regiment from the front, both flanks, and even the right rear. Shell fire from the latter direction did not cease until October 11, when French troops captured a German artillery battalion located on the opposite side of the Meuse. Record Group 120, 4th Division Historical, Box 29, Folder: 39th Infantry, Histories, Commendations & Battle Participants, NARA.

61. American Battle Monuments Commission, *4th Division Summary of Operations in the World War* (Washington, D.C.: U.S. Government Printing Office, 1944), 74. On September 30, 1918, regimental strength was noted as 2,653; by October 31, it was only 1,536.

tent mate at Camp Greene, whose body Gerdes noticed after he was killed on October 12. Despite such losses, "We captured lots of prisoners and all kinds of material including an entire electric plant as well as a supply station," he concluded.[62]

The unfathomable violence of the Meuse-Argonne made a lasting impact on the survivors. "I don't suppose that during our period on the lines . . . there was even one-half hour of freedom from the noise and smoke of those shells," wrote Lloyd Randolph, with only slight exaggeration.[63] Although the experience sorely tested the resilience of the doughboys, it also proved to be a source of regimental pride. "It was here that the 39th really showed what was in her," wrote Captain W.K. Dickson. "We took the lead and maintained it at all the time. This was some scrap and well worth being in."[64] After several days of delousing, reequipping, and visiting the rifle range, the 39th moved to Heudicourt in order to prepare for the next great American offensive. The signing of the Armistice on November 11 fortunately cancelled that operation.

With the fighting at an end, each man began "figuring down to a day the approximate date when he would land in New York."[65] Instead, "another great test of our courage, discipline, determination and stick-to-it-iveness" was required.[66] A U.S. army of occupation (the Third Army) was needed to move into Germany, in accordance with the Armistice terms, to keep watch on the Germans until a formal peace treaty could be signed. The 39th began the 330-kilometer (205 mile) march into the enemy's country on November 20 and entered Germany on December 3. It rained continuously for several days and the men were unable to dry out. The roads were impassable in some cases, forcing the Americans to change their route and adding long detours to their march. Troops carrying full equipment were often required to help push heavily loaded regimental wagons. Despite the hardships, the men made a conscious effort to keep their uniforms and equipment neat and clean, and the regimental band played and the men marched at attention through each town and village.

62. *The Wilmington* (NC) *Morning Star*, November 9, 1918.

63. *The New Castle* (PA) *Herald*, March 10, 1919.

64. *Keowee Courier* (Pickens, SC), February 19, 1919.

65. Record Group 120, 4th Division Historical, Box 29, Folder: 39th Infantry, Histories, Commendations & Battle Participants, NARA.

66. Cole and Eberlin, *The History of the 39th U.S. Infantry*, 117.

On December 8, 1918, a battalion of the 39th unceremoniously arrived in Coblenz, the American bridgehead on the Rhine, gaining the honor of being the first Allied combat troops to enter the city. Although a host of newspaper correspondents accompanied the battalion, ready to send dramatic dispatches recounting their arrival in Coblenz, the event was "no more dramatic than the entrance of American troops into any other town on any other day." Indeed, the "chief object of admiration to the natives of Coblentz [*sic*] was the field kitchen, with its remarkable prodigality of food."[67]

Nevertheless, the difficult march from France to Germany was "undoubtedly one of the most wonderful achievements of the American Army," the regimental historian believed. "We had defeated the armies of the most militaristic nation in the world, and our regiment had played an important part in this, the greatest and bloodiest of wars," one member of the regiment proudly recalled. "We had compelled the enemy to beg for peace. . . . We were very proud of our achievements."[68]

Dispersed to various billets near Coblenz, the veterans of the 39th generally enjoyed occupation duty. The men were "strictly guided by the principles of international law, justice, honor and humanity."[69] The Germans, disarmed and under close guard, "do not bother us for they know we are always ready for them," reported Captain Arthur Robinson of Headquarters Company. "In other words we are taking no chances but are constantly prepared for any emergency that may arise."[70] Despite the claims of the regimental historian that "there was no fraternization" with the local population, Howell recorded numerous instances of young doughboys attempting to become better acquainted with German fräuleins. In the words of historian Jennifer Keene, "The Germans . . . ungrudgingly offered them good meals and comfortable beds, charged reasonable prices for wine, and treated them like colleagues rather than unwelcome visitors."[71]

67. Record Group 120, 4th Division Historical, Box 29, Folder: 39th Infantry, Histories, Commendations & Battle Participants, NARA.

68. Cole and Eberlin, *The History of the 39th U.S. Infantry*, 125.

69. Cole and Eberlin, *The History of the 39th U.S. Infantry*, 130.

70. *The Corydon* (IN) *Republican*, April 10, 1919.

71. Jennifer D. Keene, *Doughboys, the Great War, and the Remaking of America* (Baltimore: The Johns Hopkins University Press, 2001), 120.

In addition to keeping the peace in Germany, the 39th performed guard duty, engaged in target practice, drills, and maneuvers, and were required to march in an occasional parade or review. Classroom instruction, athletic events, and various forms of entertainment, along with leave trips to France, Great Britain, and Italy, helped pass the time. Corporal William Bolesworth of Headquarters Company admitted in a letter home that occupation duty was a "great time," and exaggerated only slightly when he reported that "Nothing is too fine for his company soldiers and they live in the best mansions and hotels as well as castles."[72] Perhaps the highlight of occupation duty for the soldiers of the 39th came on February 3, 1919, when 4th Division commander Major General Mark Hersey decorated the regiment's colors with the Croix de Guerre with gold star, recognition by the French government of the 39th's role in capturing the Bois de Cresnes and the town of Noroy the previous July. The following month, on March 18, General John J. Pershing reviewed the 4th Division. The commanding general and the army, corps, division, brigade, and regimental commanders all complimented the men on their fine appearance.

Despite the easy duty and the honors in Germany, both officers and enlisted men were anxious to return home. "He endures the drudgery and discomfort and loneliness of each day patiently, a little absent-mindedly," wrote one member of the 39th about the occupation soldiers, "calculating what niceities of international politics may hasten or delay his return home." Overall, the American soldier longed for the day "when he shall again be a free man in his native land."[73] "I never knew what home was until I got over here and been in hell ever since," groused Raymond Crandall of the 39th's Machine Gun Company on December 30, 1918.[74] "I have had all the joys of being a soldier I want," complained Captain Dickson, "including the 'cootie,' and the sooner we get home the better."[75] "Tell grandma not to worry about me," echoed Corporal Harold Duckworth of Company A, "because I am well altho I am sure some homesick."[76]

72. *Oakland* (CA) *Tribune*, May 29, 1919.

73. Record Group 120, 4th Division Historical, Box 29, Folder: 39th Infantry, Histories, Commendations & Battle Participants, NARA.

74. *The Olean* (NY) *Evening Herald*, February 17, 1919.

75. *Keowee Courier* (Pickens, SC), February 19, 1919.

76. *Abilene Daily* (KS) *Reflector*, April 21, 1919.

Finally, the long-awaited day arrived, and on July 22, 1919, the men boarded trains for Brest, France, where they would find a ship for the return journey to the United States. On July 31, Howell and his fellow soldiers boarded a transport and began the journey home, proud of their "fine reputation," their "excellent discipline, willingness and efficiency," and the fact that "when there was still considerable work to be done, the Thirty-Ninth Infantry was chosen to do it."[77] The veterans of the 39th U.S. Infantry and the rest of the 4th "Ivy" Division had "splendidly upheld the honor of their country" as "magnificent soldiers" and "chivalrous American gentlemen."[78]

Editorial Method

Howell's manuscript appears here largely as written. Minor corrections in spelling have been made for clarity's sake, particularly foreign phrases and the names of certain cities and towns in France and Germany. On those rare occasions when Howell completely misspelled the name of a village, the correct name has been inserted in brackets "[ ]." Redundant words have been omitted. Ship names have been italicized. Capitalization and punctuation have been standardized. Brackets and a question mark [?] indicate unclear or unreadable words.

Author's Note

All the characters comprising the company squad are but prototypes of what were the actual living soldiers. While some of the names given them in this narrative are similar to those who were in the original squad, the words they speak, or the episodes described, are not actually those that the originals participated in. Otherwise these pages contain a true account of the exploits of the "Forgotten Fourth Division." A saga of unsung brigades.

I look back along the roads of hell, through the dim mists of the past, and ponder. I see endless columns of war-weary youth, slogging along the muddy pave. It is always night. Heavy pack straps cut stooped shoulders to the bone. The faces are masks of despair, their minds asleep, their bodies the controlled robots of

77. Cole and Eberlin, *The History of the 39th U.S. Infantry*, 157.
78. Bach and Hall, *The Fourth Division*, 265.

"September 13, 1918. St. Mihiel," by Kerr Eby (Library of Congress).

some pompous mortal, miles from the desolate scene. Trees without life or foliage line the road. Skies are black as jet, except for the flashes of distant rockets and guns that send whining, screeching, nerve racking shells, on through to their goal of destruction. Occasional shells strike the road—annihilation for many, but the main body of drab automatons keeps moving ever on and on to further catastrophe. This picture in the mirrors of memory is the same for all wars, past or future. All that changes, is the propaganda.

"They wear no golden lily of renown
On azure shield,
Nor mantle of aggrandizement.
Hold Clotilde! Bid them not brag
Though they slay a million monster,
The plain a deep almagra." —Anon.

Chapter 1

A Doughboy Speaks

Now that most of the generals and pseudo captains have written their memoirs telling us how they won the war by making themselves comfortable in ancient chateaus, attending dinner parties, riding back and forth to Paris and Chaumont in high priced limousines, playing polo, inspecting recruits and ordering out military bands to salute them whenever they appeared in public and otherwise catering to their egos, but never mentioning their mistakes, I think now is the opportune time to take up the subject of the down-trodden doughboy. He never believed a general was necessary to him, no sir, but he well knew he was necessary to the general, whether 'his Grace' would admit it or not.[1] For, without the lowly, uneducated, unrefined, dumb, foul mouthed, crap shoot-in doughboy, the generals could never have succeeded in a single battle or bring an arrogant militarocracy to its knees, nor have made the world safe for the international bankers.

The above paragraph and those to follow were written before the United States entered the great global war of 1941–1945,

1. Howell was obviously displaying an American enlisted man's disdain for officers, particularly generals. By 1941, a number of prominent American generals, including John J. Pershing, Hunter Liggett, Robert Bullard, James Harbord, and Peyton C. March had already published their reminiscences of World War I.

fighting two wars at the same time, east of the Atlantic and west of the Pacific. Yet, as you read these words and the subsequent narrative of episode and experience, you will be aware of a strange parallel existing therein. According to Ernie Pyle both world wars were alike but in World War II, "only the holes were bigger."

You could remove the names of World War I leaders from this narrative, Wilson, Clemenceau, Pershing, Lloyd George, Petain, Von Gallowitz, Von Bulow, Von Hindenburg, Von Tirpitz, etc., and substitute Roosevelt, Churchill, Montgomery, Eisenhower, DeGaulle, Patton, Goering, Von Bock, Von Rundstedt, Doenitz, etc., change the doughboy to G.I., Y.M.C.A. & K.C. to U.S.O., Argonne, to Battle of the Bulge and you would have essentially the same old story all over again, with the same purpose of destruction and annihilation, if not the exact situations. The slogan instead of being "to Hell with the Kaiser" would be "To Hell with Hitler."

Thousands of unknowns fought in both wars. The G.I. of the Great Global War was in many cases the son of the doughboy of World War I. Doughboy or G.I., the wars were never fought without US.[2] And by US, I mean not only those glorious regiments whose names are now clothed in legend, but also those whose record has never been noticed, because no one ever saw fit to eulogize them. Unknowns of the rank and file will always remain unknown, but they plodded steadily along through every danger and hardship doing their bit, a little dumbly perhaps but cheerfully and to the best of their ability. The spotlight of glory is never turned on them directly. They look for no emolument. In words following, I propose to tell the war story of four such glorious regiments of the 7th and 8th Infantry Brigades, World War I, who constituted the "Forgotten Fourth Division, A.E.F." 1918.

Any kind of a general could have won the war without me. That I will admit. I was just so much expense to Uncle Sam. The doughboys did not win the war all alone, like the generals. Neither were all the wars won by the United States Marines or the Army Air Force, no matter how spectacular their individual performance may have been in several well broadcasted engagements. Our entry in the First World War was a mistake, perhaps, but in the Second World War it was a necessity. But if you had inquired of the soldier as to his preference in the matter of war, he would have told you

2. Here Howell refers to American participation in World Wars I and II.

that he much preferred to stay home in Ashtabula or Hoboken as the case might be. But since he must go, he was ready for it and nothing else but.

World War I was not won by the "fighting Marines" in Belleau Wood, nor the "Lost Battalion" in the Argonne, which constitutes the average citizens knowledge and comprehension of American exploits in that war. They represent episodes only that show the character and invincible qualities of the U.S. soldier. The chief battle of that war was not fought at Château Thierry either. Men who saw action at those places were real heroes, of course, and should ever be regarded as such, but they were not the only heroes. Their spirit and tenacity of purpose drove them on to victory. Albeit, they carried out strict Army orders, but always at a great sacrifice. And when they were successful, the generals held another dinner party and did a lot of back slapping.

Stories and news carefully dispensed to our home newspapers in war time by our official correspondents and propagandists and most carefully censored and edited by the U.S. Intelligence Service, have made some of the engagements and episodes of both wars outshadow all others in a way that is all out of proportion to their real military importance. And of course they become part of the patriotic legend of our great nation. They were outstanding successes, surely, but there were others that contributed as well to the successful outcome and final victory. Numerous unknown battalions and brigades did some fighting too, besides those mentioned. Some were of the regular army, some were of the draft army. Their exploits go largely unsung, their stories never having been considered spectacular or out of the ordinary. Nor would these obscure soldiers have it otherwise. They have grown accustomed to silence and therefore forgotten is their individual reputation in the Great Adventure of 1918. The same could apply to 1942–1945. They have long since found out that a soldier is looked upon as a hero in wartime and little or nothing in times of peace. Ergo, his worth is soon forgotten as the world moves on to greater and deadlier forms of destruction, until he is needed again. However, armies will always need infantry in spite of this great mechanized age of warfare and atomic energy. The plodding foot soldier will still have to be depended on in the final phase of any future conflict to seize, occupy or defend as the case may be.

This narrative, therefore, will contain little except the simple war experience of ordinary U.S. doughboys or foot soldiers as told by one of them, an eye witness to their hardships, their joys and struggles, who trudged along with them in the 39th U.S. Infantry Regiment, 4th Combat Division, Regular Army in France and Germany World War I.[3] And what an experience it was! They wore no "lilies of renown" these boys. None of you ever heard of this particular outfit, I'll wager, yet they were the first U.S. troops to reach the Rhine in Germany, less than a month after the armistice was signed. Looking back over twenty-five years, names of individual outfits often mean nothing. Only what was accomplished as a whole remains of average interest. Can any of you tell the names and numbers of the military outfits that fought at Bunker Hill, the Battle of Gettysburg, or Richmond? A strange analogy exists, however, in the fact that the 4th U.S. Reg. Divis[ion] first on the Rhine in 1918 was also among the first in the invasions of France and the crossing of the Rhine in 1945, during the Second World War.

Our home folks never appreciated the part played by the old A.E.F. in the greatest battle ever fought by U.S. troops in this or any other war the United States was ever engaged in up to this time—the Meuse Argonne. Some will think only of St. Mihiel because it was more publicized. We have appreciated our greatest battle so little because its importance was not thoroughly advertised to us at the time of its occurrence, because of rigid censorship. Also because it was overshadowed by fast moving world events in other lines such as the collapse of Austria and the Kaiser's abdication.

Some of our soldiers too, after returning home, more readily related their pleasurable experiences in the great "Battle of Paris" (wine, women, song) rather than recite the grim details of the Argonne Woods, Grandpré, Heights of Montfaucon, Cunel and Romagne, La Tuilerie Farm, etc., all on the road to Sedan, the final U.S. objective. This attitude has given rise at home to the idea that any soldier who got across to France, did little except have a grand good time for himself, marching around and showing off. What nonsense. It was true for a few but not for the majority.

3. Howell incorrectly refers to his division as the 4th "combat" division. Divisions in the American Expeditionary Forces were simply designated by their numerical designation, followed by the word "division," e.g., 4th Division.

How about me? Well, I was just a "buck private in the rear rank." I never wore a lieutenant's uniform, so therefore, I never had an opportunity to fight the "Battle of Paris" or "Vin Blanc Ridge" as it should be fought. Being just a dumb doughboy, I was given other things to do. Most of my leisure moments when not hiking along in mud and drizzling rain, crawling around shell holes, or carrying a heavy pack with rifle and ammunition, were spent in cleaning out cowbarns for billets, sleeping on the ground in water or equally damp cellars, groping through gas filled woods and ruined villages at night, or squatting in shell holes, fox holes and vermin infested dugouts along with the rest of my squad.

I became as experienced, I'll admit, as any of my fellow soldats in the art of souvenir hunting and similar occupations. On special occasions too, I saw the mademoiselles of Armentieres and elsewhere. Also I never missed a handout from the Red Cross or Y.M.C.A., Jewish Welfare Board or Salvation Army if I could help it.[4] But no matter how I tried, I was never quite successful in my efforts to get back to Paris or the rear to join the S.O.S. (Service of Supply) where I am told they had it very soft.

And what about the officers? After the manner of soldaten of all the armies of all types and degree since time began, I both admired and equally disliked some of the officers, all according to how I was currently treated. Some of the "brass hats" were a little too brassy at times. Some were ring tailed, self-important egoists as far as their contact with mere doughboy soldiery was concerned. Il est esprit de armees ancien.

The U.S. Regular Army from the start, did not seem to have a sufficient supply of experienced regular officers to fill the demand on such an extensive wartime basis but they did what they could. They made lieutenants out of sergeants and corporals; colonels and brigadiers out of second lieutenants and so on.[5] I have noticed

4. The American National Red Cross built canteens in stateside training camps, provided surgical dressings and winter clothing items to servicemen, and assisted their families. In France, the Red Cross established hospitals and canteens and provided comfort items to soldiers. The Y.M.C.A. established recreational facilities for troops at home, and "leave areas" and recreational and religious "huts" and canteens in Europe. Organized in April 1917, the Jewish Welfare Board provided publications to army installations, supported Jewish workers in defense industries, and established more than 200 centers in training camps and overseas. The Salvation Army operated canteens and clubs in stateside training camps, established "huts" and "rest rooms" in France, and distributed food, including their famous doughnuts.

5. Although Howell wrote this statement with more than a bit of hyperbole, some officers did enjoy rapid promotions during the war. Hugh A. Drum, for example, a captain in

also that a large number of officers, lieutenants especially but even captains, majors and colonels from the National Army (draft) were brought over to France on ninety days approval, as it were, from Sears & Roebuck or some other cheap, mass production system for supplying emergency officers in quantity. The main point is that they were supplied and delivered F.O.B. France when needed, or the A.E.F. would have been handicapped in completing organization. Some of these officers turned out 100% plus. Others were good bond salesmen or military clothes models and little else. And boy! Did they look good on a parade ground! I'm for telling you they did, with their shiny new boots and glittering spurs. Anyway, the women liked them. But when they arrived at the scene of war they promptly lost most of the shine. Their chief duty as platoon leaders seemed to be that of keeping the army of doughboys entertained with work details, or should I say disciplined, when howitzers, trench mortars, minenwerfers, machine guns and crap-shootin' failed. In moments of relaxation, or when they could wrangle a pass from the colonel, these officers became ranking commanders in that ever raging, ever enjoyable "Battle of Paris," the mention of which is always passé when putting on the "hero act" before ladies and children. But don't get the idea that all the officers were like this. They were not. The former were inevitable.[6]

---

the Regular Army when war was declared in April 1917, ended the war as a brigadier general (USA) and chief of staff of the American First Army. U.S. Adjutant General, *Official Army Register, December 1, 1918* (Washington, D.C.: U.S. Government Printing Office, 1918), 598. Rice W. Means, a veteran of the Spanish-American War, was promoted from private to lieutenant colonel of the 1st Colorado Infantry (later the 157th U.S. Infantry, 40th Division) in June 1917, and served overseas. Tudor A.H. Tiedemann, also of the 40th Division, began the war as a second lieutenant and was promoted to lieutenant colonel in 1919. No author, *History of the Fortieth (Sunshine) Division* (Los Angeles, CA: C.S. Hutson & Co, 1920), 14, 83. Frederick Palmer of Pershing's staff noted that "promotions, especially for the Regulars, kept pace with the rapid expansion of the army. A captain upon our entry into the war had become a colonel. A brigadier general's star had replaced a major's leaf." Frederick Palmer, *John J. Pershing, General of the Armies: A Biography* (Harrisburg, PA: The Military Service Publishing Company, 1948), 220.

6. The first session of three-month Officer Training Camps, held from May 15-August 11, 1917, commissioned 27,341 officers, more than half of whom were in the infantry. The second session (August 27-November 27, 1917) commissioned 17,237, with again more than half in the infantry, and the third (January 5-April 19, 1918) commissioned 11,659 candidates. The fourth OTC, scheduled for May 15-September 1, 1918, was disrupted by the establishment of Central Officers' Training Schools (COTS), a four-month course. Richard S. Faulkner, *The School of Hard Knocks: Combat Leadership in the American Expeditionary Forces* (College Station: Texas A&M University Press, 2012), 36, 56, 68–69, 75–83. While 3 percent of U.S. Army officers were Regulars, 6 percent were National Guardsmen, and 8 percent were commissioned from the ranks, the Officer Training Camps furnished 48 percent of the army's officers. The remainder were specialists who received direct commissions. Edward M. Coffman, *The Regulars: The American Army, 1898–1941* (Cambridge: Harvard University Press, 2004), 205.

It has been said that the A.E.F. of both wars has sent home some of the grandest liars that ever existed. Whoever said that is more than half right. Some of our greatest self-styled "fighters" never heard a shot fired during the whole war, except a cap pistol fired around some estaminet far back in the rear areas. They never even threw a stone at the Germans. This was the class of "fighter" who brought or sent home most all of the souvenirs that the real fighting doughboy had collected at the front and then exchanged for red wine or chocolate. In this way the souvenirs got back to the hospital canteens, Y.M.C.A.'s and base camps of the S.O.S. far to the rear. Thus from here all sorts of souvenirs eventually came to the U.S. with an appropriate "tall story" to match in which the sender in the S.O.S. army made himself out to be the leading heroic figure. No real doughboy of the combat service could ever carry his souvenirs for very long as they were too bulky. If he was fortunate, he might reach a place where he could mail them home but this seldom happened. After a couple of days he was usually quite willing to part with his treasure for most anything of value in the line of eats or drink. And so it was.[7]

While I have made an effort to stick to the truth as far as possible and as I know it, still, someone with a long, pointed nose may find gross inaccuracy due to misinformation and the meagre notes I made at the time. No one man could tell all as the show was too big. If this effort therefore, chances to fall in other and more critical hands, I trust they will be tolerant. May it also prove a revelation to those readers, young or old, who have believed war to be just one grand display of infantry, artillery, tanks, aeroplanes and sabered cavalry on parade for the fickle applause of voluptuous foreign mademoiselles.

Who won the war then? Well, nobody in particular, unless it was the doughboy. It was never thoroughly decided. Time will tell who wins the peace. The U.S. turned the tide in favor of the Allies in 1918 by bringing up fresh U.S. divisions into line when the British were recuperating from a bad smash at Cambrai and the French had no reserves left after their retreat from the Chemin

7. American soldiers "lusted after German military equipment," according to historian Jennifer Keene, as those items "evoked the romance and brutality of a personal encounter with enemy soldiers on the battlefield." As Howell implies, "noncombatant salvage crews . . . often collected more marketable merchandise than combat soldiers." Keene, *Doughboys, the Great War, and the Remaking of America*, 59–60.

des Dames.[8] History again repeated itself in World War II so your Uncle Sam has twice been a good Samaritan to the above governments and still plays the role of Santa Claus, so it seems. But do we as a nation get any credit for this help, or any help. No, very little. This help is demanded and expected. In the first war we did it of our own free will to end war. In the second war we did it to save ourselves. Whatever the motive, we were more than generous. They called for help, so we gave men and treasure. As a supreme gift desired by some of our European contemporaries and the international bankers, we may yet end by absorbing all the war debts of both allies and enemy. Twenty-five years after the "war to end war" there was in progress another and greater war to save civilization, and the coming of the atomic age. There are greater although probably shorter wars in prospect which some claim will outlaw or make obsolete what we know as armies. Do you think the doughboy or G.I. will become extinct? He will be there when the crash comes, as usual.

Anyway, I've probably told a number of things that doughboys should keep quiet about as it may disillusion some of the flag wavers. I have tried to describe places and events as I found them and not as they are supposed to be, when one reads school histories or fiction.

My impression and experience is that warfare, other than to drive an invader off your native doorstep is useless folly that brings no lasting benefit to any combatant, win or lose. Misunderstandings, or the vanity and ambitions of leaders whose feet are of clay, usually causes war. Those who can least afford to carry the burden must do the fighting and then go back home and pay for it afterwards in taxes, maladjustments, blasted careers, etc. But the inciters thereof and the profiteers, are always safe behind mahogany desks

8. General Robert Nivelle, the overall French Army commander, launched the French Fifth and Sixth Armies against well-defended German positions on heights above the Aisne River between Soissons and Reims on April 16, 1917 (the Chemin des Dames, or "Ladies Road," ran along a portion of the heights). Five days later, the Tenth Army was added to the offensive. On May 15, after his troops had achieved limited gains and no decisive breakthrough despite heavy casualties, Nivelle was replaced by General Henri Petain. Further French assaults in late October 1917 led to the German withdrawal from all their defenses on the Chemin des Dames in early November. On May 27, 1918, the French in turn were quickly driven off the heights during the German Blücher Offensive. On November 20, 1917, the British launched a combined infantry-tank assault to capture Cambrai. After the British were halted, the Germans counterattacked on November 30, and, like the British assault, gained some territory before being stopped. British casualties numbered more than 40,000.

somewhere in air-conditioned offices telling everyone who will listen how patriotic they are. They direct the great armament race with billions of government money and the corporations grow richer. But the doughboy or G.I. is lucky if he gets back to Main St., U.S.A. in fair condition to start all over again.

Hatred and oppression, greed, jealousy and ambition for power have always been causes of war. It is the story of the human race since Adam. Suspicion and fear also have been rampant in most European countries. They seem to be born with it. Therefore do you believe that diplomatic bunk and bombast, notes, dickerings or formule [?] of flying diplomats and idealistic pacifists will ever end war? Not until soldiers refuse to go to war and fight. Leagues, treaties, diplomatic protest, sanctions, etc., all have seemed to be useless to stop bloodshed and will continue to be so as long as leaders and big business, greedy for gold and power continue to exploit peoples and fail to exercise the principles of the Golden Rule. This last war, however, put a heavier strain than originally anticipated on our resources and increased the national debt by many billions. Each time the expenditure of men and resources grows greater. The average individual eventually loses in war's aftermath but the corporations become richer.

Do you think our nation then, could get along without arms? The answer is NO, not as long as human nature remains as it is and probably always will be until the end of time. Therefore, I believe our nation should be adequately prepared at all times to defend itself in the air, on land or sea, including attacks from those enemies always boring from within, foreign spies and saboteurs.

We will remain a powerful nation only as long as we command the respect of the rest of the world. To help maintain that respect and keep us from war, we must have a semblance of power as expressed in an adequate military policy. That is the only language the enemy understands. We must have this even though we are trying to promote the cause of peace through new world organizations.

Our first president advised that to prevent war, we must be prepared for war but we have never been fully prepared for any war as yet. We are not militaristic as a nation until we are aroused by some turn in world events. Also we are fortunate that for decades we have had peaceful neighbors, who if they quarrel, it is solely among themselves. Likewise we have never been a territorial aggressor against any nation.

War is stupid, insensate and a diabolical illusion but there will always be war. Listen! You can hear faintly in the distance, the roll of the heavy caissons along the cobbled pavement, the clatter of horses hoofs, the drone of a heavy tank, the crisp, sharp commands of an officer, the muffled boom of exploding shells and the hideous screams of new weapons of destruction, yet unknown. But the result will be the same. Catastrophe and death. The end of our selfish ideals of happiness and civilization as we know it. Out of it may come to those who survive, the sparkling dawn of the Millennium, when all wars and strife will cease forever; when there will no longer be heartbreak and bloodshed, or death, and men will truly be brothers. "Blessed are the meek," who will inherit what is left of the earth.

Doughboy or general, private or "shavetail" lieutenant, the U.S. soldier did his duty nobly, whatever his rank.[9] Each man of the Fourth Division and every other regiment and division of the old A.E.F., as well, carried on to the best of their ability, for the honor of his country and the glory of our flag.

"Oh, how I hate to get up in the morning!
Gee, how I like to remain in bed!
For the saddest blow of all,
Is to hear the bugle call," etc.
—Irving Berlin

9. A reference to the pre-World War I army custom of shaving the tail of new army mules, "which serves as sort of a warning signal to such as may have dealings with him, that the mule has not acquired proper discipline and a regard for the feelings of others." Frederick F. Moore, *Siberia To-day* (New York: D. Appleton and Company, 1919), 108.

Chapter 2

Soldiers a La Carte

I used to think I hated the army, and army life. Who didn't? But in looking back over the years, I am proud to have been a soldier in wartime. It was exciting, even with its hardships. The United States may seemingly become economically and political unbalanced at times, but I would much rather live in its city canyons or peaceful valleys than own all the old chateaus and cathedrals, or gambol in all the flesh pots of Europe and the old world. Even the most crabby old soldier will tell you that the U.S. and our way of life is decidedly worth fighting for.

The record placed before you, therefore, is to be taken as a mixture of memoir and historical fact as it applies to the First World War of 1917–1918. Likewise, my experience with the 7th and 8th Brigades, from training camp to the war scene and beyond. You will follow with me the travels, trials and escapades of the many different characters we shall meet. That is army life, but you will be most concerned with the members of my own immediate squad who were as ribald as any soldiery in any army. Underneath this veneer, they were really patriotic, steadfast and sincere.

Names of towns and dates are given, not only for historical and sentimental purposes but also as an added interest to readers who may have traveled approximately the same roads in World War I and the new G.I. who passed along similar routes in World War II. Movements are given in unbroken sequence, so that the route followed by the 4th Combat Division, A.E.F. may be traced from the U.S. to the German Rhineland and return 1918–1919.

It was on April 18th, 1918, therefore, that my contingent left Waterbury, Connecticut amid the fanfare of the local silver-plated cornet band at 11.00 a.m. bound for the Great Whoozis.

About 4.00 P.M. the same day, we arrived at Camp Devens, Ayer, Mass.[1] where we were met with the good natured jeers and jibes of those who had preceded us, and who now come down to the station to see some of the fun which is ever present on the arrival of "rookies."

This and other days to follow are to be marked by the loss of our civilian ego, as we subject ourselves to the rigid army discipline, or basic training. Now for the first time, we learn to appreciate fully the meaning of the old army song, "yer in the Army now, an yer not behind the plow," etc. On arrival we were assigned to the Depot Brigade, 76th Division, New England National Army.[2]

Succeeding days were taken up in trying to learn the rudiments of becoming a soldier, the first lesson being to follow a duty sergeant to some obscure storehouse, get yourself a bedsack and fill the same with straw. After that you were assigned to a barracks, where you find other soldiers already comfortably situated. You learn also, that you are just in time for "chow," so it is necessary that you visit the barracks supply sergeant and secure the most necessary weapon in the army—an aluminum mess-kit, the intricacies of which you

1. Howell incorrectly recalled the date of his departure. Official records and newspaper accounts state that he left Waterbury more than two weeks earlier, on March 30. Camp Devens, located one mile south of Ayer, Massachusetts, was named in honor of Civil War Brevet Major General Charles Devens. Construction began in June 1917, and the camp was formally established the following month. The 76th Division, National Army, occupied the camp from August 1917 to July 1918. More than 1,300 buildings were erected at Camp Devens, while the cantonment area consisted of 1,800 acres. Devens reached a peak strength of more than 48,000 officers and enlisted men in June 1918. Center of Military History, *Order of Battle of the United States Land Forces in the World War*, 5 vols. (Washington, D.C.: U.S. Army Center of Military History, 1988), vol. 3, pt. 2, 695–98.

2. The 76th Division was established by the War Department on August 5, 1917, with orders to organize at Camp Devens. The following month the first draftees began to arrive at the camp and training began. Although the division numbered some 22,000 men by late October, subsequent transfers of men to other divisions meant that the 76th numbered less than half its authorized strength by March 1918. After receiving more men, the division began sailing for Europe in July 1918. The 76th was designated a depot division, and received, trained, equipped and forwarded replacements to various units. *Order of Battle of the United States Land Forces in the World War*, vol. 2, 285–95.

will soon become past master. From now on there will be plenty of drill, hiking, inspections, (open yer mouth an say "Ahr"), pick and shovel fatigue duty and inoculations. It is now that we really learn what worms we have turned out to be, owing to loud mouthed orders shouted at us on every turn by flannel-mouthed duty sergeants, who never had any authority in civilian life, but whose chief delight now is to bawl us out at the least provocation. Then too, perhaps, some pompous officer with a brand new glittering set of spurs on his boots, informs you privately and aside, at which time you must say "sir" and "yes sir," that he expects you to salute your superiors promptly or whenever the occasion demands. This is often very irksome to a green soldier who is proud or independent by nature, as he can see no sense to this military gesture. As he does not understand it, this is his first reminder of caste in the army. But of course, strict discipline is absolutely necessary in whipping a large group of easy-going civilians into shape to respect and obey military orders. Otherwise there would be no army. To salute an officer, even though you hate his guts, is part of the necessary discipline and is respectful of those things which his uniform is meant to represent—the U.S. Army and the Government of the United States.

In ancient times when soldiers passed each other in camp or elsewhere, they raised their right arms to indicate they were friendly and would not use their side weapons, such as swords and daggers, promiscuously. If the fear of the military and the desire to do our best had not held us back, some of the "would-be generals" with whom we came in contact, would now be in wooden kimonos awaiting the judgment day. Those individuals certainly lived on the fat of the land in the training camps, as they were persona grata everywhere in the camp. Men having big mouths and a good crust of 24 karat brass became non-commissioned officers, or sergeants, and picked off soft jobs before they knew it. Slow-pokes and timid souls became doughboy privates, of course. Some of the first ideas of hate for our fellow man, were instilled in our minds by the petty tyrannies of those blatant individuals called drill sergeants.

It was here that my attention was first drawn to Private McGuire, a tall, lanky, Irishman. He was No. 4 in my squad on the drill field and was being bawled out unmercifully by the drill sergeant because he missed out on the counting or "sound off," which was all Greek to him.

"Attention! Sound off in place!" orders the sergeant.

"One, two, three, —silence—, five, six, and so on, counts each man in turn, except McGuire, who was No. 4.

"Hey! You big palooka! Can't ya count above three?" shouts the drill sergeant at McGuire, "Try it over again, now."

"One, two, three, —silence—, five, six," they repeat again.

"Hey there, ya big screw! Step two paces forward! Can't ya say four, or are ya tonguetied?" raves the sergeant. "When I orders ya ta sound off, I means ta sound off! Ya understand? Try it once more, now."

"One, two, three," it starts. "Say four," says I, nudging McGuire.

"I ain't gonna say four ta please no big mouth horse-shoer," answers McGuire turning to me, red in the face. "He ain't gonna insult me, sergeant er no sergeant!"

"Oh he ain't eh?" bellows the sergeant, "Well, we'll see about that! You sounds off correctly this time, er I puts yer in the guard house! Already now, sound off!"

"One, two, three, SMACK!" The sergeant has been struck square in the eye by a cud of juicy tobacco.

"Who did that!" exclaims the sergeant, holding his hand over a smarting eye.

"I did," says McGuire stepping out of ranks with fist clenched. "You ain't gonna call me no big palooka an get away with it."

"Call out the guard!" yells the sergeant and blows his whistle three times frantically. We grabbed hold of McGuire before he did anything rash. Soon two men of the guard appear on the scene.

"You're under arrest fer insult, an assault on yer superior officer," says the sergeant to McGuire. Then turning to the guards, "Take this man to the hoosegow. I'll report later. Attention!"

We all shivered in our shoes. A few hours in the guardhouse and McGuire saw the light. Everyday thereafter he was one of the hardest working drillers on the field and became quite military. Our squad soon became very efficient in executing "squads left and right, left oblique, to the rear march" and similar convolutions. As McGuire remarked to me one day later on, "They can say what they wanna sojer, but we're the best drill squad on the field. Only sergeants is bohunks."[3]

3. According to the Oxford English Dictionary, "a low rough fellow," usually from central or southeastern Europe.

Many a civilian soldier will remember also the tricks and devices used in the training camps, and resorted to by many a homesick boy, to get permanently relieved from army service. Among these was the swallowing of a cud of tobacco, a piece of soap, or a drink of vinegar before a medical examination, to fool the doctors by simulating acute stomatitis or chronic heart disease, perhaps gaining a discharge. Some actually got by with the subterfuge too, but most of them were S.O.L. (out of luck). They were placed under arrest and further disciplined in the guardhouse. This procedure furnished still further education to the "rookie" soldier.

Occasionally a break would occur in the continuous round of squad drilling, coal shoveling, loading, or whatever else the Army could find for us to do. Once or twice we were marched down to the large camp theatre (called Liberty), for entertainment and a lecture. After the usual performance of a Y.M.C.A. song leader, who after all is only a cheap copy of a college cheer leader, we would be shown a reel or two of silent movies, followed by a vaudeville act. Acts containing women were, of course, the most popular with the embryo soldiers. At the conclusion of these preliminaries would come the real purpose of the theatre party—patriotic propaganda. We would have to sit and listen to a long lecture delivered by some officer, which was supposed to inform the green soldier who we were at war with, and why. The substance of these lectures would be somewhat as follows—

"It is most glorious to be a soldier of the U.S. because our soldiers are the best in the world. One U.S. soldier is equal to three foreign soldiers. We must therefore fight, not only to save our homes and loved ones, but because it is our sacred duty, and God will surely be with us. Our cause in this war being honorable and just, will make us the shining beacon of light for world liberty and justice, thereby ending wars for all time. To succeed, we must annihilate the invader and ruthlessly suppress imperialism, thereby becoming the arbiters of world peace. We will again ring the liberty bell of freedom for oppressed peoples."

These lectures were intended to allay fear and instill unbounded patriotism in new soldiers, and usually succeeded, for the time being at least. Whatever was said was accepted without question by all, as no one would think to do otherwise. The lecture however, made about as much impression on the "rookie" soldier as the "oath of allegiance to the flag" administered somewhat later on in the barracks dining hall in a slipshod manner, by some rubber-stamp non-commissioned officer. Not enough dignity surrounded the taking of the oath to make any patriotic impression, because it was rushed and smacked of too much routine. Anyway the soldier, more interested in canteens and mess-kits, had to be in the theatre whether he wished it or not; but he would rather be sitting in a comfortable theatre seat, than out on the hot drill field listening to the bark of some self-important lieutenant or blatant drill sergeant. All this is quite necessary of course, in any army, especially one that is raised by conscription from a civilian population composed of all nationalities.[4] It was, and still is their patriotic duty therefore, to know, fight for and respect our flag, whether or not they know anything of its history or background and under whose protection they work and live.

After an interval of several days at the camp, we finally secured complete uniforms, one piece at a time. Shoes and hats might not fit, but that made no difference. On our visits to the company supply sergeant for equipment, the greatest object of curiosity was the shiny Springfield rifle always locked in the supply sergeant's bailiwick and seen through a latticed partition. How some of us itched to be allowed to handle one of those, but we were mostly disappointed at this particular time.

It is said that a "rookie" first absorbs the spirit of a soldier from his new uniform and later from the action of his commander. This I believe is correct, because a complete uniform gave us pride in the fact that we at least looked like soldiers. Likewise, an erect, efficient, fair minded officer of good military bearing, made us wish to emulate him in military appearance and deportment.

When new men had been in the camp for about ten days and had seen everything that interested them around the large encampment, they would begin to grow uneasy and want to go down to the town of Ayer or elsewhere nearby. To give every man in the camp a pass who desired it, would be like transferring the camp all over New England. Therefore only a certain number of passes were issued each night. In our company, it was limited to three.

4. Nearly half a million members of the American Army (more than 18 percent) were immigrants of 46 nationalities. Nancy Gentile Ford, *Americans All! Foreign-born Soldiers in World War I* (College Station: Texas A&M University Press, 2001), 3.

"Geeze! I wisht I could get a pass an go ta town," says McGuire to an old army private, hanging around the canteen.

"Why don't ya go anyway, sojer?" suggests the private, interested.

"We're not allowed out of the barracks after 10 p.m., an you knows I can't get back by that time," complains McGuire.

"Well, well, well," replies the private, laughing at the seeming innocence of McGuire. "Why don't ya go A.W.O.L. then? If ya gets caught, they won't do much to you green rookies anyway."

"I'm goin' tonight then," says McGuire. "Want ta come along?"

"Sure! I'll meet ya in Ayer an show yer the town," says the old private chuckling to himself.

So McGuire goes down to Ayer that night without permission. He got through the front gate of the camp without being stopped for a pass, because he walked out practically concealed behind an automobile. On the way back about 11 p.m. however, he was stopped, his name taken and the next day he was called before the company commander to explain. For the offense, he was punished by being placed on kitchen police for a week.

"Geeze! That K.P. job is all right," says McGuire to me next day.

"That right? No kiddin'?" says I, "Guess I'll have a try at it then."

"Oh, of course, them cooks makes ya do all the dirty work, such as scrubbing all the old dirty pans, an peelin' onions an potatoes, but ya sure gits plenty ta eat, an ya don't have ta drill," says McGuire.

"I'll take the drillin' fer me," says I, "'cause I'd rather be a soldat than a scullion any old time."

"Mebbe yer right, buddy," says McGuire, "never thought of that. I wonder where that guy is that advised me ta go A.W.O.L.? I didn't see nuthin' of him in Ayer, where he promised ta meet me."

"Probably laughing up his sleeve at you right now, because he gave you a bum steer, an got you in trouble," says I.

Just then two soldiers passed our doorway that attracted our attention. One of the two was the old army private, walking just ahead and in front of the other soldier, carrying a full coal bucket. The man behind had a rifle with fixed bayonet on his shoulder and was keeping a close watch on the old army private marching with the bucket in front. It was a two man battalion with only one gun.

"Where wuz ya the other night, sojer?" yells McGuire at the old private. "I didn't see nuthin' of ya in Ayer, like ya promised."

"I got the Ayer all right," answers the private, "but I got in a fist fight wit the cheese of police, an look where I am now. In the hoosegow."

"Ho, ho, ho," laughs McGuire. "They don't do much ta you green rookies, do they? All I got wuz a week on K.P. an they're chasin' you around wit a bayonet."[5]

Camp Devens was a good camp, however, and our various compulsory duties kept us quite busy, so time never lagged. Uncertainty as to our future is what bothered us most. We wondered where and how we would end up with the army, but more often we never gave it a second thought, if we were kept moving around somewhere. Canteens were always handy too, if you had a little money and gave you somewhere to go after chowtime. The food however was usually good and plentiful with little extras thrown in from the company mess fund made from money donations of the men.

McGuire used to sleep near me in the barracks, that is, the foot end of his bed was at, or close to, the head end of my cot. Most other soldiers kept their feet covered at night, but not McGuire. When everyone was snoring and raising the shingles off the roof, it seemed to be the signal for McGuire's feet to come stealing out from under his blanket. I never did get used to that. I told him about it several times but it didn't do any good, so I must supply my own remedy. Every night, whenever his feet would steal out from under the blanket, I gave them a good whack with a ruler I kept handy. McGuire would grunt and pull them under cover, at least until I got to sleep. After that I didn't care. Sometimes the aroma would wake me again in which event I would repeat the process. Next day McGuire might complain about the balls of his feet being sore, but I never sympathized with him any.

When a few of us finally left Camp Devens sometime later without being selected to become a permanent part of the 76th Divis[ion] Nat'nl [National] Army but picked to join a regular U.S. Army regiment, we were envied and told about how lucky we were. Yeah! We got into the war zone several months ahead of the 76th Divis[ion], who were shipped across and then used as replacements in part for the Regular Army regiment I was in, after we had

5. Major General Harry F. Hodges, the commander of the 76th Infantry Division, ordered that men who were guilty of minor military offenses would train with their units in the morning, then perform fatigue duty in the afternoon as their punishment. Only those guilty of serious infractions were ordered to spend time in the camp's guard house. *Fitchburg* (MA) *Daily Sentinel*, April 24, 1918.

been four months in France and in two offensives. However we found the Regular Army atmosphere much more to our liking as there wasn't so much military blah in evidence. In that point we were lucky and so are grateful for that anyway.

Therefore on April 26th, after an all-day train ride through Wooster, New Haven, Bridgeport, etc., we arrive at Camp Mills, Garden City, Long Island, just in time for chow, but there was no mess hall or barracks there.[6] The camp was quite a large establishment of white army squad tents and located in a large field directly opposite the Garden City Hotel.

Arriving in the camp, I was assigned with McGuire and five others from various other training camps, to Company B, 39th Infantry, 4th Division, now in Camp Mills only temporarily before going across the pond.[7] And what a squad it was, too! We were all assigned by top-sergeant Painting to a separate squad tent in charge of Corporal Covey, a short, stocky, good natured, non-commissioned officer who hailed from somewhere in Texas. Besides the corporal and myself, the roster of the squad was as follows:

Private Jeffrey O'Hara . . . from a small town in Ohio.
Private William Stevens . . . garage mechanic from Bellevue, Illinois.
Private Salvatore Vinelli . . . a wop from New Haven, Connecticut.
Private Morris Belkin . . . Jewish boy from New Brunswick, New Jersey.
Private Alonzo Brizee . . . rubber salesman from Naugatuck, Connecticut.
Private Frank X. McGuire . . . plumber from Danbury, Connecticut.

6. Camp Mills was named in honor of Spanish-American War hero Major General Albert L. Mills, and was located about ten miles from the eastern boundary of New York City. Initially established in September 1917 for the mobilization of the 42nd ("Rainbow") Division, Camp Mills was ordered abandoned in late 1917, but was reestablished in April 1918 as a temporary camp to accommodate troops prior to their embarkation for Europe. The camp covered about 500 acres, with provisions for half of the transient soldiers to be lodged in barracks and the rest in tents. At the time Howell arrived (April 1918), more than 16,000 officers and men were present, with higher numbers due to arrive later that summer. *Order of Battle of the United States Land Forces in the World War*, vol. 3, pt. 2, 753–58. Some 400 men left Camp Devens and joined the 4th Division at Camp Mills, replacing those recruits who had failed to pass physical and mental tests. Bach and Hall, *The Fourth Division*, 38.

7. Company B was organized in Syracuse, New York, on June 1, 1917, under the command of Lieutenant Harry J. Holstlaw. It moved to Camp Greene, North Carolina, in late October 1917 as a skeleton organization, and there received its complement of officers, men and equipment. Record Group 120, Records of the American Expeditionary Forces, World War I, Records of Combat Divisions 1917–1919, 4th Division, 4th Division Historical, Box 29, Folder: 39th Infantry, History, [M.G., Supply, Hdrs, 1st, 2nd, 3rd Bn, and Co. A thru M], 4th Div., 204–11.4, Official History of the 39th Regiment of Infantry, 1917–1918, National Archives and Records Administration, College Park, Maryland.

Our squad was a part of the Fourth Platoon under Sergeant Patrick Nolan of Poughkeepsie, New York.[8]

Up until this time, I had never felt the trigger of a gun of any kind, and my only military training consisted of "squads left and right" (called east and west in army lingo), "about face" and "to the rear, march." We were not, therefore, considered proficient enough to drill with the rest of the company or the regiment, so Corporal Covey was under orders to teach us the manual of arms in the camp, while the rest of the company was out on the hot drill-field. We learned a little of the nomenclature; how to take the oil-can out of the rifle butt, and so on, but Corporal Covey who was out every night somewhere, was too tired to teach us much in the daytime. Also we were not keen on learning too soon either, so the corporal would delegate one of us to watch out for the "officer of the day" while the rest of us engaged in bunk fatigue duty (plain sleep) for a couple of hours.

In reality, the corporal was teaching us more than we could appreciate. We were learning the art of "gold bricking" which in Army parlance means, loafing or getting out of work whenever you could get by with it. If you were not more or less proficient in this accomplishment, you would be doing all the work, while the other

8. Jeffrey O'Hara, William Stevens, Salvatore Vinelli and Patrick Nolan do not appear in the company rosters, and are likely pseudonyms. Although Howell obviously based his characterizations and dialogue on actual members of his company, he admitted that he changed a few names, possibly because he could not locate those comrades to discuss their inclusion in his manuscript. Max Belkin (1894–1972), a native of Collinsville, Connecticut, and a resident of New Britain, Connecticut, owned a grocery in New Britain when he registered for the draft in June 1917. He claimed exemption from the draft due to "presence needed to carry on established business." He enlisted on March 29, 1918, and was discharged on August 11, 1919. State of Connecticut, *Office of the Adjutant General, Service Records, Connecticut Men and Women in the Armed Forces of the United States during World War, 1917–1920* (Hartford, CT: Office of the Adjutant General, 1941–1970?), 1496. Alonzo Brizie is likely Lee Brizzie (1895–1958), a native of Pine Plains, New York, and a resident of Waterbury, Connecticut, when he enlisted in March 1918. He was severely wounded on September 26, 1918, and discharged on July 29, 1919. *Connecticut Men and Women*, 2719. Leo Leeds Covey (1892–1967), a native of Cherokee, Iowa, was working as a laborer in Cherokee County when he registered for the draft in June 1917. He had already served two years in the U.S. Regular Army as an infantry private and been discharged from the 6th U.S. Infantry due to disability in 1915. He died in Douglas County, Oregon. Frank X. McGuire may be George F. McGuire (born in 1889), a native and resident of Waterbury, Connecticut, who was working as a forger at a metal works when he registered for the draft in June 1917. He claimed three years' prior service as a private in Company A, "National Guards." He enlisted in Company B in March 1918. *Connecticut Men and Women*, 2815. Sergeant Patrick Nolan may be Robert J. Nolan of Derby, Connecticut, who enlisted in the Regular Army in July 1917. He was promoted to corporal in Company B in March 1918 and to sergeant that June. He served with the company until his discharge in March 1919. *Connecticut Men and Women*, 641; Muster Roll of Company B, 39th U.S. Infantry, April 30-June 30, 1918, National Personnel Records Center, St. Louis, Missouri.

fellow who was a better "chiseler" than yourself, would be taking it easy except under the forced order of some superior. Corp. Covey was a soldier though and many a trick of the Old Army I have learned from him.

We had a lot of fun at Camp Mills. Two or three times we sneaked out nights before the guard was posted and went over to Hempstead, L.[ong] I.[sland] which was close by, where they passed out beer from back doors to soldiers. We couldn't go in cafes or saloons. But we were caught one night when returning to the camp. We were trying to pass the sentry unnoticed by following close behind two other soldats from a different outfit than ours. We just tagged them in the back way taking it for granted that they knew the ropes and the route as well. But a guard just coming around the corner of a mess shack, stopped us all quite unexpectedly. He asked our two friends to show their passes first. As they couldn't produce any, he called the corporal of the guard who placed them under arrest. I was more fortunate because I was with that quick witted Irishman of my squad, named McGuire. He explained to the guard that we had just arrived that day, had been out of the gate on permission and had lost the location of our outfit in such a large camp. The guard didn't ask for our passes, but seemed fully convinced with our story and even drew us a map in the sand showing the location of our company street. We knew all the time, of course, but I suppose he thought we looked and acted like rookies anyway and let it go at that. His attitude was one of annoyance because we had caused him so much bother.

Civilian cookie peddlers and pie butchers certainly must have become rich around this camp. They had a never ending supply of customers. It was at this camp also that I learned to appreciate the taste of regular army chow cooked over a wood fire and always eaten out of doors. This treatment seems to add to the flavor of any kind of food, whether it is prunes or bully beef, making it more palatable and satisfactory. You were most always well fed but somehow always hungry.

It was here also, that I first found out you had to have the permission of the Top Sergeant to talk to the company commander. I wanted to get a pass to go out to the front gate of the camp to answer a long distance telephone call, so I went to the Orderly Room for this purpose.

"What is it, soldier?" inquired Sergeant Painting, stopping me.

"I wish to speak to the company commander," says I.

"What for, soldier?" says the sergeant.

"Who wants to know?" I replied, trying to shove by through the door.

"I wants ta know!" growls the sergeant, grabbing me roughly by the blouse, "Ya can't see the company commander without my permission. Yer in the army now an don't yer fergit it!"

"I can't fergit it's none of your damn business," I said, getting hot under the collar because I had to kiss the sergeant to request a favor from the high and mighty company boss.

"Well, now looka here, soldier," continues the sergeant, "I knows yer a rookie an don't understand military etiquette very well, an so I overlooks yer bein disrespectful to yer superior officer. The Lieut. ain't in just now, so I has ta run the outfit, an ya can tell me all about it if it's important. Nobody from this company is allowed out of this camp for the rest of the week."

"Oh Hell!" says I, "it's too late to go now anyway."

Sergeant Painting and Lieutenant Holstlaw, I have pleasant memories of both.[9] They were real soldiers with plenty of Old Army experience back of them which came in handy later on.

I have now been in the service about a month. I know nothing about war as yet and very little about the accoutrements or implements of warfare. McGuire and the rest of my squad are in the same fix. But we will learn soon enough. We are about to sail for France.

The day before we are to leave Camp Mills, we are given a big feed by our mess sergeant and then marched over to the Garden City Hotel for a free bath in their large swimming pool. At the same

9. Harry Painting (1884–1964) of Boston, Massachusetts, enlisted in the U.S. Regular Army in 1908 and was mustered out three years later. He served again from 1911–1914, then reenlisted and served until 1935. Registers of Enlistments in the United States Army, 1798–1914, M233, Roll 64, 67. Harry J. Holstlaw (1873–1932), a native of Xenia, Illinois, first enlisted in the Regular Army in February 1904 and was discharged in 1907. He reenlisted in October 1908, was discharged in October 1911, enlisted again in November 1911 and was discharged in November 1914. He remained in the army as an enlisted man following World War I and retired shortly before his death. He was buried in Sunnyside, Washington. Registers of Enlistments in the United States Army, 1798–1914, M233, Roll 57, 63, 66, National Archives and Records Administration. Holstlaw commanded Company B from August 7-October 9, 1917, October 19, 1917-December 10, 1917, January 22, 1918-July 10, 1918, and from August 2-August 8, 1918. Record Group 120, Records of the American Expeditionary Forces, World War I, Records of Combat Divisions 1917–1919, 4th Division, 4th Division Historical, Box 29, Folder: 39th Infantry, History, [M.G., Supply, Hdrs, 1st, 2nd, 3rd Bn, and Co. A thru M], 4th Div., 204–11.4, Official History of the 39th Regiment of Infantry, 1917–1918, National Archives and Records Administration, College Park, Maryland.

time the 39th Infantry Band gave a concert of military music on the veranda of the hotel for the benefit of the guests, both paying and chiseling. Heavy, shiney, Wurlitzer band instruments, Corona typewriters and the green painted company headquarters trunks, are three things I'll always remember about the walking army.

"I wonder what all the activity is about, anyway?" inquires Brizee.

"Well, I'll tellya men," volunteers Corporal Covey, "It's a rumor that we're about ta sail fer a foreign country an tomorrer we hops a troop train for Long Island City and Noo York."

"I can't wait to get across and shoot the old bull Kaiser," says O'Hara. "We'll show them damn dutchmen what the U.S. Army is good for."

"Why, ya can't even hold a gun yet, ya big palooka!" remarks Belkin. "The krauts is safe. You're there with the bull, though."

"Says you!" replies O'Hara, hotly, "I notice you kikes is good bull shooters too when it comes ta sellin second hand clothes an chiselin."

"Hooray! fer the Jew boys!" exclaims Brizee, "I hopes ta kick a mule in the face if both of them don't run fer life an liberty, if they ever meets up wit a real dutchman."

Chapter 3

En Voyage

Bright and early on the morning of May 10th, we left Camp Mills behind, with its white squad tents carefully ordered inside and out, for the next contingent who would come to occupy them. A troop train took us to Long Island City where we boarded a ferryboat, proceeded across the New York waterfront, past the Battery, under Brooklyn Bridge, etc., landing at Jersey City, N.J. sometime around noon. Arriving here we stalled around and waited for an interminable time so it seemed, on the wharf opposite the Colgate Soap factory, just doing nothing at all. I recall that the girls in the factories adjacent to the wharf, seemed quite interested in us and waved from their windows incessantly, but suddenly it all stopped. They either went back to work or were ordered away from the windows because we attracted too much attention and spies might be active and our movements were supposed to be secret. But the girls helped to pass the time and kept the boys interested.

About 2.30 P.M. we boarded the Italian Cunard Liner "*Dante Alighieri*" which now lay alongside the wharf, a great high hulk of steel plates, davits and lifeboats.[1] We were immediately ordered

1. The *Dante Alighieri*, a Transatlantica Italiana steamer, was built in 1914 in Genoa, Italy. The twin-screw vessel was capable of 16 knots, had two masts and two funnels, a tonnage of 9,757, and measured 483' by 59'. Eugene W. Smith, *Trans-Atlantic Passenger*

below and were not allowed to show ourselves on deck for any reason because of our secret embarkation and departure. We were forced to stay below until the next day. We were somewhat disappointed at being assigned to this Italian ship but the men soon got over it. Before we realized it, we had pulled anchor and sailed at 5.00 P.M. but few were aware of it, except to notice the gentle even purr of the engines. When we were finally allowed to come on deck and get a breath of fresh air, we were out of sight of land and wondering about our destination.

"Where ya think we're goin in this wop bathtub, corporal?" inquires McGuire.

"Don't know a thing about it, sojer," replies Corporal Covey.

"Well, it's an eye-talian ship, so we must be goin ta Eetalie," suggests Brizee.

"That's right," puts in O'Hara, "If they wuz sendin us ta France we'd be on a French tub, or to England on an English tub, an so on. Eh, what! It must be Italy."

"I got an idea. Why not get Vinelli ta find out from the crew?" says McGuire.

"That's a good idea," agrees the corporal.

So McGuire and I started out along the deck to find Vinelli. He was presently located and we found him already talking to a member of the crew on the subject, so we broke in on the conversation.

"Ask him where the ship is goin, Vinelli," says McGuire.

"He's a say, she's a bigga ship," advises Vinelli, "an she's a goin to Bresta, France, but she may stoppa first atta Cobh, Irelanda."

"Hooray!" exclaims McGuire, jumping around, "We're goin ta France! We're goin ta France! Ring around the rosey, pick yerself a posey."

"Yeah. But mebbe the submarine, she push em up firsta," says Vinelli.

"Cripes! I hope not!" says McGuire. "I gotta date wit the Kaiser's son, der Kron Prinz, an I don't wanna be late."

And so we went back to the rest of our squad to spread the good news. We had sailed south at first, contacting warm weather, turned around and then due north until we sighted icebergs.

Ships, Past and Present (N.p.: By the author, 1947), 76. The ship was chartered by the British government to carry American troops. Bach and Hall, *The Fourth Division*, 40.

It was a sensation to see them rearing their large snow white heads along the horizon with some floating loose around our boat but not touching us. Now we were assured that our destination was France or England and could hardly wait to get there.

Restrictions on the ship were quite rigid. You could only smoke in the daytime. After dark all of the ship's lights were out, or else shaded so as not to attract the notice of a submarine, an ever present danger. We were told that a light from a single match flame was visible through a sea glass for about three miles on the ocean. Even the portholes of the ship were carefully closed after dark to shut off all possible sources of light and they shut off a goodly portion of our air supply as well. The sailors removed their white caps at night also, as these were visible in the moonlight and luminescent. The ship itself was not painted its usual spotless white because of easy visibility day or night, but was camouflaged in a variety of zigzag stripes and curves in all colors, mostly greens and blues, making it look like a zebra. With this arrangement, the ship did not stand out on the horizon, either day or night, until you were close upon it.[2] Of necessity, we wore life belts most of the time while moving around the decks, so as to be ready in case of accident or submarine attack.

After the second day out, most of the soldiers became seasick. This was expected and indicated by a series of washtubs placed in convenient positions all over the ship, inside and out.[3] The food which we thought was very poor, began to taste better about the fourth day when most of us had recovered from seasickness. But on the whole the food was not up to standard and we were fed quite frequently on what we christened "rotten rabbit" which actually was rabbit, stewed or fried a la italiane. Our friend

2. "Dazzle" painting or camouflage used patches of black or color paint to deceive German U-Boat commanders as to a ship's course, range and speed. One source also argued that the painting made a large troopship appear as two small ships, one behind the other, not an attractive target for a U-Boat captain. Bach and Hall, *The Fourth Division*, 41.

3. One of Howell's comrades noted the "funny sight" of seeing the ship's rail, crowded from bow to stern, with "fellows hanging their heads over and losing their breakfasts." He also found it amusing when, on the fourth day of the voyage, the sea became so rough that at meal times the dishes "would slide all around the table and perhaps you had your own food and perhaps some one else's." *Daily Kennebec Journal* (Augusta, ME), July 17, 1918. John A. Barnwell of Company C was one of those seasick soldiers. He reported to his sister that "I was sick two different days while on the boat. That sea sick sure gives a person a curious feeling. And I missed two meals while I was sick." John A. Barnwell to sister, Somewhere in France, June 1, 1918, World War I Service Questionnaires, U.S. Army Heritage and Education Center, Carlisle, Pennsylvania.

Vinelli became quite friendly with some of the crew, so much so, that after a short time McGuire and I passed up the regular soldier chow of the ship and got a regular handout from the crew's mess on the Q.T. I ate spaghetti until it came out of my ears, along with big hunks of black cheese and thrived on it. The ship also contained a regular coal fired brick baking oven. The odor of hot rye bread was wonderful and the taste beyond compare to a hungry soldat. The three of us therefore lushed into large pieces of this delicacy whenever we wished. One day however, we accidentally caught sight of the bakers kneading or treading the cream colored dough with their bare feet on huge mixing boards. This finished McGuire and I for any further taste for stuff, but it didn't seem to bother Vinelli any. "She's a justa like shes a made in Genova" says Vinelli biting into a big hunk with relish, "an shes a gotta ze grand arome too."

Our ship was small and somewhat overcrowded. We were continually stepping on each other in moving around and which was aggravated by the bulky cork life belts. We heard the usual rumor (same on every transport) about the Germans placing an indemnity of $25,000 for the capture of the captain of our ship, but he didn't seem a bit worried way up there on the bridge deck. One day we sighted a large whale to the left and some distance away from the vessel, having the usual fountain which seemed to spring out of the top of its head. "Thar she blows" says McGuire, speaking like an old salt.

About half way across we were joined by a Belgian Relief ship and a convoy of fifteen other troop transports carrying U.S. troops. These ships were of various sizes, shapes and nationalities. There was also one U.S. battleship steaming along ahead of us.[4]

The whole presented a picturesque marine parade. Our ship was also equipped with a small calibre naval rifle or cannon, manned by two gobs of the U.S. Navy. They would have target

4. On May 10, 1918, a convoy consisting of the cruiser U.S.S. *Frederick* and 6 transports, including the *Dante Alighieri* left New York, and was joined at sea by 8 more transports sailing from Newport News, Virginia. All the transports arrived in France on May 23, but the U.S.S. *President Lincoln* was sunk on May 31 on the return trip to the United States. Benedict Crowell and Robert Forrest Wilson, *The Road to France, Part II: The Transportation of Troops and Military Supplies, 1917–1918* (New Haven: Yale University Press, 1921), 609. According to one source, the *Frederick* eventually left the convoy and was replaced by nine destroyers. *History of the 7th Infantry Brigade*, 9. Howell probably mistook the cruiser *Frederick* for a battleship.

practice once each day about noon. A barrel was thrown overboard as a target and the gobs would shoot at it with their gun, from off the stern end of the ship, usually sinking it in one or two shots. There were 3300 U.S. Regulars aboard the *Dante Alighieri*, all being troops of the 39th Inf. Regiment and some machine gun companies. Every day aboard was much the same. We entertained ourselves as best we could.

On May 23d, the ship entered the Irish Atlantic near the mouth of the English Channel, with a full convoy of aeroplanes and torpedo boat destroyers. This was considered a most dangerous spot infested with submarines. Our spirits were exhilarated however, as we saw the U.S. destroyers in all their fancy finery of camouflage, skimming the water like swift motorboats all around us.

We were lucky. While nothing exciting had happened to us and we were safely across, another ship carrying the 58th U.S. Infantry of our division was torpedoed off the shores of England but no lives were lost and they joined us at Calais, France later on.[5]

As we caught sight of the green shoreline of ancient Brittany for the first time, it made us thrill as Columbus might, after his long and arduous voyage to the new world. We pulled into Brest harbor where the blue water was dotted with hundreds of fisher craft, small boats with one piece sails, gleaming white against the blue in the morning sunlight. We had been fourteen long days at sea and everyone was uneasy with the romance of expectancy, as we viewed the quays and warehouses of the old world port for the first time. Listen to the boys.

"When I gits ta Paris, I'm gonna find me a café with one of them wild, ravishing, dancing, seducing, mamas, I've been hearin so much about," remarks O'Hara, sort of limping along up to the ship's guard rail.

"What's the matter, sojer? Gettin that old leg trouble again?" inquires Stevens with a mock solicitude.

"Mebbe his sea legs is kinda weak, like mine," I suggested.

5. The *Moldavia*, a British ship carrying two companies of the 58th Infantry, was torpedoed and sunk by a German U-Boat on May 23, 1918. Despite Howell's claim, 56 men were killed, the 4th Division's first losses by enemy action. Bach and Hall, *The Fourth Division*, 42–45. An undated, brief history of the regiment described the crossing of the Atlantic as "thirteen uneventful days." Record Group 120, 4th Division Historical, Box 29, Folder: 39th Infantry, Histories, Commendations & Battle Participants, NARA.

"Eyah, he's weak all right! He's had the old leg trouble ever since we went to that burlesque theater back in Noo-York," wisecracks Belkin, "but his limpin would be cured quick if he was to see a nice pair of legs right now."

"Vive La Belle Frawnce, legs and all!" exclaims O'Hara, waving to a mademoiselle in a small fishing boat some little distance away from the ship.

Chapter 4

Arrival in France and Movements

The *Dante Alighieri* had crept slowly along in the harbor and sometime during the night of May 24th, we anchored directly alongside the ancient quays of Brest, France. Disembarkation began about 10.30 a.m. It was a strange, even a pleasant sensation, as we stepped off the gangplank and on to foreign soil, the first time for most of us. No doubt, but that it was also the first time, that many of the boys had ever been outside of Podunk, U.S.A. After landing, we waited around for hours so it seemed, then finally, marched over to a series of wooden shacks erected along a street back of the wharves, where we were given slum and black coffee for breakfast.[1]

After that was over, we started out on a three mile hike up a very steep hill to the town of Pontanezen (heights above Brest) and entered a small army tent camp.[2] The camp was opposite

1. "Slum" or "slumgullion" was, according to one doughboy, chunks of issue beef with "just about anything else" the cook could find, and rarely the same thing twice. Henry Berry, *Make the Kaiser Dance: Living Memories of the Doughboy* (Garden City, NY: Doubleday, 1978), 283.

2. Camp Pontanezen, located about a mile and a half from the Brest harbor, consisted of two areas. The first, about 15 acres known as Pontanezen Barracks, consisted of six large, old stone barracks and several smaller buildings surrounded by a wall. The other area, consisting of farm land around the barracks, initially covered 90 acres but was increased incrementally as needed. Many aspects of the camp were unsatisfactory in the summer of

Napoleon's old barracks, two long grey-white stone buildings facing each other endwise and two stories in height. These old barracks are still in use today. Little French urchins would run along the column of marching men, offering vin-rouge in bottles for a few sous. The soldiers bought the wine too, that is, when they thought the lieutenant wasn't looking. All were eager for a taste of the famed French wine they had heard so much about—probably the lieutenant as well.

Next day we had the honor of taking a bath in the old barracks, if you could call it a bath. The equipment consisted of a one-half inch, galvanized water pipe, plugged at one end and installed horizontally about ten feet off the floor and connected to a tank in another building. Two, one-eighth inch holes about a foot apart, were drilled in the underside of the pipe at the plugged end. This arrangement gave out two small streams about the size of a lead pencil. You were allowed to stand under this improvised two-stream shower bath until the sergeant counted fifteen, then it was shut off. If you got wet, it was O.K. but if you didn't, you were out of luck. While water was scarce in France, vin blanc and vin rouge was plentiful, as we were to find out later.

Strolling around on a road behind the old barracks, McGuire and I located a small estaminet. Outside, painted on its wall was the word "Vins," so we entered. This little place was presided over by a quite ritzy looking little jeunesse who surprised us by speaking intriguing English, which we were not at all prepared for. We had been trying hard to learn a little French on our way across, but the minute we saw the little mademoiselle, we promptly forgot every word of it and hardly knew how to address her.[3]

"How do ya do, mademoiselle?" says McGuire, speaking in a jerky manner.

1918, as the small permanent garrison struggled to make improvements while new troops rapidly increased the population of the camp. Many men were forced to live in shelter tents outside the barracks in "tenacious" mud. M.W. Ireland, *The Medical Department of the United States Army in the World War*, 15 vols., 1921–29 (Washington, D.C.: U.S. Government Printing Office, 1927), Administration, American Expeditionary Forces, 2: 465–71. Colonel Smedley Butler, who arrived at Pontanezen a few months after Howell, noted that the camp was "a hell of a place" with "acres and acres of mud flats" where troops "wallowed in ooze." Lowell Thomas, *Old Gimlet Eye: The Adventures of Smedley D. Butler* (New York: Farrar & Rinehart, 1933), 245.

3. Sgt. Earl J. McWilliams of Company I noted that by early July 1918 he had "picked up enough French" to get along well in the markets or ask for most anything to eat, but could not carry on a conversation, although he tried "awfully hard sometimes" when he met an attractive mademoiselle. *The Alta Vista Journal* (Alma, KS), August 8, 1918.

"Comment alle vous, Messeurs," replies the mademoiselle seriously, and then with a ghost of a smile, "How are ya, boys? Two vin blanks, tout de suite, eh?"

You could have knocked us over with a feather, this outburst was so sudden and unexpected.

"Do you really speak English, mademoiselle?" says McGuire in surprise.

"Oui, oui. Soldier Eengleesh I understand a leetle," replies mademoiselle.

"Give us a nice big kiss, then," says McGuire, leaning toward her.

"Kees? Ah non. Eet iz too zoon. I not know ze naughty soldats. Beeg bad boyz too frash," coos mademoiselle smiling, but trying hard to scowl.

So McGuire leaned over the little bar and kissed her anyway, and got his face slapped for his trouble.

"Beeg bad boy! I hope I not hurt heem much," says mademoiselle in a voice of sugar, stroking McGuire's raw boned chin with a soft white hand.

"Got any whisky?" queries McGuire.

"Wheesky?" says mademoiselle, perplexed. "Non. I not got wheesky. I got plenty of ze cognac. Beaucoup, zee beeg boy?" holding up a green bottle to the light.

"Two coneyac then, toot sweet," says McGuire.

Mademoiselle then places two small glasses on the little bar and pointing to each alternately with her dainty index finger, began reciting "Un, deux, bottan ze schoo" and gave us a melting smile as we poured out our drink from the green bottle. McGuire was completely hypnotized and lost in the fog. Well, I might as well say we both were. Here we are, on French soil not more than five hours and already talking to a friendly mademoiselle, enjoying ourselves immensely. We visited the little estaminet only about twice afterward, as we moved from this camp in about two days time. We found out that Mademoiselle's name was Marie. Also, she was not French, but Belgian, having been born in Ghent.

Our camp was now only a mushroom camp of about fifty army squad tents. When we came back in 1919 on our way home, we found an enormous camp of long wooden barracks, complete in every particular, of which more later. Camp Pontanezen, Brest and its environs are located on the coast of ancient and picturesque Brittany and the De la Manche of the Three Musketeers.

Therefore, two days after arriving, we are on the move again. We are now going up to Calais, in northwestern France, where a large English Army camp is located. Calais is on the English Channel about fifty miles from the Belgian border, near Dunkirk and Ostend, opposite England. Our train out of Brest therefore, was made up of boxcars, very small in size and containing no airbrake equipment such as we are accustomed to see and hear in the U.S. Instead, they employed a system of spring bumpers between each car, making the train noisy and jerky, amusing us with its erratic performance. You couldn't "ball the jack" into a switch with one of these cars without throwing the whole train off the track.

This was our first introduction to the famous "40 Hommes-8 Chevaux" (40 men-8 horses) the wartime legend painted on each car.[4] With our full equipment on our backs and draped around us, it was a hard matter to get forty men inside one of these dog houses. This fact caused some choice language to flow from the lips of the future heroes trying to squeeze inside, and you can lay to that.

"How the hell do they get that way, thinking they kin squeeze forty men an eight horses inside one of these piano boxes!" exclaims Stevens.

"That forty hommes, eight chevox means forty men alone or eight horses alone, not all together," explains Corporal Covey.

"Well, Judas Priest!" says Stevens, "There's only eighteen men in here now, an ya can't move a gahdamn inch! Get yer damn helmet and gas mask outta my face, wil ya?" he continues, glaring at O'Hara.

"Pipe down, you birds!" orders Sergeant Nolan, "Yer in here an yer gonna stay in, if yer likes it er not until we gets ta Chartres. Then ya kin stretch yer legs. Git away from that door, ya big bohunk! Ya wanna git killed before ya sees the Kaiser?"

"Get kilt! Not me," says McGuire, "I kin run faster'n this flat wheeled baby carriage is go'in."

4. The famous "40 and 8" boxcars transported many American soldiers in France. The side-door cars could haul 40 men or 8 horses. A member of the 39th noted that Americans used to traveling in Pullman cars found the "discomfort and degradation" of riding in "40 and 8s" to be "an introduction to life in war-ridden France. From that moment the American soldier left comfort behind." Record Group 120, 4th Division Historical, Box 29, Folder: 39th Infantry, Histories, Commendations & Battle Participants, NARA. Another doughboy recalled that "It seemed that all the wheels of the car were flat from the noise it made and the way it was bouncing over the narrow track we were hard put to stay in the car, let alone trying to get any rest." E.J.D. Larson, *Memoirs of France and the Eighty-Eighth Division* (Scott-Mitchell Publishing Co., 1920), 21.

"Eyah. Flat an squeaky, like the sergeant's voice," says O'Hara from a safe distance way back in the corner.

"If I could get at ya, private, yer head would be flatter'n two pancakes, an I don't mean maybe!" retorts the sergeant.

Our journey from Brest, through old Brittany and Normandy to Flanders, consumed two days and one night. We stopped for a whole afternoon at Boulogne-sur-mer, a small seaport on the English Channel and were fed by an English contingent located there. This is the town where General Pershing first set foot on French soil in June 1917, being greeted by President Paul Painlevé and Marshall Joffre of the French Republic.[5] From Boulonge, our next and last stop is Calais, opposite Dover, England. On our long journey up here we had passed through many famous towns of the ancien regime, the scene of some of the early stages of the French Revolution and one time ruled by English kings. A few towns are as follows:

Morlaix (finistère dep't)
St. Brieuc (côtes-du-nord)
Rennes (ille-et-vilaine)
Laval (mayenne)
Le Mans (sarthe)
Chartres (eure-et-loir)
Dreux (eure-et-loir)
Rouen (seine)
Amiens (somme)
Abbeville (somme)
Étaples (pas-de-calais)
Boulogne-sur-mer (pas-de-calais)

Arriving at Calais, we march through part of the town to the outskirts where there is an English rest camp, with canvas squad tents reinforced with sandbags about half way up the sides all the way around. This camp usually experienced air raids nearly every night from the German lines, now located about seventy miles to the northeast. The sandbags gave some protection from flying shrapnel. Part of the English Army of the Somme was here recuperating and being reorganized after their disastrous retreat

5. Pershing landed at Boulogne on June 13, 1917, where he was greeted by numerous French officers and officials and British Expeditionary Force Adjutant General Sir George H. Fowke. Pershing met War Minister Paul Painlevé and Marshal Joseph Joffre later that day in Paris.

of April 1918, so you can see we were in good company for green soldiers.[6] The eats, our chief worry, were excellent. We had good old English cheddar cheese, plenty of breakfast tea and marmalade, with great hunks of delicious white bread and butter, if you could grab it quick enough. Each man was issued a strip of meal tickets in advance, good for just so many meals. McGuire and I found several extra strips, probably lost by some unfortunate soldat whom we could not possibly identify, so we promptly made use of them. What we couldn't use, we gave away.

This is one place that I can say we actually got enough to eat. Our stay at this camp, however, was short. Because of the way they moved us around the camp from tent to tent, we knew it wouldn't last long. The truth is, according to records since perused by the writer, the Army didn't exactly know what to do with us at the time. Anyway, after an inspection, we turned in our large barracks bags, containing all our treasures such as cameras, knitted socks and sweaters given us by friends and sweethearts back home. We were told that they would be given back again at the next town we stopped at, but of course they never were. It was ever our opinion that the labor battalions and quartermaster outfits that handled them in the S.O.S. traded off our stuff to the Frogs (French) for vin blanc and cognac.[7]

Here also, we turned in our American Springfield rifles in exchange for English Enfields, a heavier and clumsier weapon.[8] The new rifles were stacked in an open yard of an armory

6. On the morning of March 21, 1918, the Germans launched the "Michael" Offensive. The German 17th Army struck the British Third Army, while the German Second and Eighteenth Armies attacked the British Fifth Army, forcing them to retreat some 40 miles. A combination of British and French reinforcements and German logistical problems halted the drive on April 5. Casualties numbered nearly 240,000 for the Germans and more than 250,000 for the British and French. On April 9, the German "Georgette" operation began further north, and the British First and Second Armies likewise were forced back from the Armentieres area with significant losses. As with "Michael," failed German logistics and a stiffened Allied defense forced the German offensive to sputter to a halt on April 27. Again, casualties were high—86,000 for the Germans, 112,000 for the British and French.

7. Despite Howell's dim view of the S.O.S., or Services of Supply, the organization was absolutely critical to stockpiling and moving millions of ship tons of necessary supplies to A.E.F. units at the front. The S.O.S. established base sections around major French ports such as Brest, St. Nazaire, and Bordeaux, where rail lines could then move supplies to an intermediate section in central France and an advance section near the front. More than 644,000 men served in the S.O.S., or about one third of the American Army in Europe.

8. The highly regarded American Model 1903 30.06 caliber Springfield rifle was an extremely well-made, accurate, and reliable infantry weapon. The British Short Magazine Lee Enfield (SMLE), No. 1 Mark III, caliber .303, admired by the British soldier, was issued to some U.S. troops, particularly those who trained or served with the British. As Howell indicates, the Enfield was thoroughly disliked by the American doughboy. Bruce Canfield, *U.S. Infantry Weapons of the First World War* (Lincoln, RI: Andrew Mowbray Co., 2000), 98–99.

on the opposite side of Calais, just like ordinary cordwood. They were not protected from the weather by as much as a tarpaulin. The only protection they had was Vaseline or cosmoline and rust. We, of course had to clean these weapons thoroughly before the daily inspection. If they were not clean then we would get a blast from the captain. While this gave us something to do, it made the detachment extremely crabby. English Enfields were issued because we were expected to train with the British within a short time. On our way across town to get the new rifles, we marched through the main street of Calais. On this street I noticed a small red front Woolworth 5 and 10 store, probably a foreign buying agency. Also we passed a Singer Sewing Machine store. These things are unimportant, but they impressed us at the time and made us think of home.

Decoration Day, May 30th, we moved out of Calais late in the afternoon for Samer, a short train ride to the south. After detraining, we hiked a short distance out of Samer to a hamlet called Doudeville [Doudeauville] and prepared to stay a while. We have now become a part of the reserve of the British 5th Army with Passchendaele or Cambrai in prospect.

At Doudeville [Doudeauville], we went into cow barns for billets. This was our first experience with this type of bivouac since we had been in the army. We were compelled to police up (clean out) these barns, inside and out, before we were allowed to locate in them, according to army sanitary ideas and much to the chagrin of the French who didn't want them disturbed. We also had a payday here, my first since joining the army.

Our stay at Doudeville [Doudeauville] was for about a week altogether. We practiced open warfare maneuver and bayonet drill every day in a stony wheatfield just outside the village. There was plenty of vin rouge to be had nights at the local estaminet up until 9.30 P.M. but no one became intoxicated. Several buxom peasant girls, daughters of the village in wooden shoes and quaint and picturesque costume, did their best to entertain us. Ancient and historic old Normandy and Flanders has not changed much in dress or custom since the days of the Franks and Normans or the wanderings of Philip the Bold.

On June 7th we left our cowbarn billets and hiked to Breens [Brêmes] close by. There we entrained (40 hommes-eight chevaux)

[for] Meaux, located in the Marne Valley, twenty-six miles from Paris. The reason for our movement at this time was because General Foch had told Pershing we were more urgently needed for the French reserve before Château Thierry, than idling in an English rest camp.[9] This, of course, made the English General Staff quite angry as they had been promised the use of U.S. troops as replacements to fill the roles of decimated regiments forced back to Calais back in 1916. Naturally they hated to see us go to the French.[10] As far as we were concerned, we were as green as grass in warfare and wouldn't have been of much use in case of an actual attack, anyway. We needed a lot of training, especially on a rifle range.

Traveling southeast toward Paris, our train was raided by huge bomber planes around Arras and Amiens in the Somme. The krauts had probably noticed our movement and suspected our destination. We were forced to stand idle in railroad yards daytimes, traveling only at night with all lights extinguished and no smoking. All that showed was the stack and fire-box of the engine, not even a headlight. When raided, the train would come to a dead stop. While we were never directly hit, several times we were caught in a heavy shower of stones and shrapnel bursts close to us which very much excited our heroes cooped up in the train.

"Geez! Lookit that guy in that crate up there!" exclaims O'Hara peeking out through a crack in the boxcar door. "Sure is makin a hell of a racket. Gives me the shivers."

"What's the matter, Harp? Is you afraid of pineapples and sky rockets? That show is especially fer our benefit," says Stevens.

"It's no benefit ta me, Mug. That bird is roamin too damn close wit his egg crate ta suit me," replies O'Hara, "I'm gittin so's I cai'nt sleep nights no more."

9. Marshal Ferdinand Foch (1851–1929) was appointed supreme commander of all Allied armies in March 1918.

10. As historian Harvey A. DeWeerd explained in his study of American participation in World War I, "No other problem took up more of General Pershing's time and attention or appeared under a greater variety of forms" than the "prolonged and bitter" controversy over amalgamation of American troops into the French and British armies. From April 1917 until late July 1918, Allied military commanders and civilian leaders never urged, as Howell suggests, that individual American soldiers be placed under foreign command, but that companies or battalions be assigned to Allied units. British officers no doubt hoped that the 39th Infantry would remain under British command, particularly in the wake of the devastating German offensives of March and April 1918. Harvey A. DeWeerd, *President Wilson Fights His War: World War I and the American Intervention* (New York: The Macmillan Company, 1968), 300–311.

"Aw gwan. Yer half asleep most of the time anyway, so what's the difference?" says Stevens.

"Says you. Its gittin so a sojer can't sleep a'tall when theys boiler makers and garage mechanics blowin' an braggin' around day and night," snaps O'Hara.

"If blowin yer horn was music, you an Stevens could make more noise than a whole bugle an drum corps combined," ventures McGuire.

"Listen to the shanty Irish poppin off," says O'Hara.

On our way toward Paris and our final destination of Meaux on the Marne River, we passed through the following towns, some of which were famous in the earlier stages of the war, 1914–1916.

Lille (nord dep't)

Arras (somme)[11]

Amiens (somme)

Beauvais (et oise)

St. Denis (Paris suburb)

Meaux (seine-et-marne)

26 mi. from Paris on the Paris-Soissons road.

11. Arras is actually part of the Pas-de-Calais Department.

Chapter 5

Behind the Front

It was on the night of June twelfth, that we detrained at the town of Meaux. No one seemed to know we were coming and the officers didn't know where we were supposed to go. So we stood around and waited, and kept on waiting. Some of the men lay down alongside the road and went to sleep. Others stood around and crabbed about the fine army we were in. Finally, a motorcycle dispatch rider drove in from somewhere with orders for our company commander, Lieutenant Holstlaw. The order said, that we were to hike to the village of Acy-en-Multien, which was about seven to twelve miles northwest of Meaux, its nearest railhead. To find our way to this town in the dark and without maps, we needed a guide, or at least an interpreter. So the company was combed for men who could speak passable French. The choice therefore, narrowed down to two men, Private Stevens and Private Apoulos. The latter, a big Greek, was selected and the company moved out in the dark for Acy, with the rest of the battalion following.

After an hour's hiking without once having come on a village or other source of life, Lieutenant Holstlaw became somewhat worried and halted the column and the battalion. After consultation with the officers and sergeant of the four companies of the battalion, it was decided to continue on for another half hour and then stop for the night, wherever we might be. Before fifteen minutes had passed however, we entered a small hamlet and halted. Arousing one of the burghers, Private Apoulos then attempted to find out where we were and the location of Acy. As it turned out, the Greek was such a whizbang of an interpreter that he couldn't even make himself understood. His French was probably a mixture of Greek, Latin, Italian and Walloon. So they called on Stevens to see if he could improve on the situation. His French was only a little better. Anyway, he could understand the gesticulating Frenchman who was now angry because we had called him from his bed. Stevens soon found out that we were on the wrong road and traveling in the opposite direction, or away from Acy, so we had to retrace our steps and took another road back.

"Well, whadda ya know about that?" wails O'Hara. "That fatheaded goldbrick Greek, Apoulas, thought he could parlevoo French, an now has got us hikin' all over France in the middle of the night. I'm fed up with this man's army."

"Fed up! Me too! Why the hell did General Pershing pick on us fer a promenod all over the back areas?" says Brizee. "I thought we wuz supposed ta be up at the Front, lookin' fer krauts."

"Cripes! All this hikin' an no chow in sight. I could eat a horse an wagon, bones an all," moaned McGuire.

"Crabbin' about it won't do any good," says I. "An besides, if they orders ya to hike all over France, day or night, yer a soldier an gotta do it, whether ya likes it er not."

"Quiet men!" orders Lieutenant Holstlaw. "Complaining won't get us there any sooner. Com-pan-ee halt! Fall out for five minutes rest!"

So we halted by the roadside for a short rest and subsequently resumed hiking again. When we finally got on the right road, daylight was peeping through the clouds as we sighted the town of Acy in the valley, its long slender church steeple now prominent on the horizon. Soon we were passing through Vincy-Manoeuvre and then through the main street of Acy-en-multien, encamping in a small woods above the town.

Acy was to become the particular training area for my battalion. The balance of the regiment, as well as the three other regiments comprising the 4th Infantry Division under Major

General Cameron, were all located in the vicinity at the towns of Lizy-sur-Ourcq, Rosoy-sur-Ourcq, Trilport, Quincy and May-en-multien, all hamlets, with divisional headquarters temporarily at Lizy-sur-Ourcq. While this was our training area in the French sector, actually we were in Army Reserve for the 2d and 3d U.S. Divisions (regular) and the 26th Division (New England National Guard) who were brigaded with the French VIth Army holding back the German Feldensturm [Friedensturm] and preventing a break-through to Paris.[1]

The above troops were located about twenty-five miles south and east of Acy, in the vicinity of Château Thierry and Belleau Wood. The 26th U.S. Division was toward the northwest of us at Montdidier. Those of us at Acy did not know that we were in reserve at this time, as we had heard very little about the progress or developments of the war in our travels. Had we known of our close proximity to such a strong, hotly contested sector, we would probably have felt less secure. Even as it was, we could faintly hear the distant rumble of cannonade and the sky was red at night with the scarlet sunset of war to the east. Therefore we were aware that we were not too far from the actual scene of war, but of its ramifications we were in virginal ignorance, not realizing that we might become a part of it at any instant.

Acy itself, was only a crossroads village like hundreds of others in France. Its chief reason for any distinction at all, lies in the fact that it contains a church built in the twelfth century, which

1. The "Friedensturm," or "Peace Offensive," began on July 15, 1918. George Hamilton Cameron (1861–1944), a native of Illinois, graduated from West Point in 1883. He rose steadily through the ranks and was promoted to brigadier general in the National Army in August 1917 and to major general that November. Cameron went to Camp Greene, North Carolina, in December 1917 and began organizing the 4th Division. He led the division until August 1918, when he took command of the Fifth Corps. During the Meuse-Argonne Offensive, Cameron's troops failed to capture the critical high ground of Montfaucon on the offensive's first day, and he was relieved of command that October. He retired from the army in 1924. U.S. Adjutant General, *Official Army Register, January 1, 1925* (Washington, D.C.: U.S. Government Printing Office, 1925), 690. On May 27, 1918, the German Seventh Army, supported by the First and Eighteenth, struck the Allied line near Soissons in Operation "Blucher." Early on May 29, they captured the city and continued to advance toward the Marne River. By May 31, they reached the Marne River village of Château Thierry. Allied reinforcements, including the U.S. 2nd and 3rd Divisions were rushed to halt the German drive. The 3rd helped French units hold the south bank of the Marne, while the 2nd, in position north and west of Château Thierry, blocked the main road to Paris. On the morning of June 6, the 2nd Division counterattacked and captured several important German positions, including a portion of Belleau Wood (although the wood was not cleared of Germans until June 26). On June 9, the 39th Infantry entrained at Maresquel and Hesdin and went into camp on June 15 at Acy-en-Multien. The regiment was attached to the French 4th Division for training. Cole and Eberlin, *The History of the 39th U.S. Infantry*, 21.

is still in use and in excellent condition. Many of the men of my battalion attended services there and will remember the picturesque old cure.

In Sept. 1914, troops belonging to the 7th French Corps descended on Acy from the Nogeon Farm to drive out the Germans. There was ferocious fighting in the streets and the little woods on the hillside where we are now encamped. The village changed hands several times.

Acy had seen many a gay royal hunting party in the dead, faraway past. The DuBarrys, Maintenons, LaValliers, Pompadours and Madam royals, with their Louis's have passed its gates without number, but not stopping for very long, except to change horses. Their destinations were usually Soissons, Villers-Cotterêts, Forêt-de-Retz or Forêt-de-Compiègne. All this was prior to the French Revolution. At the present time, Acy is less than an hour from Paris and is in the Multien section, noted for its cheese and poultry products, a quiet rural community in peacetime.

The 1st Battalion, 39th Inf. (co's A-B-C-D) bivouacked in "pup tents" set up in the woods at the top of a small hill to the right of the village toward the Etavigny Plateau, between the upper and lower roads. The LaGargogne River, which is but a small brook, runs through the end of the town and furnishes its chief water supply.

Our stay at Acy was for about a month. During this time we built a rifle range, dug some useless trench, practiced bayonetry, hand grenade throwing and the use of the Chauchat automatic rifle.[2] We now turned back the English Enfields issued to us up at Calais and again received the good old Springfield, which pleased us immensely. We were also completely reoutfitted here.

2. The French Model 1915 Chauchat automatic rifle was chambered for the French 8mm round, and was capable of firing about 300 rounds per minute. The American Army purchased nearly 16,000 Chauchats. Although generally reliable, the Chauchat gained a somewhat undeserved reputation for failure among the doughboys because the rifle used circular magazines with open sides which could become clogged with mud, and was prone to overheating and jamming. Believing their 30.06 caliber round was superior, and wishing to reduce supply problems, the Americans developed and produced their own version of the Chauchat, designated the Model 1918. Although more than 19,000 were produced, few were issued, as the American version was even more problematic than the French. Canfield, *U.S. Infantry Weapons of the First World War*, 147–56. An undated brief history of the regiment noted that "the men were put through a stiff course of training and thru rifle practice on a range constructed of such materials as could be picked up in the neighborhood." Record Group 120, 4th Division Historical, Box 29, Folder: 39th Infantry, Histories, Commendations & Battle Participants, NARA.

Gen. Pershing and Maj. Gen. George H. Cameron, commanding 4th Division, leaving 4th Division Headquarters after a conference and a visit to 4th Division units. Lizy-sur-Ourcq, France, July 11, 1918. U.S. Army Signal Corps Collection, National Archives, 17612 [2100J8].

One item was the new overseas hat or trench cap, which we had long coveted. We had been wearing the wide brim campaign hats of the Spanish American War. These had made us feel sort of out of place or inferior to the other army outfits we occasionally observed in the vicinity, wearing new trench hats. Along with the hats came also new rolltype leggins, steel helmet, gas mask, etc. Altogether we felt like regular A-1 soldats now and were growing impatient for some action. As McGuire says, after putting on his new hat and leggins and grabbing the trusty old Springfield, "Well boys! I guess we're ready to go out an get 'em now!" And we were. "Sure-a!" says Vinelli, "Now we looka for da Boche, an he's a looka for Guiseppi."

I had finally learned the manual of arms as well as some more "squads east and west," so I have been progressing as a soldier. In fact, all the squad had grown quite military. But actually, I know very little of the military, even at this stage. I was however, considered proficient enough to be placed on my first regular guard detail around an honest-to-goodness military camp in a foreign land. I am supposed to know and be able to repeat verbatim, the twelve General Orders of the U.S. Army.[3] About all I knew then, or can repeat even now, is General Order No. 2 which reads, "To walk my post in a military manner, keeping always on the alert and observing everything that takes place within sight or hearing." Anyway I did know enough to order "halt."

An incident in connection with my first night on guard duty might be of some interest. My job was to patrol two sides of the camp rectangle, outside and around the camp enclosure. The night was inky black, not a star in the sky. At two places on my patrol, I would meet the sentry who was patrolling the opposite two sides of the camp rectangle. When we met we would exchange a few words and then turn back to our beat. Directly behind the camp to the rear, was a dense woods or thicket of heavy undergrowth, quite eerie at night and full of strange noises and rustling of leaves. I had to pass directly across the front of these woods on my patrol and therefore moved deliberately, but without loss of time, until I became somewhat used to it. Just outside the camp rectangle also, was the tent quarters of the Battalion Sergeant Major. I had to pass between his quarters and the edge of the camp while on patrol. Things are now quiet all around. Not a sound except the measured beat of my hobnails on the gravel. The early part of the evening went fast and nothing happened. But sometime in the early morning hours while passing near the Sergeant Major's tent I heard, or thought I heard, the sound of footsteps creeping slowly and cautiously toward me. Yet, when I stopped and stood quiet, the sound of footsteps ceased. I then proceeded on my beat as before, past the eerie woods and back again. Down by the woods, I heard a mule's bray and the whinnie of a horse in the distant valley.

3. The following orders comprised the Twelve General Orders for sentinels: 1) to take charge of this post and all Government property in view; 2) to walk my post in a military manner, keeping always on the alert and observing everything that takes place within sight or hearing; 3) to report all violations of orders I am instructed to enforce; 4) to repeat all calls from posts more distant from the guardhouse than my own; 5) to quit my post only when properly relieved; 6) to receive, obey, and pass on to the sentinel who relieves me all orders from the commanding officer, officer of the day, and officers and non-commissioned officers of the guard only; 7) to talk to no one except in line of duty; 8) in case of fire or disorder to give the alarm; 9) to allow no one to commit a nuisance on or near my post; 10) in any case not covered by instructions to call the corporal of the guard; 11) to salute all officers, and all colors and standards not cased; 12) to be especially watchful at night, and, during the time for challenging, to challenge all persons on or near my post, and to allow no one to pass without proper authority. Office of the Adjutant General, *Manual of Interior Guard Duty, U.S. Army, 1914, Corrected to April 15, 1917* (Washington, D.C.: U.S. Government Printing Office, 1917), 34.

Coming closer to the Sergeant-Major's tent again, I distinctly heard footsteps again. So I stopped and looked around, keeping my rifle at the alert position for possible use. Standing behind a tree I could see dimly about a hundred yards away, what appeared to be four legs, or two men walking together and moving slowly toward me. I didn't know what to make of it, so I let them come closer for better observation. I had been told previously by the corporal of the guard to watch out for the "officer of the day" who as a test would probably try to take my rifle from me. I was therefore on the alert and half expected something like this to happen.

The legs kept moving closer and closer, slowly and more deliberately it seemed, so I challenged, "Halt! Who goes there?" says I. There was no answer but I imagined I heard whispers. Again I challenged and pulled the bolt on my rifle. Those legs kept right on coming, closer, slowly, always closer in the dim light. "Halt! I'll fire!" says I, somewhat frantically, placing the Springfield at my shoulder. No attention whatever was paid to my final challenge, so I fired into the night air. It made a loud report on a stilly night, roused the other sentry near me as well as the corporal of the guard. Both came running on the double to see what all the shooting was about. I then pointed out the dim outline of two pairs of gray legs creeping slowly toward us.

"Cripes!" the corporal whispered, "looks like the damn Boche!" moving off to one side in a hurry to investigate.

The corporal returned soon, however, frothing at the mouth. The brimstone invective he unloosed was classic. He blew up everything connected with the army, the generals, the officers, the brigade, etc., consigning them to places he thought was proper. Then turning a scornful eye on me, he bawled, "Who the hell let you in the army, ya big raw boned recruit? That was only the Sergeant-major's horse ya gahdam fool. Good thing fer you ya didn't shoot him er the whole damn army would be on your tail."

I was very meek, of course, so after that I always investigated such things more thoroughly myself.

At this stage, the Germans were still on the offensive between the Aisne and the Marne. U.S. soldiers were just beginning to arrive in large units and were being given hurried training like we were receiving at Acy. You would see occasional aeroplanes in the sky day times but always they would be marked with the Allied insignia. One day however, a plane much larger than we had usually seen, appeared in the sky but flying low. We were attracted by the low even drone of its motors. As it came closer, we noticed two black crosses painted on the underside of its wings. It was a Boche all right but as there was no anti-aircraft guns near us, the plane cruised about unmolested. After circling low a few time[s] near our camp, it disappeared over the horizon. As it had made no effort to fire on us or drop any bombs, we figured it must be a captured German plane being given a tryout by French airmen and forgot the incident.

Shortly after this episode, a new officer appeared in our midst. This was not unusual and we gave him only a casual glance. He talked to some of the men and asked various questions, all of which seemed in the line of duty. His uniform was apparently O.K. and therefore we noticed nothing irregular. One of the battalion sergeants however, had noticed that he was carrying a small camera of peculiar design in his hand and acting sort of funny about it. This was unusual, as we were not allowed to possess cameras and no one except the U.S. Signal Corps was allowed to take photographs of troops or anything else connected with the U.S. Army. Therefore the suspicious sergeant questioned the trim looking officer about his camera. The officer was incensed of course at being questioned but as he gave no satisfactory answer about the camera, the sergeant called out the guard and placed the protesting officer under arrest. This was an unusual unprecedented procedure, but the sergeant had made no mistake. The supposed U.S. officer had turned out to be a German spy dropped from the aeroplane we had recently seen. He was among us to get information and photographs of newly arrived U.S. troops. This incident caused much excitement among us at the time and we marveled at the Boche nerve, but nothing further was ever heard about it.[4]

On July 4th, we had a big Field Day for the whole battalion at Rosoy-sur-Ourcq, a small town near Acy.[5] Early in the morning we

4. The insertion of spies by parachute from an airplane or balloon was rare during World War I. George A. Hill, for instance, was a British agent and pilot who flew his aircraft behind enemy lines to drop and retrieve agents. Nigel West, *Historical Dictionary of World War I Intelligence* (Lanham, MD: Rowman & Littlefield, 2014), 129–30. Also see Captain Henry Landau, *Secrets of the White Lady* (New York: G.P. Putnam's Sons, 1935). No corroborating information could be found to verify this particular incident that Howell reported. It could be that Howell was merely repeating a rumor that the spy arrived by parachute.

5. The 7th Infantry Brigade's "Field Meet' on July 4 consisted of sports in the morning and a baseball game in the afternoon. The 39th Infantry's baseball team was soundly beaten by the team from the 47th Infantry. *History of the 7th Infantry Brigade*, 12.

were marched over and then given a big roast pork dinner with real mashed potatoes and gravy, a ball game, etc., but no pink lemonade or peanuts. Some of the soldats however, loaded up on vin blanc from the estaminet in the town. My sidekick McGuire got plenty. So did Vinelli. However, Mac was just good enough to win us boo-coo (beaucoup) franc in a crap game with the mule skinners of one of the "horsemanure outfits" close by. Mac and I had been buddies ever since the Camp Mills sentry episode back in the U.S. so we went fifty-fifty on everything. "C'mon snake eyes! Catch yo papa a new pair of hobnails! Wham! You're faded!" We liked the army now but we had a feeling we were being groomed to move elsewhere soon where it wouldn't be quite as pleasant as now. The late summer twilights in France are fascinating. The clouds rise high and white in skies of pale blue. It is almost broad daylight at 9.30 P.M. and you can read a book or paper until almost 10.00 P.M. in the summer.[6]

On July 4th also, a part of the 1st Battalion 39th Regiment, went with Lieut. Haney of A Company to Paris to form a section of a composite regiment, which was made up of the best drilled and best groomed soldiers from various units located in the vicinity.[7] None of my squad were selected, their pants didn't hang right. The "scrubs" therefore were left behind. Those selected were to parade in Paris to show the French that the U.S. Army had arrived in strength and was well disciplined.[8] This was of course more or

6. Kansan Paul R. Parrish of the 39th wrote home that "it stays light until 10 o'clock," which made it rather hard to go to bed early. At 9 p.m., he reported that he could see almost as well as at 4 p.m. back in Kansas. *The Topeka* (KS) *Daily Capital*, July 14, 1918.

7. Mathias Willoughby Haney (1883–1931), a native of West Virginia and resident of Philadelphia, was later awarded the Distinguished Service Cross for his actions on September 26–28, 1918. Haney "displayed exceptional skill in extricating his company from a perilous position" while in a dense fog, capturing more prisoners than the number of men in his command in the process. The next day, he took command of his battalion at a critical time, stopped a threatened retreat, and reestablished the line under heavy machine gun and artillery fire. Finally, on September 28, Haney led his battalion forward through heavy fire, advanced his line one kilometer, and held his line against enemy counterattacks until he was relieved. Haney was also awarded the French Croix de Guerre with palm. U.S. Adjutant General's Office, *American Decorations: A List of Awards of the Congressional Medal of Honor, the Distinguished-Service Cross and the Distinguished-Service Medal awarded under authority of the Congress of the United States, 1862–1926* (Washington, D.C.: U.S. Government Printing Office, 1927), 324; *Philadelphia Inquirer*, July 26, 1919. An undated history of the regiment described Haney as one of the most "able and fearless officers in the regiment." Record Group 120, 4th Division Historical, Box 29, Folder: 39th Infantry, Histories, Commendations & Battle Participants, NARA.

8. Lieut. Harley B. Gaston of Company K was one of the "biggest and best-drilled" soldiers selected to march in Paris. Gaston's account of enjoying the sights of the city may be found in *The Gastonia* (NC) *Gazette*, August 7, 1918. An enlisted man in the 39th made

less propaganda, as the Parisians were then a trifle nervous and panicky due to the close proximity of the German Army now just outside of Château Thierry. Also because of the dramatic incidents and annoyance of the "Big Bertha" long range gun then firing on the city at certain intervals from the vicinity of Laon in the Forêt de St. Gobain, north of Soissons.[9]

Members of 39th Infantry marching down Avenue de President Wilson between Place d'Yena and Avenue Montaigne on Independence Day. Paris, France, July 4, 1918. U.S. Army Signal Corps Collection, National Archives, 15889 [513J8]

---

extensive preparations in order to be chosen for the parade, including shaving, receiving a haircut, scrubbing his clothes and equipment in a nearby creek, mending his uniform, and cleaning his rifle and sidearms. His detailed account of the parade may be found in *The Daily Northwestern* (Oshkosh, WI), August 14, 1918.

9. The legendary "Paris Gun" (actually three guns) began bombarding Paris on March 23, 1918. Howell confuses the "Big Bertha" 42cm howitzer (withdrawn from service by 1918) with the "Paris Gun." The German long-range bombardment of Paris began on March 23, 1918, and continued until August 9. A total of 303 of the 264-pound projectiles landed in the city, killing or wounding 876 Parisians. U.S. Army Ordnance Department, *Railway Artillery*, 2 vols. (Washington, D.C.: U.S. Government Printing Office, 1921), 723–740. The guns were located in three positions, including near the city of Laon, about 122 kilometers from Paris; at Ham, 100 kilometers from the city; and at Fère-en-Tardenois, about 10 miles from Château Thierry and 80 kilometers from Paris. H.W. Miller, "The German Long-Range Gun," *Army Ordnance*, November-December 1923, Vol. IV, No. 21, 167–76.

"Can ya imagine that?" says Stevens, "The one place in the hull world I wants ta see, an that goldbrick Mahoney of the second platoon wuz selected in place of me ta go ta Paree."

"Ya don't hold yer mouth right, that's why," says McGuire, "An ya gotta talk through yer nose too."

"Phooey!" says Belkin, "No numbskull private is ever selected ta go anywhere 'cept the trenches. Wish I wuz a corporal or a sergeant. They allus gits the gravy."

"That ain't the real reason," says I, "Ya gotta be a goldbrick soldier an have yer pants pressed. You birds can't even march at attention without stubbin yer toes. How do ya expect them ta see-lect us?"

"Yer more 'n half right," agrees McGuire, "I ain't gonna worry no more wrinkles on my youthful face on account of that. When I gits ready ta see gay Paree, I goes A.W.O.L. an takes the consequences."

"Me too" says Belkin.

"Same here," says Stevens, "But I hopes that Big Bertha whizbang ain't work'in when I finally gets there."

Shortly after the 4th, General Pershing visited us quite unexpectedly in person, in the woods above Acy. We were all lined up under the trees and the General came slowly along the column and inspected each man, expressing his satisfaction afterward on the general appearance of his new troops. Some of the men however, had been sick from the food but no mention of it was made at the inspection or elsewhere, except to crab the mess sergeant for serving rotten chow. We had been subsisting for several days past on "monkey meat" (Argentina canned beef & carrots) which was part of the French ration then issued to us. By way of inquiry, the General asked one soldier how he liked the food he were getting. Being a "bohunk" and seeking to please the high officer, he answered "fine." But before Pershing left however someone else advised him of the poor condition of some of the men caused by the canned food. In less than an hour after he left we received a truckload of hindquarters of good old western steer beef frozen as hard as a rock, from some army refrigerator nearby. The cooks had to use an axe to cut it in pieces, prior to cooking. With the meat also came plenty of potatoes, some chocolate, chewing tobacco, one or two other knicnacks and a large supply of bread.

If we had nothing else, we always seemed to have plenty of white bread baked by the army soldiers in France. I have seen it numberless times during the war, arranged in huge piles or stacks, sometimes out in the center of a muddy field, or on railroad station platforms with a dirty tarpaulin carelessly thrown over it. Sometimes it would drop off from the back of supply trucks passing us on the march. If we were hungry there would be a scramble to pick it up off the road. It always tasted good, even if frosted with black mud and horsemanure.

Along with the truckload of supplies came two medical officers, who inspected us again. Now we knew, we must be going somewhere, with the general inspecting us, the big feed and so forth. They always fed us plentifully just before a move toward the front. As we soon learned, heavy eats usually meant heavy duty just ahead.

Shortly after this episode, we were routed out one evening just after midnight and hiked up to the front, a little northwest of Château Thierry. Some of our officers had made a mysterious journey a few days before to scout the new location, so we heard whispers about what they saw. We were told by way of explanation, that we were going into a quiet sector to be under fire for a few days, just to see how we reacted. That was to be for training and also that we might get used to the racket of the big guns. We were further informed, through the sergeants and the latrine route, that after this tryout, we would come right back to our nice woods again at Acy. We never did, though. We moved right up across the Etavigny plateau, through Boullarre, then east past the famous farm De La Grange Aux Bois, thence to Mareuil a few miles above Château Thierry.[10]

At Mareuil, I remember, there was a French sentry, with long slender, knife-edged bayonet on his gun, stationed at one end of the Ourcq River bridge. A German sentry with a jagged saw-tooth bayonet on the end of his rifle also, stood guard at the opposite end of the bridge. The Germans would come down on their side of the stream to wash their clothes, right in broad daylight and the French soldiers did likewise on the opposite side. Neither molested the other and none tried to cross the bridge over the Ourcq. This, therefore, was a nice place for potential trouble and

10. Grange-aux-Bois Farm was the scene of heavy fighting by the 37th and 91st Divisions during the Meuse-Argonne Offensive in September 1918. American Battle Monuments Commission, *American Armies and Battlefields in Europe* (Washington, D.C.: U.S. Government Printing Office, 1938), 321.

perhaps a possible breakthrough—and we were in the trenches right back of the town.[11]

The town of Mareuil itself was a deserted village and partly in ruins. A French fire engine of ancient design stuck out of one of the doorways into the main street. McGuire and myself rummaged around all over town and finally came upon a French canteen located in one of the abandoned cellars. After much bargaining, ouis, m-wahs and combiens, we induced the Frog soldat to sell us two cans of condensed milk at a fabulous price. Having acquired them, we then went back to our muddy trench and had a banquet with the thick milk spread on hunks of a loaf of bread we had previously swiped from a crabby mess sergeant. Did it taste good? Just like bread, butter and sugar to a small boy after a hard schoolday.

There was no action of any kind at Mareuil while we were there. The nights were quiet, almost too quiet. We moved from there shortly without hearing a gun fired, except the occasional far off staccato of some isolated machine gun post to the east. But we were in the war to stay and are to be in action most of the time from now on until the armistice. We found out later that our moving-up had been a necessary precaution, as army reserve, to help stop an expected breakthrough, should it occur and if the much heralded second Feldsturm [Friedensturm] of the Germans should materialize. They are now just outside of Château Thierry, with Paris as their objective.

"You're in the Army, now.
You're not behind the plow.
You'll never get rich,
You son of a bitch,
You're in the Army now.
"So what the hell, and how.
You're in the Army now.
You'll soon get the itch,
And die in a ditch,
'cause you're in the Army now."
(Unexpurgated version of famous old army song)

11. Howell was mistaken about the French and German sentries. Although the 39th was stationed only a few miles from Mareuil-sur-Ourcq at La Villeneuve-sous-Thury and Thury-en-Valois on July 15–17, Mareuil-sur-Ourcq was located several miles behind the front lines in July 1918. Cole and Eberlin, *The History of the 39th U.S. Infantry*, 25.

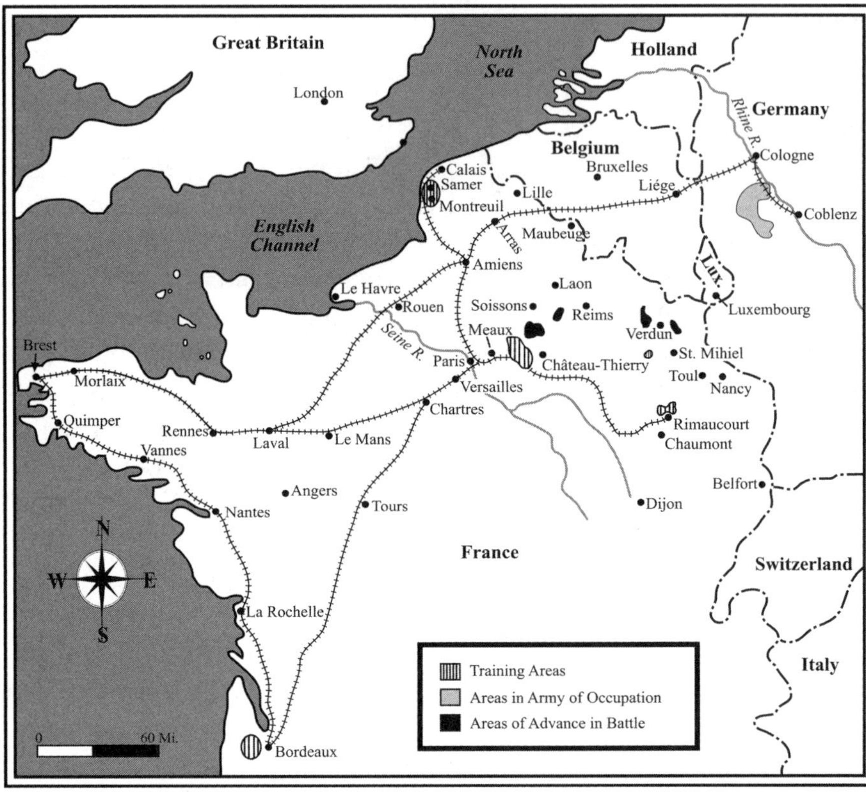

4th Division in Europe

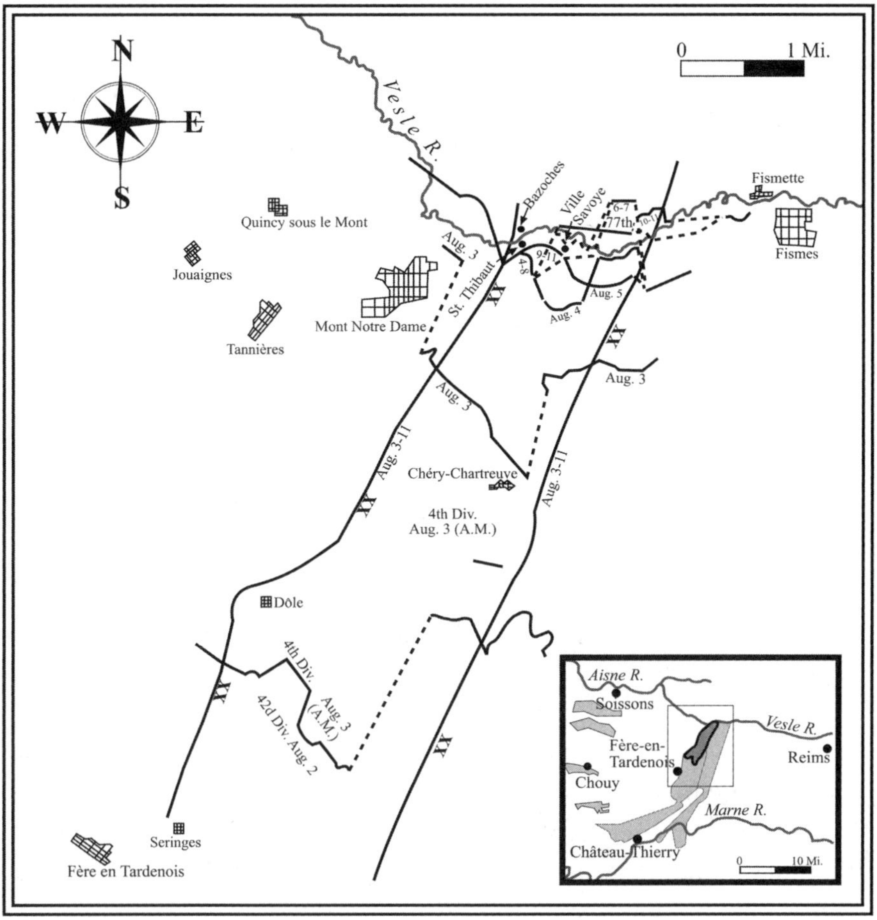

Aisne-Marne/VESLE sector

Chapter 6

Aisne-Marne Defensive (July 16th to 24th 1918) Second Battle of the Marne[1]

While my battalion was located at Mareuil-sur-ourcq, or about July 16th, the Fourth Division, less artillery, had been assigned or brigaded with the French 33rd Division at La Ferté-sous-jouarre and divisional headquarters was moved there. The majority of the division with General Cameron as commander, went into trenches in the hills above Crouettes and were a part of General DeGoutte's 6th French Army, IXth Corps, under General Dimitry.[2]

On the above date, we of the 1st Battalion, 39th Inf., moved out from Mareuil-sur-ourcq under cover of darkness on camouflaged roads, turned west, then north and thence to the Bois de Retz

1. On July 15, 1918, the Germans launched their last offensive of the war, designed to push forward on either side of the city of Reims. East of Reims, the attack quickly ground to a halt. West of the city, the Germans were able to cross the Marne River. On July 18, Marshal Ferdinand Foch launched a counterattack to eliminate this German salient in the Allied line. Eight American divisions participated in the Aisne-Marne Offensive, and gradually the Germans withdrew from the salient and the Allied attacks ended by August 6. The 7th Infantry Brigade and the 39th Infantry were assigned to the French Second Corps for the operation.

2. General Jean-Marie-Joseph Degoutte (1866–1938) took command of the French Sixth Army in June 1918 and led that army during the Second Battle of the Marne. He became chief of staff of the Flanders Army Group that September. General Marie Antoine Henri de Mitry (1857–1924) actually commanded the French Ninth Army during this period. Spencer C. Tucker, ed., *World War I: The Definitive Encyclopedia and Document Collection*, 5 vols. (Santa Barbara, CA: ABC-CLIO, 2014), 2: 458–59, 1108–09.

(Villers Cotterêts wood). There was a drizzling rain which continued throughout the night. Great pools of mud and water were on the roads. It was pitch black in the forest as we entered. Here also, the mud and water was up to our knees and in the darkness we had to hold on to the man in front of us in the column, to keep our direction, maintain contact and not become lost. It was an all-night forced hike and very exhausting, but necessary in order to get the troops to the jump-off place and in position before the start of the coming drive. Clothing and packs were sodden with rain and mud, which made them twice as heavy for the weary men to carry, but they moved steadily on in ragged formation.[3] We were in complete ignorance, of course, as to what was taking place, but the plans called for a surprise attack and a drive east through the German flank, to cut the lines of communication between Soissons and Château Thierry. There were to be 150,000 U.S. troops in line in this attack. General Gouraud, famous one armed French general and his 4th French Army, had already stopped the so-called Feldsturm [Friedensturm].[4] After terrific struggle before Reims, the attack of the German armies had been completely broken. Not having any reserves left, the planned German offensive toward Paris could not therefore be renewed for some time. Generals Foch and Pershing, sensing this, agreed that now was an opportune time to attack the weak left flank of the enemy, take the offensive and get the feldgrau on the run, thereby turning the tide from four long years of trench warfare to quick moving open warfare. This was the right idea as was subsequently proven, so the Allies strained every nerve to make the attempt successful.

After tramping all night through the woods, the company had come out in an open velvet mossy clearing along toward morning. Here we were ordered to pitch our pup tents and had an all day sleep. The deep woods themselves had an ominous quiet about them that was provocative of a sense of danger. Not a sound except

3. Regimental Field Order Number 1, issued July 16, 1918, directed that "full field equipment" would be carried, including "two days reserve rations." After the 39th relieved the French 11th Infantry Regiment, "each man will be equipped with 200 rounds [of] ammunition." Only one blanket was to be carried, the other was to be collected by the battalion supply officer. Record Group 120, Records of the American Expeditionary Forces, World War I, Records of Combat Divisions 1917–1919, 4th Division, 4th Division Historical, Box 30, Folder: 39th Infantry, Field Orders, 204–32.1, National Archives and Records Administration, College Park, Maryland.

4. General Henri Joseph Eugene Gouraud (1867–1946).

the occasional falling of branches or the twitter or rasp of some forlorn insect. Toward late evening our rolling kitchens came up and we had a good feed of hot chow, which put the men in good spirits once more. Just before dusk we were ordered to roll our packs, break camp and then moved a mile or so further on to the east rim of the woods. Here we stopped at some half trenches, fox holes or dugouts located just inside the wood and skirting the edge of a waving, greenish yellow wheat field. It was now hinted that we might "go out and get 'em" in the morning. Two men were selected from each platoon to watch the wheat field with instructions to fire on anything they saw moving in the wheat if they thought it looked like a Boche.

Brizee and I were selected from our platoon and we took turns in watching across the wheat. About two a.m. I was straining my gaze against the dim opaque haze rising above the wheat in the

Building occupied by 4th Division Headquarters. La Forte sous Jouarre, France, June 29, 1918. U.S. Army Signal Corps Collection, National Archives, 15140 [429J8]).

remote pall of the sky. It is the time, they say, a man's resistance is at its lowest degree. Twice I had lunged forward and stopped short at something I now saw in the field ahead of me where before there had been nothing. Now there was movement only ten paces in front of me. It was only a ripple, as if beneath it, men moved, bayonets fixed, ready to lunge at me. I fingered the trigger of my rifle and waited with baited breath. As it came closer I noticed a blue, French type helmet slowly rise above the level of the wheat. Even then I was somewhat skeptical but they turned out to be a squad of French soldats returning from a reconnaissance of the German lines on the other side of the wheat field. As they saw our guns pointing at them, they began wildly waving their arms and stood up so they would not be fired on. Of course we were much relieved to find out they were allies.

About 4.30 A.M. on the same morning (July18th) I was still crouched in the same wheat field looking up at the leaden gray sky of early dawn. There was no sound of anything, not even the buzz of a wheat moth. I felt as though suspended in a vacuum, yet there was a feeling of heaviness, of premonition. Suddenly, without warning, an enormous barrage cut loose from field batteries located in the woods all around us. It lasted, a thundering continuous inferno of sound for nearly one hour, engulfing everything in a colossal roar, inexplicable, atomic. We had been entirely unaware of these guns located in the dark woods all around us as we had seen none of them previously. It was French field artillery manned by mixed American and French gun crews, firing at random. The early morning sky was soon lighted by gun discharges and shell bursts. Red and green rockets were seen to rise from the German lines but it was quite some time before the enemy starting answering with artillery. Then, he sent over only a few feeble shots from isolated field pieces. The Germans were either surprised and off their guard, or else they were busily engaged in moving to a safer position farther to the rear.

With the barrage still going on but slackening down somewhat, we moved out about 5.30 A.M. in our first action across the wheat. We were plenty worried, of course. Every man is, whether a potential hero or coward. Even the general, miles back in the rear is plenty worried until he actually sees from the incoming reports just how the battle is going. Most of the men of our company were sick from diarrhea and we had just began to collect "cooties," both of which stayed with us continuously until the end of the warfare on French soil.[5]

"Attention, you men of the fourth platoon! Attention fourth platoon!" repeat Sergeants Parker and Nolan, moving about among the men. Soon the platoon was assembled and grouped around Lieutenant Spence, a fine upstanding officer.[6]

"Attention men," says the lieutenant, slowly and deliberately. "We've got a little dirty work to do, over on the other side of the wheat. Fix bayonets and be ready! Remove your packs and leave them here, but take one blanket, shovel and raincoat, emergency ration and ammunition. We'll come back this way later."

So we did as ordered and waited for the signal to move out. The men were strangely silent now. Not a word was spoken. This was our first engagement. There were no wisecracks from O'Hara, McGuire or Belkin. Vinelli was tonguetied. The corporals as well as the sergeants were visibly nervous. Soon we heard Lieutenant Spence's whistle. It was the signal!

"Take it easy now, men, and follow me!" orders the lieutenant. "Column of squads! Three yard intervals! Forward!

I can see those shiny bayonets now, glistening in the early morning sunlight. It seemed as though there were thousands of them, instead of the paltry one hundred and fifty or so of our

5. "Cooties" were body lice.

6. Howell apparently changed this officer's name from Pence to Spence. Company B's Second Lieutenant Charles W. Pence (1894–1961) was a star athlete before the war. While a student at DePauw University in Greencastle, Indiana, "Six" Pence was a member of the football, basketball, track, and baseball teams for three years and "won a letter in each branch of sport during all three years." He was described as "one of the best backfield defense man [*sic*] in the state" in football, and the top-scoring basketball player for two years. Named captain-elect of the 1917 football squad, Pence left the university at the end of his junior year to attend the officers training camp at Fort Benjamin Harrison in Indianapolis. Commissioned a second lieutenant, Pence joined the 39th Infantry at Camp Greene. *The Indianapolis Sunday Star*, September 8, 1918. Wounded severely in France, Pence remained in the army until 1952, gaining fame as commander of the Japanese-American 442nd Regimental Combat Team during World War II. He retired as a brigadier general and received the Distinguished Service Medal and Silver Star. Record Group 120, Records of the American Expeditionary Forces, World War I, Records of Combat Divisions 1917–1919, 4th Division, 4th Division Historical, Box 32, Folder: 39th Infantry, Rosters of Officers of the 39th Infantry, Officers, Historical Section, 204–65.1, Roster of October 7, 1918, National Archives and Records Administration, College Park, Maryland; U.S. Adjutant General, *Official Army and Air Force Register, 1 January 1948*, 2 vols. (Washington, D.C.: U.S. Government Printing Office, 1948), I: 1418. Sergeant A.C. Parker of Company B (1891–1976) was a native of Gaffney, South Carolina, and was wounded in the Argonne. *The Gaffney* (SC) *Ledger*, November 25, 1948, November 10, 1976. A letter from Sergeant Parker to his parents, expressing his belief in God, may be found in *The Gaffney* (SC) *Ledger*, October 3, 1918.

immediate company of four platoons. When we reached the other side of the trampled wheat, we came to a small stream called the Savier [Savière] River, which flows along in front of a small rise of ground in this position. We were ready for immediate action. We expected it. Imagine our surprise at seeing, instead of the Kaiser and the whole German Army, only a handful of French soldiers calmly strolling up and down the banks of the small stream, calmly smoking their cigarettes with the languid puffs of nonchalance, as if nothing mattered. What had happened to the Boche?

As we crossed the stream on hastily felled trees and started up the slope into the Buisson de Cresnes, we suddenly pushed into a heavy enfilade fire of machine guns. Long, blue barrels, sticking out through bushes and moving with a sweeping motion, but mostly the guns were located in trees. Mr. Boche had been waiting quietly and patiently for us to show up, so he could take us at a disadvantage as we came up the side of the little hill. He proved to be only the rear guard, however, and our men made short work of driving him out. Nearly all the feldgrau abandoned their guns or were killed or captured after a short interval. The Fritzies of the main contingent who had seen us coming, had moved out hurriedly when they felt the effects of our artillery barrage, which had been terrific. Broken trees and the bodies of the enemy were strewn about in wild confusion. Ghastly looking legs and torsos hung in trees along with scraggly shreds of uniforms. Some of the Germans had died drinking their coffee, backed against a tree. Shrapnel from our shells had played havoc with them. Our barrage and the subsequent attack, had therefore been a complete surprise to the enemy. Now for the first time, we, almost green recruits, saw the results of war.

We followed the enemy most of the day through woods and underbrush, but never came in direct contact with them in any great number. They were always just a few yards ahead of us, always on the run, retreating back to some more favorable spot to make a stand.[7] Toward the middle of the afternoon, however, the enemy artillery became quite hot, firing from behind the

7. Regimental Field Order Number 3, issued at 3:40 p.m. on July 18, confidently declared, "The German Army have been defeated all along the line." Record Group 120, Records of the American Expeditionary Forces, World War I, Records of Combat Divisions 1917–1919, 4th Division, 4th Division Historical, Box 30, Folder: 39th Infantry, Field Orders, 204–32.1, National Archives and Records Administration, College Park, Maryland.

village of Noroy. We also had trouble with our own artillery, with shells falling short behind us, catching us between two fires which was quite unhealthy. This was soon remedied by a rocket shot in the air, showing our location to our own gunners, so they raised their range to shoot ahead of us.

Earlier in the day our third battalion had failed to advance on the right of us, therefore, Co.'s A, B & C of the First Battalion, 39th, were ordered to extend to the right in line and it was here that some of the heaviest resistance of the enemy was felt. The Germans were finally driven out of the woods. Lieutenant Haney of A Company, later received the Croix-de Guerre for heroic action in this fight, the first decoration in the regiment. Our first day's action resulted in the capture of about seventy-five prisoners. Twelve machine guns, two trench mortars, six field guns and a large amount of ammunition was captured by the regiment. That night we stayed in the woods where we were, after "digging in." Only two men of my company had been injured and none killed. We had actually met the Germans and had seen the feldgrau on the run. All this was a source of satisfaction to the men and gave them confidence and courage. We had been engaged opposite the XIIIth Württemberg Regiment (Watters).[8] While our men were troubled with diarrhea, a lot of the enemy were found to be suffering from the flu. However, they fought us with all the best German efficiency and tradition and gave us our first baptism of fire.

By the next day, the enemy was pushed back through the edge of the villages of Noroy and Chouy or about four kilometers from his original position. There was a large hill for our company to ascend in front of the village of Chouy. After reaching the crest of this hill through a strong enemy barrage, from artillery located in the town and controlled by a sausage balloon high over the hill, we advanced over and down the hill with heavy losses. Men would be running forward and down the hill toward Chouy. Suddenly a shell would explode in front of them and they would drop and curl up like little brown earth-worms, or fall like a bag of chaff. Some would squirm a little and that was the end. Corporal Covey of my squad lost his knee cap here. I saw him reach down and hold it in place, while smiling and joking about it. The German barrage was so intense that we had taken it on the run down the hill,

8. Probably the 13th Royal Württemberg Corps, commanded by Theodor von Watter.

to the shelter of some stone houses on the edge of Chouy and out of range of the artillery. Here we formed again, attacked and took the town with a handful of Frenchmen who had beckoned to us to rush down the hill. Seeing us, the enemy pulled their guns and retreated farther back toward the Aisne River.[9]

Earlier the same day and also the previous day, a buddy who had formerly been a streetcar conductor in New Haven, kept tagging close to my heels like a small child. He kept telling me that he would surely be hit. So strong was his premonition and belief, that he begged me to take his silver cigarette case and watch, with the promise that I would deliver them to his mother in case I came through the war O.K. To humor him I accepted the articles. Going down the hill before Chouy, he was hit by shrapnel and killed, just a few feet from me. Many records have come to light since the war of similar premonitions felt by soldiers going into battle. Of such is the grist of war. On this and succeeding days the battalion gained the towns of Melroy, Noroy and Chouy, all small hamlets. We were held up continually by the German rear guards, who were using machine guns and the vicious cross firing with little one-pounders.[10]

By the second night, the 4th Division had gained over six kilometers, advancing most of the time against machine gun nests in concealed positions and through dense undergrowth. Sergeant Lawless of the 39th Infantry, voluntarily carried an important message through to battalion headquarters, across a wide, open field, more than a thousand feet away, in full sight of the enemy and under a blistering machine gun fire.[11]

9. Captain Walter Smith witnessed Company B's advance on Chouy. "None of the officers or men who witnessed the scene which took place during the ensuing five minutes will ever forget it," Smith recalled. He confessed that no other incident made a greater impression on him during the war. Company B's long skirmish line advanced slowly, the men carrying their rifles at "high port" and keeping their alignment and interval, not moving faster than a walk, for almost five hundred yards. "It seemed that a shell fell among them almost at every step, throwing up clouds of smoke and dirt and bowling men over like ten-pins," Smith remembered. "The moral effect was certainly terrific, and the steadiness shown by the men was nothing less than marvelous." Captain Walter B. Smith, "Operations of the 1st Battalion 39th Infantry (4th Division), in the Aisne-Marne Offensive, July 18–20, 1918," 18–19.

10. "One pounders" probably refers to either the 3.7cm Grabenkanone or the 3.7cm Sturmbegleitkanone, both of which fired a 1-pound shell, although it could also be the Granatenwerfer 16, a mortar that fired a high-explosive grenade. Herbert Jäger, *German Artillery of World War One* (Ramsbury, UK: The Crowood Press, Ltd., 2001), 134–36, 140. Company B lost several men during this period, including Privates Roman Borofski, G. DiBernardino, Thomas Fitzgerald, Frank Gonyea and Mike Podlesney. Cole and Eberlin, *The History of the 39th U.S. Infantry*, 94.

11. Edward Russell Lawless (b. 1892), a native of Leominster, Massachusetts, was a candidate at the Reserve Officers Training Camp at Plattsburgh Barracks, New York, when

Another soldier hit in the knee and lying in a shell hole, heard several wounded comrades calling for water. He roused himself and found he could walk a little, though painfully. In spite of his injury, he made a number of trips to a nearby brook under great difficulty, bringing back full canteens of water to his injured and dying comrades. This was Private George Boardman.[12]

The above serves to illustrate the heroism and fortitude of civilian soldiers, who but a few days before, had never been on a battlefield and who had been sent up to the lines about half trained, just to get them "acquainted with the shelling."

After a few hours experience under heavy shell fire and battle, the men became articulate again. They had now lost all sense of fear and were soaked in the spirit of combat.

"Geeze! Did ya see that kraut I speared?" exclaims O'Hara breathlessly. "He was gonna decapitate me wit his bayonet, but I parried his thrust an damn near lost me own gun. Then I clubs him in the shins wit the butt of me gun ta make him bend over, which he does. Then I speared the bastard in the keck an lookit! The blood is all over me hands! Cripes! I'm sick to me stommick!"

Another soldier—"Where the hell is all the lieutenants and sergeants? Here I gits me a Boche Kapitan cornered in a wire entanglement, an he won't surrender. He was one of them damn ferocious Prussians, callin' me 'pig' an 'Americain swinehund.' I runs around him an pokes him a coupla times with my bayonet, but he won't come out of the wire at me. I was about to shoot him cold, when I sees he has no leg, an is really caught in the wire. All of this time he is still pointing his pistol at me, so I rushes him, but he don't even shoot. Finally the gun drops out of his hand an I kin see he is dead, 'cause his head drops over his breast. I goes over, picks up the Lugar pistol an finds out it wasn't even loaded. Geeze! He was a game bird! Here's his papers. Where the hell is our gahdamn lieutenant!"

---

he registered for the draft in May 1917. As the regimental sergeant major of the 39th Infantry, Lawless was awarded the Distinguished Service Cross for his actions near Troësnes, France, on July 18, 1918, when he carried an urgent message across some 500 yards of open field while under a murderous enemy fire. U.S. Adjutant General's Office, *American Decorations*, 398.

12. Private Guy W. (not George) Boardman of Company A, 59th U.S. Infantry, a native of Ohio and resident of California, was awarded the Distinguished Service Cross for his actions near Courchamps, France, on July 19, 1918. Although wounded in the ankle, Boardman made several trips under heavy machine gun fire to a small stream to fill the canteens of his wounded comrades. Boardman was later killed in action. U.S. Adjutant General's Office, *American Decorations,* 169.

Another soldier—"I could a captured him an let him live. He said 'kamerad' an then dropped his rifle on the ground. But afore I knows it though, he wuz shootin' at me with a small Luger pistol. So I fires point blank at him wit my Chauchat automatic, level wit me waist. Part of his guts falls out on the ground. He utters a sickly groan, reaches down ta grab them an falls in a heap. What more could I do? He would a done the same ta me. Here's a picture of his wife an little girl back in Oldenberg, just like me wife an kid back in Chi. Cripes! I didn't wanna kill him!"

By July 20th, we were in the Bois-de-Chatelet. In this wood there is more action. The feldgrau are still on the run but as usual they left a sizeable rear guard of machine gunners up in the treetops and behind bushes to hold us back as long as possible. These of course had to be cleaned out. But mostly the Boche had stampeded. Their dead were lying around in all shapes and conditions. All of them were horribly mangled as a result of our heavy artillery curtain fire. Men with arms and legs missing, headless bodies, carcasses of dead horses, stench, little round pancake hats, hairy arms with hands only attached, in a death grip on a rifle, odd little pieces of brains. It was a sickening sight, but this is war and we must carry-on.

Lieutenant Spence sent me out on outpost duty here in a field, about two hundred feet in front of the edge of woods, where our company was dug in and waiting. I thought I was out there all alone and expected to meet a Boche patrol any minute, but when I finally raised my head above the top of the shell hole I had selected to hide in, I could see French and U.S. helmets bobbing up all around me. Seeing that I was not alone made me feel a lot more comfortable. Fritz was sending over a barrage of one pounders from a small village near the woods and making a terrible racket. We had expected a counter-attack, hence the outpost duty. The attack failed to materialize, however. A shell whizzed and whined like a screeching bumble bee overhead and then struck the earth directly in front of my shell hole. I hugged the bottom of the opposite side, waiting for the end of everything, but lucky for me, it failed to explode. Before morning, we were relieved by a company of French Blue Devils and withdrew back to the hill above Sillie-la-Poterie for a couple of days rest.[13]

13. Chasseurs Alpins, or French mountain troops, wore a distinctive blue beret and were known as "Blue Devils." Casualties in the 39th during the fighting on July 18 and 19 were two officers and 54 enlisted men and 9 officers and 218 wounded. Major M.S. Eddy, "Machine Gun Company, 39th Infantry (4th Division) in the Aisne-Marne Offensive," The Infantry School,

We of the 39th Infantry are a part of the 7th Brigade. The 58th and 59th U.S. Infantry regiments of the 4th Division constituted the 8th Brigade and were in action at the same time to the south of us around Hautevesnes, Courchamps, Priez and Sommelans. They experienced some tough hand to hand combat in the Bois-de-L'Orme and at the above points where they lost many dead, especially north of Hill 193, or north of Château Thierry.

By July 24th, we are back in action again under French command, this time in the Bois-de-L'Ogons [des Ogons] another wood. We are still mopping up machine guns, some planted in little houses located in treetops, from which they could fire down on you and had a clear view of the surrounding woods.

In this wood we took several prisoners, perhaps fifteen. Among them was a young feldwebel (sergeant) about seventeen years of age. Another pair captured, was a father and son. They believed

Captured German guns in the square at Villers Cotters. Captured by the French and Americans during the July offensive. Villers Cotters, France, July 27, 1918. U.S. Army Signal Corps Collection, National Archives, 19020 [1084G8].

Advance Course, 1929–30, Maneuver Center of Excellence Libraries, Donovan Research Library, World War I Student Paper Collection, Fort Benning, Georgia, 18.

we intended to kill them after we had ransacked their pockets for information and souvenirs, so the father pleaded with us to kill him first but to spare his son. Neither was harmed as they were sent back with others to the rear and safety. This German outfit was a part of the 102d Saxonians Machine Gun Battalion.[14]

In crossing a road running through the thick woods, Catlin and I were fired on by a machine gun concealed high up in the branches of a tree about fifty yards away. Catlin carried the Chauchat automatic rifle and I had the ammunition clips. We were not aware of the enemy gun until it fired on us from the tree. At the first few shots from the machine gun, we hurriedly crossed the road and fell on our bellies in the ditch alongside the same.

"Cripes! Lookit! There he is up in that tree ahead!" says Catlin. "I can't see nuthin'," says I. Just then he fired another salvo, which passed barely over our heads. If I hadn't pulled in my feet, I would easily have been hit.

"Set er up on the tripod," says I, "but don't raise yer head." As he did so, I shoved in a circular clip of shells and Catlin pulled the trigger. The lone German gunner fell from the branches of the tree at almost our first shot and with a thud like a dead bird. We hadn't even taken time to aim the gun properly but our random shot had reached the mark. This episode impressed Catlin so much that he grew sick to his stomach and vomited. McGuire happened along just then and gave him a swig of sour vin rouge that he had in his canteen, putting Catlin on his feet again. But thereafter, he could never quite forget the incident. After the armistice later on, I saw him in Bendorf, Germany. He still spoke in a nervous way about "that bird falling from the tree."

Our exploits thus far, have taken us from the vicinity of Villers Cotterêts and Troësnes (aisne) through Sillie la Poterie to the vicinity of Oulchy-le-Château (aisne). We are now slated for a few days rest and start back toward the rear while the French held the line.

We were held in reserve for a few days at Neuilly-St. Front, doing nothing in particular, having advanced too far in the previous action

14. Probably men from the 104th Regiment of the 40th Division, a Saxon division that faced the French 33rd Division and American 4th Division on July 18, 1918. On the other hand, the 102nd Infantry Regiment (3rd Royal Saxon) was part of the 32nd Division and assigned to a quiet sector at Eix-Bezonveaux starting July 15. U.S. War Department, *Histories of Two Hundred Fifty-One Divisions of the German Army which participated in the War, 1914–1918* (Washington, D.C.: U.S. Government Printing Office, 1920), 399–401, 442–45.

Building occupied by 4th Division Headquarters from July 23 to July 28. Building was struck by a shell which carried away the entire center of roof and top floor. Bourneville, France, July 25, 1918. U.S. Army Signal Corps Collection, National Archives, 19015 [1079G8].

without adequate artillery support. What artillery we did have was in scattered units manned by the French. We were supposed to stay at Neuilly until our own artillery (4th Field) could join us from the rear. They had not as yet had time to reach us from their training sector at Camp de Souge, near Bordeaux, way down in southern France. But they were on their way, partly by train, and Nash Quad trucks (4 wheel drive).[15]

Finally after about two days at Neuilly-St. Front, we were suddenly ordered to another reserve position northwest of Beuvardes (aisne). We marched into a wood in this position, late at night. The sky ahead was red with rockets and flares and there was the sullen boom of heavy artillery not far away. We were here in

15. Charles Nash of Nash Motors developed the Nash Quad, or four-wheel-drive truck. More than 9,700 Quads were produced for Army use in 1918. Charles K. Hyde, *Storied Independent Automakers: Nash, Hudson, and American Motors* (Detroit: Wayne State University Press, 2009), 43–45.

Interior of top floor, 4th Division Headquarters, where direct artillery hit carried away center of roof. American soldiers souvenir hunting. Bourneville, France, July 25, 1918. U.S. Army Signal Corps Collection, National Archives, 19016 [1080G8].

support of the 42d, Rainbow Division (National Guard), but as we were not immediately needed, we lay down on the ground in our blankets to sleep as best we could. At daylight we awakened to find ourselves in a beautiful wood of white birch saplings. Our soup gun was already steaming away, exuding the savory odors of slum and black coffee. The men were taking it easy. The shelling ahead also seemed to have quieted down somewhat. This was in the Bois-de-la-Tournelle.

Just before chow call, Lieutenant Holstlaw, our company commander, received an order by battalion runner to advance the company on ahead at once and to pick up a liaison officer, who would join us at a certain point later on that day. So urgent seemed the order that the cooks were not even allowed to dish out our morning chow, all prepared and ready. However, the men were allowed ten minutes to collect everything and be ready to march. We could get our coffee but had to drink it on the move.

Soon the entire company was spread out and deployed through the trees. We were ordered to watch everything, the brush, the tree tops, etc. All morning long we proceeded slowly through the wood and underbrush and saw nothing but rabbits. At noon we came to a road running crosswise through the woods. Here we stopped and were allowed to have our chow, our soup cannon having followed us by another road. Here also, we picked up the expected liaison officer.

After about an hour's wait, we moved on through the woods in the same manner as in the morning. Holstlaw and the liaison officer were leading on ahead. The ground was now carpeted with a rich green moss and this, with the white birch saplings made a most beautiful piece of woodland. It was probably someone's private shooting preserve but we were after bigger game now.

Some little distance further on, the woods opened up on a stone quarry and a few old buildings. It was about dusk as we arrived in this position. We move in the quarry and shortly after we were halted by close-up enemy artillery fire, the first we had heard since morning. We noticed also that our liaison officer guide had left us. Lieut. Holstlaw ordered us to halt and spread out. We waited all night for further orders but none came and the German artillery peppered us most of the night. None of us were hurt however as we had stopped just out of the range of the guns and the enemy didn't think to change his trajectory which could have caught us easily.

Next morning we received orders to about face and proceed to the rear, then march to the Forêt de Fère (Fère-en-Tardenois

Wood). Just what occurred or what we were supposed to do in this quarry episode, I never found out. It was evident to all of us however, that we had been led within the range of the enemy artillery quite unexpectedly. Perhaps we luckily escaped further injury, or even annihilation, because of Holstlaw's good judgment in halting our advance at the first sign of hostility. We all knew that there was something peculiar about the whole procedure, because the lieutenant was heard to remark about the delay, in the return of the liaison officer, who never did show up again. Had we been a little farther on, toward the center of the quarry, we would have been squarely in the middle of a dangerous box barrage, with results you may well imagine.[16]

"Whadda ya 'spose we came in here fer, corporal?" inquires Stevens of Corporal Andrews, who had just been made corporal of our squad in place of Covey, who was wounded at Chouy.[17]

"How does ya expect a ribbon clerk from Philadelphee ta answer that one?" demands O'Hara. "Even the lieutenant can't answer it."

"Well, no harm in askin', is there?" replies Stevens. "Ain't a corporal 'sposed ta know everything privates is ignorant of?"

"Yer ignorant all right. An that ain't no dream," says O'Hara. "Anybody kin see that the lyceum officer who joined us yesterday, wuz a fake."

"So wuz St. Patrick a fake," puts in Belkin, impishly. "But the Irish, of course they knows everything."

"Now fellas, be care . . ." begins Corporal Andrews, talking like a sissy.

"All the Jews is lousy, an all the Belkins' is got big feet," snaps O'Hara.

"My stars! Now fellas, don't commence . . ." tries Corporal Andrews again.

"Aw, shut up!" says O'Hara. "Wait until yer has been a corporal mor'n a week, afore ya tries ta advise any of us privates. I'll bet yer pants is wet yet, from that heavy shellin' last night."

"Stop that talking, afore I slaps ya down!" snaps Corporal Andrews. "I may be a ribbon clerk, an talk like a sissy, but take that!

16. As the name implies, a box barrage enclosed an enemy position on both flanks and the rear, preventing them from receiving support or withdrawing from the area.

17. Perhaps Hubert Paskell Allred (1895–1975), a native of Van Zandt County, Texas.

An that! Ya gosh damn Irish smart alec!" continues the corporal, as he knocks O'Hara flat with an uppercut under the chin.

"Lookit the great O'Hara now!" exclaims Belkin in high glee. "I'll bet he's dreamin' about the bogs of Ireland, er the stars of Broadway."

"Wuz that a whizbang hit me?" says O'Hara weakly, as he slowly picks himself up from the ground. "You win, corporal. You sure is got a hell of a wallop fer a softie!"

"Well, my stars! Look! He's bleeding!" exclaims the corporal.

In the 2d Battle of the Marne, the Germans had entirely lost out in their first battle of a series of planned offensives. Their about face therefore, from their hilarious joy of previous victories in the Marne and on the Chemin des Dames, has now resulted in a much lowered morale that usually springs from defeat. Our attacks had been felt principally by the German 7th Army under the command of General Walter von Reinhardt. Many of the soldiers of this army, it is true, were sick with the flu and dysentery which contributed to their loss of driving power. But in some of his writings, Gen. Von Reinhardt has discussed the fighting qualities of the U.S. soldier as he observed them and of whom he speaks appreciatively as follows:

> "The American troops brought across something more important than training and experience. Something that must be inborn. The will to attack, the firm resolve to kill or get killed. These are warlike qualities which brave men have never hesitated to praise. My opinion of the U.S. soldier may be summed up in the words of Frederick the Great, who once remarked of his own legions, 'they may not look so good, but Hell! how they can fight.'"[18]

The German war chancellor, Von Hertling, also has something to say. Asked a few days before his death the question, "When

18. Walther Reinhardt (1872–1930), entered the army in 1891 and was appointed to the General Staff in 1913. A major when the war began, Reinhardt was eventually promoted to Chief of General Staff of the Seventh Army. Howell slightly misquoted the German officer: "However, the American troops brought with them across the ocean something much more important than training and experience, something that cannot be taught, but must be inborn: The will to attack, the firm resolve 'to kill or get killed'—warlike qualities which brave men never hesitate to praise even in the enemy!" A later paragraph in Reinhardt's account states, "My opinion of the American soldier may be summed up by quoting King Frederick the Great. Some two hundred years ago, the potentate of a neighbouring country criticized Frederick's troops before he had seen them in action. Prussia's great monarch remarked: 'They may not look so good—but hell, how they can fight!" George Sylvester Viereck, *As They Saw Us: Foch, Ludendorff and Other Leaders Write Our War History* (Garden City, NY: Doubleday, Doran and Company, Inc., 1929), 123–24, 315.

was it that the German Gov't first realized that the war was lost to them?" His reply was as follows: "At the beginning of July 1918, I was convinced, I confess it, that before September our adversaries would be sending us peace proposals. We expected grave events for Paris before the end of July. That was on the fifteenth. On the eighteenth, even the most optimistic among us knew that all was lost. The history of the world was played out in three days."[19]

This will illustrate the status of mind of the German high command before and after the 2d Battle of the Marne, but they still continued to make the German people believe, through propaganda and the magnification of minor successes, that they were winning the war. Thus, there was to be over three months more of hard fighting before the German war machine was to be thoroughly crushed.

Two hundred and fifty thousand U.S. soldiers actually participated in the second Marne battle, brigaded with French divisions. You will appreciate, therefore, how impossible it is for any single line soldier or officer, to know all that is taking place, except at his immediate position on the Front. Each soldier is but a small cog in a great wheel designed to hold, push back and finally bring a stubborn, arrogant and ruthless enemy to his knees.

The 1st, 2d, 3d, 4th U.S. Regulars and the 26th and 42d National Guard Divisions participated and held fast at the Marne. The 2d, with its Marines, had become famous at Belleau Wood. The 3d, under General Dickman, doggedly held the bridges at Château Thierry.[20] The 26th, (New England National Guard) was at Montdidier to the north, making history. The 4th Division was in reserve for all of the above near Meaux at the start of the battle, just prior to July 18th, but itself moved into action on

19. Georg Friedrich von Hertling (1843–1919), chancellor from November 1917 to October 1918. Howell made a few minor errors in transcribing Hertling's statement, which appeared in its entirety in *The New York Times* on January 11, 1919.

20. Joseph Theodore Dickman (1857–1927) graduated from West Point and saw combat in Cuba, the Philippines, and China from 1898–1900. A brigadier general in May 1917 and a major general in the National Army that August, Dickman took command of the 3rd Division in November 1917. He led that division to France and into combat at the Second Battle of the Marne. Given command of the Fourth Corps, he led that organization during the St. Mihiel Offensive, then led the First Corps in the Meuse-Argonne Offensive from October to November 1918. He took command of the Third Army (Army of Occupation) in November 1918 and after occupation duty in Germany and promotion to major general, returned to the United States and retired in 1921. Anne Cipriano Venzon, *The United States in the First World War: An Encyclopedia* (New York: Garland Publishing, Inc., 1995), 202–3.

Members of 39th Infantry digging in just after the Boche had left. Near Fresnes, France, July 31, 1918. U.S. Army Signal Corps Collection, National Archives, 18680 [415G8].

Members of 39th Infantry digging in just after the Boche had left. Near Fresnes, France, July 31, 1918. U.S. Army Signal Corps Collection, National Archives, 18681 [416G8].

the 18th. What happened thereafter, I have related in so far as it concerns the necessary part played by the 39th Infantry Regiment and the 7th and 8th Brigades, driving through the enemy flank toward the east and successfully cutting off the Château Thierry salient. The Germans were now moving back toward the Vesle and the Aisne to consolidate new positions and make a more determined stand. They are on the run, so we have now taken up the offensive.

Chapter 7

What Happened in Fère-En-Tardenois Wood

Leaving Beuvardes and traveling east, August 1st found us moving up through Fère-en-Tardenois Wood (Fôret de Fère) located near the town of the same name. The 42d, Rainbow Division was then in line near Sergy and Coulonges (aisne). On July 28th to 30th, the 42d, assisted by the 47th Infantry, 4th Divis[ion], had advanced through the Bois Colas, over Hills 184 and 212 and taken Sergy and Seringes-et-Nesles. Two old regiments of National Guard, the 167th Alabama and 168th Iowa, who had opposed each other in the U.S. Civil War and who were now a part of the 42d Divis[ion] A.E.F., were now fighting a common enemy side by side on this front.

Back through the woods and roads to Villers-Cotterêts, Neuilly-St. Front and La-Ferté-Milon, and Château Thierry, there was now an incessant troop movement. Men struggled along under heavy packs. Troops were coming out of the lines, others going in. We of the 39th were here at Fère-en-Tardenois to relieve the 42d Division who would go to the rear for a rest. It is night and the roads are full of moving troops. Walking infantry is mixed with guns, limbers and all sorts of transport. French camions, U.S. motor trucks and water carts are bobbing about as they slowly edge their way through the congested road. Traffic would be halted in what seemed a hopeless tangle and then suddenly proceed to other halts. Hard-bitten mule skinners loudly curse their mules, the war and the U.S. Army. Men stumble and fall flat in the mud, only to rise wearily and continue on, cursing and crabbing about everything as they go. Ahead, through the woods, at the crossroads, there is the ominous boom of a high calibre German gun whose shellbursts are making the spot unhealthy for moving troops.

All night long B Company struggles along on foot. I or any of my comrades could have gotten out of the war easily, just by reaching out a foot sideways to the right or left, to be run over or smashed by the endless stream of heavy caissons and wagons moving along the road on all sides of us. But why should we do that? Such, however, is the almost irresistible desire of war weary men, to get a small injury of some kind, so as to be sent back to a hospital for a long rest and thus escape the incessant proximity of war. As we continue on, the night becomes putrid with the profanity of troops, pressing ever on and on under the most unspeakable hardship. We didn't know our destination, of course, but we knew it was war and more war. We must carry on.

Suddenly, we were stopped alongside the road and turned in the wood on the left of us. It was near morning. Strangely enough, as daylight came, there were scarcely any troops, or movement, visible on the road outside. There would be only an occasional watercart doping along, while the road was otherwise deserted and quiet. All day long we remained hidden in the woods, not venturing outside. A troop of newly mounted French cavalry, seldom used in this war, but resplendent in clean, new uniforms and wonderful black mounts, passed us, riding through the trees and going toward the northwest. Few of them would ever come back. Mounted cavalry was too conspicuous and sort of out of place in this war.

Our rolling kitchens (chow guns) now with us in the woods, got busy and gave us a good feed.[1] Smoke from them was screened,

1. There were four main types of rolling kitchens available for use in the A.E.F. (the Magor, with two boilers, the Steinburn with four boilers and two small ovens, the Taylor No. 29 with four boilers and a large griddle, and the Taylor Number 30 with six boilers), but it is impossible to determine which type was used by the 39th Infantry. All were "very hard on men and horses," "traveled poorly," and supplied poor meals because the

but it must have been somewhat visible above the treetops, as there seemed to be numerous Boche planes always passing overhead. McGuire and I busied ourselves digging a hole in the soft, sandy earth and then crawled into it for a good snooze. The rest of the squad were all about, engaged in whatever pleased them. Thus passed the day.

That night, after dark, we moved across to the wood on the opposite side of the road, one man at a time. The major of our battalion had become leery of the aeroplanes seen above us all day. So we must move for safety, or so he thought. Everyone was cautioned not to light a match or cigarette, but some wise boy who just couldn't wait, disregarded orders and because of his own selfishness, got us all in trouble. A Boche bomber plane, probably looking for a large U.S. naval gun located in these woods, spotted us from the glow of the cigarette or match.[2] Suddenly, close above the treetops, sounded the low heavy drone of a Boche motor. The plane passed by but was soon back again, cruising around above the trees. Quickly the night was turned to daylight as the plane dropped several magnesium flares, which revealed the path in the woods just below, overflowing with moving infantry in close-up formation. Another deft swing of the plane. All eyes are now turned upward in consternation. Then, without warning, came several heavy bombs, crunching and screeching as they plopped to earth and exploded. More followed in quick succession, while the men below on the path scatter in hopeless confusion.

"Everybody down on your bellies!" yells Sergeant Nolan frantically. Some of the men remain standing as if stunned. Others fall, groaning and writhing in terrible agony. Others were lying motionless and still, never to rise again. Still more bombs crash behind us. The plane is following the path back to the road along the whole column of infantry, bunched together on this single pathway. The result is terrible.

---

cooking was practically limited to stews or "slum." In addition, the smoke they produced drew enemy artillery fire, which forced them to be located far to the rear, requiring the food to be carried great distances. M.W. Ireland, *The Medical Department of the United States Army in the World War*, 15 vols., 1921–29 (Washington, D.C.: U.S. Government Printing Office, 1926), 6 (Sanitation): 710–12.

2. Howell is mistaken. The five U.S. Naval Railway Batteries did not begin operations until September 6, 1918.

One little Jewish soldier in my company, a native of San Francisco, who was always looking for a quartette among us to sing "Down by the Old Mill Stream" or "When You Were Sweet Sixteen," was directly behind me in the column moving into the woods. He had been telling me just before we crossed the road to these fateful woods, about his darling sweetheart back in the U.S.A. He was imparting intimate thoughts on what he planned to do when he got back to God's Country again. And, as he expressed it, "I feel that we will soon be home." He was to go home, poor fellow, but not to San Francisco. That same night he was shot through the heart with a piece of jagged shrapnel from the aeroplane bomb, along with many of our comrades.[3]

Altogether about thirty men were killed or wounded by flying shrapnel from bombs in my immediate company, including our temporary commander Cap't V.P. Rousseau who was seriously wounded. The entire First Battalion of four companies, lost about 125 men in less than ten minutes on this spot.[4]

The air raid was our first real experience at close range with this type of destruction. Being trapped thus without a chance to escape, unnerved all of us. Yet, somehow, we didn't hate the enemy.

3. Three men of Company B were killed during this period: Private 1st Class John Murray and Privates Emil Boudreau, and Tommy Franks. Cole and Eberlin, *The History of the 39th U.S. Infantry*, 94. Murray, who died on August 1, 1918, was reinterred in the San Francisco (CA) National Cemetery.

4. Vincent Paul Rousseau (1893–1972), a native of Vermont, was commissioned a second lieutenant and first lieutenant in June 1917. He was promoted to captain (temporary) that August. He attended the army service schools at Fort Leavenworth, and was assigned to the 39th Infantry at Syracuse and traveled with the regiment to Camp Greene. On the night of August 1, 1918, Rousseau was seriously wounded when he was struck by a fragment of an aviation bomb. The fragment tore through Rousseau's helmet and lodged in the left side of his brain, paralyzing his right side. He underwent an operation in a field hospital, but it was not until two months later that he gained partial use of his side. He was sent to a base hospital in France and then returned to the United States. There Rousseau underwent a second operation, replacing a portion of his skull, and when he developed double ether pneumonia and empyema, his surgeons removed two sections of ribs in order to drain his chest cavity. The seriously underweight Rousseau was retired in November 1919 due to his disability. He was recalled to duty in World War II and retired again as a major in 1944. U.S. Adjutant General, *Army Register, January 1, 1920* (Washington, D.C.: U.S. Government Printing Office, 1920), 994; U.S. Adjutant General, Army *Register 1 January 1945* (Washington, D.C.: U.S. Government Printing Office, 1945), 1361; 74th Congress, 2d Session, Senate Report No. 1568, Calendar No. 1633, "Vincent P. Rousseau, Report to Accompany H.R. 4777," 1936; *Burlington* (VT) *Weekly Free Press*, March 7, 1918. Rousseau commanded Company B from July 11–August 1, 1918. Record Group 120, Records of the American Expeditionary Forces, World War I, Records of Combat Divisions 1917–1919, 4th Division, 4th Division Historical, Box 29, Folder: 39th Infantry, History, [M.G., Supply, Hdrs, 1st, 2nd, 3rd Bn, and Co. A thru M], 4th Div., 204–11.4, Official History of the 39th Regiment of Infantry, 1917–1918, National Archives and Records Administration, College Park, Maryland.

Rather, it brought home to us the folly and useless sacrifice of the institution called war, especially as we saw the white waxen faces of good American boys, their eyes staring, their uniforms covered with blood and slime and mud, looking up at us from the cold, wet, ground, their lives cut off in the flower of young manhood—and for what? Because men in their greed or ambition had exploited their fellow man, to further their own selfish ends. Because we must help stop the four long years of hell and carnage by sacrificing ourselves, if need be, in the cause of humanity. Among the fallen were some of our closest friends. My pal McGuire, became a bit panicky in the excitement, but soon snapped out of it. Vinelli and Stevens, O'Hara and Corporal Andrews were still shakily on the job but ready for anything. Belkin was sobbing beside the body of a fallen friend and comrade.

After our grim experience of the night, we left next morning for the hell hole of the next front—the Vesle River sector. We were a solemn procession on our way out, as we passed slowly by our dead comrades. They were wrapped in mud-caked blankets, shelter halves and raincoats and would be laid at rest like the legion of others in the bosom of France, far away from mothers and sweethearts.

Yesterday there was glamour and glory, but no longer is there any glory in war, as such. After the Fère-en-Tardenois Wood episode we are thoroughly disillusioned. It is only our duty and loyalty to our country's flag that drives us onward, to whatever may be our fate.

Soldiers demand little praise from commanders for courage. Often they never have a fighting chance. But now and then, they may be severely criticized for apparent cowardice. Either can become a part of any soldier's make-up, however, under certain conditions. Great heroism is often the result of accident and the soldier-hero himself is least able to relate what motivated him. Certainly not patriotism alone—he doesn't even think of it. He is sometimes compelled to go through with situations that reflect great heroism in spite of himself, and often in sheer panic he drives through and wins. There will be other situations subsequently to overshadow Fère-en-Tardenois.

As the U.S. Army, in conjunction with the French, have now taken up the offensive, in the words of that illustrious officer,

Major General Chas. H. Martin (86th Divis[ion]), "From now on we are going to be just as damn offensive as possible."[5] And that was our spirit and sentiment as well.

The Vesle River sector, where we are now headed, is located between Soissons and Reims along the Paris-Soissons railroad, running parallel with the Vesle River. We are pushing the Hun steadily back, but he is showing stubborn resistance.

5. The purported quote is, "The spirit of this army is the spirit of the offensive and we are going to be just as damned offensive as we can!" Martin supposedly uttered the quote during the division's training days at Camp Grant, Illinois. James C. Russell and William E. Moore, *The United States Navy in the World War* (Washington, D.C.: Pictorial Bureau, 1921), 264.

Chapter 8

Aisne Marne Offensive (July 26th to August 15th, 1918) Battle of Vesle River-Soissons

We're the U.S. Army privates.
We don't amount to much,
But we're a damn sight better;
Than the gahdam Dutch.
Early in the morning,
We get our slum and stew.
And before the day is over,
We'll get a kraut or two.
—Army Rhyme

The strategic German positions on the Marne and the Ourcq were now lost to them. The remainder of their divisions therefore, had stampeded north, back to the heights of the Vesle River about fifteen kilometers away, to establish another line of resistance to try and hold back the ever pressing advance of the intrepid Americans and French.

We also, now leave the fateful Fère-en-Tardenois woods and proceed to the Vesle River sector through small sections of woods, keeping off the roads as much as possible, except at night. I remember distinctly on two occasions, being followed by Boche raiding planes at night while marching along the roads. The French roads in the moonlight are like long, white bands, silvery and luminous. Anything on them is a contrast and therefore quite easily visible from the sky. When the drone of a German aeroplane motor came uncomfortably close to us, we would drop on our bellies alongside the road until the danger would pass. This happened to us a number of times en route to the Vesle. The planes acted as a sort of Boche rear guard, intended to molest and hold back advancing troops as much as possible. To all of us the sight of the huge bombing plane close above our heads was fascinating, as we lay in the ditch alongside the road, practically concealed in the deep shadow of the weeds and foliage.

"There's the Kaiser again," remarks Corporal Andrews.

"If he's the Kaiser, I'm Frederick the Great," says Belkin. "That bird is just snoopin' and crusin' around lookin' fer another place ta lay some more iron eggs. He's probably got his eye on us, too."

"You got right, Belkie," retorts Stevens gazing upward. "Better keep yer head down."

"Say corporal," says Belkin, "ya didn't fergit that Fère-en-Tardenois Wood yet, did ya? That bird'll find out he's Philip the Last, instead of the Kaiser, when we opens up his guts up on the Vesle.

"Phooey on you an the damn Boche, too," remarks Stevens.

"Hey, you birds! Pipe down!" orders Sergeant Nolan. "Do you want him ta lay some more of his black eggs on us? Keep a little more quiet!"

WHAM! SWISH! PLOP! BANG! Several heavy projectiles drop from the air.

Complete silence. Nobody hurt. Everyone nervous.

"Jeeze! Ain't that bird got a mean disposition, though?" remarks Stevens, dropping his mess tins with a loud bang.

"Hey, you! Keep quiet! No more talking from now on! Ya understand? Yer in the army now, an don't yer fergit it. Forward, March!" orders the sergeant.

"Aw, pipe down yerself," says Stevens.

At Seringes-et-Nesles (aisne) we moved into a dark clammy section of Forêt de Nesles woods late at night. Here we found evidence of recent German occupation and hurried departure. The woods were full of ill smelling carcasses of dead horses and men, victims of artillery. Large quantities of unused shells, still in their original baskets or cases were strewn about. There was war debris of every description belonging to the German army. McGuire and Belkin lay down together in the pitch dark woods, too tired to look around much at their surroundings. But in the morning when they awoke, they noticed there were three of them, the third being a dead Boche. So they rolled him over, only to find that he had no face and what was left was covered over solid with a host of green-blue flies. In the morning therefore, we moved out to another section of woods around the corner that was in a much cleaner condition. Every day now our taste for the glories of war were more and more on the wane. I know of no odor that is more repellent to such thick skinned individuals as soldiers usually are, than the smell of human dead bodies left in the open to mortify and decay.

Sergeant Billy Burch, who was always using the expression "blowed up" around our company, certainly had a good chance to be blowed up as he was going alone through the woods acting as a company runner.[1] He was armed of course but only with a pistol and was moving along a narrow path in the woods listening to the birds, to deliver a message to A Co's P.C.[2] Just as he was about to round a turn in the path, he suddenly heard the guttural sounds of Germans talking. Almost immediately they came into view in front of him on the path and proved to be an Herr Hauptmann (captain) or a lieutenant strolling nonchalantly along the path with two orderlies directly behind carrying his baggage. They were apparently unarmed and probably thought that they were traveling in a safe zone. Burch jumped quickly behind a tree, clicked the safety on his Colt Automatic and yelled at the Germans to halt and surrender. Did they throw up their hands? No. They dropped their luggage and made a quick dive for the brush along the path instead. Sgt. Burch fired, killing one man, but the officer and his remaining orderly escaped through the trees. After waiting for a short interval, Burch concluded that they were just an isolated party as no others had shown up at the sound of the firing. He then searched the Herr Offizier's baggage, so hastily dropped, found and brought in the offizier's papers to

1. William Burch is not listed on Company B's muster roll. Muster Roll of Company B, 39th U.S. Infantry, April 30-June 30, 1918, National Personnel Records Center, St. Louis, Missouri.

2. Post of Command, the field headquarters of the commanding officer of a unit.

the captain of A Co., which may or may not have been of value to our intelligence section.

On his way back, returning to B Co., Sgt. Burch again inspected the officer's baggage for other souvenirs. He brought in to us, some [of] his buddies, a small supply of tinned honey and a quantity of German cigars. He was all "blowed up" after his exciting experience in the woods and we were almost blown up by the cigars. The honey, however was a real luxury.

Biting eagerly into a cigar, but not lighting it, Burch remarked, "I never did like the looks of Boche officers, or their cigars either. This gahdamn cabbage tastes like it has got cayenne pepper in it."

"Let's see it sarge," said Belkin, suspiciously, "looks funny to me." It was handed over.

Carefully he unwrapped the outside and skillfully concealed under the wrapper was a short fuse leading to some high explosive material packed in with the tobacco. It made a neat little incendiary bomb to light and toss in some convenient place. None of us smoked any of the cigars, you be can be sure of that. We buried the whole bunch underground and touched them off. They made a loud detonation.

Shortly after, we left these woods and moved to a new location nearer to the Vesle River Front, or in the Bois-de-Dôle. We did not go into action at once but stalled around for several days awaiting further orders. I can see the old water cart now, standing there among the trees with its phills propped up on a stick. The company chow gun is also close by steaming away with a savory odor. Then, there was the old Lister Bag (chlorinated water) suspended in a tree, swaying two and fro in the breeze. A few yards away among the trees can be seen the swishing tails of the mules, which are used to draw the ration and water carts, and the chow gun of our company.

While thus waiting, we spent most of the time cleaning up and puttering around with our equipment. I had only one razor blade left and it was too dull to use. While I borrowed safety razors from the other men, I found them to be little better than mine, even with new blades. Something about shipment of these blades across the salt water of the Atlantic dulls them, or else they were made of poor steel and were never sharp anyway. In an old ruined farmhouse just on the outside of the woods, I picked up a small concaved bit of pottery similar in texture to a common flower pot but somewhat closer grained. I poured a few drops of gun oil on the same and used it to hone my razor blade. It worked like magic, so afterward I never had any trouble to shave with hard, cold water and Ivory soap for lather.

Often at night, the Boche would harass us in the woods with shells from field pieces close by. The noise was nerve racking, but no one was hurt as the gunner's trajectory was set a bit too high, his shells falling short and leaving us just out of range. He was, however, concentrating his fire in and about Mont St. Martin, Ville Savoye and the crossroads at Chéry-Chartreuve farm, using G.I. cans (high explosive) and gas.[3] Occasionally a series of Austrian 88s would give a vicious crack close to us and then down would come branches from the trees without however doing much harm, except to knock over some private's pup tent. Considerable gas lurked in the woods at times, but we paid little attention to it as it didn't seem strong enough for us to get excited about. It was too much bother to get out our gas masks. A green outfit would probably have clanged all the gas alarms within reach and had their gas masks on and off a hundred times in a like situation.

August 3d to 13th we were in action trying to cross the Vesle River between Fismes and Bazoches Wood, near St. Thibaut. The days were hot and there was little air stirring, making us sticky and uncomfortable. Before reaching Bazoches, we had passed through another wood that was a veritable Hell. This was about August 6th. Shells cracked over our heads and tore up the ground all around us. We were pelted with stones, shrapnel and gas with the high explosive shells making great gouges in the woods, up-rooting trees and scattering heavy branches across our path.

This held us up considerably. "Dead Man's Curve," a section of the road near the little hamlets of Ville Savoye, St. Thibaut and Tannières, was a regular slaughter house. Austrian 88s would land on the curve of the road back of Ville Savoye and crack without warning, annihilating anyone who tried to round the bend of the road leading to the Vesle River. H.E. shells would come over

3. One member of the 39th described a "'G.I. shell' as a shell of gigantic proportions." "G.I." stood for "galvanized iron." "There are many slang names for shells," he explained, including "whizz bangs," "G.I. cans," and "duds." *Modesto* (CA) *Evening News*, March 7, 1919.

Streets of Sergy crowded with Infantry and Artillery from 4th Division, on way to the front. Sergy, France, August 3, 1918. U.S. Army Signal Corps Collection, National Archives, 18804 [613G8].

the hill and crunch in the field alongside the road while men hugged the foxholes in the hillside on the right. I remember being stopped here by an officer-priest who made hurried inquiry as to my religion. "Geeze!" I thought to myself, "must be some stiff action ahead. I've never been stopped like this before." When the priest learned that I was protestant, he passed me hurriedly on with some kind of a blessing. All Catholics, however, were detained a few moments, but joined us presently. Some were in the Great Beyond only a few moments later as they moved too close to the bend in the road.

It was the intention of the command to await a quiet moment in the shelling, concealed in foxholes, and then rush around the bend in the road, a few men at a time, until the whole company was in the shelter of a sunken road (Grande Savert), just around the bend, offering some temporary protection. There we were to re-form in column of squads and proceed with a rush to the Vesle River embankment at a time to be scheduled later in the day. A few men attempted this movement but were promptly picked off

Close up of Brig. Gen. B.A. Poore. commanding 7th Infantry Brigade, 4th Division. Chéry Chartreuve, France, August 9, 1918. U.S. Army Signal Corps Collection, National Archives, 19023 [1087G8].

by snipers. Then would come another salvo from the 88's and a few more shells from the field pieces would pass over the hill and land alongside the road as before. Our every movement was watched through enemy field glasses.

Many of our company were shell shocked here also and acted like crazy men or went limp on the ground. These were carefully carried back to a zone of safety. My old pal, McGuire went back to the rear from here badly shell shocked. I never saw him again after this but I heard from him later at St. Mihiel.

Unable to get around "Dead Man's Curve" in any great numbers, we now moved back off the road to the right and entered some woods on a high ground unobserved. This position was to the rear of the sunken road that we had been trying to reach from the curve but with an open field between the woods where we were concealed, the sunken road, the Soissons-Reims railroad and the Vesle River itself, our real objective.

Just at dusk therefore we rushed out of the woods to the attack across the Vesle. We got across the open field and to the shelter of the sunken road which was similar to a large trench with the road in the bottom. This was accomplished before the enemy artillery opened up. Presently we were over the top of the road, across another large field and rushing the railroad position, intending to skip over the rails and get across the Vesle River in the valley beyond. This sort of movement was being carried out all along the Vesle by the rest of the 39th Inf. and the 32d Division on our right. In a few isolated instances they got across but turned back. We got as far as the railroad embankment and across the rails but had to fall back behind the railroad as it was too hot. We were stopped by artillery firing at point blank range, so we couldn't get across the Vesle and the hill beyond. Star shells and flares illustrated the whole position as bright as day. The noise set up by the German artillery all along the Vesle was terrific. They knew the Americans and French were coming and wished to hold us back long enough to allow their retreat back to the Aisne River.

It would have been just too bad if we had been caught by this artillery fire in the valley along the Vesle. Lieutenant Holstlaw of B Company and Haney of A Company consulted and decided not to attempt a further crossing of the Vesle at this time in a hopeless attack. It was useless at this time to attempt to swim the stream, as the German snipers had the field too well covered. We would have to wait for our own artillery to blast them out and it was not yet in position. Therefore we lay behind and were somewhat protected by the railroad embankment itself. If a soldier cautiously raised his head above the level of the tracks, "ping" would come a rifle bullet close to him with a whipping sound, more often than not, picking him off. After dark, the enemy kept burning red flares to light the position so he could watch us.

Down in the valley on the shore of the Vesle below the tracks, was a handful of Army engineers striving to construct a bridge. The Boche (Prussian Guards) would allow these engineers to fell trees and drop them across the Vesle almost without molestation. When a bridge was completed for us to cross however, they would blow it to pieces with uncanny accuracy. Otherwise they didn't bother the engineers but busied themselves with keeping us back behind the railroad tracks.

The whole Vesle River sector was in truth a hell hole. Mud up to your knees, shell-shock victims, wounded, dead, etc. A single battalion of the 58th Infantry, 4th Divis[ion] got across the Vesle and stayed there in spite of heavy enfilade fire from Château Diable. Next morning we were relieved here by the 47th Infantry, 4th Divis[ion] and fell back to the sunken road at daylight. The Boche strafed us unmercifully with his artillery firing at point blank range all the way back across the field to the sunken road. Subsequently the 47th then took up our position at the tracks and finally got about three hundred men across the Vesle at a great sacrifice. Hundreds of this regiment were slaughtered as they were trying to wade or swim the stream encumbered with full packs and ammunition. This was a useless sacrifice as the enemy shortly withdrew to positions farther to the rear toward the Chemin des Dames.

Unburied dead of the 4th Division also lay in Ville Savoye and the paths above the town in large numbers. This was proof of the intense struggle and the resistance put up by the enemy for the possession of the hamlet. The same condition was also in evidence at Fismes, where the men of the 4th Division, assisting the 32d Division, captured and recaptured the town several times by stubborn street fighting. The towns near Chéry-Chartreuve farm and St. Gilles were completely destroyed, mostly by artillery.

Lieut. Col. C. A. Bach, chief of staff, 4th Division, questioning German prisoner of the 259th Prussian Reserve. Left to right: Capt. Restrand (French), prisoner, Capt. Cothereau (French), Capt. Le Bourkis (French), Lieut. Col. C. A. Bach, and E. W. Savage, United States Army. Chateau Belle Vue, France, July 14, 1918. U.S. Army Signal Corps Collection, National Archives, 17622 [2110J8].

The former, being in the zone of the advancing Americans, was therefore a target for direct artillery concentration which was not only fatal to large groups of infantry but took particular toll of ammunition and supply trains, their animals and drivers.

Some German prisoners were taken in these struggles, of course, but the main body of the German Army was across the Vesle. These regiments were summarily dealt with by the 77th and succeeding U.S. divisions who relieved the 4th on August 12th, advancing to the Aisne River only after intensive hand to hand combat at Château Diable and around Fismette.

The fighting, with us of B Company, took place mostly at night or in the late afternoon and could not properly be called fighting, just a series of rushes and advances. Action in the towns, however, was usually in broad daylight with hand to hand encounters against bayonet and machine gun in the open streets and in the shelter of demolished buildings, made more difficult and horrible

Two German prisoners 18 years of age, having been in the army six months and were captured on their first day in the trenches, (Aug. 9). Left to right: Yochom Dudsenski and Frank Yoshkko, 1918 reserves. Mont St. Martin-Fismes Road, France, August 10, 1918. U.S. Army Signal Corps Collection, National Archives, 19003 [1057G8].

by Boche planes bombing from the air. As far as my company was concerned, there were only a few Germans visible to us and those were always on the run, retreating to the rear a few hundred yards ahead. They usually wore the red bands of artillerists.[4]

August 16th found us moving to the northwest through the large city of Soissons (aisne). This town had been freed from German

4. It is unclear exactly what Howell means by "bands." For most of World War I, a colored band on the German wool field cap signified the wearer's branch of service, with a red band for infantry, black for artillery, etc. In 1917 a universal green band was introduced, although soldiers still continued to wear colored bands for the remainder of the war. If the Germans were wearing these field caps, he might have mistaken the red infantry cloth bands for an artillery designation. Red was the branch color of the U.S. Army artillery.

Fourth Division Field Hospital. Receiving wounded at tent wards, which are on both sides of the road. Chateau in center. Chateau De Le Foret, France, August 10, 1918. U.S. Army Signal Corps Collection, National Archives, 19005 [1059G8].

occupation nearly three weeks previously by the Marines of the 2d U.S. Division.[5] After an all-night hike, we stopped here early one morning for breakfast. I had my repast sitting on top of a rock pile in the center of the road in front of the ruined Soissons Cathedral. The meal was ordinary, consisting only of our emergency ration, a tin of which every soldier carried in his pack.[6] We just sat there in the road, gazing at the famous cathedral and wondering about it. No one was saying very much.

Finally Private O'Hara broke the silence. Turning to Belkin who was busy munching on a piece of corn-willie he says,

5. French troops captured Soissons. The U.S. Marines fought south of the city.

6. The emergency or "iron" ration, intended to be eaten only in "dire extremity" or by order of an officer, was packed in a small can to be carried in the soldier's upper left-hand coat pocket. It consisted of three 3-ounce cakes of a mixture of beef and ground cooked wheat, three 1-ounce cakes of chocolate, three-quarters of an ounce of salt, and a dram of black pepper. The components were packed into oval, hermetically sealed, lacquered tin cases. The bread and meat cake could be eaten dry or boiled to make a soup or porridge. The chocolate could be eaten as candy or made into hot chocolate. Benedict Crowell, *America's Munitions, 1917–1918* (Washington, D.C.: U.S. Government Printing Office, 1919), 444.

"Hey Max, do ya suppose they has synagogues in Jerusalem as good as this here one in Soissons?"

"Mebbe," answers Belkin, not very enthused.

"I'll bet some of my early ancestors musta carried hod on that job," observed O'Hara. "Yes sir! That's why it's such a damn good job."

"Listen, Irish! Did ya ever see a synagogue with a gentile cross on the top of it?" questions Corporal Andrews, smiling.

"No, an neither did Moses Belkin, either," replies O'Hara.

"By the looks of you, yer ancestors wuz a swell bunch of broken down hod carriers, all right," says Belkin, turning a cynical eye on O'Hara.

We now pass on through Soissons and thence northward toward the Chemin des Dames (road of the ladies, Louis XV) as a support for the 32d U.S. Division. This road was bitterly fought for by the French and lost when they retreated back to the Marne in the last days of April 1918 and was still in German hands before the 32d Division attacked and drove them off and moving them farther back.[7] After moving about six kilometers on this road toward Chavigny [Juvigny] we halted, as the 32d was now dug in. We were not needed, so we made an "about face" and started back toward the rear for reorganization and rest.

We hiked back through the famous wine country of the Champagne. Vinyards were everywhere in evidence, indicative of the leading industry of this locality. While there appeared to be many wine cellars, we were not given the opportunity to inspect any of them thereby creating disappointment in a few cases.

"Geeze! I wish't we'd a went on-a to Reims," remarks Vinelli, longingly, "so's we could-a got some-a-good-a wine."

"Plenty of vin-blanc and vin-rouge, that's me, too," says O'Hara. "This is one place where the wops can't drink up all the wine. There was plenty left by the Boche, who couldn't take it with them, but the U.S. Marines has been here so now there ain't none left for nobody."

"Sacri Bleuie! Phooey on the gahdamn Marines!" says Vinelli.

As we were now on our way back to rest billets there will be no more war for us for awhile. Just a lot of moving around. At our

7. Howell is mistaken. The Germans captured the Chemin des Dames position on May 27, 1918.

final destination we will secure replacements to fill up our much depleted battalions. Replacements, too, will mean some additional drill, inspections and instruction before moving to the St. Mihiel salient as a unit of the 1st U.S. Army under our own exclusive leadership instead of liaison with the French. In all previous engagements under French command, their conservation and difference in language, prevented complete success in a number of glaring instances. This removal from French control, therefore, brought on a quarrel between Foch and Pershing, which was not patched up until some time later, or not until after we had more than proved ourselves capable of fighting as an independent army.

The seemingly long trek on foot from Soissons (aisne) back to the rear as far as Château Thierry consumed about four days time but it was a welcome hike. Our route was via the Forêt de Deringes and Forêt de Fère and passing through the following towns, all in the Aisne.

Ciry
Septmonts
Vailly
Braine
Mareuil-en-dôle
Jaulgonne
Château Thierry
Étamps-sur-marne

We were much pleased to be going back for a rest and away from the Front. Every soldier is, even though it means more drill, inspections and the rest of the rigmarole connected with a foot soldier's life.[8]

Of the original squad assembled at Camp Mills, L.I., we have lost Corporal Covey and Private McGuire, wounded and shellshocked

8. As one member of the 4th Division's 58th Infantry poetically wrote, "Just as it is necessary for a boxer or wrestler to rest and recuperate after one match and to train and recover before the next one, so must a combat unit rest and reorganize before it can again enter the battleline." In addition to giving the men "both physical and mental" recreation, replacement troops had to be integrated into units, equipment issued to replace items lost or damaged, and animals "restored to maximum usefulness by rest, food, and proper exercise." For the average doughboy, the most common desire in a rest area was to "get clean," as weeks of campaigning had allowed few opportunities for washing one's face or hands, let alone bathing. Uniforms, worn continuously for days, had been "soaked with water" and "stained with mud and blood." "The St. Mihiel Drive," Record Group 120, Records of the American Expeditionary Forces, World War I, Records of Combat Divisions 1917–1919, 4th Division, 4th Division Historical, Box 36, Folder: 58th Infantry, Histories, Commendations & Battle Participants, 4th Division, 204–11.4, National Archives and Records Administration, College Park, Maryland.

respectively. Stevens, O'Hara, Belkin, Brizee, Vinelli and myself are still going strong along with Corporal Andrews.

Some of the boys would ask for furloughs but even though they were refused, there would be a welcome relief from the atmosphere of the front line and a certain freedom to move around.

"When I gits back ta Paris, I'm gonna git me a swell skirt an just promenod, just promenod on ze boo-le-vard and drink boo-coo vin-rouge," says Corporal Andrews, happily.

"I'm gonna climb the Eiffel Tower," says O'Hara, "so's I kin spit down on all the damn corporals an shavetails in this man's army."

"And when I finally gits promoted to sergeant," brags the corporal, "I'll make it my dooty ta drill all the privates ragged, so's they can't git ta Paris or anywhere else."

"When you gits ta be a sergeant, which ain't likely," retorts O'Hara, "you'll probably git full of coney-ac an be reduced ta buck private again, like the rest of us. Only 24 karat goldbricks ever gits ta be non-coms, anyhow."

Chapter 9

Formation of the First American Army

On August 18th, we arrive at Château Thierry after our long hike from the Chemin-des-Dames and the Vesle River sector. This famous town is located on the Marne River and the Paris-Soissons road about two hours from Paris.[1] On our arrival we find it occupied by Pioneer Infantry (work battalions) who are engaged in cleaning up the debris of the town and salvaging war materials, both German and American.

Having entered the town from the northeast, we now slowly move south through the winding main street amongst disorder and ruins that shows the heavy hand of artillery concentration and the destruction of what once had been prosperous business establishments and homes. Stores were gutted and pilfered. Glass and mortar, feather beds and cooking utensils, German and American army accoutrements, grenades, crockery and picture frames, all lay in wild disarray in the streets, along with hundreds of empty wine bottles strewn about. In our entire march through the town we did not see a single civilian, indicating that the town was entirely deserted, except for the battalion

1. Technically, Château-Thierry is located on the Paris-Reims road, although a road does link Château-Thierry with Soissons.

or two of U.S. troops now putting the town in order and looking after sanitation.

"Looks like they wuz a fight around here," says O'Hara."

"Yer damn right," agrees Stevens, "an they wasn't all Irish that wuz fightin' either. I kin see that."

"Geeze-a! I wish't I hadda some of that vin-a-rouge that wuz in all them bottles once't," exclaims Vinelli.

"That wasn't no ordinary vin rooge," says Stevens. "I kin see some of the labels, an they says coneyac an champagne."

"Let's fall out an see if we kin find some," suggests O'Hara.

"Naw!" says Stevens. "The lieutenant would miss us, an we don't rate any too well now, with him, as it is."

Just at this moment a squad of Pioneer Infantry passes us, marching up the road with shovels, headed for the north.

"What outfit?" yells O'Hara.

"391st Pioneers," they reply. "What army are you?"

"Salvation Army," says O'Hara. "Got any chewin'?"

"Sure Mike!" answers a big husky, picking up a long bone and tossing it to O'Hara. "Chew on this awhile."

"Take it out an bury it along wit yerself an the other stiffs," retorts O'Hara, tossing it back.

After passing through the town of Château Thierry down hill, we crossed the Marne River bridge and then hiked up another long hill to the southwest. Some of the men became exhausted and fell out alongside the road long before we entered the town of Étamps-sur-Marne, an overgrown hamlet. We did nothing here in the woods outside the town, except pitch our pup tents for shelter and wait, as it was expected that we would entrain soon for some other un-named destination. While waiting thus, our company commander, Lieutenant Holstlaw, old army officer and original organizer of the 39th Inf., was accidentally injured. We were sorry to see him sent to the rear, as he had been with us ever since leaving the U.S. and was well liked. He returned to our regiment later on however, just before we started for Germany.

Next morning, we left Étamps early and hiked back down the hill to Château Thierry. There we entrained in the usual boxcars (40 & 8's) for Andelot (haute-marne), located about two hundred fifty kilometers to the southeast near Chaumont (haute-marne), General Pershing's headquarters.

"Where we goin' this time, corporal?" inquires Belkin.

"Dam 'fi know," replies Corporal Andrews, "But it ain't Paris. I knows that."

"We're just off'n one front, so I 'spose now we gotta go back to another," says Stevens. "They ain't no rest fer privates in this man's army, nohow. Gotta be movin' soemwheres alla time."

"Well, if yer don't like it, why don't yer ask fer a discharge?" says Belkin.

"A discharge? Says you! I'm gonna do something so's I kin git put in the hoosegow in Bar-le-Duc, an have a good long rest. Savey?" replies Stevens.

"They ain't no war where we'se goin', anyway," says Belkin. "Lookit all them pretty towns we is passin' through, wit their red tiled roofs an flower gardens. That don't mean war. We is goin' away from it."

"Hope yer right," says Stevens, doubtfully.

On arrival at Andelot, we were billeted in the new type Adrian wooden barracks, instead of cowbarns or woods.[2] These were so scrumptiously clean as to be a great joy to cootie infested soldiery. Also, they were equipped with double-decked chickenwire bunks, which was extreme luxury after being accustomed to sleeping in the mud and wet clammy woods for days and weeks past. We were paid here too, this being my second payday in the U.S. Army.

As there was no estaminet in the town (probably closed under orders) where we could spend any of our newly acquired French francs (cigarette coupons), Belkin, Stevens and myself, nosed around to see if we could find some obliging Frenchwoman who would cook us home fried potatoes or eggs. We finally went up to a house having the largest manure pile in front, as this would indicate greatest prosperity of the inhabitant. Stevens informed us before hand, that he would do all the talking necessary and banged loudly on the door. The same was quickly opened and just as quickly slammed in our face again. Undaunted, we went around to the back of the house, out of sight of the street, and knocked again. This time the door was opened gently by Madam, who smilingly beckoned us inside to a room where the three of us sat at a

2. Adrian barracks were easily assembled and disassembled one-story barracks buildings that measured 20 by 100 feet. One type was all wood, while the other had corrugated iron sides and roof.

table covered with a red checkered tablecloth. On one side of the room were shining copper pans and kettles. A little French window opened out coyly on a picture garden.

Madam soon came over to us with a bottle of amber colored wine and three stem glasses which she sat before us.

"Avevoo de les oeufs, Madam?" inquires Stevens.

"Ah! Oui, oui!" responds Madam, graciously.

"Avevoo pommes de terre?" continues Stevens, showing off his lingo.

"Oui, oui, Monsieur," answers Madam.

"Dees donc pomme-de-terre, avec oeufs, wreck 'em," says Stevens, waving his hands wildly over the top of the table.

"Reek im? An, non, non!" exclaims Madam. "Omelette?"

"Omelette? Ah, we-we!" says Stevens, pursing his lips and holding up both hands twice to indicate the quantity of eggs desired.

"Oui. Omelette, tout-de-suite," says Madam beaming, and hurrying away.

"Allay! Allay!" says Stevens impatiently, as we started sipping the wine.

"Say! Where did you learn ta parleyvoo frogpond so good?" asks Belkin.

"Why, I learns it from my sweetheart, the original lady of Armentieres," answers Stevens. "Can't you parleyvoo atoll?"

"Sure," says Belkin. "Listen. Donny m-wah, dees donc o-see m-wah, horsefeathers."

After a short interval in which we were still occupied in sipping our vin-ordinaire, Madam came back with a large sort of platter heaped high with steaming, savory, omelette, made with eggs and potatoes. We helped ourselves on the three plates set before us and it was a real pleasure. I ate so much that I had the bellyache. Belkin and Stevens admitted for once that they had had enough to eat and couldn't eat any more.

After we had finished the omelette, along with a second bottle of wine, Stevens again beckoned to Madam.

"Combien francs, Madam? Des omelettes de les vins?" asks Stevens.

"Sank franc," answers Madam, pointing to each of us, individually.

We paid her five franc each and left highly satisfied with the world and ourselves.

We also found a confeiture establishment later on. Here I was able to purchase a hatful of English walnuts and a can or two of preserved peaches from Spain. Hot dog! All this was ecstatic luxury for doughboys who were more than starved for some of the creature comforts of civilization, a taste of sweets and a little home cooking.

We went through some intensive drilling here at Andelot, a supposed rest camp. But this was mainly a workout for new replacement soldiers just arrived and was to be expected. However, our nights were free to do as we wished around the camp.

After several days of this useless parade stuff at the behest of a certain pompous officer (who once had a grenade hurled at him by his own men as he sat on a horse), we moved out of Andelot and through a much larger town called Rimaucourt, thence to a woods outside of another hamlet called Manois, high on the hill above Rimaucourt. These two hamlets and the one large town, were within ten minutes walking distance of each other (Andelot, Rimaucourt, Manois), but while we were at Andelot, we had no inkling of the larger town close at hand around the bend of the road. This kept our francs in our pockets for the time being anyway.

This was a beautiful, lush country, untouched by the destructive hand of war. The picturesque, cozy houses, deep green foliage lining aged streets and old cobbled pavements, would remind one of scenes from a childhood fairy book.

At Rimaucourt there was a regular U.S. Commissary (not a Y.M.C.A.) where officers and men could purchase most anything regulation required in army accoutrement and also quite a few knicnacks as well, desired by soldiers. Here the boys could and did purchase enough chewing tobacco (Standard Navy and Brown's Mule), Fatima cigarettes and Hers[h]ey chocolate, in bars or cans, to last for weeks to come, or to use as money in future crap games.

In the woods at Manois, we pitched our pup tents in company street formation and prepared for an extended visit, as the whole battalion was here in this locality. There was plenty of green grass, beautiful young trees with wavy green leaves on them and not blackened skeletons of dead vegetation such as you would see at the front. You could pick green hazelnuts from the bushes and hear songbirds warble, instead of the screech and whine of an H.E. shell or whizbang.

Here, I became a student bugler. I would practice all day practically alone strolling through the woods at my ease, while the rest of the battalion was out in the hot sun drilling (squads east & west) with replacements from the 76th Division (New Eng. Natn'l [National] Army) and others. This drill routine went on for several days, much to the disgust of O'Hara, Stevens, Belkin and the others. I still took it easy. Along with my bugle, I also had a signal lantern to play with, on which I practiced the Morse telegraph code when I felt like it.

The 1st U.S. Army is now being assembled, to be under the personal command of General Pershing.[3] We are getting ready for St. Mihiel, but we of the rank and file are still unacquainted with any war news or plans for the future drive at this time. Nor were we concerned about them to any great extent. Our life these days was just too sweet and easy.

Something happened to our food supplies here at Manois. We were not getting enough of the right things to eat. Here we are, in the midst of a lush beauty, a few more battles to live for and starving, so to speak, although it was never quite as bad as that. The emergency ration (hardtack, corned beef, salmon, hash, tomatoes), one or two tins of which every soldier was required to carry in his combat pack, was called for by our mess-sergeant and turned in at the company kitchen to be heated up and prepared for regular chow. Under these conditions, we had "cornwillie stew" for breakfast, fried "cornwillie" for lunch, fricasseed "cornwillie" for dinner, mixed with hardtack and hot-air promises and a goodly supply of watery stewed tomatoes.[4] This lasted for about four days, or until we commenced to have cramps, bellyache and worse. We were as sick of watery canned tomatoes and "cornwillie," as the Germans must have been of their usual cabbage and turnip soup. The boys even ate all the chocolate bars they had recently purchased down the hill at Rimaucourt, and which they

3. The First U.S. Army began to be organized on July 4, 1918, and General John J. Pershing assumed nominal command on August 10, 1918. From September 12–16, 1918, this independent American army participated in the successful St. Mihiel Offensive. For that operation, the army consisted of the First, Fourth and Fifth Corps (U.S.), and the French Second Colonial Corps, a total of 14 U.S. divisions and 3 French divisions. *Order of Battle of the United States Land Forces in the World War*, vol. 1, 82–85.

4. Canned corned beef. Willis Rowland Skillman, *The A.E.F.: Who They Were, What They Did, How They Did It* (Philadelphia: George W. Jacobs and Company, 1920), 169. A member of Company F proposed to write a book entitled, "A Million Different Ways to Cook Corn Willie." *The Iola* (KS) *Register*, August 9, 1919.

had been carefully saving for future consumption, when sweets would be unavailable.

This sort of thing had happened to us before, so we were patient, but there was no excuse for it now, we figured, back here in the rear areas, with so many quartermaster depots around the vicinity and the General Army Headquarters close at hand. We knew, of course, that we would eventually get a square meal, but the delay was getting on our nerves, while our stomachs touched our backbones. Too much red-tape somewhere.

Finally the platoon sergeants, after getting themselves all worked up about it, decided that an army couldn't be expected to perform a lot of useless squad-drilling, if it were only half fed, just for the sake of drilling. They couldn't get any action or satisfaction from our mess sergeant who disclaimed all responsibility, or the then company commander who was in awe of his superiors, so they decided to take matters in their own hands and acted accordingly.

Therefore, one fine morning when thin watery tomatoes and corned beef was served again for breakfast, without bread or coffee, things blew up around the company. When first call for drill sounded, every private soldier was busy doing bunk fatigue (plain sleep) and the sergeants and corporals made no effort to get the men out of their tents for drill. The company commander heatedly ordered out all the platoon sergeants and even routed out a few privates himself, but the majority of the company did not stand drill formation that morning. Our lieutenant was very angry with the whole company, because we had gone on a laydown strike, as it were. He raved all over the camp, calling us slackers and mutineers, and even threatened to have the ringleaders of the so-called mutiny, courtsmartialed and shot. He ordered the entire outfit placed under arrest and confined to quarters. Phooey! Who cared? We certainly didn't as long as there was no useless drill exercises. We could lie around and smoke, even if we couldn't eat.

Company A of our battalion, right alongside of us and in practically the same fix in regard to food, was forced to go out and drill as usual. But their commander was an iron fisted executive and kept his company on its toes, food or no food. However he promised his men action with the quartermaster, and got it. In a short time the colonel of the regiment appeared on the scene, but having only a vague idea of the true situation. When he found out the real state of affairs however, he proceeded to raise hell with everyone who even attempted to address him without permission. And he didn't need a loudspeaker to amplify his voice either, as he could bellow louder than a coast guard foghorn. That was why he was such a good colonel, at least according to O'Hara, who knows everything.

In less than two hours after the colonel had left the battalion, a big army lorry drove in at our P.C., loaded to the rafters with a generous supply of rations, enough to please everybody. Besides frozen meat and good white bread, there were even such luxuries as Chocolat Menier, smoking and chewing tobaccos.[5] Our lieutenant even got his marmalade and jam, which is most necessary to keep some lieutenants good natured in war time.

The kitchen got busy right away too. Soon they were serving us beef-a-la-steak, cornmeal mush with molasses, and boiled rice for dessert, flavored with nutmeg and lemon extract that the cooks didn't even have time to get drunk on. It tasted as good to us then, as chicken or ice cream would to you right now perhaps, and we could have all we could eat. We made regular pigs of ourselves and had to lie down to digest it. So hooray! for the sergeants, the lieutenant and the colonel, the old pot-bellied frozen-face. The boys had another word for it.

The colonel was quite all right as a soldier, however. He was just good enough to get a D.S.C. [Distinguished Service Cross] for himself later on unsolicited, in the Meuse-Argonne at Septsarges Wood.[6] In the previous Vesle River campaign, he had succeeded

5. Chocolat Menier was introduced in 1821 by Jean-Antoine Brutus Menier. His company marketed chocolate bars in France beginning in 1836.

6. Frank Crandall Bolles (1872–1955), a native of Illinois and resident of Rolla, Missouri, graduated from West Point in 1896. He saw action in the Spanish-American War and Philippine-American War, and was awarded the Distinguished Service Cross while a second lieutenant in the 18th U.S. Infantry for his actions in the fighting at Jaro, Panay, Philippine Islands, in February 1899, where he exhibited "conspicuous bravery and skill" in leading his troops even after being wounded in the leg. Bolles also took part in operations against Moro tribesmen in the Philippines in 1906. Promoted to major in 1916, Bolles was ordered to Hawaii in May 1917, but in March 1918 was ordered stateside and assumed command of the 39th U.S. Infantry. Bolles led the regiment in combat in France, and was awarded an oak leaf cluster for his Distinguished Service Cross for two additional instances of heroism. On September 26, 1918, near Septsarges, France, Bolles "personally directed the assaulting battalion of his regiment when the line was temporarily held up by hostile fire," and led the troops forward to their objective. Once their objective was reached, they came under withering machine gun and artillery fire, and Bolles courageously encouraged his men to hold steady. Two days later, he rallied his men under heavy fire, and was wounded, but assisted with reorganizing their positions. He was also awarded the Distinguished Service Medal for

only in getting himself bottled up for several hours in a cellar of a ruined house at Fismes, along with three other soldiers with whom he was putting on the grandstand hero act for a possible decoration. The way he attracted artillery fire on this occasion, shows that he was really in the army. Anyway, the Boche artillerists seemed to think so. The way they shelled him would have done honor to an officer of much higher rank. The German Komandatten must have thought our colonel was General John J. Pershing himself, as they gave him everything from G.I. cans to one-pounders, whizbangs and gas, before they stopped shelling his particular dugout. A few telephone wires running into the dugout may have been the real reason for it however and an officer should have known better than to hide in a place where the wires were visible. Anyway, the colonel came through it all unscathed.

A story is told of this officer, relative to the first time the regiment was ever in action, near Troësnes (aisne). The colonel was observed walking around behind some of C Company's pup tents back in the woods. He was overheard talking to himself, although I may not be quoting his exact words. Puffing on a big black cigar and walking back and forth with his head down, he spoke somewhat as follows:

"Did you see 'em Frank? Well, well, well. The sons-a-bitches won't drill, but they sure can fight! Ya got a damn good outfit, Frank. Yes sir, a gahdamn good outfit! Wish't you'd a had 'em in Cuba. You'd a been a brigadier by now. Yes, sir!"

Amen, Colonel Frank, and orchids to you. I never saw anyone that looked as much like a Regular Army colonel as you did.[7]

---

his leadership of the 39th Infantry. Bolles was promoted to brigadier general in 1928 and to major general in 1935. He retired the following year. U.S. Office of the Adjutant General, *American Decorations*, 170, 679; *Assembly* 16, no. 3 (Fall 1957): 63–64. One unidentified member of the regiment wrote that Bolles was much missed by the men after his wounding, for they were accustomed to seeing him leading the assaults "with an indifference to personal safety." He was universally regarded as the best fighter in the regiment and no one was more deserving of a Distinguished Service Cross. Despite his loss, Bolles "had formed the regiment into the aggressive fighting organization which it was on the front line and it continued his spirit after he had to withdraw." Record Group 120, Records of the American Expeditionary Forces, World War I, Records of Combat Divisions 1917–1919, 4th Division, 4th Division Historical, Box 29, Folder: 39th Infantry, Histories, Commendations & Battle Participants, 4th Division, 204–11.4, Official History of the 39th Regiment of Infantry, 1917–1918, National Archives and Records Administration, College Park, Maryland.

7. According to 39th veteran Private Oscar Kindred, Colonel Bolles called his men "hooligans," and when a general once tried to stop the regiment from making a charge, Bolles reportedly said, "How can I stop the damned Hooligans when the German army can't." *The Bloomfield* (IN) *News*, December 26, 1918.

Our stay in the woods at Manois was cut short soon after the food episode. Sergeant Nolan said it had been decided that it would be much better to move us back to the front lines without further delay, to give us something to do that would be more exciting. Well, we were scheduled to go back soon anyway, so we didn't feel bad about it.

The last Sunday that we were at Manois, a high platform and altar was constructed in the woods complete with lace altar cloths and candles. The 39th Infantry Band was brought over and a memorial service conducted complete with a Mass, for our comrades who had passed on in the Vesle Rive sector, Fère-en-Tardenois Wood and the Marne. Mass was celebrated by an officer-priest, while a protestant chaplain as well as the colonel and several other officers spoke impressive eulogies. It was indeed very dignified, appropriate and patriotic. It gave us something to write home about.

Our route from Château Thierry to Andelot and Manois had been somewhat as follows:

Château Thierry (aisne dep't)

Épernay (marne) Big wine cellars here.

Châlons-sur-Marne (marne) Battlefield of Attila the Hun.

St. Dizier (haut-marne)

Ancerville (haut-marne)[8]

Joinville (haut-marne) Center of French movie industry

Andelot, Rimaucourt, Manois (haute-marne)

On August 30th, 1918, we broke our camp at Manois to start moving toward the St. Mihiel sector to the northeast, to become part of the 1st American Army under the direct command of General Pershing. As we marched out to the road and sat down on our packs waiting, we could see the long lines of grey French camions approaching us far back over the hill, in what seemed an endless column. These trucks were driven by little Indo-Chinese chauffeurs (Anamites) who couldn't speak a word of French or English, but simply followed their leader.[9] Each camion could hold a squad of eight men comfortably, along with their rifles and

8. Ancerville is the Meuse Department.

9. Some 50, 000 colonial troops were recruited from French Indochina during World War I. Many doughboys commented on the use of these men as truck drivers on the Western Front. Richard S. Fogarty, *Race and War in France: Colonial Subjects in the French Army, 1914–1918* (Baltimore: The Johns Hopkins University Press, 2008), 27.

Men of 3rd Battalion, 39th Regiment Infantry, Company I, 4th Division, entering French trucks to be taken to the front. Trucks and soldiers can be seen along the road waiting their turn to load. Rimaucourt, Haute Marne, France, September 1, 1918. U.S. Army Signal Corps Collection, National Archives, 24375 [2415S8].

equipment. But sometimes a dozen or more would be crowded in, if there was a scarcity of trucks.[10]

Soon we were all aboard and hour after hour we passed through glorious country, over gorgeous old Roman roads and through long lanes of tall poplars. We rode all one day, all night and all the next day, with only an occasional halt for the men to get out and stretch themselves. The trucks seemed devoid of springs and were extremely tiresome. Some of the men were lulled to sleep by the monotony of the road rattle and dust, and the incessant drone of the motors. Conversation was spasmodic, sometimes even fretful. We had nothing to eat except our emergency ration, but the men quickly grew tired of that, too.

10. One member of the 58th U.S. Infantry recalled, "The troops soon became begrimed, their faces showing from the rear of the trucks as gray masks." "The St. Mihiel Drive," Folder Record Group 120, Records of the American Expeditionary Forces, World War I, Records of Combat Divisions 1917–1919, 4th Division, 4th Division Historical, Box 36, Folder: 58th Infantry, Histories, Commendations & Battle Participants, 4th Division, 204–11.4, National Archives and Records Administration, College Park, Maryland.

American troops of 3rd Battalion, 39th Regiment Infantry, 4th Division, and French trucks by the roadside. French officers in the foreground, who have charge of loading of troops. Shows the perfect cooperation of French and Americans. Rimaucourt, Haute Marne, France, September 1, 1918. U.S. Army Signal Corps Collection, National Archives, 24376 [2416S8].

"Geeze! Ain't these French chariots rough ridin' though?" says O'Hara with profound disgust.

"Yeah! The old hay rick, and the runaway team of sorrel mares back home in Indiany, was heaven compared to these Paris busses," says Stevens.

"Git yer damn foot out of my eye, will ya!" exclaims Belkin to O'Hara, who was squeezed in tight behind him.

"What ya squawkin' about, rookie? When I gits on terra firma again, I'll put both my hobs right through yer 'sophagus," replies O'Hara.

"The two fairies is fightin' again," remarks Stevens sarcastically.

Just then their camion came to an abrupt stop and the three men fell over the tail board and landed square in a heap on the road.

"All out you men! Line up fer chow!" orders Sergeant Nolan, coming alongside the camion at that instant.

Looking down road. American troops entering French trucks to be carried to the front. Shows long line of troops and trucks in line. Third Battalion, 39th Regiment Infantry, 4th Division. Rimaucourt, Haute Marne, France, September 1, 1918. U.S. Army Signal Corps Collection, National Archives, 24377 [2417S8].

"As usual, the Irish is always first, sarge," wise cracks O'Hara, picking himself up off the road.

"Yeah! Everywhere 'cept the front line trenches," says Belkin.

Some of the towns passed through enroute were as follows:

Neuf Château (vosges dep't)

Gondrecourt (meuse)

Vancouleurs

Ligny

Bar-le-Duc (meuse)

Triaucourt

Bannoncourt

As a brief summary of the previous operations of the 4th U.S. Division up until the formation of the 1st U.S. Army, let me mention that there were 4,912 wounded and 752 killed in the Aisne-Marne Defensive and Offensive in the Marne, Fère-en-Tardenois and Vesle River sectors. We advanced a total of 17 kilometers against active machine-gun nests, heavy artillery bombardment, gas and the veteran Prussian Guards. We also helped prevent a breakthrough to Paris on July 18th and nullify the great German Friedensturm to the satisfaction of the French command.[11] U.S. troops were now firmly recognized as good soldiers even by the Germans, who were surprised, chagrined and stupefied with their own commands. Under these conditions, with fresh, aggressive U.S. soldiers in line, how could it have been otherwise?

Between August 13th and Sep't 1st, the 1st U.S. Army was being collected and assembled from all over France where they had been either actively engaged or were in training with French and British armies. Most of them assembled in southern central France near Chaumont.[12] This mobilization had been General Pershing's ambition ever since he had first organized the A.E.F., but its final accomplishment was no easy matter. He had been opposed repeatedly in carrying out this plan, part of his original army orders from Washington, by Haig of the British, Foch and Clemenceau of the French, who wanted to employ U.S. soldiers for replacements only, for Allied armies, filling losses in their own front line divisions. Thus, you see, in case of a complete Allied victory, whatever glory was attached to the same would be credited to English and French, with the United States holding secondary place in any peace conference. But General Pershing just couldn't see it their way, and for a good reason.

Differences in language had made liaison arrangements impractical in fighting under French commanders. The Americans were aggressive, while the French were conservative in warfare. All this had brought on repeated and unavoidable friction in administration and commands. Prior to August 13th, U.S. soldiers brigaded with the French died in large numbers, through inefficiency in translating or carrying out some ill-advised French combat order. Most of this, therefore, was unnecessary sacrifice.[13]

11. Howell is mistaken. Although the last great German offensive was launched on either side of Reims on July 15, the attack was stopped by July 17, and the following day the French and Americans launched their counterattack south of Soissons.

12. Chaumont is in eastern France, not the "southern central" part of the country.

13. Although American losses prior to mid-August 1918 had been heavy while under French command, as Howell indicates, they cannot be blamed on the French alone. As General Hunter Liggett recalled after the war, the brave but inexperienced "American Army endlessly took chances that no French soldier in his right mind would have chanced; nor would our men had they been fighting since 1914." Hunter Liggett, *A.E.F.: Ten Years Ago in France* (New York: Dodd, Mead and Company, 1928), 130. On the other hand, Frederick

Pershing's original Army Staff orders from Washington, before he set foot on foreign soil early in 1917 had been, "keep the identity of U.S. troops intact and form an all American Army under American command as soon as you consider it practicable." The wisdom of this clause in his original orders has, I think, been amply demonstrated. U.S. troops may not have been as experienced perhaps, as other veterans of four years warfare at this time. But without the freshness, natural speed, initiative and enterprise of our soldiers, an Allied victory would certainly have been impossible. Without us, their manpower and reserve would have been completely vanished. Thus, they would have lost the war.

According to the best German generals, our entry decisively and effectively turned the tide against them.[14] Our long suit is and always has been open warfare, as against a war of attrition. Warfare had become stagnant after 1917, with no great gains on either side before July 1918 when we entered the picture in large numbers.[15]

The new 1st U.S. Army, therefore, is now being made ready for a real demonstration of its effectiveness and worth, under its own supreme command, to settle once and for all, the idea of using U.S. troops as replacements only for depleted Allied battalions. But later on, even after we had reached the Argonne, the French again tried to break up the successful U.S. Army by going over Pershing's head direct to Washington. For this presumption of the

---

Palmer of Pershing's staff wrote that French General Degoutte "subjected our troops to unnecessary sacrifice by some pretty bad generalship." Palmer, *John J. Pershing*, 283. Pershing agreed, noting that many American officers who had served under him on the Vesle "felt that because of his orders American troops had been unnecessarily sacrificed." In addition, those American divisions dependent on the French for the care of their sick and wounded experienced "very grave difficulty" and "no little dissatisfaction." Pershing, *My Experiences in the World War*, II: 245, 249.

14. German First Quartermaster General Erich Ludendorff recalled following the war that because of the "timely assistance" of the United States, the Allies were eventually able to gain "military ascendancy." This did not force Germany's eventual surrender, however. "Rather," he explained, "it was the result of the collapse of the German home front." Likewise, General Max Von Gallwitz noted that "it was the astonishing display of American strength which definitely decided the war against us." Viereck, *As They Saw Us*, 27, 287.

15. Howell is correct that neither the Allies nor the Germans enjoyed major successes in the latter half of 1917 (British efforts "had no decisive effect on the military situation," and French attacks, although successful, were "limited"), his assertion that the front was stagnant in the first half of 1918 before significant American intervention is incorrect. The first of a series of German offensives drove British forces back more than 30 miles in Picardy (March 21-April 4), while another against the British in Flanders (April 9-29) resulted in an approximately 12-mile penetration of the Allied line. A drive against the French along the Aisne River (May 27-June 4) forced the French to retreat about 30 miles. American Battle Monuments Commission, *American Armies and Battlefields in Europe*, 22–23.

French Premier, Clemenceau, they were as promptly referred back to Pershing again by President Wilson.[16]

To make doubly sure, therefore, of success at St. Mihiel, General Pershing took personal command of the 1st Army and left no important detail to subordinate staff officers.[17] During the process of collecting and assembling the scattered U.S. divisions, we of the rank and file took things fairly easy, except as I have stated in preceding paragraphs. We are now ready for another push into enemy strongholds.

16. By late September, Marshal Foch became convinced that too many American troops were concentrated in the Meuse-Argonne and at St. Mihiel, and he proposed that two or three American divisions would be sent to the French XVII Corps east of the Meuse, and the same number to the French XXXVIII Corps west of the Argonne Forest. Pershing naturally objected, and Foch relented. Later in the Meuse-Argonne Offensive, however, Foch planned to increase the number of American divisions serving with Allied armies, and decrease the number under Pershing's command. Donald Smythe, *Pershing: General of the Armies* (Bloomington: Indiana University Press, 1986), 203–04, 217.

17. Although Pershing was meticulous about his work while in command of the A.E.F., and, as Major General James G. Harbord noted, "edits everything he signs, even the most trivial things," and "does nothing hastily or carelessly," Pershing did in fact delegate a great deal of work to his carefully selected aides. James G. Harbord, *Leaves from a War Diary* (New York: Dodd, Mead & Company, 1925), 124.

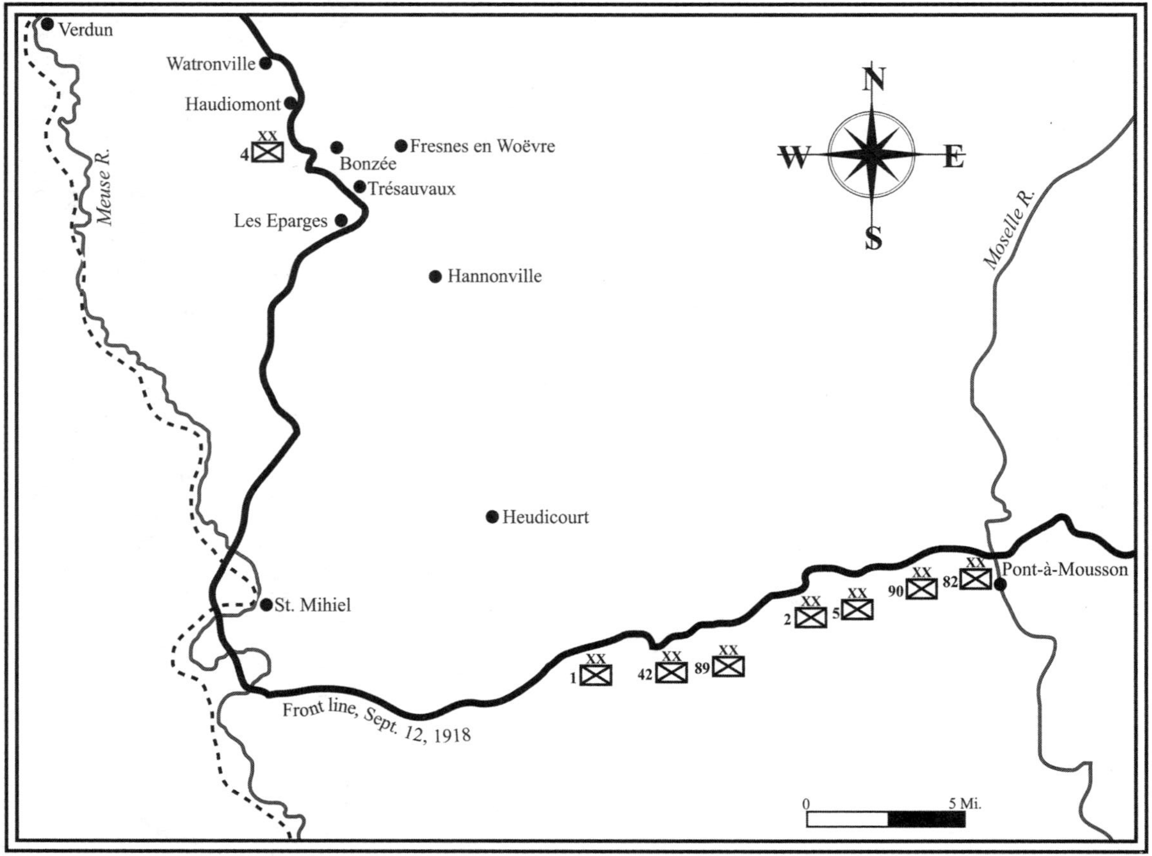
Verdun
Watronville
Haudiomont
4
Bonzée
Fresnes en Woëvre
Trésauvaux
Les Eparges
Meuse R.
Hannonville
Heudicourt
St. Mihiel
Front line, Sept. 12, 1918
1
42
89
2
5
90
82
Pont-à-Mousson
Moselle R.
N
W
E
S
0
5 Mi.

St. Mihiel

Chapter 10

St. Mihiel Offensive (Sep't 12th to 26th 1918)

"The cannoneers have hairy ears,
They slap their leather breeches.
They sleep all day,
And bang all night,
A hell of a bunch of quinces."
—Infantry vs. Artillery.

About Sep't 10th, 1918, we of the 1st Battalion 39th Infantry are located in a series of small wooden barracks in the woods behind the St. Mihiel front. These barracks, I remember, were left in a very unclean condition by some previous outfit, probably French, as they were full of old straw and cooties. This was at Haudiomont (meuse) near Fort du Rozellier, and Mesnil-sous-les-côtes in the Forêt de Amblonville. Since Sep't 1st we had been moving about, always closer to the front, stopping for a short time only in various places on our hike from Bannoncourt (meuse), so as to get here in time for the start of the big American drive.

On our way up we had bivouacked at Génicourt, Sommedieue and Haudainville, places well known in the earlier fighting, 1914 to 1916. At Sommedieue there was a large number of wooden shacks and dugouts scattered around on the hillside, built originally by the Germans themselves. They had cobbled sidewalks, porches with railings of rustic design and stone steps, all of which gave the place quite a homey appearance. Later these were occupied and improved by the French. We stayed here one night in comparative safety from shelling and while we were fairly close, the Front was quite inactive at this time.

At Mesnil-sous-les-côtes we also stayed overnight. Here the dugouts were made of huge iron pipes about ten feet in diameter. The sections were riveted together and extended for about forty feet in the hillside. They were like huge iron smokestacks, laid horizontal, pushed edgewise in the side of the hill and covered over. Nothing showed except the entrance which had a stone facing like a cemetery vault but was a good piece of work. These dugouts, however, were cold and damp and were originally lighted by electricity. We had to be content with a few candles. Moisture condensed on the iron ceilings and walls and was continually dripping down on us. Some of the men couldn't stand the damp, inside of these bomb proof shelters and therefore slept out in the open. In case of shelling, they could have easily rushed inside where there was double-deck chickenwire bunks on each side, with a board walk in the center. Nothing happened however. Each bombproof would accommodate a platoon of about thirty men and there were several of this type in the vicinity. We amused ourselves by inspecting them. In one there was a lively crap game in progress. Souvenir hunters occasionally found a German coal-scuttle helmet, a few buttons or a pancake hat which pleased them as much as a child with a new toy.

The towns in this sector were long since deserted by civilians and were mostly in ruins. At Haudainville, there were a few houses and we caught the sight of an old woman pawing in the rubbish. When a soldier went up to speak to her, she ran away and disappeared among the ruins, shaking her fists at him as she ran. She probably thought the soldier was going to arrest her and send her to the rear while she preferred to stay here.

While waiting in barracks along the road in the woods near Haudiomont, we did nothing except practice gas-mask drill and wait for orders to move up to the line. It was here that I heard from my old pal McGuire, who you will remember, was shell shocked back at the Vesle River sector early in August. His letter informed me that he was now a "steam fitter" around some quiet far hospital or other, far to the rear. He was in a safe spot, but itching to get back to his old outfit again to see some of the boys, especially O'Hara and Belkin.

He was seeking my best advice on the subject of joining-up again at the front. My answer was to tell him that the chow was rotten and without any pate de foie gras and champagne like he was having, that a lot of the old guard was gone and that we had a new officer and were full of replacements. If he knew when he was well off therefore, I advised, and was having such a swell time of it back in the S.O.S., he should stay there, as things were expected to get real hot up here very shortly. If he came it would be at his own risk. Whether he took my advice or not I never knew, as he didn't report back to B Company again. But he probably did join some outfit or other where there was good "crap shootin'," rather than continue to be a "goldbrick" around some base hospital and safe in the rear areas. I was glad to know he was alive, anyway.

Our regiment is now in active reserve close to the western end of the St. Mihiel salient. The 1st U.S. Army will now be subject only to the orders of its own commander, "Black Jack" Pershing, and the Generalissimo of all the Allied Armies, Marshall Ferdinand Foch. In the approaching offensive, it will be Pershing vs. Von Gallwitz, with Von Fuchs in immediate command of the feldgrau at St. Mihiel.[1]

500,000 men (13 divisions) are to be engaged in this operation. It is the largest single army ever assembled anywhere in the world, up to this time. Great preparation has been made for its success, as I have previously stated.

Germans at Sedan, war against France, 1870. . . 250,000 men

Grant's Army of the Potomac, U.S. Civil War, 1865. . . 125,000 men

Russo-Japanese War, Army at Mukden, 1906. . . 310,000 men[2]

1. General Max von Gallwitz (1852–1937) commanded the army group (Army Group Gallwitz) that manned the St. Mihiel salient. His subordinate was Lieutenant-General Georg Fuchs, who commanded Army Detachment C.

2. Although Howell is correct that the American First Army was likely the largest single Allied army in the field, French armies, although smaller, were more numerous. Likewise, the French Army contained more divisions than the A.E.F. The approximate average combat strength of an American division in 1918 was 25,500, while a French division numbered 11,400. Actual combat strength of the entire A.E.F. on September 12, 1918 was 999,602 and 1,078,222 on November 11, 1918, with a total in the A.E.F. of 1,981,701 on November 11, 1918. American Battle Monuments Commission, *American Armies*

It was anticipated that the St. Mihiel offensive would result in a series of hard fought battles as the Germans had held it for four long years. It was considered well-nigh impregnable by the French. During their long occupation, the Germans had strengthened the natural defenses with dense acres of barbed wire and extensive fortification. Every effort was made therefore to keep the exact date of our hammer blow a state secret as well as our planned point of attack. Complete surprise was necessary to make it a success.

The U.S. Intelligence or secret service played its cards skillfully in liaison with the General Army Staff so as to make it appear that our attempted breakthrough would occur at Belfort, far to the northeast, near the Swiss-Vosges frontier. The German high command became so convinced of this that they hurried five of their best divisions, which they could ill afford to spare from off the Western Front, in a big rush to this locality to stem the breakthrough and possibly save the Rhine further on. Phoney generals, both U.S. and French were moved purposely around the fake front. Telegrams and fake orders were stage managed and allowed to be copied and intercepted. The U.S. Intelligence strategists therefore created the impression of great activity and preparation in that section. The strategy worked to a T. While the Germans were expecting us in the Vosges, the 1st U.S. Army struck at St. Mihiel, taking them completely by surprise.

Three regiments of the 4th Divis[ion] (39th, 47th, 58th) were in reserve here for our 59th Infantry. We of the 39th were in active reserve near Trésauvaux directly behind the 59th which was concealed in the front line and grouped before the towns of Fresnes-en-woëvre, Bonzée and Watronville.

On the morning of Sep't 11th our company was detached from active reserve with the 39th with orders to report at once to the 8th

---

and Battlefields in Europe, 501–02. There is disagreement among historians on the total number of French troops on the Western Front. According to one source, by October 1918 the French Army numbered 1,670,000, and by the time of the Armistice contained 102 infantry divisions and six cavalry divisions in all theaters. Anthony Clayton, *Paths of Glory: The French Army, 1914–1918* (London: Cassell, 2003), 162. Another authoritative work states that French combatant forces on the Western Front numbered 1,688,000 on October 1, 1918. David Stevenson, *With Our Backs to the Wall: Victory and Defeat in 1918* (Cambridge: The Belknap Press of Harvard University Press, 2011), 269. A third study claims more than 2.5 million French were serving on the Western Front in late 1918. Elizabeth Greenhalgh, *The French Army and the First World War* (Cambridge: Cambridge University Press, 2014), 367.

Brigade in the front line for active duty. We therefore moved out through the woods to join the 59th Inf. near Fresnes-en-woëvre.

"I bet I gits me a kraut this time," says Stevens, moping along, "An if he has an Iron Cross, I'll send it back to my mother-in-law to show her I ain't yeller no more like she said I was."

"Mebbe he'll a getta you furst," advises Vinelli, "witha one of thema saw tooth bayonets."

"Not me," says Stevens, "Them Germans is only overgrown boy scouts ta me, an I got two good hand grenades besides."

"An you'll probably throw them the wrong way too," puts in Corporal Andrews.

"Quiet!" orders the lieutenant. "Fall out along the path men. Remove your blanket roll and make ready with combat packs only. Sergeant Nolan, leave a guard on the rolls and we will pick them up on the way back."[3]

"Jesu Cristo!" exclaims Vinelli, "supposa we no comeaback!"

At 5.00 A.M. on the morning of Sep't 12th, we began entering the towns which were lightly held. What Germans there were had started for safety in their deep underground dugouts at the start of our short, but vicious, preparatory artillery barrage. There was a drizzling rain and the sky was lighted by burning supply dumps, shell bursts, green and red rockets and flares, making a terrible and awesome sight. The U.S. infantry left the old trenches or whatever shelter they had and started out across great gaps in the barbed wire with intervals of about six to eight feet between men in column of single file and met with little or no resistance for several hundred yards.

Coming slowly up a small hill at Fresnes and meeting no Germans, Stevens, Vinelli and O'Hara suddenly saw a stone quarry in the opening just below them. They immediately fell on their stomachs so as not to be seen and peered cautiously over the edge of the quarry. They saw here and there a slinking form disappear into the entrance of a dugout directly below them.

"Here's where I gits me a kraut at last!" exclaims Stevens reaching for a hand grenade.

"Wait a minute, men!" orders Sergeant Nolan, who had just crawled up behind them.

3. The blanket roll, carried in a pack carrier, could be detached from the upper haversack to form the less bulky combat pack.

"Looks like the whole German Army wuz down in that dugout," says O'Hara.

"Don't make a move until we sees what's down there, then!" orders the sergeant. "If ya shoots now, they'll know our position. We has the drop on them here, so I'll go down an reconnoitre a bit. Vinelli, you move over ta the left an cover me with the Chauchat gun! Stevens, you be ready with a Mills grenade! When I signal, ya drops it directly on the dugout roof. O'Hara, you go around ta the right of the dugout an creep toward it, but look out for a machine gun! I'll move down ta the left, but everybody keep down'till I gives the signal."

"O.k. sarge, here's where I practices a little pitchin'," says Stevens, winding up.

Sergeant Nolan then started moving cautiously over the edge of the quarry to the left and down into it unobserved. There wasn't a Boche in sight. Presently he signaled to Stevens to drop a grenade on the dugout roof. There was a terrific explosion and almost immediately the Germans came on the run out of the dugout, two or three at a time. Vinelli picked off five of them with his first clip in the Chauchat while O'Hara kept up a steady rifle fire from behind. The Boche thought they were surrounded by a large company and began throwing up their hands, yelling "kamerad! kamerad!" Vinelli, Nolan, O'Hara and Stevens soon closed in on them, ordering them to lay down their arms if they had any and surrender. In all there were about thirty-five Germans, including a lieutenant, with about ten more killed or wounded.

When they were all rounded up and it was ascertained that they had all of them, Sergeant Nolan delegated Stevens and O'Hara to escort the prisoners back to Battalion Headquarters in the rear. Sergeant Nolan and Vinelli then went on toward the town of Fresnes with the Chauchat gun between them, looking for more Germans to capture or fight.

After proceeding back a couple of hundred yards with the prisoners, Stevens, who was marching importantly at the head of the column with the German lieutenant, while O'Hara marched behind them with fixed bayonet, suddenly called a halt of the column of little round gray hats and leather boots.

"I'm a general, now," says Stevens to O'Hara, strutting around and throwing out his chest. "So I begins by inspectin' the company."

"Oke with me," answers O'Hara. "But a gineral has gotta give orders."

"Lieutenant, do you'se sprechen se English?" inquires Stevens.

"Ja, Ja" replies the German lieutenant, turning and facing his men.

"Kompany Attenzione!" commands the lieutenant.

Heavy boots clicked together and the Boche company stood as erect and stiff as a flagpole, facing their officer, while Stevens and O'Hara looked on.

"Inspection fer souvenirs! All pockets inside out!" orders Stevens, walking along in front of the Boche company.

"Ja, Ja" says the slim lieutenant, adjusting his thick glasses and giving the necessary orders to the prisoners.

O'Hara pulled the bolt on his rifle and stood at port arms while Stevens walked slowly down the length of the Boche column. Out came silver watches, pocket knives, rings, money, postcard nudes, tinned honey, hunks of bread, iron crosses, fancy pencils, English uniform buttons and so on. Through all this the German lieutenant stood as stiff as a ramrod, gazing ahead, while Stevens passed down the column taking what he wanted and passing the balance to O'Hara. Then he walked back to the lieutenant and unceremoniously jerked the Iron Cross from off his uniform.[4] Next, he proceeded to cut off the bars or shoulder epaulettes of grey-green, trimmed with red, from the officer's coat, carefully tucking the same away in his blouse pocket.

Turning and facing the company, who were now slyly grinning at him, Stevens pulls himself erect and shouts importantly,

"Company, attention! About face, right oblique, left oblique, to the rear, forward, march!"

The Germans were bewildered. Some turned, some stood still, some looked foolish, some walked backward a few steps, but none attempted to run away.

"Jumpin' jiminy! Halt!" orders Stevens wildly throwing his arms about. "What the hell kinda soldiers are you krauts, anyway? Ain't ya never been in an army before?"

4. Established by Prussia's King William Frederick III in 1813, the Iron Cross was authorized in three grades, a Grand Cross and 1st and 2nd Class. It could be awarded either for heroic actions on the battlefield or distinguished service in wartime. Because few Grand Crosses were awarded, and the Iron Cross 2nd Class was normally represented by a ribbon on the uniform rather than the actual medal, Howell's comrades probably secured 1st Class medals.

"Ja, Ja," says the lieutenant, saluting. "XVth Jaager Mazchine Gun Battalion. Gun kapoot mit grenade."[5]

"Kapoot? What the hell does that mean in Irish?" says Stevens, turning around toward O'Hara.

"It means, that the Boche machine gun wuz knocked outta commission by your hand grenade," explains O'Hara. "A good shot, I calls it."

"That so?" says Stevens. "Then I gits me another Iron Cross fer that, ta send home ta the old lady."

"Yeah? Why not? An I gits me a week in Paris fer capturin' the whole damn battalion," brags O'Hara.

"We'll both go, then," says Stevens, "'cause I sure got me plenty a French francs off'n the Boche lieutenant, enough ta last a month."

"Hot ziggadee!" exclaims O'Hara.

"Forward, March!" orders Stevens, turning to the Boche company.

So they took the Boche prisoners back to the battalion P.C. and turned them over to Major Wilmerding, who in turn sent them on to brigade.[6]

By eleven o'clock on the morning of Sep't 12th, the fighting was over in our section of the front, as the 4th Division had been ordered to advance only a few kilometers. News from other sections indicated success of the drive. The majority of the St. Mihiel salient was pinched out on this first morning without too much difficulty. The men encountered little resistance and advanced as fast as they could walk. However, in spots, there was fierce grenade fighting and smaller skirmishes which continued for a day longer, with corresponding losses.

5. Howell was possibly describing a unit of either the 8th or 13th Landwehr Division, which occupied the general area the 39th moved through during the St. Mihiel Offensive. On the other hand, the 195th Division's 14th Jaeger Regiment also contained the 15th Reserve Jaeger Battalion. The division was engaged northeast of St. Mihiel after entering the line on September 14. U.S. War Department, *Histories of Two Hundred and Fifty-One Divisions*, 636–39. An American intelligence document (Summary No. 159, dated September 7, 1918) likewise placed the 15th Reserve Jaeger Battalion in the 195th Division in late August 1918. Summary of Information, Second Section, General Staff, General Headquarters, American Expeditionary Forces, September 1918, Numbers 153 to 182 Inclusive, 1061.

6. Major William E. Wilmerding (1874–1948), a native of Texas and an 1899 graduate of Sewanee Medical College, accepted a commission as a first lieutenant in April 1917. Promoted to major that November, he commanded the 4th Division's Sanitary Train. He remained in the army following the war, was promoted to lieutenant colonel in 1937, and retired in 1938. U.S. Adjutant General, *Official Army Register, January 1, 1940* (Washington, D.C.: U.S. Government Printing Office, 1940), 1190.

The 59th Infantry, 4th Divis[ion] during the St. Mihiel advance was under the command of that frank and fiery Marine officer, Colonel Frederick M. Wise, hero of Belleau Wood, who became famous for his trite and typically Yank retort to a pudgy French major of infantry. The latter had suggested to Colonel Wise, that he should retreat after taking over the sector from the French, as it was too hot to hold longer.

"Retreat? HELL NO! We just got here!" was Colonel Wise's crisp reply.[7] The colonel was now in command of a Regular Army regiment, instead of Marines, because of some difficulty he had experienced with Major-General Harbord over disposition of some Marine battalions in Belleau Wood. After Belleau and a short rest with his wife in England, he left the Marines and was assigned to the command of the 59th Infantry at his own request.

At Watronville, the Germans didn't even know that the doughboys were at their doorstep. Advance elements of the 59th Infantry quietly slipped into the town square without molestation, or the firing of a single rifle. As they started looking around in some of the houses, the surprised Germans were amazed to see them, as they had not known they were in the town. In a number of instances, the Germans were caught and forced to surrender right at their card games.

After the first few hours of the attack, the 59th Infantry had gone souvenir hunting in the towns, or wherever they happened to be. They just couldn't find any more Germans to play with. In their advance, they had taken hundreds of prisoners with little effort, including whole battalions who surrendered en masse.

The 39th Infantry, therefore, which had moved up from active reserve on the night of Sep't 13th, was no longer needed as a support

7. Although many Marines are given credit for this quote, and Wise claimed to have uttered it, historians believe that Captain Lloyd Williams of the 5th Marine Regiment was probably its author. Frederic May Wise (1877–1940), U.S. Marine Corps, a battalion commander in the 5th Marine Regiment at Belleau Wood, took command of the 58th U.S. Infantry on September 4, 1918, and continued in command until January 30, 1919. He was awarded the Distinguished Service Medal for his "skill, ability, and gallantry" in leading the 59th, including personally directing an attack of his regiment during the St. Mihiel Offensive, and again during the opening days of the Meuse-Argonne Offensive. His "personal courage and aggressive attitude" during the latter offensive was an important factor in the success of the 8th Infantry Brigade. Bach and Hall, *The Fourth Division*, 283; U.S. Adjutant General's Office, *American Decorations*, 788. Brigadier General James G. Harbord commanded the 4th Brigade of the 2nd Division at Belleau Wood. An account of the "difficulty" between Harbord and Wise may be found in the latter's memoir. Frederic May Wise and Meigs O. Frost, *A Marine Tells It to You* (New York: J.H. Sears & Company, Inc., 1929), 202, 240–41.

Rolling kitchen of Company D, 311th Machine Gun Battalion, 79th Division, cooking in the town of Les Eparges, Meuse, France, October 14, 1918. U.S. Army Signal Corps Collection, National Archives, 27461 [1764T8].

for the 59th, so it withdrew. The 4th Division as a unit, continued to hold its position for several days longer, but with little or no action, until all other spots in the salient were completely occupied by the other U.S. divisions participating in the drive on our right. These were the 1st, 2d, 5th, 26th, 42d, 82d, 89th and 90th. All these had been working on the east of our position. We were located at the hub end of the spoke of the great wheel comprising the salient to the southeast. Of the above divisions, the 5th, 82d, 89th and 90th had never before been engaged in offensive combat. The Army Reserve consisted of five divisions, the 3d, 35th, 78th, 80th and 91st.

St. Mihiel, contrary to expectation, proved to be one of the easiest drives of the war, as far as it went. Its success was widely heralded in the press of the United States at the time, as it was our first big drive. This has given rise to the idea in the average public mind, that it was our greatest battle, which it certainly was not, except up to that time. What we did at St. Mihiel is commendable and satisfactory, but it was only a pop-gun as to what would follow in the Meuse-Argonne.

It had been the intention of General Pershing and his staff to continue on through the Briey iron basin of Lorraine, thus taking the valuable coal and iron mines which furnished much of the necessary sinews of war to Germany. If they had been allowed to carry out this plan, perhaps thousands of good U.S. doughboys might now be enjoying life and the pursuit of happiness, instead of "pushing daisies" at Romagne cemetery, in the Argonne. Marshall Foch would not agree to any such plan at the start of the drive and set the objective of the 1st U.S. Army just short of Metz (German stronghold, Lorraine) insisting that we should stop here and then move the attack in the opposite direction through the Argonne toward Sedan. After he saw how successful we were, he then wanted to know why we hadn't continued on through Lorraine. This in spite of his previous order to move to the Argonne as soon as we had pinched out St. Mihiel.[8] The abandonment of further advance at St. Mihiel at this time unduly prolonged the war and cost thousands of American lives lost in the Argonne, although the strategy was successful in the end. As the Germans were stampeded at St. Mihiel we could have kept them going clear back to the Moselle Valley and possibly the Rhine, cutting off their other

8. On August 24, 1918, Pershing submitted a plan to Foch to eliminate the St. Mihiel salient and capture Metz. Although Foch initially agreed, within a few days he changed his mind and, in a stormy encounter with Pershing on August 30, Foch cancelled the operation. In another meeting on September 2, both commanders agreed to proceed with the St. Mihiel offensive, but without continuing the operation toward Metz. Edward G. Lengel, *To Conquer Hell: The Meuse-Argonne, 1918* (New York: Henry Holt and Company, 2008), 50–51. Major General Hunter Liggett wrote in his memoirs that "it was argued by quite a number of excellent solders in our Army that Marshal Foch, in limiting our advance at St.-Mihiel, was in error; that we might have gone on and captured Metz and the vital railroad in September." Liggett, *A.E.F.*, 159. Col. George C. Marshall, assistant chief of staff (operations) of the U.S. First Army, concluded that Metz could have been captured on September 14. His view was shared by Brig. Gen. Douglas MacArthur of the 42nd Division. David F. Trask, *The AEF and Coalition Warmaking, 1917–1918* (Lawrence: University Press of Kansas, 1993), 112. General Pershing agreed, believing that if the St. Mihiel advance had continued, it would have "carried us well beyond the Hindenburg Line and possibly into Metz, and the temptation to carry on was very great." Pershing, *My Experiences in the World War*, II: 270. There is no indication, however, that Foch asked why the American advance had not continued after he witnessed the success at St. Mihiel, as Howell implies.

armies and before they could locate in sufficient number to effectively hold us back.

St. Mihiel had not been all "apple pie" however. There was plenty of hard fighting with German rear guards who put up a stiff resistance and counter attacked at several places, notably Hannonville (meuse), Vigneulles and Thiaucourt. The high hill of Montsec and Loupmont were passed up by the 1st Divis[ion] who used a smoke screen at these places and passed unnoticed around them, cutting them off and meeting their first resistance at Nonsard (meuse) and the Bois de Vigneulles. The artillery of the 32d Divis[ion] effectively removed the menace of Montsec, the main German observation post in the sector and drove out the large garrison established on the rear of the hill.

The strategy of attack having caught the enemy unprepared, he therefore had to quickly abandon a large amount of war materials. The capture of large numbers of prisoners and war materials shows how successful we were in blocking their retreat. There were ten German Landwehr Divisions and two brigades in line with seven divisions in reserve.[9] When the enemy retreated, he set fire to some of his largest supply dumps as well as the town of Thiacourt and several lesser hamlets to hold back our advance.

General Pershing omitted only one thing in his calculations on the drive—the effect of a sufficient number of machine guns. We could have used and ought to have had more of them if they were available. That is one point all the way through the war where the enemy had the advantage of us. We had our Vickers, Maxims, Brownings, and Chauchats but the enemy had some of these as well as thousands of his own special brands. He had more of them than we and knew how to use them as well. They were planted in every brush pile, every old ruin or hole in the ground where they could be used to advantage, even in trees and church steeples. He would hide them in dugouts along with himself and then let us pass by, then he would come out and shoot us in the back. But toward the last he didn't have so many, it seems. His ammunition was getting poorer and his morale and nerve were steadily on the

9. Howell is incorrect. The salient was held by three Landwehr and five other divisions, with four divisions in reserve. Under German military law, Landwehr members were second-line reservists generally between 27 and 39 years of age who had already served a period on active duty and in the reserves.

wane. We were therefore, able to blast him out with H.E. shells and gas. It was the American horde that was following, that made him wish for but one thing—to get back behind the Rhine and save the Fatherland from the destruction and shambles that he had forced on Belgium and northern France.

The spirit of our troops was certainly tested at St. Mihiel and the operation, an outstanding success, was a model of quick and effective organization. The rapid advance over fortified positions and territory so long held by the Germans and considered impregnable by the French, proved how effective the U.S. Army could be with an all American administration and command.

With the salient closed off, the 1st U.S. Army made an immediate "left oblique" turn and started for the Argonne sector, leaving a few divisions to hold the front at St. Mihiel.[10] And they had to be in the Argonne for the start of the drive which was scheduled for Sep't 26th. This left turn movement was a stupendous undertaking but was carried out successfully by the American staff, not without difficulty, however. The importance of what was accomplished, the obstacles that were surmounted, the strain on the men, transport service and supplies can only be appreciated by military men, who can visualize such a manoeuvre, without parallel in history. There was just two weeks to move 500,000 men and supplies, all under the cover of darkness, for another attack a little over sixty miles away.

The 1st U.S. Army succeeded in taking 16,000 prisoners and 433 cannon at a cost of 7,000 doughboys killed and wounded, and could have continued on to a greater success if it were permitted, instead of going so soon into the Argonne and intending to continue on from St. Mihiel with a 2d U.S. Army later to be assembled from tired divisions in the Argonne.

Sept'16th to 24th therefore, the 4th Division was engaged in moving out of the St. Mihiel sector. We went by way of Les Eparges,

10. Technically, Howell is incorrect. Although the jumping-off line for the Meuse-Argonne Offensive was northwest of St. Mihiel, thereby requiring a "left oblique" march for seven of the American First Army divisions involved at St. Mihiel in order for them to take part in the opening stages of the Meuse-Argonne, only two divisions (the 1st and 82nd) were involved in the initial assault on September 26, 1918, and then only as army reserves. Howell's own 4th Division (located on the west side of the St. Mihiel salient, and therefore not required to "left oblique"), was the only one in combat at St. Mihiel that was involved in the opening days of the Meuse-Argonne. Eventually, however, all the remaining divisions that had fought at St. Mihiel joined the Meuse-Argonne drive.

Maj. Gen. John L. Hines, commanding 4th Division, and staff. Haudainville, Department of Meuse, France, September 15, 1918. U.S. Army Signal Corps Collection, National Archives, 24393 [2433S8].

Vigneulles, Dommartin and LaCroix on our long hike back to Bannoncourt (meuse). On our way out we could see transport moving in every direction. Limbers and guns, supply trains of ammunition and food, foot soldiers and water carts, the whole a conglomerate mass enlivened by the lashing tongues of the mule skinners who gee'd and haw'd and gahdamned the mules, the U.S. Army and the Kaiser on whom they sought to put the blame for their predicament.

Some fighting was still in progress on the front we had just left, but there was very little artillery bombardment. We fancied we could hear long range guns firing in Verdun, far to the northwest of us.

One day about noontime, going along a road, we saw a French captive balloon about six- hundred feet in the air, attached to a truck that we were about to pass on the roadside. Just before reaching the truck however, we heard the drone of a Boche aeroplane motor. Soon it came into view quite high in the air, while the Frenchmen commenced to work the wench hurriedly on their truck to haul in the captive balloon while they had time. Too late. The Boche plane circled around the balloon and started shooting fire into it. The French anti-aircraft batteries etc., on the ground kept up an awful din but it didn't bother the Boche. Three times he circled around the bag belching fire at every turn. "I betcha the observer drops out soon," says Corporal Andrews. "If he don't drop soon he'll drop with the bag anyway" remarks Sgt. Nolan. Sure enough the balloon soon caught fire and the observer was seen standing on the rim of the basket, his parachute opening and taking the air beautifully and allowing him to make a safe landing in a field close by. The Boche plane disappeared unmolested. "Well, that's one bag less to move around," says Stevens. "Too many olda bag in the Frog Army anyway" observes Vinelli.

Later on, just before dusk the same day, the company had fallen out for a brief rest along the roadside. Suddenly we heard the drone of a heavy German plane some distance away. We looked up at what appeared to be a heavy bomber and you could see a long barreled machine gun sticking out over the rear observer's seat. Soon from high in the sky above comes a plane no bigger than a mosquito and dropping very fast. It made a wide circle and finally came up under the big bomber. Soon three other little ones appeared on the scene from nowhere and all began pestering the big bomber with machine guns. We could see red fire belching from the machine gun of the bomber but apparently it wasn't hurting anything. We all watched the cat fight breathlessly, making appropriate remarks and conjecture as to the outcome.

"Four little flies after a big black spider," observes Belkin.

"I bet on the flies," says Stevens.

Soon we saw the bomber take a quick nosedive and expected to see him straighten out to get from under and away from the flies. He straightened out all right but he didn't get away as they were too fast for him.

They pestered him for what seemed a long time and finally one little machine suddenly left. Almost at the same instant, the big plane started what looked like a barrel turn. It rolled over and over and suddenly nosedived to the ground and out of sight, while three little mosquito planes disappeared into the night.

"Hooray for our side!" says Belkin, gleefully watching the show.

"To hella witha the Kaiser!" says Vinelli with great gusto.[11]

Finally arriving at Bannoncourt, we found a long grey truck train of French camions drawn up alongside the road through the main street, awaiting us. It was not a long ride, but our destination was to be the Forêt-de-Hesse to the northwest, and the Meuse-Argonne sector. We rode from Bannoncourt through Souilly to Triaucourt and St. Menehould (marne). After a short interval we continued on through Clermont and Dombasle to Montzéville (meuse) where we left the trucks and starting hiking again to Esnes, through Chattancourt, to Cumières (meuse) located near La Mort Hommes and Hill 295. The last hike from Esnes was over rocky, shell torn roads, blasted by four years of warfare. In some places there was no road visible at all, only deep shell craters and dead vegetation.

On Sep't 25th, we arrive at Béthincourt (meuse), a small hamlet just west of Verdun. This was at dusk and in time to enter some old unused French trenches of 1916. We were all ready now for the big jump-off the next morning—the start of the Argonne Drive. This is a reputed quiet sector now. The night was quiet, too quiet, to suit us as it meant trouble brewing. Across from us in the German lines, we could hear a little switch-engine, probably a

11. An unidentified member of the 58th U.S. Infantry interestingly noted that news of the American success at St. Mihiel was "met with indifference that was almost apathetic," because a "soldier in the field does not cheer wildly over the big things," he continued. "He will make ten times the demonstration when a well-directed shot brings down a hostile avion than when he learns of the success of a corps attack." Likewise, a shell burst among the enemy or a "successful long-range pot-shot" from a rifle "will evoke more satisfaction than the signing of an armistice." "The St. Mihiel Drive," Record Group 120, 4th Division Historical, Box 29, Folder: 39th Infantry, Histories, Commendations & Battle Participants, NARA.

narrow gauge, puffing away for all it was worth. Next day we were to see it lying on its side in a ditch, abandoned.

This sector was the scene of some of the heaviest fighting in the earlier stages of the war (1914–1916) around Verdun, where legion were lost on both sides through useless manipulation of guns and men by the German Crown Prince, so successfully stopped by Marshall Petain of the French.

It's A Lovely War
"Up to your waiste in water.
Up to your eyes in slush,
Using the kind of language,
That makes a sergeant blush.
Who wouldn't join the Army?
That's what we all inquire.
Don't we pity those poor civilians at home,
Sitting by the fire?"
—Fawcett's Battle Stories.[12]

12. Lyrics from the 1917 song, "Oh! It's a Lovely War," written by John Long and Maurice Scott.

Chapter 11

Meuse-Argonne Offensive (Sep't 26th to Nov. 11th, 1918)

"Bang away at Lulu,*
Bang-er good an strong.
Whadda yer gonna do,
Fer a bing! bang! boo!
When Lulu's dead an gone?
Bang-er in the morn-in,
Bang-er ev'ry night.
If Lulu quits er bang-in,
We'll never win a fight.
Oh! Bang away, etc., etc.,"
—Loud mouthed gunnery sergeant's song.

At one half minute before eleven P.M. on the night of Sep't 25th, 1918, a lone lieutenant of artillery slowly extends his right hand high over his head, watching closely the second hand of a timepiece held in his other hand. Standing close by him in the woods, a gunnery sergeant holds the lanyard of a small field gun. This isolated battery has just moved in on the Meuse-Argonne front.[1]

*Lulu Belle was the name once given to a famous Civil War cannon.

1. More information on the entire Meuse-Argonne Offensive may be found in several

All is quiet around them as far as the sector is concerned. The stars above give out the only luminescence visible on this peaceful autumn night.

The instant the second hand of the lieutenant's watch ticks in the hour of eleven P.M., the lone officer as quickly drops his hand, while the waiting sergeant suddenly jerks the lanyard of the field gun. The gun barks and recoils. On that instant, as the shell leaves the muzzle of the gun, the greatest battle ever to be fought in the world's history is under way and which is to be extended until it reaches from Calais on the English Channel near Belgium, southeast to Belfort in the Vosges near Switzerland.

At first there is only a shot fired here and there intermittently as if they were trying out a few guns. Gradually more and more batteries join the ever increasing chorus until at 2.30 A.M. on the morning of the 26th there are 3,928 guns of all calibres, standing hub to hub on a thirty-five mile front, firing in unison. This intensive artillery concentration continues without let-up for over three hours longer or until 5.30 A.M. when it stops more abruptly than it started. This avalanche of Hell is as one continuous roar as from the bowels of the earth, lighting the sky as bright as day and vibrating the ground on which we stood like a continuous earthquake. It completely destroys the concrete dugouts and gun emplacements, barbed wire and trenches of the supposedly impregnable Hindenburg Line in the Meuse-Argonne, the toughest section of this long battlefront.[2]

---

excellent, modern works. These include Mitchell Yockelson's *Forty-Seven Days: How Pershing's Warriors Came of Age to Defeat the German Army in World War I* (2016), Edward G. Lengel's *To Conquer Hell: The Meuse-Argonne, 1918* (2008) and *A Companion to the Meuse-Argonne Campaign* (2014), and Robert H. Ferrell's *America's Deadliest Battle: Meuse-Argonne, 1918* (2007).

2. Howell implies here that the intense preparatory Allied artillery barrage of September 25–26, 1918, was effective in destroying German forward positions. A brief history of 39th Infantry noted that the bombardment, "the like of which was never before seen," was so amazingly accurate that it "tore the ground and the enemy positions beyond recognition." Record Group 120, 4th Division Historical, Box 29, Folder: 39th Infantry, Histories, Commendations & Battle Participants, NARA. As American artillery units tried to advance with the infantry, however, they began to suffer from "many handicaps," meaning that close support to destroy the subsequent German defenses was not always available, leaving the task to infantrymen like Howell and his squad. A thorough analysis of American artillery during the offensive may be found in Justin G. Prince's "Artillery in the Meuse-Argonne," in Edward G. Lengel, ed., *A Companion to the Meuse-Argonne Campaign* (New York: John Wiley & Sons, Inc., 2014), 340–356. Historian Robert H. Ferrell believes that most of the preparatory fire on September 25–26 was wasted, and the American artillery brigades "displayed egregious errors" during most of the offensive. It was not until November 1, 1918, Ferrell argues, that artillery units were well coordinated and most effective. Robert H. Ferrell, *America's Deadliest Battle: Meuse-Argonne, 1918* (Lawrence: University Press of Kansas, 2007), 149–51.

Doughboys of the 1st U.S. Army were given the task of conquering this almost impregnable front and they were to continue without let-up at this task for forty-seven terrible days until the enemy was brought to his knees begging for an armistice and finally peace.

Thus the Meuse-Argonne became in fact, the greatest battle ever fought by U.S. soldiers in this or any other war in U.S. history—a fact little known or appreciated in the U.S. This is because it was little advertised in the press of the U.S. at the time of its occurrence, due to strict censorship and the simultaneous happenings of world events which overshadowed its importance in the public mind.

1,390,000 U.S. soldiers (28 divisions) engaged in this offensive—the largest single army ever assembled in the world's history under a single command. It was now to be Pershing vs. Von Hausen.[3]

The original line of attack was from the Meuse River near Regnéville (meuse), thence west to LaHarazée (marne), where it liasoned with the IVth French Army under Gouraud. The attacking units were made up of National Army divisions, some of whom had just arrived in France, others had very little battle experience except that briefly gained at St. Mihiel. The veteran 4th Division, U.S. Regulars, was placed in the line between the 79th Divis[ion] on the left and the 80th Divis[ion] on the right, close to the Meuse River. Their purpose was to "set the pace" (History A.E.F.) for the other less experienced divisions, and they did. They went so fast that after the third day, they had to wait four days longer at Septsarges Wood for the 79th Divis[ion] on the left to catch up. This exposed the left flank dangerously, but no great advantage was taken of it by the enemy, as he was too busy with other immediate problems.

The use of several all green or semi-experienced army divisions, except the 4th, at the opening of the great Argonne battle, was made necessary because of Marshall Foch's decision to cease further attack at this time on the St. Mihiel front and move to the Argonne.

3. Howell is incorrect, in that 21 entire divisions and one regiment from the 92nd Division were credited with combat service in the Meus-Argonne Offensive. American Battle Monuments Commission, *American Armies and Battlefields in Europe*, 327–28. Most historians believe that about 1,200,000 Americans participated in the offensive. Pershing's opponent in the Meuse-Argonne was General Max von Gallwitz, who commanded an army group that controlled the area from Metz to the Meuse-Argonne. The Meuse-Argonne itself was defended by the Fifth Army, led by General Georg von der Marwitz.

Therefore, a majority of the Regular Army and National Army divisions of the 1st Army were left at St. Mihiel, either to hold the line already established or to remain temporarily in active reserve, until we could get the Argonne drive well under way, thereby diverting additional German divisions away from St. Mihiel and relieving more of our own for duty in the Argonne. In the later and succeeding phases of the Argonne battle after October 15th, these divisions again came into action and took over some of the hardest fighting of this famous drive.

The jump-off for us of the 39th Infantry was at Béthincourt (meuse) early on the morning of Sep't 26th, 1918. This town, or ruin, was a few kilos northwest of Verdun on Forges Brook, just over the crest of Hills 304 and La Mort Hommes 295, scene of the fierce fighting of 1916 (Feb. 21st) when the French defender of Verdun, General Petain, exclaimed, "Ils ne passeront pas!" (They shall not pass!).[4] This sector therefore, was assigned to the 4th Division with the difficult task of breaking the enemy line at one of his strongest points.

We started out as scheduled, in the misty dawn at five a.m. through the old rusty barbed wire entanglements into "no man's land," after the heavy artillery and machine gun preparatory barrage. Everything on the German side was literally torn to shambles by the heavy six hour barrage, which gave the enemy little time or opportunity to properly man his guns. I doubt if he could even get at some of his guns to fire them. Even if he had, it would have availed him little as numerous gun emplacements and ammunition dumps were shelled completely out of commission.

When we reached the first line trenches of the Von Hindenburg Stellung behind our machine gun advance, with bayonets fixed and ready for action, the Boche, Hienies, Jerrys, Fritzies, Allemagnes, feldgrau, knubs, or whatever you should choose to call them, came out to meet us in large numbers.[5] You bet! But they carried no rifles or bayonets. This time they were actually pleased to see us

4. This quote was attributed to French General Henri-Philippe Petain (1856–1951), who was charged with the defense of Verdun in 1916.

5. The German defenses in the region consisted of the front line, the Hagen Stellung, Etzel Stellung (including the heights of Montfaucon), Giselher Stellung, Kriemhilde Stellung (part of the Hindenburg Line), and the Freya Stellung. American Battle Monuments Commission, *American Armies and Battlefields in Europe*, 170.

Group of German prisoners taken by 39th and 47th Regiments Infantry, 4th Division, stopping for rest in Montzeville on their way back from the front. Montzeville, Meuse, France, September 26, 1918. U.S. Army Signal Corps Collection, National Archives, 26078 [1420T8].

after passing through the grueling artillery strafe of extinction a few hours before. Now they carried only their gas masks, leather boots or a loaf of bread, and had thrown away their arms and ammunition. They were through with the war and glad of it. Out they came to meet us, hands high above their heads, yelling "kamerad! kamerad! Amerikaners!" and put up no resistance whatever at these first line trenches.

Some of our men would could speak German, kidded the prisoners. Some of the Germans were laughing, some were very serious, some were scared. Others were filled with remorse at the disgrace of surrender, and were sobbing. However, all were glad to be taken prisoner by the "Amerikanisher Soldatten" as we were called, instead of the French. A lot of this was due to the printed propaganda previously dropped by our airmen over enemy lines, which offered three meals per day, with pay, tobacco and clean quarters to any Entente soldier who surrendered.[6] After endless weeks on turnip soup,

6. Howell clearly meant "German" or "Central Powers" rather than the Entente, or Allied nations.

German prisoners arriving from the front at Montzeville They were captured by the 39th and 47th Regiments Infantry, 4th Division, near Cuisy, Montzeville, Meuse, France, September 26, 1918. U.S. Army Signal Corps Collection, National Archives, 26082 [1424T8].

this must have been an inducement worth consideration. General Army Orders covering this matter read, "Prisoners shall not be employed nearer the Front line than 30 kilometers. Hot soup and tobacco must be given them as soon as possible after capture."

One German offizier of high rank, was so pleased at being captured by Americans that he requested that he be "sent to New York immediately as I've always wanted to see it," he said. Instead he was ordered to grab a stretcher and help carry a wounded man back to a field dressing station. This was, of course, much beneath his dignity as a high ranking Prussian offizier. He complained loudly, but that made no difference to us so he was forced to grab hold of a stretcher with the others and work alongside the lowest private in his own former command. Officers were quite useful however in making the handling of prisoners somewhat easier for, as a rule, they understood some English.

Also, there is a story of another German prisoner, captured the first day, who was much pleased because he was an American captive. He was very talkative about it too. He gives us his impressions and observation of the fighting qualities of the various Allies in an amusing manner, somewhat as follows. Speaking to a U.S. Intelligence officer, he said, "The Frenchman. Ach! the swinehund! He booms himself for half an hour in one place, then switches his trajectory, eats a sandwich and then boom! booms! for a half hour in some other place.

The Englishman. He is somewhat different. He comes out after breakfast with his walking stick and boom! booms! in one spot continuously until it is time for afternoon tea. After this, he will fight methodically until dinnertime. And, when dinner is over, which takes a long time, he comes out and boom! booms! for a few times and is kaput for the night, which is well."

Ah! but the Amerikainer! Ach! du lieber! He iss crazy! He has big guns. He booms! early and he booms! late. You can't tell anything about him. He booms! anytime he feels like it. Sometimes he goes on a regular Geschellchaft Abend (society evening) and boom! booms! all over the verdamft sector. He makes me nervously nervous."

In the Verdun sector of the Hindenburg line, the Germans had constructed numerous deep dugouts as a protection against heavy artillery fire. Some of these had large rooms, deep underground and many had shafts extending diagonally down in the earth as much as 200 ft. from the surface. Soldiers in these holes had not been seriously harmed by the heavy artillery concentration of the previous night and morning. It was therefore our duty when we came to the mouth of one of these dugouts, to yell down in them somewhat as follows, "come on out of there you lousy kraut eaters, etc.," as suited the mood of the doughboy. Some of the Boche however, showed fight of course. Others would remain patriotic however and refuse to surrender, for which they must be respected. Most of them would rather be live cowards than dead heroes after four long years of warfare and did the sensible thing—they came out. After fair warning to those remaining inside a deep dugout, a Mills hand grenade was dropped in the shaft which was sure death to those who choose to remain "for Gott und Vaterland." We had to do this as we couldn't afford to run the risk of having them come up behind us after we had passed by (an old Boche trick) and treacherously shoot us in the back with machine guns and even artillery.

"Geeze! I never saw so many krauts in all me young life," says O'Hara, walking the ties of a narrow gauge railway and closely eyeing every old shack.

"Yeah, an they comes right up out of the ground like angle worms after a rainstorm," says Stevens.

"Ifa we gits atime, we'll taka looka in one a dem deepa dugouts fer souvenirs," says Vinelli.

"Not me," says O'Hara, "I'm takin all me chances right on top. They might be mined."

"Why be so careful? You'll probably get bumped off anyway," says Stevens.

Just then a sergeant's whistle blew somewhere to the left. The three doughboys took it on the run in the direction of the whistle, looking for Germans. As they rounded the corner of a long low shack, they saw Belkin, Andrews, Sgt. Nolan and Brizee in mortal combat with about eight Germans. O'Hara and the rest rushed in. O'Hara clubbed one kraut on the head with the butt of his rifle, just as he was about to push his bayonet in Belkin's ribs. Sgt. Nolan jabbed his bayonet in another Kraut to save getting jabbed himself and had to put his foot on the body and pull hard in order to get the bayonet out again. The rest of the Germans were either taken captive or shot. The whole bunch had proved to be more hard boiled and vicious than any the boys had yet seen. They were quite excited over the encounter.

The first day, Sep't 26, the 39th Inf. advanced as far as the town of Cuisy (meuse), just north of Malancourt (meuse) and there Gen. Hines established divisional headquarters.[7] This town is located on high ground and was guarded to the southeast by treacherous machine gun nests, some of which were in round concrete shelters or "pill boxes." These were supposed to be impregnable except for a direct hit on them by heavy artillery. However, they could be surrounded and taken from behind, if you could conceal

7. John Leonard Hines (1868–1968), a native of West Virginia, graduated from West Point in 1891. A lieutenant colonel by May 1917, and a colonel (temporary) that August, Hines became a brigadier general in the National Army in April 1918 and a major general that August. He commanded the 4th Division from late August 1918 until that October, when he assumed command of the Third Corps. Hines retired from the army as a major general in 1932. He was awarded the Distinguished Service Cross for his heroism near Soissons on July 21, 1918, and the Distinguished Service Medal for his wartime service. U.S. Adjutant General, *Official Army Register, January 1, 1933* (Washington, D.C.: U.S. Government Printing Office, 1933), 847; U.S. Adjutant General's Office, *American Decorations*, 343, 717.

your movement somewhat and enough men could get through the barbed wire entanglement. Otherwise you would be mowed down like grass in the front lawn.

The three "pill boxes" on the hill in front of Cuisy were arranged for deadly cross firing. As we approached them slowly and cautiously, to within about 300 yds., a lone machine gunner suddenly appeared on top of the center "pill box," wildly waving his arms and shouting "Kamerad! Kamerad!" He had, no doubt, read some of the propaganda dropped behind the lines by our airmen and wanted to surrender his gun without further bloodshed. Perhaps, also, he wanted to get us closer in, so as to wipe out the whole company. Anyway, one of our company hotheads took a pot shot at Mr. Boche as he stood there and without warning or command to fire. He missed, but Mr. Boche was angry and probably said to himself, "the verdamte Americain swine! If they want fight, I'll show 'em." He thereupon ducked back in his "pill box" and let us have it to the tune of about thirty casualties.

At this point I will digress, to reminisce for a few paragraphs.

Back in August 18th, after we had been relieved from the Vesle River Soissons sector and had hiked back to the rear through Château Thierry and Étampes-sur-Marne, there awaiting transportation for Andelot, you will remember that our company commander was injured and sent to the rear. Since then and up until a short time before we entered the St. Mihiel sector, we had no regular company commander for any length of time. Rather, we had all kinds of lieutenants assigned to us for a day or two or a week as the case might be. Among them was a certain lieutenant, a replacement officer from some National Army cantonment back in the States. He had just recently arrived in France and had little or no battle experience. Our impression of him at that time was, that he looked like a big bag of wind, was pompous, impatient, aloof and haughty toward privates as required by military ethics. He was a good example of a 90 day "Sears-Roebuck" officer, had a glistening new uniform with all the accoutrements, etc., but his mind was still back in the National Army camp from which he had lately matriculated via England. He was full of parade discipline, etc., which has no real place in actual front line warfare and was assuming command of a company of veterans in a Regular Army outfit who had been under fire many times within the last two months. Naturally, he had a lot to learn—things that are never taught in training camps. In justice to him, I will say that before the war was over, he finally did learn them and to his credit. But I must get on with my story.

At this time I was in the company headquarters staff as a runner.[8] The new lieut. had been used to having his personal valet or "batman" back in the States, so he asked me to be his "dog robber" or "striker" which mean the same thing. In other words, he wanted me to be his body servant. English regimental officers in war books and movies have a yen for this too, only their "batman" is a sort of "wet nurse" to them. This luxury had not been indulged in by our previous commander, an old Regular officer, so we weren't quite used to the idea. We felt that it was sort of out of place in the front line anyway where every man is for himself and his buddy only. Therefore, I declined the job of "dog robber," even though it meant extra pay and certain other privileges. As the lieut. could get no one else in the company for obvious reasons, he had to do without. This and other little annoyances he must have experienced, made him a little irritable at the time with our company, especially the hard boiled platoon sergeants. We were a little too crude for him. He therefore started out to find fault and discipline us whenever he could to suit his own petty ideas, therefore getting "in wrong" or more or less disliked in his own command. It isn't easy to be an officer, even under the best of conditions, but he made things worse.

Every man in the company is supposed to carry a certain amount of iron (emergency) ration in his combat pack at all times, which is as it should be. When the lieut. made his first inspection of the company at the Front, he found out much to his displeasure, that there wasn't a can of iron ration in the whole outfit. As you will remember, we had turned it all back to the kitchen at Rimaucourt-Manois where we had experienced a food shortage. We had not as yet received a re-issue from the quartermaster and here we were right up at the front. We were worrying about that ration too. The lieut. therefore proceeded to show his pompous authority and ordered that the company would proceed to dig trenches all one day on a blank hillside as a punishment for eating, as he thought, our iron

8. Runners engaged in the hazardous work of delivering messages. Perhaps the two most famous runners in the 39th Infantry were Corporal Thomas Blindwoman, a full-blood American Indian from Oklahoma, and a "little Frenchman" identified only as "Frenchy." *Oakland* (CA) *Tribune*, December 31, 1918.

ration on the way up to the front, and not having it in our combat packs where it was supposed to be. The platoon sergeants were angry at the supercilious of the order and so got together in the matter. They resolved that the company would not dig any useless trench that would never see war, just to satisfy the ego of our lieut. or any other "goddam Sears-Roebuck officer" and told him so. They also informed him as to why it was that we were minus our iron ration. Also what had taken place at Manois, leaving out no colorful detail. The lieut. was at once apologetic, saying that he did not understand the situation correctly and advised that his trench digging order was countermanded. Accordingly we received a new issue of emergency ration without delay. Anyway, by this time the lieut. was "in wrong" with his company and it is not always healthy to be that way at the front for obvious reasons. He meant well, no doubt and I am telling this story only because our lieut. was representative of other like officers in the A.E.F. the result of our preparedness for war, who had never been under fire and thought that war was just parade stuff with a flock of boot licking orderlies about. This may be all right in its place, but not at the front. The men proceeded to educate him soon enough around the St. Mihiel sector and I am sure that he overheard many disparaging remarks in such amorous terms as "gold brick, jam eating lieutenant," etc.

The day before we entered the lines for the Meuse-Argonne Drive, he was observed sitting in the corner of a ruined estaminet in a small village near the front, holding his head in his hands and sobbing as he received the order to move the company up for action in the old trenches near Béthincourt. What touched him emotionally, I do not know. He may have been high minded and idealistic. Perhaps he hated war. Well, who didn't? This, no doubt was to be his first real combat experience, even though he had been with us at St. Mihiel. I do not believe, however that he was actually afraid at any time, just a bit nervous about the unknown. As the news of this spread around the company, the men were not slow in expressing themselves privately. They didn't have much confidence in a leader that showed weakness and disliked "going in" with him.[9] I will also state that at this time, as before every

9. 1st Lieutenant (later Captain) Harmanus Fenno Neff commanded Company B from September 12, 1918, to December 22, 1918. Record Group 120, Records of the American Expeditionary Forces, World War I, Records of Combat Divisions 1917–1919, 4th Division, 4th Division Historical, Box 29, Folder: 39th Infantry, History, [M.G., Supply, Hdrs, 1st, 2nd, 3rd Bn,

other battle we were in, very few of the buck privates of the rank and file had any idea as to where we were in France, the importance of our position in the offensive or what was just ahead of us. Information as to war plans and policy was carefully kept from filtering through to us, although the lieutenants and possibly the platoon sergeants knew something of what was to transpire. Most of the time we were in complete ignorance as to the reasons for our movements. But we did know from past experience, that it was more war and the sooner the action was over the better. Then we could rest and eat regularly again. This brings us back to those "pill boxes" before Cuisy.

After the machine guns had fired on us and we had lost about 30 men, the company had spread out over the terrain and was waiting further orders. The losses in the regiment before Cuisy was small compared to later ones. The lieut. and I were in a shell hole together. He turned to me and said, "you're a runner, aren't you?" I replied in the affirmative. "Find the sergeant of the 4th platoon and tell him that the company commander orders him to send a corporal and a picked squad of men to take the center 'pill box' on the hill." I crawled out, leaving him in the shell hole alone, started out on my belly with head down, toward the location of the 4th platoon. Every time I would raise my head a little and go a few yards, there would be a rain of machine gun bullets all around me. I would stop a minute and then continue on, when the same thing would happen all over again. Mr. Boche was following me through his glass. Toward the last I got up and started to run, reached the 4th platoon unscathed and delivered the verbal order to the sergeant. Five of the eight men selected became casualties. Some were hit in the groin, others in the legs as they stood up and rushed the wire in front of the "pull box" on the hill. But three got through all right and captured the gun and gunner after they had cut through the wire with their bayonets. This was in broad daylight. Seeing what had taken place, the other two "pill boxes" on the right and left peppered the company to a standstill to keep

---

and Co. A thru M], 4th Div., 204–11.4, Official History of the 39th Regiment of Infantry, 1917–1918; Box 32, Folder: 39th Infantry, Rosters of Officers of the 39th Infantry, Officers, Historical Section, 204–65.1 , Roster of September 26, October 7, and November 30, 1918, National Archives and Records Administration, College Park, Maryland. Neff, born in Dorchester, Massachusetts, in 1885, survived the war and retired from the New England Mutual Life Insurance Company. He died in Dedham, Massachusetts, in June 1955. *The Boston Herald*, June 18, 1955.

us down. As we moved in closer toward them however, they pulled their guns and retreated. These were rear guards and held us back a good hour or more. We were not long in covering the rest of the distance over the hill and through another short ravine where we encountered another gun which was silenced with hand grenades and entered the town of Cuisy shortly afterward.

After I had delivered the lieut.'s verbal order to the platoon sergeant, I hurried back to the shell hole to report back to the officer, but he was nowhere to be found. None of the soldiers in the locality seemed to know anything about him either. He had completely disappeared, that's all. Both of his two lieutenants, who were regimental dental officers assigned to fill out for the drive only, were also missing. They had either been killed, wounded or went A.W.O.L. This left the company temporarily in command of Sgt. Nolan. I felt that our company commander had not been hurt and that he had simply taken a walk for himself, considering his previous actions. However, I will give him the benefit of the doubt, as there was so much confusion among the various outfits who became mixed at this stage of the game, that anything was possible. Whole companies lost their direction. Green support outfits pushed up into our sector, yelling and firing off their Enfields, they were so excited. They shot in the air at nothing, shot down in dugouts that we had already inspected. They just went crazy with the heat and didn't seem to have any officers or leaders and didn't know where they were, or what they were doing. We let them run through our position and after they were a little distance ahead, some sort of runner or orderly overtook them and headed them off to the right in a different direction out of our sector.

When we entered the town of Cuisy in the late afternoon of the 26th, along with elements of the 47th Infantry, Stevens, Belkin and myself, who usually stuck together as closely as possible in the front line, were all tired out. Continuously on the battlefield since the dawn of daylight, the excitement and hardship, with little water and nothing to eat, began to take effect on us. We were all dragged out and couldn't go much farther without dropping in our tracks. We must rest. It had been a tough racket getting through to Cuisy, across the Forges Brook, in and out of ravines, the clatter of machine guns and the other obstacles we had to pass. Belkin was also somewhat nervous after his close encounter with the Boche, earlier in the day.

We decided therefore, the three of us, to say in the town of Cuisy awhile and await further developments. The rest of our company, however, kept right on moving up without encountering much resistance. There was very little artillery firing, but night was coming on. We didn't seem to be in a battle at all, it had become so quiet. Anyway, we knew that our company would stop in the next town about three kilos farther on, so we could join them in the morning.

We had discovered too, that one of the 47th Infantry's chow guns was moving into Cuisy. We caught a whiff of it as we passed them on the road. It smelled like mother's kitchen back in the dear old U.S.A. with its sweet aroma of good old stew. We just couldn't pass it up, we were so hungry. The 47th Infantry had been right alongside us all day long a little to the west. Our two regiments constituted the 7th Brigade. The 8th Brigade (58th & 59th Inf.) were right behind us as support. We were sort of run in together, but it wasn't any of the 8th Brigade who went crazy and fired off their rifles in the air as I have already mentioned. That was some green National Army outfit. The 8th Brigade was delegated to leapfrog us at Septsarges on the second day and they were headed in that direction now. They would carry on the advance, relieving the 39th and 47th Infantry temporarily.

My two buddies and myself, however, knew nothing of this arrangement when we decided to stay in Cuisy. It was chow we were after. As any old soldier will tell you, chow always tastes better when secured from some other strange outfit besides his own, whom he always believes feeds better and gives more "seconds" than is obtainable from his own outfit, whether it is true or not.

"I'm gonna git me some of that stew over at the 47th," says Belkin, "Damn me, if it don't smell good!"

"Damn me too," says Stevens. "I want a handout of them good old army beans, if they's got any."

"I could use some hot, black, coffee right now," says I. "And damn me if I wouldn't like to dunk a crust of army bread in it too."

"All right then, let's go!" says Belkin. "But keep yer eyes peeled fer officers."

"They're lining up fer chow, already!" says Stevens, excitedly.

So we got in the chow line and when we reached the rolling kitchen, the mess sergeant gave us the dog-eye and the once-over. We didn't know if we would get any chow or not, the way he looked at us.

"Where you birds from?" says the sergeant to Stevens, sarcastically. "Do you think we feeds the whole damn U.S. Army?"

"No, Sir!" replies Stevens. "We knows you by reputation, which is that you're the only honest mess officer in the whole 47th Infantry. All the rest is chiselers and goldbricks."

"That's right," puts in Belkin. "We heard about you over in the 39th."

"Well, O.K. then, sojers. Step right up," says the mess sergeant smiling all over and filling our mess tins. "If ya comes from the 39th, yer all right. And say, if yer happens ta have any of them Boche Luger pistols in yer souvenir kit, I'll slip yer a little extra chow fer 'em. Come around later."

"All right, sarge," says Belkin, grabbing his chow, "an nuts ta you."

"What's that you said, sojer?" asks the sergeant angrily.

"I said, ya got swell-elegant stew," replies Belkin, as we made a somewhat hasty retreat.

That same night the three of us slept beneath the front steps of the demolished Catholic church at the crossroads, in the center of Cuisy.[10] I had been carrying a heavy brass Very pistol (flare gun), besides my own rifle and ammunition. I also had an electric signal lantern (reflector flash lamp), together with a bag of colored flares for signaling the artillery when we should reach our objective. I forgot to use the flares as my objective was chow and a good sleep. It didn't make much difference now, anyway, as the Army objective had been reached the first day, instead of taking two days as originally planned. All this superfluous junk or trappings of war that I carried, was becoming too heavy and cumbersome and wasn't needed anyhow, so I selected what was necessary for my own safety and left the remainder behind. The Pioneer Infantry outfits would salvage it later on, when they came up to clean the battlefield.

10. An unpublished history of the regiment explained that "practically nothing" remained of the towns of Haucourt, Malancourt, and Cuisy, particularly in the case of the former two, and "few stones remained to show that on the site had once been a village." Record Group 120, 4th Division Historical, Box 29, Folder: 39th Infantry, Histories, Commendations & Battle Participants, NARA.

Next morning, the three of us, still stiff and tired, crawled out from under the church to look around. As we were again browsing around close to the 47th Infantry chow gun again, we accidentally bumped into the 39th Infantry chaplain, of our own regiment.[11] This was quite unintentional on our part as we were technically A.W.O.L. or "straggling" as it were, away from our company. We heard also that General Hines, then commanding the 4th Division, was moving his headquarters into Cuisy. Therefore, this was no place for us with a lot of "brass hats" around. No, Sir! So we must move out toute de suite (in a hurry) before we were discovered. But the chaplain had recognized our regimental markings, as he spotted us. So he just naturally asked us what we were doing in Cuisy, when the rest of the battalion was near Montfaucon or Septsarges. We had no satisfactory military excuse to offer. We just told him that we had become lost from our company and stayed there after the fighting of the previous day. This was about half true and sounded plausible enough, but it brought a wee flicker of a smile to the chaplain's face. Addressing us with an air of authority, he said, "I've got work for you birds, and after it is done I'll see about

11. It is uncertain which one of the regiment's two chaplains Howell and his comrades encountered. Chaplain and 1st Lieutenant James Robinson Shanks (1883–1961), a native of Richview, Illinois, left his career as a telephone lineman and entered the ministry at age 23 and was ordained a Baptist minister in 1908. He received a bachelor of arts degree from Shurtleff College in Alton, Illinois, in 1915. He attended Newton Theological Seminary in Newton, Massachusetts, the following year. When World War I began, Shanks served with the Y.M.C.A. at Great Lakes Naval Training Center, then joined the U.S. Army in May 1918. He was discharged from active duty in July 1919, but remained a reserve officer (but saw no more active service) until 1928. *The Bureau County Tribune* (Princeton, IL), October 30, 1925; *Alton* (IL) *Evening Telegraph*, April 24, 1961. 1st Lieutenant William Francis Odell (1880–1948), the regiment's other chaplain, was a native of New Britain, Connecticut. After attending St. Charles College in Catonsville, Maryland and St. John's Seminary in Brighton, Massachusetts, Odell was ordained to the priesthood in 1907. Appointed a first lieutenant and chaplain in June 1918, Odell served with the A.E.F. from July 1918 to July 1919. Discharged in July 1919, he returned to Connecticut and remained in the priesthood for the rest of his life. Record Group 120, Records of the American Expeditionary Forces, World War I, Records of Combat Divisions 1917–1919, 4th Division, 4th Division Historical, Box 32, Folder: 39th Infantry, Rosters of Officers of the 39th Infantry, Officers, Historical Section, 204–65.1, Roster of September 26, 1918, National Archives and Records Administration, College Park, Maryland; *The Hartford* (CT) *Courant*, September 7, 1948; *Connecticut Men and Women,* 1107. Howell and his comrades were not alone in straggling. Straggling proved to be a serious problem for the American Army during the Meuse-Argonne Offensive, not only sapping the strength of front line units but also forcing the diversion of valuable resources (military police and cavalry units) to look for absent soldiers, units that could have been used elsewhere. According to one estimate, 10 percent of the American First Army straggled or went AWOL during the offensive. Although some soldiers simply became lost, and others left the front to avoid combat, many stragglers, such as Howell, went in search of food and water. For a thorough discussion of this issue, see Richard S. Faulkner, "Disappearing Doughboys: The American Expeditionary Forces' Straggler Crisis in the Meuse-Argonne," *Army History*, Issue 83, Spring 2012, 6–25.

getting you back to the 39th." He was so very nice and sarcastic about it too. We didn't like the way he said it and had visions of courtsmartial or worse. We all shivered in our boots. But nothing ever came of it as we had not deserted in the face of the enemy. No, Sir! The enemy had deserted rather than face us so what could the chaplain do about it?

The chaplain wanted to use us for a burial detail. He gave me the job of standing guard over a pile of salvaged clothing, personal belongings and accoutrements taken from dead soldiers collected on the battlefield, so I had it soft. But Stevens and Belkin along with some others he had also corralled, were put at work collecting all of our dead comrades in one spot, removing their "dog tags" (identification disc worn on string around neck) for checking with the records. We stayed with this officer about two days and lived mostly on the emergency ration taken from dead men's packs.

View from hill looking down the valley, showing the shell-ruined town of Cuisy with Americans in the foreground. This town has been constantly under shell fire, and is the headquarters of the Fourth Division Post Command. The main thoroughfare to the front leads through this town. Eightieth Division. Cuisy, Meuse, France, October 11, 1918. U.S. Army Signal Corps Collection, National Archives, 26504 [1549T8].

We were comparatively safe here too. There was now very little shelling and the front was about 4–6 kilos away.

We came across an Austrian artillery crew's dugout built in the side of a knoll. It was equipped with double chickenwire bunks and had a charcoal stove for cooking and warming the place. German and Austrian army accoutrements hung about the walls inside along with helmets, gas masks, etc. There were yellow silk tasseled bayonets, a frying pan, photographs and postcards of "der Vaterland," leather boots, clothes and books. This was a real homey place and looked like the occupants had been here a long time as there was a vegetable garden outside. We also found a few cigars and tinned honey belonging to the Austrian artillery officer who now lay dead just outside across our doorstep. The close proximity of dead soldiers made no difference to us now as we were used to seeing them. We just rolled him out of the way to get inside. As we did so a French soldier came along, pulled off the Austrian's leather boots, went through his pockets, took his money, Luger pistol and big silver watch. We simply looked on, not knowing what else to do. The French soldier then picked up the leather boots, spit in the dead Austrian's face, says "adieu messeiurs" and disappeared in the gully.

The Austrian 88 gun, with its half empty racks of shell cases and baskets, was located close by. We examined it with interest before returning to the dugout. Once inside however, we shortly had a fire built in the charcoal stove and began frying hardtack in some of the bacon grease that Stevens always carried in his condiment can. We three then enjoyed a front line culinary treat and spent the evening at home with our cigars and honey.

"Did ya see that Frawg frisk the Austrian?" says Stevens. "They wouldn't think of doing a thing like that in our army. No, Sir! Got more sense of decency and honor."

"I read in a history book somewheres, that the Duke of Wellington's men frisked the Frawgs after the Battle of Waterloo," says Belkin. "So there is nothing new about it."

"I feel sort of sorry for that officer lying alone out there in the wet," says I. "Mebbe he has got a pretty young wife and kids at home waiting for him. Who knows?"

"Don't worry yerself about him," says Stevens. He ain't even married, er a gentleman either. Lookit all these naughty female postcards, I jest found."

"Well, anyway, they knows how ta build good dugouts," says Belkin, curling up comfortably in a chickenwire bunk. "Good night, sojers."

I picked up and carried for a long time, the diary of the dead officer who lay outside. It dated from 1914 and the translation of the same would probably have made an interesting volume, but it soon became wet and torn and I had to discard it. I remember also that there was a copy of Goethe's *Faustus* in the dugout, printed on thin parchment or bible tissue [?], which we used of necessity in lieu of a good mail order catalogue.

Speaking of artillery, some of the enemy guns captured by the 39th Infantry near Cuisy, were taken over immediately by the 13th Field Artillery. After organizing special batteries, they turned these same guns against their late owners. One battery taken by the 39th on Sep't 27th, was turned over to the 77th Field Artillery and more than three thousand rounds of German shells were turned back on the enemy before they were finally discarded.[12]

Parts of the Argonne which we have now passed through, has been mostly open, though hilly country. It has been thoroughly plowed over by exploding shells and scarcely any vegetation except weeds is visible in this particular section. From now on the terrain will be more difficult and treacherous for fighting, as we come to the more wooded section, which seems to have escaped excessive shelling. There will be old abandoned trenches. Heavy undergrowth with long snake grass will now be visible in deep dark ravines which seem to resound with low ominous echoes at night. Everywhere there is now to be seen old rusty barbed wire entanglements and German "potato masher" hand grenades (grenades with long handles and large bulb or canister on one end). Also discarded rifles and ammunition belts from machine guns are strewn about. The trees also in certain areas are now mere blackened skeletons and look like bean poles sticking out of the ground, bare from three years of heavy shelling in the sector. The whole is an indescribable conglomeration of fresh and ruined vegetation mixed together with

12. The use of captured German equipment by American forces had occurred earlier in the year. One of the 39th's officers reported on August 19, 1918, that he had "gun crews following us to take over the Hun guns; and we are still using them, so plentiful is the ammunition." One platoon of his company was equipped with German Maxim guns, "with a big supply of ammunition." *The Charlotte* (NC) *News*, September 15, 1918.

Battery F, 16th Field Artillery, firing on German positions just over the hill. On road between Cuisy and Septsarges, Meuse, France, September 27, 1918. U.S. Army Signal Corps Collection, National Archives, 45812 [2296V8].

the debris of war. Such is the Argonne sector, a collection of small woods long occupied by the German Army who have built numerous shacks and dugouts therein. Some of these were very luxurious, even containing mattresses, furniture, pianos, etc. Some were equipped with electric lights and in one or two instances, tiled bathrooms. These shacks were scattered everywhere throughout the Argonne sector but were more numerous between the Hindenburg and Kreimhilde Stellungs.

On Sep't 30th, we of the three A.W.O.L. group returned to our company again. We found them waiting, with the rest of the 1st Battalion, for the orders to move to the attack through the woods above Septsarges which was another wooded section called the Bois de Fays. In the meantime, on Sep't 27th, the division had taken Nantillois and lost it again. On the 28th they recaptured it again and moved further on.[13]

13. Howell and his fellow stragglers had missed some vicious combat in the taking of Nantillois. According to an unpublished regimental history, the unit began its assault on the

Battery F, 16th Field Artillery, Hill No. 295, firing French 75's at German battery in woods opposite, where 39th Regiment Infantry are facing Germans. A German shell can be seen exploding in background. The open position of battery gives idea how fast they have been advancing to keep up with Infantry. Near Septsarges, Meuse, France, September 28, 1918. U.S. Army Signal Corps Collection, National Archives, 45813 [2297V8].

No one asked any questions of me or my buddies as to where we had been, so we knew that we had not been missed by the top sergeant, at least he said nothing about it. Anyway we had been working with the chaplain, so everything was O.K. and we were glad to be back with our outfit again.

As we were waiting here, my company received an order from Battalion Headq[uarters] to stay behind, while the balance of the battalion would be engaged cleaning up to the left around

morning of September 28. "Jerry . . . put down a curtain fire with machine guns," the unidentified author noted, "and followed up with a stiff fire of H.E. [high explosive] and shrapnel." After the village was taken, heavy combat patrols moved into the Bois de Fay, but German machine gun fire from the flanks drove the patrols back to their own lines. The 39th held on for two hours at the edge of the woods, despite a "terrific fire" of Germany 77mm guns from across the Meuse River. Finally, the regiment was forced to withdraw to a position south of the woods. On the 29th the regiment took position as the 4th Division's reserve. Record Group 120, Records of the American Expeditionary Forces, World War I, Records of Combat Divisions 1917–1919, 4th Division, 4th Division Historical, Box 29, Folder: 39th Infantry, Histories, Commendations & Battle Participants, 4th Division, 204–11.4, Official History of the 39th Regiment of Infantry, 1917–1918, National Archives and Records Administration, College Park, Maryland.

Montfaucon chasing rear guards which they had passed more than a mile beyond two days previous. This was good fortune for us to be withdrawn from further combat action at this time. We were now detailed to go back to the rear about five kilos to the town of Malancourt (meuse) for military police traffic duty. The town was totally destroyed, but located on a crossroads of the main and only supply road for the U.S. Army in this sector. The road was jammed solid with immovable traffic. In looking over the town for a P.C. location, we decided on the ruined wine cellar of the local estaminet which was long since sans vintage and was in fairly good condition. Although full of debris, the walls offered good protection from shelling and flying shrapnel even though a trifle damp. We lost no time therefore in cleaning it out and making it the company headquarters.

We were under orders to clear the traffic and get it moving on this road by any means available. We had to get it moving both ways at once. The road had been shelled until it was full of holes and shell craters, making it well nigh impossible, but the 4th Engineers filled these holes with rock and sandbags carried from everywhere by hand, graded and leveled a road over which it was possible to advance ammunition and supply trains toward the front and ambulances full of wounded back toward the rear. They worked day and night feverishly, filling the crevices between sandbag and rock with mud and in a short time it had dried sufficiently to allow passage of supplies for the 200,000 men ahead in the front lines.

Soon we started pulling out guns and heavy ammunition carts and ordering other vehicles off the road into the fields on either side. This left space to get traffic moving again. Our chow gun, which we had not seen since Sep't 25th, was discovered locked in the traffic on the road and we lost no time in pulling it out and moving it to our new P.C. for immediate action.

Mule skinners and truck drivers were frequently found sitting bolt upright in their seats sound asleep, their vehicles wedged in the hopeless tangle and at a standstill on the road. We had to get them moving and keep them moving as well. As the engineers were building and repairing our road another group of 4th Engineers was building another road through Esnes to Montfaucon so as to allow two way traffic over different routes and stop congestion, a procedure absolutely necessary for success of the drive.

"Hell! This is worse than war!" exclaims Stevens to Corp. Andrews, "I never worked so damn hard in this man's army before."

"What seems to be the trouble?" inquires Andrews.

"Trouble!" says Stevens, "lookit that bird on the ammunition cart over there. I've pulled and prodded and pinched him. Even twisted his nose, I have, but all I can get him to do or say is 'yes sir,' like I was an officer. And there he sits, alive but dead to the world. What the hell am I going to do? Guess I'll go over an prick him with my bayonet an see if I can bring him ta life long enough ta start moving."

"I'll go over with you," says Corporal Andrews.

So the two soldiers went over to the ammunition cart and finally, after Stevens had slapped the driver's face, and Andrews had jerked his arms and kicked at his feet, he was eventually awakened, much bewildered and mouth agape.

"Pull in toward the center of the road, ya big bohunk, an get goi'n," orders Stevens. "Allay! Allay! Toot sweet!"

"Yes, sir!" answers the driver, saluting. Then turning to his mules, "Gee! Gee! Giddap ya striped sons a bitches!"

"Looks like we wuz gittin' some action, at last," says Stevens, going away satisfied.

Long lines of camouflaged heavy artillery, wagon trains full of supplies of all kinds for line soldiers, camions, foot soldiers, ambulances full of wounded now passed by in endless parade along this single road to front and rear.

Farther up to the northwest of us could be seen white smoke of the shell bursts of battle. As we looked along the road, we could see in the distance, drivers hastily leaving the shell torn roads and starting across open fields at a gallop. These were either ammunition carts, or batteries of field guns moving to some new position in a hurry. In one instance we saw a lone caisson or wagon galloping across a field. Instantly, so it seemed, the Boche caught sight of him and down would come a rain of G.I. cans all around him. In a second the horses reared and stampeded. The driver pulled and jerked, but soon was astride the horses backs, lashing them in panic. On would come another rain of shells, the bursts throwing up great quantities of rock and smoke all around them. What was left of the caisson would disappear into some ravine. Shortly along would come some other type of vehicle and go through the same performance. But they all seemed to get by.

A high calibre gun used to fire on us every day at exactly ten minutes before twelve noon. This gun was stationed across the Meuse River some fifteen kilos distant. We could hear the gun fire, then count one, two, three, slowly and the shell would whizz over our heads and directly over our kitchen. It would land with a loud detonation in the open field across the road. It never did us any damage and we found out later that it was one of a number of old worn-out guns that were being utilized by the Boche to harass or scare the traffic on this single arterial road. It would fire a half dozen shells and then remain silent until the next day when it would repeat the performance.

"One,-two,-three,-Bang!" counts O'Hara listening to the big gun.

"That's the first time I ever knew you could count anything except two sixes" says Corp. Andrews sarcastically.

"Thanks, Corp. for the compliment," says O'Hara, "but I've made more noise on the fourth of July with my toy brass cannon than that Boche makes with his whizbang."

"An you has been makin a big noise ever since" remarks Stevens who was standing close by.

Road through ruined town of Malancourt, Meuse, France, showing congestion of roads leading to the front. September 28, 1918. U.S. Army Signal Corps Collection, National Archives, 34889 [377T8].

"That's right," puts in Belkin. "Boloney is his specialty. Just a big hunk a Irish boloney."

"Oh yeah? Says you! You'd a been a hunk of kosher boloney or a wart on a wienerwurst if I hadn't a clubbed that Boche who was about to get you over near Forges Brook," says O'Hara heatedly.

"I've got to admit that," says Belkin. "You sure saved my life that time, old Pal. Shake an fergit the slander."

"Aw shake yer ashes outta here" replies O'Hara. "I'd do it again even if I had ta eat kosher boloney on Friday."

Top Sergeant Nolan was still commanding our company when we reached Malancourt. We had been here about three days when in walks our missing lieutenant—our company commander and the one I lost in the shell hole before Cuisy. He explained to Sergeant Nolan that he had left our company on verbal order to take command of C Company, during an emergency and had just been relieved. Such a condition did occur with A Company around Montfaucon, so we took his word for it and let it go at that. Seeing that there was no dissent, he then resumed command of the company with big gusto. Next day in walks two other A.W.O.L.'s only they happen to be privates instead of officers. The lieutenant drew himself up to a great height and a light like the Statue of Liberty enveloped his face. Filling his lungs full of the damp air, he bellowed,

"Where the hell were you men for the past week? I'll have you two court-martialed for desertion in the face of the enemy and shot! Where were you? Answer me!"

"Sir," one of the men meekly replied, "we were six kilometers back to the rear in the same town you were. An we only got half shot."

The lieutenant fumed at the mouth, spluttered around, told the men they were under arrest and ordered the company clerk to take down their records. Very shortly, he announced that he had to see someone or other on the outside. Nothing further was ever said to the privates about the matter, however.

About this time also, Sergeant Painting returned to our company. There was a soldier for you! He was not of the spectacular, hurry-up and get 'em variety that you see in the movies or fiction, but a good level headed veteran of the old 30th U.S. Infantry, who had seen service in Mexico and the Philippines. He was red faced and hard

View of Malancourt from the interior of church. Ruins of church wrecked by Germans in foreground, after capture from Germans by Third Army Corps. Malancourt, Meuse, France, September 28, 1918. U.S. Army Signal Corps Collection, National Archives, 26079 [1421T8].

boiled but always a model of neatness at all times—a regular dude soldier. And his command of adjectives too, was simply superb. He was one of the most entertaining talkers I've ever listened to, with a flow of the most delicious profanity on tap at all times. This he would use as occasion demanded, especially when drilling a bunch of "rookies." You would think that privates were as scum under his feet, to hear him rave at them, but only on the drill-field. He was a better drill-master than most of the two-cent lieutenants we had already met in our brief army career.

Sergeant Painting had left the company shortly after the Vesle River campaign to attend an officer's training school somewhere around Gondrecourt. When he was about to graduate, he went A.W.O.L. to Paris as he had suddenly made the decision that he didn't want to become a "shavetail" (2d lieut.) after all. After he had seen the nights and sights of Paris to his own satisfaction, he allowed himself to be found by the Paris military police and brought back to Bar- le-Duc. For this episode he was forced to spend some time in the "brig" along with some German war prisoners from whom he learned their lingo.

When he finally matriculated at Bar-le-Duc, he was ordered to return to the company at the Front which he was glad to do and started to hitch hike back to us in the Argonne. On the way back he learned that we were doing M.P. duty at Malancourt, so he decided that he wanted to see the famous fortifications at Verdun to the east of us which he had heard so much about and therefore included that town on the return itinerary. We therefore received from him piecemeal a complete description of the town and its underground construction and a regular travelogue of all his experiences to Paris and back. Sgt. Painting had therefore hiked most of the way alone from Bar-le-Duc near Nancy to Malancourt near Verdun, about 250 kilos, getting his food from army outfits encountered along the roads and some transportation by occasional truck rides picked up en route. He was one of those gifted ones who can talk themselves into a feed or a lift anywhere. But up in the wet and slime of the Argonne woods he was strictly a soldier, always ready at the appointed time to take part in the attack. While he would be as nervous as any of the rest of us, he was always there taking the lead, giving orders and moving against nasty machine gun nests with uncanny success.

War is full of little episodes. In the confusion of battle for instance, a seemingly unimportant action by some individual may have a far reaching effect. I speak of this because there seems to have been much criticism of the 39th Infantry and the 4th Divis[ion] for their conduct around the town and hill of Montfaucon (meuse-argonne). Post war biographers and historians have raised the question as to why it was, that the 39th Inf. apparently passed up Montfaucon when they could have taken it. Instead, they had circled around it for more than a mile beyond without effort to capture the same until the following day, when they assisted the 79th Divis[ion] in whose zone of advance it lay, in taking the village.

The best answer to the moot question of the performance of the 39th Regiment at Montfaucon is given in the record of A Company of the 1st Battalion of which Lieut. M.W. Haney (later Cap't) was then commanding[?]. I quote from the record of the company as it appears in the official archives, Historical Section, U.S. Army War College at Washington, D.C. as follows:

"When we hit Montfaucon hill (A Co., 39th), we were moved to the left in the sector of the 79th Divis[ion] and were abreast of the 3d Battalion (39th) on the firing line.

Lieut. Haney took the 3d and 4th Platoons of A Co., and worked them around to the right and flanked the top of the hill and captured over 100 prisoners. But, Col. Bolles (commanding 39th Inf.) came along and took these platoons, pushed ahead to the town of Septsarges (meuse) and left only the headquarters platoon. After the prisoners had been sent back and Sgt. Keller with four men sent to the left as a patrol, only one runner was left. We had to send him back to B & C companies and get a platoon each and then work about two hours to get back to the same sections of trenches that we had been in earlier with the headquarters platoon and secured prisoners. Because immediately after we left, the enemy came out of their dugouts, mounted some machine guns on the left flank and caused many losses. Had we been allowed to have another hour, before we were finally ordered to march on to support the 3d Battalion (39th), we could have taken the entire defences of Montfaucon as we had almost entirely encircled the hill. We lost 82 men and took over 100 prisoners here as well as several machine guns, eleven of which were in one pile."

Such is the story of Montfaucon where the German Crown Prinz had his headquarters and an armored observatory giving unobstructed vision for miles around the sector. The 39th Inf. therefore, with only part of a battalion available, could not have been expected to take this stronghold, bristling with machine guns, entirely alone. No French or British outfit would have done it either. Next day, the 39th assisted the 79th Divis[ion] who were lagging behind, in taking the town as they came abreast of it.[14]

14. Montfaucon, or Mount of the Falcon, was a seemingly impregnable 342-meter limestone height that dominated the Meuse-Argonne battlefield and the First Army's zone of attack. It was invaluable to the Germans as an observation post from which they could direct artillery fire on the advancing Americans. Montfaucon was in the 79th Division's zone, so that division was charged with taking the height. The veteran 4th Division was ordered to advance in an adjacent zone, east of the 79th. American planners hoped that the 79th's attack would pin Montfaucon's defenders in place, while the 4th would overcome light resistance in their front and encircle the height from the east and north. Inexplicably, the 4th quickly moved forward and continued to advance without encircling Montfaucon, while the 79th was delayed by heavy German opposition, finally captured the height a day later than planned and suffering heavy casualties in the process. The delay allowed the Germans to rush reinforcements into their line further north. Members of the 79th Division were harshly criticized for the delay. In reality, Major General Robert L. Bullard, commander of the American Third Corps (including the 4th Division), chose to ignore the order to assist the 79th, instead urging that his corps drive forward as quickly as possible and disregard what was happening in other sectors. He intentionally ignored two opportunities to assist the 79th Division. An excellent summary of this event may be found in William T. Walker, Jr.'s "The Chance of a Miracle at Montfaucon," in Edward G. Lengel, ed., *A Companion to the Meuse-Argonne Campaign* (New York: John Wiley &

By Oct. 6th, we of B Company have now finished our military police duty at Malancourt and rejoined the 1st Battalion, 39th again at Septsarges Wood where they have already seen action, been relieved by the 58th Inf. and are now in Brigade reserve. Major Winton of the 1st Battalion had been wounded on the night of Sep't 28th when the regiment was trying to push into the Bois de Fays.[15] The command of the battalion then passed to Lieut. M.W. Haney, previously mentioned. We stayed here several days more as brigade reserve, under almost continuous artillery bombardment and at night slept in holes we hollowed out of the ground. It rained most of the time. You would go to sleep despite the bombardment and awake in the morning with your feet and body partly submerged in water.

The 47th Inf., the other regiment of the 7th Brigade is now somewhere ahead in the Bois de Fays woods, alternating with the 3d Battalion 39th Inf. in holding on or trying to push through.

The slowness of the 79th Divis[ion] in coming abreast of us had exposed the left flank of the 39th Inf., holding the Bois de Fays woods, for several days and catching the withering, incessant artillery fire. In these days, both the 7th and 8th Brigades (39th, 47th, 58th, 59th Inf.) alternated in holding this position. Sometimes both flanks were exposed in the southern edge of the woods to a devastating machine gun barrage. The enemy was strictly on the defensive and fighting with his old time tenacity. He made perpetual counter attack but our losses were mostly from artillery and machine gun.

It was almost impossible to get food or reinforcement to these battalions in the daytime and almost equally so at night due to the almost continuous bombardment. Ammunition was scarce and whole companies became disorganized and scattered. Men were straggling about the woods everywhere, not knowing where they were or were supposed to be, except that they still hung on in the Bois de Fays.

Sons, Inc., 2014), 39–58. The full case against Bullard may be found in William Walker's *Betrayal at Little Gibraltar: A German Fortress, a Treacherous American General, and the Battle to End World War I*, published in 2016.

15. Roy Walter Winton (1883–1949), a native of Indiana, served as an enlisted man in the Regular Army from 1906–08. In the latter year, he was commissioned a second lieutenant in the infantry. Promoted to captain in May 1917, Winton served as major (temporary) of the 39th Infantry from February to December 1918, then was promoted to lieutenant colonel. He was wounded on the opening day of the Meuse-Argonne Offensive while leading the regiment's 1st Battalion. U.S. Adjutant General, *Official Army Register, January 1, 1920* (Washington, D.C.: U.S. Government Printing Office, 1920),674; Cole and Eberlin, *The History of the 39th U.S. Infantry*, 61; *The New York Times*, January 5, 1949.

Shows Battery A 16th Field Artillery, in foreground and troops of 47th Regiment Infantry in background, going forward to relieve men of 39th Regiment Infantry, who are in action on opposite slope. Near Septsarges, Meuse, France, September 28, 1918. U.S. Army Signal Corps Collection, National Archives, 45814 [2298V8].

Sergeant Painting and part of a squad including Stevens, O'Hara and Vinelli were lying on their bellies along a rusty narrow gauge railroad track in the Bois which was overgrown with weeds. Behind them in a deep shell hole among the trees was an overturned French tank. There was a machine gun in front of them but they could not quite locate its exact position as it only fired when the men moved or rustled the branches of the undergrowth. But it had to be captured and put out of commission so that the line could continue to advance.

"Get ready, you men," says Sgt. Painting, "We're gonna get that goddam kraut before he gets us."

"Where the Hell is he?" questions Stevens, "I can't see a thing that looks like a nest."

"Mebbe hes a uppa da tree," suggests Vinelli.

"I'll go over to the right a few yards and blow my whistle," says the sergeant. "That will attract his attention and draw fire. You birds keep down but keep yer eyes open and try to locate his position. When you find it we'll all move in quickly."

So the sergeant moved over to the left about 25 yards and blew his whistle. The machine gunners expecting an attack started shooting in panic in the direction from which they had heard the whistle. The three men crawled slowly forward until they could see the location of the gun which had raised out of the ground not twenty feet away from them. Vinelli then stood up and hurled a Mills grenade directly at their position. There was a loud explosion and flying debris. Sergeant Painting and the others then rushed up on them, charging with fixed bayonets. When they reached the trench they found the two gunners dead but the machine gun itself was untouched. The gun was concealed except when firing.

As they looked down the trench around a small bend, they saw another machine gun, partly concealed, pointing toward the right, away from them. As they looked, they saw the gun rise out of the trench and fire toward the right center. Our men were still unnoticed by the gunners, so O'Hara grabbed the handle of the captured machine gun, after pushing the dead gunner off to the side, swung the gun around so it pointed directly down the trench at the other gunners and ran a belt through. Painting, Stevens and Vinelli then rushed around behind the Boche gun and as they came close they found three of the four gunners wounded. Vinelli bayoneted the fourth as he refused to surrender. But their work was not yet over.

As they looked up they now saw about six Germans rushing them from behind through the trees with fixed bayonets. There was a short skirmish, but with two Germans down, the other four surrendered. After going through their pockets for souvenirs and information, O'Hara took them back a few hundred yards and turned them over to a corporal of E Company, who took them back to Battalion Headquarters at Septsarges.

A few yards back of the gun trenches was an old wooden shack camouflaged with branches and well hidden in the trees. Sergeant Painting and the others crept cautiously toward it but soon found it was deserted, although showing signs of recent occupation. It was probably the shack of the machine gunners just captured. German equipment of all kinds lay about. Even a pot of stew was sizzling over a perforated iron salamander of glowing hot embers. A few loaves of black bread lay on a crude table.

"Geeze! Who'd a thought we'd ever find hot chow in these God forsaken woods?" remarks O'Hara.

"Yeah, but look how lucky we've been all day," replies Stevens, "capturing guns an krauts. Wish the damn shellin' would quit. Gives me the jitters."

"Phooey! Turnip soup!" exclaims O'Hara, tasting the stew.

"Put in yer can of cornwillie an make it a real Irish stew, then," suggests Stevens.

"Righto," replies O'Hara, jabbing his bayonet into a tin of corned beef and dumping the contents into the stew.

About fifteen minutes later, all sat down to a hot savory stew, although a little salty, and smacked their lips because it proved palatable; above all, it was hot. It revived their spirits wonderfully.

About this time also, Vinelli was outside the shack fumbling around for nothing in particular, except to be on the watch for more Germans. Presently he came rushing into the shack all excited. The rest of the men made a quick grab for their rifles as they thought there was another raid on.

"Jesu Cristo!" exclaims Vinelli. "At last I founda! At last I founda!"

"Found what, you crazy headed Sicilian wop?" says Sergeant Painting. "Calm yerself! Calm yerself! More Boche coming, or what?"

"I'sa founda at last! Come on-a sarge! Come on-a Steve! Come on O'Hare!" excitedly entreats Vinelli. "I'll a showa you I'se a founda!"

So all followed Vinelli outside the shack. There, he pointed proudly to a large object hidden among the weeds.

"Looka de barrel, sarge! Vin-a-rooge! Vin-a-rooge!" says Vinelli with flaming, wide open eyes.

So they rolled the barrel out in the open and each man got out his aluminum mess cup to sample whatever it might prove to be.

"You tap it, Vinelli!" orders Sergeant Painting.

So Vinelli drove the butt-end of his rifle against the bung, knocking it in at the first blow. There was then a small explosion, a swish and a rush, and out comes a foamy brown liquid that hit Vinelli directly in the face and splashed wet all over his uniform.

"Sacristi bleuie! Figlio di puttana!" exclaims Vinelli. "Olda potato beer! Sacre Maria! Olda potato beer!"

All then rushed over to the barrel and captured some of the foamy liquid in their mess cups, drank it hurriedly, re-filling again and again.

"So this is Paris, eh Vinelli?" finally says Sergeant Painting.

"This is a Paree, a Vienn, Roma, Munica, alla togedder," replies Vinelli delightedly. "Ah one-a, two-a, three-a, feefty glassa already."

"I'sh can liksh the Kaisher an the whole dammit Germish Army," brags O'Hara with a thick tongue.

"Pipe down an pull in yer neck," orders Sgt. Painting. "Er does yer want the hull Kraut army on top of ya?"

"Bringa on the Knubs," says Vinelli passing gently into a glamourous slumber among the empty meat tins and papers strewn on the ground.

But heavy shells still continued to drop regularly among the trees.

As the division and the corps moved forward, they began to catch heavy shelling from the hills to the right of the Meuse River, toward Brieulles—another strong point of the enemy. This fire was continuous and was slowly devastating the Brigade.

The 3d Corps commander, Gen. Rob[er]t Lee Bullard, after several days of this, ordered the U.S. artillery and all the aeroplanes he could collect to bombard Brieulles Fort across the Meuse.[16] They were successful in silencing the fort thereby relieving the 4th Divis[ion] bottled up in the Bois de Fays and other small woods. The strain of cross firing from the Fort and the bombardment on the left flank of the Division had been tremendous but they had held on in these woods for over a week. Now they could be fed, reinforcements sent up, also a chance to relax somewhat and grab a little sleep.

Yes, we were reinforced and fed, but also made ready for some further work before we could get relieved on this Front. These last

16. Robert Lee Bullard (1861–1947), a native of Alabama, graduated from West Point in 1885 and saw service in the campaign to capture Apache leader Geronimo. He served as colonel of the 3rd Alabama Infantry during the Spanish-American War and the 39th U.S. Volunteer Infantry in the Philippine-American War. Bullard continued to serve in the Philippines and later in Cuba. Promoted to brigadier general in June 1917, and to major general (temporary) in August 1917, he led a brigade of the 1st Division to France, and commanded that division from December 1917 to July 1918. In the latter month, he assumed command of the Third Corps. In October 1918, Bullard took command of the Second Army and was promoted to lieutenant general (emergency) and major general (permanent) in October 1918 and November 1918, respectively. The Second Army was demobilized in April 1919, and Bullard returned to the United States the following month. He retired from the army in 1925. *Assembly* 7, no. 2 (July 1948): 3–5.

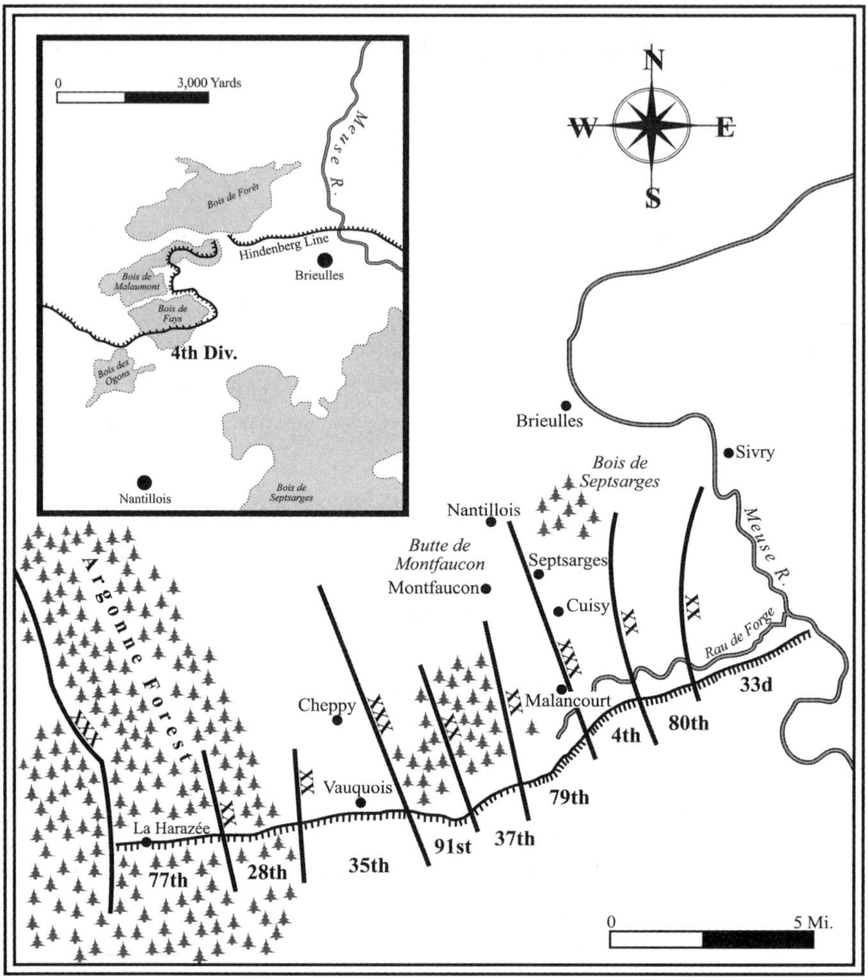

Meuse-Argonne

few days were only a drop in the bucket, as against what would follow for the 4th Divis[ion], in the Bois des Rappes, Bois de Forêt, Bois de la Côte LéMont and Bois de peut-de-Faux.

After the Bois de Fays was cleaned out, Maj. Gen. Bullard was promoted to lieutenant general and given command of the 2d U.S. Army then being formed in Lorraine on the St. Mihiel front for a belated push in the Briey Iron Basin, and toward Metz. General Hines of the 4th Divis[ion] was promoted to fill Gen. Bullard's place as commander of the III Corps (1st U.S. Army), he in turn being succeeded by Gen. Cameron and later by Gen. Mark L. Hersey. So, you see, all the Generals got promoted because we hung on in these treacherous woods.[17] All we got was the itch and additional promotion further up in the line where there wasn't a "brass hat" in sight but plenty of coal scuttle helmets.

After the 79th Divis[ion] had come up alongside of us back at Nantillois, we had then proceeded with the drive that took us through the Bois de Fays, Bois de Malaumont, Bois de Forêt and Hill 299 toward Aincreville. In all of these positions, it was the same old story of woods fighting such as was experienced by the Marines at Belleau Wood and other outfits and the same as we had just experienced in the Bois de Fays. There were numerous machine guns which must be surrounded and taken by frontal attack, almost continuous shelling by artillery, with gas, high explosive and everything the Germans had available. Shelling from the sides and even the rear. No shelter at night. Wet, dripping trees, gas burns and cooties. No warm food of any kind. The staccato of machine guns echoing through dark ravines and the acrid odor of chlorine and high explosive shell bursts floating on the air. It was a continuous performance, night and day. No rest, no sleep, no warm food, no shelter. Just holding on with our teeth.

The Bois de Forêt also, will always be remembered as a symbol of the heroism, the invincible progress and fortitude displayed by the men of the 4th Divis[ion]. The 39th Inf. attacked this position on the night of Oct. 9th, 1918. Gas shells, G.I. cans and machine gun bullets rained on us from every side. We lay under constant fire and advanced only by inches, it seemed. The enemy was determined to hold us back at all costs. There was a steady downpour of rain every day as it was late autumn. What sleep we did get was snatched momentarily. Paths through the woods were strewn and lined with dead. In one spot there were more than thirty including Germans. In another spot more than two hundred were scattered

17. Mark Leslie Hersey (1863–1934), a native of Maine, graduated from West Point in 1887. Hersey saw service in Cuba during the Spanish-American War, in China and the Philippines, and was promoted to colonel in July 1917. He was appointed a brigadier general, National Army, the following month. He trained the 155th Infantry Brigade and accompanied it overseas. Promoted to major general in October 1918, and assigned to command of the 4th Division, Hersey remained with the division during the occupation of Germany. Hersey was awarded the Distinguished Service Medal for his leadership of his brigade during the Meuse-Argonne Offensive and for his handling of his division during the occupation. Hersey became a brigadier general in the Regular Army in 1921, a major general in 1924, and retired the same year. *Sixty-Fifth Annual Report of the Association of Graduates of the United State Military Academy at West Point, New York, June 11, 1934* (Newburgh, NY: The Moore Printing Company, 1934), 153–56; U.S. Adjutant General's Office, *American Decorations*, 716.

around. German gun crews lay across their guns with fallen Americans all around them. Walking wounded came straggling back toward the rear. Some of the men were temporarily blinded from the effects of yellow cross gas, others groped along the paths.[18] Those with injured legs or feet, or no feet and who couldn't walk, crawled back to dressing stations or other places of safety. Other companies of new troops were constantly going in the lines to feed the roaring furnace of war. Old abandoned guns and tanks could be seen overturned in the ravines or along the paths. The German war machine slowly backed away but was fighting for every inch of ground that they relinquished to us.

For four horrible days the 39th struggled to get possession of the Bois de Forêt with the assistance of the 47th and 132d Inf. The only food available came out of cans. The nerves of the men were at the breaking point. Shells from U.S. batteries raced themselves to get over into the enemy lines and as quick in retaliation would come the shrill whine of H.E. shells as they struck plop! bang! in back and in front of us among the trees. All along the line there would be the clatter of automatic rifles and guns as they spit their venom toward the enemy who would quickly answer with the staccato of machine guns or the quick bursts of one pounders.

The first we knew of the nearness of the enemy was when Stevens raised his rifle and fired through the trees. He had caught sight of a single fleeting gray uniform as it darted about in front of him.[19] As we waited the Germans would come out at us through the trees in squads of a dozen or more with fixed bayonets. But after short vicious skirmishes in which a few would be killed, we would still hold on and even gain a few inches. The Boche would then withdraw as quickly as they had come. They watched every movement we made and counterattacked at any hour or all hours, so determined was their resistance.

We held them back with Mills grenades, Chauchat rifles and bayonets. The sight of the Germans infuriated the men. They were

18. Yellow cross, also known as mustard gas, was so called because the Germans marked the gas shells with bright yellow crosses.

19. Surviving 39th Infantry "Summary of Intelligence" reports note "visibility fair to poor" from October 5–8, 1918. Record Group 120, Records of the American Expeditionary Forces, World War I, Records of Combat Divisions 1917–1919, 4th Division, 4th Division Historical, Box 30, Folder: 39th Infantry, Summaries of Intelligence, 204–20.1, National Archives and Records Administration, College Park, Maryland.

Corpl. Erland Johnson. Company L, 58th Regiment Infantry, 4th Division, in first line trench, hastily constructed along the edge of a wood. On the northwest edge of the Bois de la Cote Lamont, Meuse, France. Fourth Division. October 2, 1918. U.S. Army Signal Corps Collection, National Archives, 24617 [920T8]. "Rigors of War. Note the drawn features, the result of more than a week under continuous machine gun fire and the blasting of heavy artillery, day and night without warm food or shelter," Howell wrote.

no longer just soldiers but demons intent on only one thing—to kill or get killed and have it over with. Men ran about blubbering to themselves. The ranks thinned out but the battle continued on.

As the Germans withdrew, mud caked ashen ghosts would frantically dig themselves holes in the side of the ravine and lay in wait exhausted for the next attack. Perhaps up the ravine would come a wheezing tank or two, creaking at every joint and making more noise than a street roller. All the time shells, timed to clock like accuracy, would continue to drop all around us. When the next attack came, the tanks would plow through a squad of the enemy or run down a machine gun, then move on to some other position along the front line.

This sort of fighting would continue on, hour after hour, without let-up. The men could not rest. There was no shelter, no water, no warm food. At intervals between the attacks the men would lay in their wet holes and pray for relief. But no relief came.

While here in the Bois de Forêt, we received by battalion runner, a citation from Gen. Bullard, the Corps commander previously mentioned, extolling us for the gallant conduct of the 7th and 8th Brigades in the Bois de Fays (Oct. 5th) over a week before. It ended with the words, "You are there. Stay there."[20] We expected we would have to stay here anyway as we did in the Bois de Fays as you would have to die to get relief. Instead of citations, we would rather have had a belly full of good hot chow and a chance to sleep a little while unmolested. But we finally drove through to hill 299 and won. We cleared the woods entirely of the enemy and reached the Army Corps objective on Oct. 11th, 1918. We held this position until the 13th against further counterattack and heavy artillery bombardment, some of which was directed at point blank range almost annihilating the regiment.

But on the night of October 13th however, the 39th Infantry was finally relieved by the 3d U.S. Division and went back to the rear as far as Septsarges Wood as division reserve. Other units of the 4th Division (58th & 59th Inf.) then proceeded on toward Bantheville, through Cunel, the Bois-des-Rappes in the heights of Cunel, and also aided the 3d Division at Romagne (meuse). Colonel Parsons of the 58th Infantry and his entire regimental staff were gassed here.[21] Colonel F.M. Wise, famous Marine

20. As General Bullard later explained, "The words were warm, but the reasoning cool. . . . Withdraw and you are lost. Enemy morale leaps, your own declines. You lose heavily. You are withdrawn. The incoming division loses heavily, regaining ground the enemy has had time to consolidate." Bullard, *American Soldiers Also Fought*, 107. General Orders No. 29, issued by Third Army Corps on October 5, 1918, cited the 4th Division for its "gallant conduct" in the seizure, "against great difficulties," of the Bois de Fay [*sic*] and holding it against "repeated and determined counter attacks" between September 26 and October 5, 1918. Cole, *The History of the 39th U.S. Infantry*, 73. One unidentified member of the 39th answered Bullard's "stay there" order by stating that remaining in position was costly and a tremendous test of nerve. Record Group 120, Records of the American Expeditionary Forces, World War I, Records of Combat Divisions 1917–1919, 4th Division, 4th Division Historical, Box 29, Folder: 39th Infantry, Histories, Commendations & Battle Participants, 4th Division, 204–11.4, Official History of the 39th Regiment of Infantry, 1917–1918, National Archives and Records Administration, College Park, Maryland.

21. James Kelly Parsons (1877–1960), a native of Alabama, served as a lieutenant in the 3rd Alabama Infantry during the Spanish-American War. He was commissioned a lieutenant in the Regular Army in 1899, and held the rank of major when the United States entered World War I. Promoted to lieutenant colonel in the National Army in August 1917 and to colonel in July 1918, Parsons commanded the 39th Infantry from September 28, 1918, until he was gassed on October 11, 1918. He remained in the army following the war, and was promoted to brigadier general in 1930 and to major general in 1936. He retired in 1941. Parsons was awarded the Distinguished Service Cross for his service from

commander of Belleau Wood, was now commanding the 59th Infantry in Brieulles Wood. These units of the 8th Brigade, in face of intense resistance and innumerable hand to hand encounters, had forced through the Bois-des-Ogons, Bois-de-peut-de-Faux, Bois-de-la-côte-LéMont, and Bois-de-Brieulles. They were held up somewhat at the town of Brieulles and could not take it but finally circled around it.

Their display of fortitude and courage was beyond compare in these dense woods against bayonet, machine gun and artillery bombardment. Colonel Wise says,

"Here in these woods had taken place a fight even more desperate than that of the Marines in Belleau Wood. There, we took twice our number in prisoners, but here, the prisoners were few. It was a fight to death. By now, I couldn't see any difference between civilian soldiers in the Regular Army, and professional fighters in the Marines. The last two weeks had taught me something that I had not learned in twenty-one years in the Marine Corps. I knew now that the civilian soldier can make good."[22]

On October 22d, the now thoroughly worn out 4th Division was ordered relieved from the sector, after being in action for twenty-four consecutive days and nights—a record never equaled by any other U.S. division in the World War I.

Most of this time it had rained, and there was sunshine for only three to four days out of the three week period. There was no protection from the dripping wet of the trees except such crude shelter as could be constructed on the spot. During this time we had been subjected to an almost continuous flank and rear artillery fire, had innumerable encounters with machine gun nests in frontal attack and in hidden positions, contested foot by foot by the famous Jaeger regiments (Kaiser's Own) and repulsed frequent counterattack. The Germans had brought against us in all, eight of their best divisions. The bulldog tenacity and fortitude displayed here by the men of the 7th & 8th Brigades, of the 4th Divis[ion] in holding and

September 27-October 11, 1918, when, knocked down by shellfire, he rallied his men and kept them well organized. The following day, he took command of the 39th Infantry and commanded it during successive attacks, and refused to be evacuated, even though he was so badly gassed he was unable to see. He was also awarded the Distinguished Service Medal for commanding the embarkation camp at St. Nazaire, France. U.S. Adjutant General, *Official Army Register, January 1, 1942* (Washington, D.C.: U.S. Government Printing Office, 1942), 1193; U.S. Adjutant General's Office, *American Decorations*, 490, 751.

22. Wise and Frost, *A Marine Tells It to You*, 262.

advancing for 24 continuous days and nights under constant pressure of the enemy without relief, can only be appreciated when it is considered that the French and English never kept their combat divisions in front line positions to exceed a week's time.

As we had been the only U.S. divis[ion] to pass the first and second line positions of the enemy on the first day of the drive (Sep't 26th Hindenburg Stellung), we are now the first division to pierce the Kriemhilde Stellung, another great enemy stronghold and which occurred in the Bois de Forêt, northeast of Cunel (meuse) on Oct. 11th, 1918, after several painful repulses.[23] The 1st, 3d, 32d, 80th and part of the 90th Divis[ion], with heavy artillery support, struggled along with us up the slopes toward the heights of Cunel and Romagne as part of the IIId and Vth Army Corps of the 1st U.S. Army, thus ending the second phase of the Meuse-Argonne battle.

The 4th was also the last of all the original divisions who started the Argonne drive (Sep't 26th) to be relieved. While the 8th Brigade (58th & 59th Inf.) was technically relieved by the 3d Divis[ion] of part of their sector about Oct. 15th, the actual relief was the then quite new and very weak 5th Division (U.S. Reg.) made up of draftees from Camp Logan, Texas. Up to this time, these boys have had very little battle experience under grueling heavy artillery fire.

As we of the 39th started back toward the rear, we commenced to see stragglers from the division supposed to be relieving the 8th Brigade of our division. This was unusual. All that we heard from these men coming away from the front, was not to the unmitigated credit of American arms either. There had been distressing losses in men and terrain for two days, through the inexperience and inefficiency of newly made officers (Sears-Roebuck), three month training camp products who became confused and in whom the men themselves had lost all confidence.

It became necessary, therefore, to place the 5th Division under the same command as the 3d Division, for a time, to hold them steady and maintain the line. Under the crunch and boom of heavy

23. According to the American Battle Monuments Commission, "The first penetration of the Hindenburg Line made by the First Army was on October 4 when in a dashing assault troops of the 4th Division captured the Bois de Fays." American Battle Monuments Commission, *American Armies and Battlefields in Europe*, 259–60. Many historians give the 32nd and 42nd Divisions credit for capturing the Côte Dame Marie and the Côte de Châtillon respectively, both key strongholds on the Hindenburg Line.

Second Lieut. A. S. Murray, liaison officer, with the mobile headquarters. Thirty-ninth Infantry Regiment, receiving orders from the Colonel, Col. Bolles, who is with the soldiers in the first line. Fourth Division. Near Nantillois, Meuse, France, September 28, 1918. U.S. Army Signal Corps Collection, National Archives, 24616 [919T8].

artillery bombardment, the whine and snap of machine gun bullets through the trees in deep dark ravines, and the gas shelling, their officers were useless, although they had probably looked good on some college parade ground. Under conditions at the front, the unwarning crack of an Austrian 88 or a machine gun concentration, the men would stampede in all directions. They even threw away their rifles—their only protection.[24]

Some of the units of the 8th Brigade (4th Division) were therefore forced to turn back to the old sector and again hold their old

24. Howell is unnecessarily harsh in his criticism of the 5th Division. As he indicates, the division was technically a Regular Army organization and contained some Regulars, but like the 4th Division, was brought to full strength with volunteers and draftees from all parts of the country, or "at large." The division participated in the St. Mihiel operation and suffered more than 1,500 casualties. On October 14, 1918, the 5th began an assault under heavy enemy machine gun and rifle fire but managed to capture the town of Cunel and the Bois de la Pultière. The next day, the doughboys managed to reach the Bois des Rappes, but their confused commander ordered them to withdraw on the morning of October 16 (an order that led to his removal). Finally, on October 21, the 5th captured the Bois des Rappes, but was withdrawn the following day, after having suffered more than 3,500 casualties.

positions for several days longer, or until the 5th Division stragglers could be rounded up in the back areas by military police and reorganized. This was accomplished around the town of Malancourt, where you will remember my company had previously cleared traffic on the road. There, General Pershing placed the 5th Division under the command of Major General Hanson E. Ely and a few other selected officers, with orders to make good—and they did.[25] They re-entered the lines once more as a division, regained all the terrain previously lost and went on with success, clearing the woods north of Cunel and took the town of Aincreville (meuse) on Oct. 30th. On Nov. 11th, they were at the Stenay-Jametz line.

Bois de Foret, looking east toward Meuse River. On road running north out of Brieulles, Meuse, France, November 21, 1918. U.S. Army Signal Corps Collection, National Archives, 40075 [865D8].

25. Hanson Edward Ely (1867–1958), a native of Iowa, graduated from West Point in 1891. After service in the Philippine-American War, Ely commanded the 7th Infantry during the Vera Cruz Campaign in 1914. After America entered World War I, Ely served as chief of staff of the 1st Division, then took command of the 28th Infantry and led it in the Battle of Cantigny. Promoted to brigadier general in the National Army in June 1918, he assumed command of a brigade in the 2nd Division. Promoted to major general that October, and given command of the 5th Division, Ely led that division through the remainder of the war. He was promoted to major general in 1923 and retired in 1931. He was awarded both the Distinguished Service Cross and Distinguished Service Medal. *Assembly* 18, no. 1 (Spring, 1959): 83–84; U.S. Adjutant General's Office, *Official Army Register, January 1, 1932* (Washington, D.C.: U.S. Government Printing Office, 1932), 815.

My division, now all worn out, is already started back toward the rear. The men are sick from diarrhea, flu, colds, gas burns and cooties. We are a scurvy lot and have earned a well-deserved rest. We are absolutely filthy, officers and all, and are a sorry looking lot, but we had advanced over thirteen kilos in combat under fire, at a cost of some 6,000 dead to take 2,737 prisoners. Some companies lost all their officers twice. Other companies were commanded only by corporals. My company had forty men and one officer left, out of the one-hundred fifty men and three officers we started out with on Sep't 26th at Béthincourt. And what a sight these men were. Watery, red-rimmed eyes, heavy from loss of sleep, gas burn and hardship. Mud-covered from head to foot, with their muddy tin helmets askew. Ragged, torn uniforms and bristling mud-caked beards. Our lieutenant, now a seasoned veteran, was as ragged as the rest. He had been promoted to a provisional captaincy for his action and courage on the field in this treacherous woods fighting. This sort of redeemed him in the eyes of his company.

It is almost inconceivable, that men could stand the rigors of three weeks continuous fighting, day and night, under the most nerve-racking and exhausting conditions, without warm food or shelter, retain their happy spirit and still live through it. But we did and became known thereafter as the "Bull Dog Fourth."[26]

Major General Cameron, who had originally organized and commanded the 4th Division and brought them over to France, again took command, succeeding Major General J.L. Hines during the progress of the drive. When he saw the condition of his men, he began quibbling with the High Command for their long overdue relief without success. Finally, in desperation, he informed

26. Correspondent and A.E.F. Colonel Frederick Palmer referred to the "bull-dog 4th Division" and its "bull-dog commander" Major General John L. Hines. Frederick Palmer, *Our Greatest Battle (The Meuse-Argonne)* (New York: Dodd, Mead and Company, 1919), 340. The division was more commonly referred to as the "Ivy Division," a reference to the green, four sided ivy leaves adopted as the division's insignia before the 4th left the United States. Prepared by General George H. Cameron, the design was derived from the Roman number IV, with the ivy meaning "steadfast and loyal." Bach and Hall, *The Fourth Division*, 37–38. According to Captain G.C. Sergeant, Howell's Company B contained only about 40 officers and men at the end of the Meuse-Argonne Offensive. Record Group 120, Records of the American Expeditionary Forces, World War I, Records of Combat Divisions 1917–1919, 4th Division, 4th Division Historical, Box 29, Folder: 39th Infantry, History, [M.G., Supply, Hdrs, 1st, 2nd, 3rd Bn, and Co. A thru M], 4th Div., 204–11.4, Official History of the 39th Regiment of Infantry, 1917–1918, National Archives and Records Administration, College Park, Maryland.

General Pershing that "either the 4th Division goes back to a rest area, or I'll be relieved of its command." Both occurred. We were sent back, and the command of the division was turned over to Major General Mark L. Hersey. We now become part of the 2d U.S. Army in Lorraine, our old sector near St. Mihiel.

As it is the end of the 1st and 2d phases of the great Argonne battle, the 3d or last phase will be started immediately by rested veteran divisions, ending the war. These divisions are part of the original 1st U.S. Army and had been left at St. Mihiel when we opened the Argonne drive. They will now come forward and take up the last phase of the famous battle, whose objective is the famous town of Sedan (Ardennes) and which controls the railroad running southeast between Maubeuge and Metz. The railroad was the main outlet of the German armies in France and Belgium. U.S. troops were opposite the gates of Sedan as the armistice was concluded. The 1st and 42d Divisions could have entered the town, and in fact a few of its stragglers did enter, but the official honor was reserved to the French, for sentimental reasons.

While the above divisions were pushing back and following the enemy in these last few days, we are on our way southeast to the Toulon sector of Lorraine. As there is no available transportation, we must hike, over old shell craters and mud and through deep dark woods to the rear. As we go farther back, we take the roads by day and sleep in the woods at night.

While this hike was a hardship and continued for nearly eight days, it was pleasant to me at least, as it was a relief from the grim actuality of war. The country through which we now marched was new and bizarre to us. It presented new towns, new scenes and possibly new hope. We hiked at an easy pace and passed through the following towns, some of which have known the tramp of soldier's feet for centuries past, in history.

Malancourt (meuse)
Forges
Regnéville
Fresnes-en-Woëvre
Charny (meuse)
Hattonchâtel
Vigneulles
Buxerulles

Apremont (meuse)
Bouconville
Gironville
Jouy-sous-les-côtes (et Moselle)

"In the next war, if I gits through this one O.K., I'm gonna join the Salvation Army an do all my fightin' wit a doughnut," muses Stevens out loud, hiking slowly along with the column.[27]

"Aw, gwan," answers Brizee. "Ya don't fight wit a doughnut, you'se eats 'em."

"Yep, that's right," says O'Hara. "You eats 'em if you sees any, same as yer supposed ta do wit a Boche."

Silence for a few moments as the company continues hiking along toward the south.

"If I ever sees a doughnut lassie again, I'm gonna eat her too," says Stevens, speaking up suddenly.

"Yud have ta take a bath furst," remarks O'Hara.

"Well, mebbe. Per'aps I'm lousy an needs a tub, but you're twice as worst as me," replies Stevens.

"Ho, ho, ho," laughs O'Hara. "If ya ever gits them cockle burrs outta yer hair, an yer face washed, I'll think ya are a woman an probably wanna kiss ya myself."

"Mebbe you'll try, but probably you'll die," replies Stevens. "They just ain't no cheek kissin' Irish frawgs allowed ta live in this man's army."

At the head of the column of war weary soldiers, moping silently along the road with the rest of us, is our grandiose lieutenant. He seems more dead than alive. His face is covered with bristle in thick patches of black. Every step on the dusty road seems to give him pain and his eyes are expressionless. He bows his head like the defeated Napoleon he is not, as the flaps of his ragged trench coat flutter statically in the breeze. At last—relief from the monstrosity called war. Temporary relief perhaps, but a chance to live and breathe again in the glorious sunshine, far to the rear.

27. Salvation Army "doughnut lassies" and their doughnuts were legendary among American forces in France. See Evangeline Booth and Grace Livingston Hill, *The War Romance of the Salvation Army* (Philadelphia: J.B. Lippincott, 1919).

Chapter 12

On Furlough in Southern France

Having completed the long hike from the Argonne battlefields southeastward, we have now arrived at the small, picturesque, village of Jouy-sous-la-côtes (muerthe et Moselle), near Commercy (meuse), about October 28th. We enter the village from the rear, where the low hills contain old abandoned trench systems and a fort, which had been in use in the earlier stages of the war, 1914 to 1916. Here our time will be taken up in resting, cleaning equipment while awaiting further orders, as this town is probably just a temporary stop in the zone of the 2d U.S. Army Reserve.

There were thick vineyards on the hillsides to the left of the village. We roamed at will through them, looking for an occasional grape that might still be hanging on the vines, overlooked by the vintners. We found quite a few too. They were small, and of the sour, white, variety used in the making of dry wines and champagne, but they were a great treat to us, because we had not been favored with fruit desserts of any kind since leaving the U.S. Knowing the care bestowed on vineyards by their owners, we were careful not to break or otherwise injure the vines.

Sergeant Painting is now the Top Kick of the company once more, as Sgt. Nolan has just left us to attend officer's training school near Gondrecourt. Our lieutenant, too, has disappeared again, but we suspect that he has gone over to Toul or Nancy to get a bath, a square meal, a new set of captain's bars or a clean uniform.

Only the sergeants knew where we were. The men had no idea of our location. They were indifferent anyway, but they knew there was no war around here as the village was too clean. All the houses were occupied by thrifty burghers and there was no other army outfit in the town except us. Our chow-gun also, was lost somewhere in the fog behind us but we knew it would show up presently, and then life would be complete.

A butcherie or butcher shop, located on the corner of the main street of the village, was selected for our company headquarters. Belkin, O'Hara and myself, with Sergeant Painting, Stevens and the company clerk, occupied the place as a billet. We hung our guns and accoutrements on the bare meathooks around the walls, using the counters to sit or sleep on. It was the cleanest, driest, most comfortable place we had known in weeks. But you can get used to anything in the army in wartime.

"I wonder if they've hung any real meat on those hooks since back in 1914?" muses Belkin, surveying the inside of the butcherie.

"Dunno," says O'Hara, "unless mebbe it wuz a rasher of kosher ham."

"Who ever heard of kosher ham, anyway?" questions Stevens sneeringly.

"How about smoked dried beef then, without any rind?" replies O'Hara. "Looks like it, don't it?"

"Tell us if he's right, er not," says Stevens, turning to Belkin. "You wuz a schochat butcher in New Brunswick, afore you wuz a Chauchat gunner in the Army."

"Aw shut up!" exclaims Belkin somewhat peeved. "You birds can't kid me. Phooey on all you mackerel snatchers, anyhow."

Just at that moment our rolling kitchen rattled over the cobbles in the street outside, with Vinelli and several others chasing along behind loudly clanging their mess kits. Soon O'Hara, Belkin and the rest of us were lining up for chow.

"Hey, Vinelli! Whatta they got fer chow tonight?" yells O'Hara to Vinelli, who was first man at the head of the chow line.

"Bacon, goldbricks," answers Vinelli, moving away with a full mess tin.

"Aw nuts! Bacon on Friday! I can't eat that!" says O'Hara.

"I can't eat bacon on Friday er any other day," says Belkin, Jewishly, as both soldiers came alongside the mess sergeant who was dishing out the chow.

"Yer eats it an likes it, er ya goes without," says the mess sergeant. "Do ya think we has patey de froy grass every day, just fer you two birds?"

"How about a few army beans then, sarge?" says Belkin.

"You'll take mush, an keep yer clam shut," replies the sergeant. "An yer lucky ta git two extra spoonfuls of molasses fer dessert, too."

"Have it your way, sarge. But who is the jam for?" says O'Hara, spotting a couple of cans of jam on a box close by.

"Its fer the lieutenant, if he shows up," replies the sergeant. "An if he don't show up, I gits it. Catch on?"

"Sure. Goldbricks allus gits the gravy," says O'Hara, shuffling off in the dark with his tin of mush and molasses.

Belkin sits alone on a nearby rock drinking black coffee, in which he occasionally dunks a big hunk of bread.

Next morning, orders came through to send some of the oldest veterans selected from each company of the regiment, on a long looked-for furlough.[1] Combat outfits seldom if ever got to Paris. That delight was reserved for lieutenants and others of higher rank. A combat soldier had to go A.W.O.L. to see the Champs Elysees or the Rue de Dieu. But some of us were now going to get a vacation anyway and that was something.

Being in the company headquarters at the time, I pulled strings with Sergeant Painting to be among those selected, along with six others including Belkin and Stevens. More would be selected also from the battalion and the regiment, to go along at the same time. Soon we will leave the company temporarily and start on this welcome junket which is proving a pleasant anticipation. Those who would have to stay behind, now begin to tell us how lucky we are in being selected. It is to be our first play spell since we joined the army. Uncle Sam is not such a bad scout after all.

1. The first leaves were granted on October 19. About 85 men were taken to Le Mont Dore, where they were quartered in "excellent hotels and treated in every way as other guests would be, except that they didn't pay the bill themselves." Record Group 120, 4th Division Historical, Box 29, Folder: 39th Infantry, Histories, Commendations & Battle Participants, NARA.

Therefore, in the early morning of Oct. 30th, we leave Jouy-sous-la- côtes in a motor truck, later joining a cavalcade and picking up men from other battalions enroute.[2]

"Wonder where we're bound for, anyway?" worries Stevens.

"Dunno," says I. "Orders reads, it's a seven day furlough."

"Hot ziggadee!" exclaims Stevens. "Seven whole days to eat an play."

"I can't believe it!" says Belkin.

Our motor truck now passes through Toul (et Moselle) and after about one and one-half hours, we enter the proud city of Nancy. This is a famous lace, glass manufacturing, garrison and university town of about 120,000 inhabitants, dating back to the 16th century and has matchless 18th century architecture, all of which we were then in complete ignorance.

We entered through one corner of the town via the Rue de Toul, finally arriving at a place called the Parc St. Marie, which is located on the Avenu de Garenne facing the Ecole de Beaux Arts or arts college. It is very beautiful here. Well-kept lawns, parkways and trees, with a magnificent wrought iron gateway at the entrance of the parc.

Directly back of the Parc, or at one side, is the Nancy Thermal or public baths. These were located in an ornate building of Greco-Roman design, in white sandstone. The baths were taken over and operated by the Y.M.C.A. who met us here with hot chocolate and sandwiches. I am not ashamed to say that I got in line three or four times. Before we could get a handout however, we must take a bath and get some of the cobwebs of war out of our systems.

2. Howell was fortunate to leave the company at this time. Training Schedule Number 1, issued on October 29, 1918, directed that from October 30 to November 2 the men of the 39th Infantry were to engage in close order drills, instruction in saluting, and "other military courtesies." Clean arms and equipment were required at all formations, and "neatness" expected "at all times." Drill periods were to last from 30 to 60 minutes, while "snappiness of movement and precision as to detail will be required." Saturday mornings were to be devoted to the inspection of the men, their arms, equipment and billets, and to "competitive tests." Training Schedule Number 2, issued on November 1, directed that from November 4–9, the men would engage in ten minutes of "setting up exercises" in "a snappy manner and without rest," followed by an hour of squad close order drill. Rifle companies were then required to conduct an hour of squad drill in attack formations, an hour of individual and group instruction on weapons, and an hour each of platoon close order drill and attack formations. Record Group 120, Records of the American Expeditionary Forces, World War I, Records of Combat Divisions 1917–1919, 4th Division, 4th Division Historical, Box 32, Folder: 39th Infantry, Training Memos and Schedules 50.4, National Archives and Records Administration, College Park, Maryland.

On the lawn to the rear and left side of the thermal, we stripped naked on the grass, practically in full view of the Y.M.C.A. ladies who had their tables of eats on a porch running around the thermal building. Had they cared to turn their heads, they would have been properly shocked. But modesty, private dressing rooms or civilian inhibitions, had no place here. We left our old war soaked, mud caked, cootie infested clothing in a pile on the grass, went into the thermal for a hot bath and then received a complete, new, clean, outfit of clothing from the army quartermaster located in the cellar. Then and only then, were you allowed to get in line for your handout. This procedure, therefore, took the greater part of the day, as there was several hundred men altogether from the regiment to be accommodated. To kill time, we just strolled around the parc and took it easy, wondering what was to come next.[3]

Along about five p.m. all were taken care of and ready to be on our way. We marched down to the LaGare (R.R. station) where we found a long black train awaiting us. It was a first class Continental train, too, with compartments a-la-old-country and not the usual 40 & 8 boxcars we were accustomed to and had expected. This train was fully provisioned for a long run as we soon found out, but none of us had the slightest inkling as to our destination. What surprise! What thrills of expectation! We were like schoolboys just starting out on a picnic, instead of old soldiers on a binge. Our only thought was pleasure, but we knew we were being treated to "real class" this time and that pleased us immensely.

We stayed on this train a night and a day, with frequent stops to allow the men to get out, stretch their legs and fill their canteens with water. The supply officer came along the train at one of the stops enroute and told us that there was plenty of extra hardtack and sugar a few cars ahead. If we cared for any of it, all we need do was to go forward and help ourselves. I didn't care for hardtack or

3. The recreation center at Nancy, opened in September 1918, was described in one report as "one of the outstanding features of the Y.M.C.A., A.E.F." The Nancy Thermal, located about half a mile from the heart of the city, contained a gigantic swimming pool capable of accommodating 400 men at a time. American authorities successfully negotiated for the use of the pool every day, after noon. More than 200,000 American soldiers were given baths in the Thermal. As Howell indicates, the Quartermaster Department installed a salvage plant at the Thermal as well, so that incoming soldiers could be provided with fresh clothing. According to one report, "The popularity of this experiment was instantaneous and widespread." In addition, the Y.M.C.A. provided coffee and sandwiches. James Albert Sprenger and Franklin Spencer Edmonds, eds., *The Leave Areas of the American Expeditionary Forces, 1918–1919* (Philadelphia: The John C. Winston Company, 1928), 28–29.

dogbiscuit, but I took my messkit cup (canteen cup), which holds about a pint, and filled it full of white granulated sugar. It must have been two to three pounds at least. This certainly was a great luxury for a soldier as hungry for sweets as I was. I took the sugar back to the compartment and showed it to Belkin and Stevens. Their eyes bugged out of their heads. They just couldn't believe you didn't have to steal it. So up they went also and got some of the same, along with three cans of Carnation milk that Stevens had discovered. This we poured over the sugar and ate with rare satisfaction and relish.

Later on, after we had reached our destination, this gorge of milk and sugar affected me. My legs and knees swelled up to about twice their normal size. When you stuck your finger in the swelling, it would leave a nice dimple or depression, but there was no pain of any kind.

I thought I had contracted inflammatory rheumatism after our long exposure to the wet and slime of the front line. This was not the case however. I didn't want to report to the medical officer as I had no pain and could walk O.K. Neither did I want to be sent to a hospital in a leave area when I could be out enjoying this new found freedom. So I just did nothing about the swelling and in less than two days it had completely disappeared as mysteriously as it had come so I was myself again. The way I figured it out, I had absorbed so much sugar that nature couldn't take care of its proper distribution and assimilation all at once, so it was stored in cavities around the leg muscles until it could be properly used. The fact that it didn't make me sick to eat it, showed that my system needed the sugar and used it up as quickly as possible. We were always hungry anyway and could eat anything as long as it was palatable.

The trip into southern France was itself uneventful, but a feast for the eyes. The grass was getting greener every day. Quaint and picturesque tiled roof brick houses in a variety of colors, some all stone houses, funny telegraph poles with white porcelain insulators, lethargic cattle with peculiar long horns, also sheep and long whiskered goats. The goats were usually attached to little two wheeled carts carrying from two to four milk cans in side baskets over the wheels. Dogs were also used for the same purpose. There were also women railroad gate crossing tenders. All this was interesting panorama to us. And what a lot of fun we had trying to figure out our destination, by deciphering French signs along the route. Most of them however were advertising for vins and Chocolate Menier. The station names meant little to us as we had no maps to follow our course.

This part of France was untouched by war and was peaceful and quiet. Even the native peasants were picturesque in their manner of dress. We knew that we were heading south in the general direction of the French Jura, the Carcasonne, the Basque country or the Riviera but couldn't make out for sure.

"I betcha we're in Switzerland," volunteers Belkin.

"Gee! Looka the real snow up on that mountain," says Stevens, "I'm gonna take a long ski ride if I gits a chanct to go up there."

"I'm gonna buy a big Swiss cheese an eat it all by myself," says Belkin.

Our ultimate destination however was Le Mont Dore (puy de dome) a rather small village or town, but a famous watering place high up in the Auvergne Mountain Range near La Barbour [La Bourboule] (puy de dôme). This section was near Spain, Switzerland, Italy and not far from the Mediterranean.

Suddenly our train came to a dead stop in front of a long rambling station made of fancy colored rococo tile. It had shiny white ramps and a gendarme or two slowly strolled up and down in front of the same.

"Looka the funny engine!" exclaims Stevens as we saw another train waiting on a siding.

"Just like I saw in moving pictures," says Belkin. "This is a swell part of Yurrup all right. Listen to the conductor blow'in his fish horn."

"He's got more gold braid than Admiral Jellicoe," says Stevens.[4]

"Boy! Are we lucky, or are we lucky? Just think of O'Hara smudging around the mud back there in Jouy," remarks Belkin.

At Clermont-Ferrand near the base of the mountain range, we now change trains and then proceed slowly up the mountain to Le Mont Dore. Our route from northeastern France had been somewhat as follows:

Nancy (et Moselle dep't)

Langres (haute marne)

4. Admiral Sir John Jellicoe (1859–1935) was commander-in-chief of the Royal Navy's Grand Fleet during the Battle of Jutland (1916).

Dijon (côte d'or)
Charolles (saône et loire)
Moulins (allier)
St. Germain (allier)
Vichy (allier)
Clermont-Ferrand (puy-de-dôme)

Le Mont Dore itself is noted for its healing curative waters. This Thermal and others of which there are several in this section, was well known to the old Romans who first located here and built numerous baths of which they were very fond. It is near the high peak of Mont de Dore and also the famous Puy de Dome peak of the Auvergne Mt. Range. Most of the soldiery had never heard of this place before but this section is well known to all tourists in southern France. The town of Le Mont Dore was taken over entirely by the Y.M.C.A. and the U.S. Army as a leave area for soldiers on furlough. All of its several large hotels, pensions, etc., were operated by the U.S. Army or rather under its supervision as the regular owners and staffs were still on the job as employees of the U.S. The large Casino or gaming house was operated by the Y.M.C.A. who passed out hot chocolate gratis and sold cookies at the bar instead of ze grande liquer. The former gaming rooms and the lounge were now reading rooms supplied with American, French and English periodicals and magazines, many of which were of ancient vintage. There were also writing tables and supplies handy for the soldiers. Many a delayed, long overdue billet-doux or message home was written here. As to games, the boys had to be content with checkers or ping pong instead of boule, baccarat or roulette. Card playing was not allowed either. If ping pong became boresome, the boys just went out somewhere away from the eyes of officers and enjoyed a game of good old army craps, but never around the Casino.

The Casino itself was constructed of about two thirds glass and was very ornate and elegant in appearance. Most of its rich, luxurious velvets and tapestries had been removed for obvious reasons. Hard boiled soldiers of the line were none too careful with their hob nail shoes or anything else, so expensive furnishings were taken out and replaced with heavy duty furnishings. The Casino Bldg., also contained a fully equipped theater seating about 700 persons. Here we were invited to see without charge, mixed British, American and French vaudeville acts sent direct from Paris.

In a leave area, most of all you need a little money to buy whatever may be for sale such as souvenirs, chocolate bars, cigarettes, wines or food. On arriving at a leave area, usually the boys would be without this commodity due to long overdue paydays. Therefore there was an Army Quartermaster Paymaster in each leave area where you could draw a stipulated amount of your back pay. This made everybody happy and a furlough would have been a blank without it.

It was not my privilege to stop at one of the large resort hotels in Le Mont Dore of which there are several good ones. These were already filled to capacity. Belkin, Stevens and I were assigned instead with six other soldiers to a small but exquisitely appointed Pension operated by a widow who had lost her husband and two sons in the war. I have forgotten to mention that up until we had arrived in Nancy, we had not seen a woman of any kind for a long interval. For weeks at a time while we were at St. Mihiel and then later in the Argonne, all that we had seen day or night was men. Our lives were just a routine of war and destruction. We had partly forgotten what a woman looked like. It may seem strange to you, but when we saw these clean, smiling American Y.M.C.A. women at the Nancy Thermal Baths, they appeared almost as sacred as Madonnas to us and we could have kissed their hands in worshipful reverence. Sex didn't enter into it then. They were just clean women to us, like our mothers and we respected them. It was in a like manner that we regarded the widow of the Pension. She was so motherly and kind to us that we all loved her. As we moved around Le Mont Dore however, we soon saw other women such as bar maids, shoppe workers, milliners, Y.M.C.A. women, etc., so the spell soon wore off. Always hungry for forbidden sweets and excitement of any kind, the soldiers looked around for strange pantries to rummage in—and a lot of the boys found them too.

It was here that we had our first taste of a French feather bed since we had entered the country. Oh! Boy! The feathers were about two feet thick and you would sink way down in their luxurious warmth and downy mass as if you were being covered with gobs of beach sand or rolling in bread dough. All this was some contrast to the usual mud hole called a dugout or barracks with chickenwire bunks. We hated the thought of ever going back to the wet and slime of the Front, dead men, noise and cooties.

This was a peaceful paradise and we wanted to stay as long as possible.

One bright morning, Stevens, Belkin and I visited the elite bath house or Thermal to try out the mineral water baths. The Thermal was run by the Y.M.C.A. and you were given two white towels, soap and the service of a native male attendant, all for the small sum of ten cents. The center aisle or foyer of the bath house was like the knave of a cathedral with a high ceiling and a system of stone arches and pillars. Off from this aisle on each side were private bath rooms. The bath itself was set level with the floor like a swimming pool, faced with cut stone or tile and rectangular dimensions of approx. 5 X 8 ft. It was about three to four feet deep. A little stairway led down into the bath, which was filled with water up to your knees. While the water was not actually hot, it was not artificially heated either but just as it came piped in from the rocks at a temp. of approx. 100–110 F. It was sort of yellowish in color and the steam smelled a little of sulphur. I was told it contained such minerals as iron, bicarbonates, arsenic and salicylates. There were eight to twelve of the springs supplying the Thermal, each spring being given a name such as the Madaleine, the Caesar, the Chanteurs, etc., the first being the most famous for its curative properties. There was real "old country class" to this bath house and we were fifteen cent millionaires enjoying our whims and taking the cure.

"I'm gonna get gassed," announced Stevens, after we had dressed.

"Won't be the first time" says Belkin. "Er the last either."

"I mean I gonna get gassed in here" says Stevens opening a door leading into a small alcove.

"How do ya do it?" says Belkin. "They ain't no vin-rooge in there."

So we entered. Around the walls of the rectangular room at certain intervals hung a rubber tube about a foot long, attached to a gas cock, with a place for a mouthpiece. You just grabbed the rubber tube from the wall, turned on the gas and inhaled the gas vapor that was piped in from the rocks surrounding the mineral-water springs. Inhalation of these gases was popular with the old superstitious Romans, who placed great faith in their curative properties for asthma, colds and lung affections. Also bronchitis, hay fever and headaches.

The mineral water from the springs is bottled and sent all over the world. Two confections, called pectoral paste and barley sugar, are both made from the waters of the Madeleine spring. Taking everything into consideration, Le Mont Dore was one of those European watering places you read so much about in travel books, but seldom have the opportunity to visit. While it is not as pretentious perhaps as Cannes, Nice, Biarritz, Aix-la-Bains or Dieppe, it was highly pleasing and satisfactory to us as the guests of Uncle Sam. We enjoyed it the same as though we were making a high priced continental tour. While we had no valets or maids and did not put up at the Sarciron, Metropole or the Hotel-des-Sapins where more fortunate soldats were billeted, still, you could feel quite exclusive at the Villa Jeanne-de-Arc, which suited Belkin, Stevens and myself to a T, with its winding wrought iron staircase and French casements. We would like to have stayed here indefinitely. Boy! How we envied a small battalion of transport soldiers and military police who were quartered here for the duration of the war. They had it soft, but when we talked to any of them, they were all dissatisfied and wished (so they would have us believe) they could be at the front where there was more excitement.[5]

One day, Belkin and I took a stroll up a narrow mountain path, just to view the panorama of the valley below. After we had gone some distance, we came upon a little old lady seated outside the doorway of a small stone house. She held a circular or half round, crescent shaped contrivance in her lap, on which was mounted between eighteen and twenty-five small spools filled with thread. As we soon learned, she was engaged in fabricating a form of handmade lace. We watched her deft fingers for some time with interest. Finally, pointing to the lace I inquired, "combine, madam? (how much).

5. In September 1918, the commanding general of the Services of Supply requested the establishment of thirty Leave Areas and tasked the Y.M.C.A. with recommending locations for the facilities. Ultimately 19 leave areas and 39 leave towns were established. The Y.M.C.A. offered La Bourboule and Mont Dore, which combined would be known as the Auvergne Leave Area. Casinos at both locations were rented "after great difficulty" and opened about September 15, 1918. The area was a summer resort, and had just experienced a successful season, so the hotelkeepers and workers were reluctant to keep the facilities operating through the winter. In addition, both locations were somewhat inaccessible for supplies and Mount Dore suffered from "mountain dampness." In January 1919 the facilities were closed due to the impossibility of heating the hotels and "other difficulties connected with administration," including the failure of the mayor and local authorities to prevent the sale of cognac to American troops and to cooperate with "the proper regulation of moral conditions." Sixty Y.M.C.A. personnel operated both La Bourboule and Mont Dore. Sprenger and Edmonds, *Leave Areas*, 19–21.

She arose smiling and entered her little house, presently returning with an assortment of her handiwork which was of the most beautiful workmanship. We selected and purchased a number of pieces, as the cost was insignificant, and also because we thought our people back home in the U.S. would appreciate receiving some of this excellent product, direct from France.

Later we took it down to the Y.M.C.A. in the casino, to mail it home. The Secretary informed us that we would have to mark the nature of the contents on the outside of the package. Therefore I labeled mine "lace" as instructed, being somewhat of a bonehead. Belkin purposely forgot to label his package, except the address, being of a race with a shrewder nature than me and not so quick to obey static suggestion. Some months later after we had moved into Germany, he received a letter from his people stating how pleased they were to receive the lace. Mine has never arrived to this day. Draw your own conclusions.

A Y.M.C.A. uniform, like that of a soldier, conveys every form of human estate. There were all kinds of people working with the Y in France in 1918. I believe however, that the Y actually did many things for the welfare and entertainment of the A.E.F. soldat that they never got proper credit for, because the soldier did not know if these gratuities came from the Y, the Red Cross or the Army. The Y was active and effective in many leave centers behind the lines, hospitals, and so on, but the men expected to see more of them at the front. Because we seldom saw them, on our front at least, the men were quick therefore, to condemn. If they did appear occasionally with chocolate bars or cigarettes for sale, the officers were always given the first opportunity to purchase and very often took the meagre supply available before half a company could even purchase a stick of gum. This would often cause the men to utter such remarks as "gahdamn Y" or "goldbrick officers get everything."[6]

6. Surprisingly, this was not one of the three most common soldier complaints made against the Y.M.C.A., according to General Johnson Hagood, chief of staff of the Services of Supply. Those complaints included overcharging for goods, selling tobacco intended as gifts, and turning soldiers away from canteens because they did not belong to particular organizations. Sprenger and Edmonds, *Leave Areas*, 80–81. In his collection of interviews with former doughboys, author Henry Berry recounted a story of an American serviceman who was charged for cigarettes by a Y.M.C.A. worker. Berry believed that "While much of the criticism about it was unjust, the fact does remain that the Y never did make it with the Doughboys," and "to the large majority of the AEF they became 'that damn Y.'" Even sixty years after their service, fairly or not, the veterans had not changed their opinion of the organization. Henry Berry, *Make the Kaiser Dance: Living Memories of the Doughboy* (Garden City, NY: Doubleday, 1978), 84–86.

It was here at Le Mont Dore that I was nearly run down by the only automobile in the town. Belkin and I were going up a small hill, swaggering along in the middle of the street, swinging the fancy canes we had just purchased. I was looking around everywhere, except ahead. There was apparently no life on the street, but suddenly around a small bend and down the hill comes the auto, four wheels, no brakes, headed straight for me. Belkin yelled, "Look out!" A woman screamed from a nearby doorway, the driver frantically squeezed the bulb of the brass horn and I looked around just in time to see the danger, and reach up and drape myself on the big brass headlights. I was unharmed, but the French officer with a goatee on his chin was very excited, also apologetic. "Pardon, M'sue, Pardon," with several m-wahs and oui's. He proved to be the owner of the local Chocolat and Gifte Palace where we had just bought the canes and presented his card. After much gesturing and monkey business, kissing me on the cheek, and so on, he invited me to call on him at my convenience, writing something on the back of his card in French that I didn't understand. Stevens couldn't make it out either, so later, the three of us went to the shoppe, showed the Frenchman's card and were hospitably received. They also presented us with enough hot chocolate and bon bons to last a week. A neat little jeunesse who looked after us, was also a source of satisfaction. Stevens fell in love with the little mademoiselle at once and tried to "parley voo" her, but she would only smile and run away. He was a big raw-boned recruit anyway. We soon left without further incident.

Stevens couldn't get the little French maid out of his mind however, and wanted to return. So the next day we were back again.

"Chocolat, Messeuirs?" asks the maid sweetly.

"We, we. Bon chocolat, mademoiselle," answers Stevens.

"Oui. Kis, kis, casse," says the maid somewhat coquettishly and hurries away.

Stevens thought she said "kiss me" and made a grab for her but she eluded him. Soon she was back again with the chocolat, placing the neat little cups in front of us along with a packet of madeleines each. She stood there smiling at Stevens and looking at each of us in turn, pressing her little white apron coyly against the table. Just hanging around as it were.

"Promenod avec moi, babee? says Stevens.

"Ah non, mon cher. Fache," says mademoiselle pouting. Then as her face lights up, she continues, "Desirer tout mon coeur donner a rendezvous la petite soldat," looking at Belkin.

"Aw nuts! Just my luck! Can you beat that?" says Stevens. "She won't promenod with me, but her heart's desire is for a date wiz ze itzy bitzy Belkin."

Belkin's face turned as red as a spanked baby's bottom on hearing this, but he was immensely pleased never-the-less.

"Tell her it will be a real pleasure," says Belkin, rising and bowing from the waist.

"Mademoiselle, c'est entendu a plaisir," answers Stevens somewhat jealously and rising also.

"Oui bon," responds mademoiselle, smiling happily at Belkin who continues to blush furiously. "Comment vous, appelez vous Je m'appele Marie."

"She wants ta know yer name, ya big sap," says Stevens. "She says her name is Marie."

Stevens then introduces Belkin and myself to Marie in French, but of course I was a blank and didn't know a word he said.

"Ask her where I shall meet her and when," says Belkin impatiently.

"All right. An yer better take me along fer interpreter too," says Stevens. "I won't tell her what a big fathead you are."

"Love is the same in any language, so I won't need you," replies Belkin.

"Well, here's twenty franc. You'll probably need that," says Stevens by way of reprisal.

"Phooey! I spit on you. You, you-you dirty Irish stinker, you," says Belkin somewhat angrily.

"Careful, mon cher," cautions Marie touching Belkin's arm.

"Do you speak English, Marie?" says Belkin somewhat startled.

"Oui, a leetle cherie. I desire you at first sight," answers Marie, looking at Belkin with melting eyes. "Revenir, tonight at nine o'clock. Oui?"

"Adieu then, babee, till nine," says Belkin blushing and stubbing his toe on the way out.

"You mean a Jew, baby," says Stevens trying to rub it in.

Once outside, we then continued down the street to the Casino, where for some time the three of us sat at a table, doing nothing in particular.

"Gee, ain't you a lucky stiff though!" remarks Stevens to Belkin.

"Boy! She's got the prettiest legs I ever saw on a French dame. An ta think she picked out a kibitzer like you."

"Aw fergit it," says Belkin. "It's all a fake anyway."

"There won't be any fakin' fer you, old timer," replies Stevens. "An she can speak English too."

"I knows my onions, but if I needs any help, I'll send fer you," says Belkin.

"O.K. sojer. Put er there," replies Stevens extending his hand.

The next day after the chocolat shoppe episode, Belkin, Stevens and myself were strolling idly along a side street of the town, just looking around. Belkin would tell us very little of his rendezvous with Marie on the previous night, except, that she was the sweetest, most lovable girl he had ever known in France. We tried to get him to fix up a date for us also, with two of her girl friends.

"Nothin' doin' fer you birds," says Belkin. "I keeps her all to myself as long as I am here. Think I'm gonna let you'se guys spoil it all?"

"We got more manners'n you," replies Stevens. "Besides, one rotten apple in a barrel spoils all the rest anyway."

"Soldats is always selfish with their women," says I.

"Once a kibitzer, always a kibitzer," observes Stevens.

"Aw you'se guys is just jealous, that's all. Phooey!" says Belkin.

At this particular moment we stopped suddenly to look. A funeral was just emerging from a church across the way. As it passed by, we noticed that all the civilians removed their hats, so we did the same.

We had also stopped unintentionally in front of what looked like a store, except that the curtains were drawn down over the front windows. As we stood there, we also heard music coming from within—soldier music.

"What kind of a joint do ya think that is?" asks Stevens.

"Dunno," says Belkin. "It sounds something like a café but ya can't see nothin.'"

"Yer right," agrees Stevens. "Smells like vin-rooge ta me. I'm goin' in right now and see what it's all about. Comin' along?"

So we went up to the door which was locked and Stevens rattled the latch violently. Soon a female face peered out through the curtain and then opened the door about three inches. Stevens put his foot in the space so she couldn't close it again. We pushed right in without further ceremony, the little maid gesticulating and trying to keep us out without success.

Well boys, this place was no Y.M.C.A. or Y.W.C.A. either. In fact it was running in opposition to them, in furnishing entertainment to soldats. The place contained about fifty or so soldiers and officers, all making whoopie, sitting around tables and drinking some sort of clear white liquid in little stem glasses. Once inside, we sat down at one of the tables too. The little mademoiselle, seeing that she couldn't keep us out soon brought us three glasses of the same stuff. It was thick and sweet, tasted like anise and you could feel it way down to your toes. It cost us two franc each.

"Don't taste like coneyack ta me," says Stevens, smacking his lips.

"Looks like melted rock candy to me," says I.

"It must be absinthe, then," says Belkin. "We'll be drunk fer a week, an I can't see Marie."

Just then a big fat major of Engineers got up in front and started singing in a loud manner. He was leading the others around him in a song that went something like the following, with everyone clinking glasses after every verse of which there were several.

"The soldat says to the pretty bar maid,
'Jiggy 'd jig'," says he.
But the maid, she only smiled at him,
So he thought, 'she no compree'."
"'Oh, gimme a glass a rum,' says he.
'Veuillez vous, coucher?' says she.
But the soldat looked the other way,
So she knew, 'he no compree.'"

As our eyes became accustomed to the heavy smoke, we could see directly into a little side room that had escaped our notice before.

"Holy mackerel! Lookit, ya big sap!" says Stevens loudly, turning to give Belkin a quick punch, and pointing.

"I can't see anything," says Belkin. "What's all the noise about?"

"Just looka the swell lieutenant in the side room," answers Stevens slowly, to add mystery.

We looked, and then looked again. There was our Marie leaning back on the lap of a big husky second lieutenant of artillery, her arm around his neck holding a glass, her legs kicking her skirt high above her knees and giggling because she was being tickled.

"Ho, ho, ho," laughs Stevens. "Just look at that. The swellest, most lovable girl in all France. An yer gonna keep her all ta yourself. Ha, ha, ha! Whoo-pee!"

Belkin looked and was speechless.

"Looks like the fille de regimente," I suggested.

"Eyah. A chanson de amour ta lieutenants and kibitzers, but not to white men," says Stevens. "Let's go over an take her away from the shavetail. Whadda ya say, Belkin?"

"I'm goin' over myself, right now," replies Belkin. "An ta think I gotta salute the gahdamn shavetail too."

So Belkin went over, but Stevens and I got out while we could still walk, as the place was getting loud and boisterous.

Presently Belkin made a forced exit behind us, landing hard on the sidewalk.

"What's the matter, Belkie? Did yer fergit ta salute the shavetail?" inquires Stevens, gleefully.

"Why didn't ya stay an help a feller out?" answers Belkin, his hands holding the seat of his pants. "Fine pals you'se turned out ta be."

"Well, ya said ya didn't need no interpreter, an wuz afraid we'd spoil it all, an ya wanted ta keep her all ta yerself. You knows yer onions an if yer needed help you'd call us, that's the way we figgered," says Stevens sarcastically.

"Your figgers is mixed, an so wuz mine," says Belkin. "I took a poke atta shavetail, missed, an hit a colonel. That's why I'm here."

While some outfits of the A.E.F. were granted a fourteen day furlough, we were only supposed to have a week and then return. However, owing to the congestion on French railroads, busy hauling supplies for the armies at the time, we had to stay several days longer than our allotted time. This was very welcome to be sure. Belkin paid no more attention to Marie, so the three of us just moped around as usual. On leaving Le Mont Dore after a most pleasurable ten days, we passed black troops of the 93rd Divis[ion] coming in.

Chapter 13

Formation of 2d U.S. Army (Fini La Guerre)

The short furlough that we had enjoyed so much now being over, we are on our way back to rejoin the 39th Infantry. "Fini la Guerre." The war is over. "Fini la Guerre," that is what the "frog" soldats had been telling us all the way up from southern France. At every station so it seemed, some French soldiers would come alongside the troop train and say "fini la guerre" and then try to swap us rum or vin ordinaire for American hardtack, cigarettes or rubber raincoats. The French soldier was very covetous of the latter article and would swap a week's rum ration to get one. We didn't have much faith however as to the war ending so soon. We believed these soldiers were just trying to be friendly and pleasant or were just kidding us. We expected the war to continue all through the next winter at least and if it did—God help us all! While away on furlough, we had been quite out of touch with any of the recent developments of the war and did not know the Kaiser had abdicated and flown to Holland, or that the German Plenipotentiaries were at that minute in Marshall Foch's railway coach in the Forest of Compiègne (oise).

We had expected of course to be put off the troop train at Toul or even Commercy but we detrained instead at an obscure hamlet that had no name that we could discover. A sign post pointing northeast read "To Conflans" so we knew we were somewhere around St. Mihiel. Altogether there were probably 150 of us belonging to the 1st Battalion 39th Inf. who detrained here. The little hamlet contained only a small store and about a dozen or so houses and cowbarns combined as is the custom in French villages.[1]

As we arrived late in the afternoon of Nov. 10th, we prepared to stay in the village overnight, hence we were assigned to haylofts in the barns.

Just after we had arranged our billets for the night, a company of green recruits marched into town. They were probably intended for replacements in companies of the 39th. Their officers lined them up in two rows facing each other in the center of the main street, for a personal medical inspection. A medical officer moved slowly down between the columns inspecting the men. As they were doing so, two French girls came running out of the store to see the new soldiers. Before anyone could stop them, they were abreast of the head of the columns and saw everything. Did they blush? No—but the soldats did. They made the quickest and funniest left oblique turns I ever saw and not to be found in the book of drill regulations. Stevens and I laughed our heads off. The girls simply giggled a little realizing it was a faux pas and went back in the store again. The inspection then continued as though nothing had happened. As there were no billets in the little town for the new men, they moved on to the next town just before dusk. We hit the hay.

"Where do ya suppose we are, anyway?" queries Belkin.

"I don't know exactly," answers Stevens, "but we're somewhere around Metz. From feather ticks to lunatics. Some comedown fer the jew boys, eh, Belkin?"

"Eyah. Cooties again too. Say!" says Belkin, "I heerd some of them recruits talk'in about an armistice."

"Mebbe them frawgs wuz right about finne la guerre" observes Stevens. "I don't believe it though. Just another latrine rumor."

"An they says the old Kaiser has flown the coop, too," says Belkin. "Whadda ya know about that?"

"Aw gwan, ya can't make me believe that the 'all highest' has quit his army, cold turkey" replies Stevens.

1. Sergeant Earl McWilliams of Company I informed his parents that the French "house and barn are consolidated. Most all that I have been in, you could step right out of the kitchen into the barn where the milk cows and oxen are kept, which would not be very appealing to most of the housekeepers in the States." *The Alta Vista* (KS) *Journal*, August 8, 1918.

"I can't believe it either," says Belkin. "Whadda ya suppose we're behind this front for?"

"Dunno," answers Stevens, "but I wish we were back with O'Hara an the company again."

"Hock the damn Kaiser!" says Belkin. "Looka all the trouble he caused us."

"Yeah, that's what Heinie ought to do, hock der Kaiser in a pawn shop," advises Stevens.

"Wouldn't bring five cents fer old [?]," says Belkin.

"Der cream of today iss der limburger chizz of tomorrow," philosophizes Stevens, as they lay in the hay listening to the bats in the rafters.

While we had been on furlough our company had moved to a new location somewhat further north from Jouy-sous-la-côtes. Early next morning therefore, on the 11th of November, we hiked down the road from the hamlet on our way to report to our old regiment and company who are located in the Bois de la grand Emaente, a woods just outside of Heudicourt (meuse). This town is between Vigneulles and St. Mihiel and south of Conflans-Jarnisy. Conflans (et Moselle) is a railroad town of Old Lorraine, northeast and close to Metz, the main railhead and distribution point for the German armies in France.[2] Our regiment is here in support or reserve for the 28th U.S. Division who are holding the Front in this sector. Altogether there are thirteen U.S. divisions grouped before the German stronghold of Metz. These divisions constitute the newly formed 2d U.S. Army under the command of Lieut. General Rob[er]t Lee Bullard, with orders to move on Metz if the Germans fail to sign the Armistice as scheduled. The 1st U.S. Army of which we had formerly been a part is now steadily advancing in the Meuse-Argonne near Sedan (Ardennes) far to the north of us.

While we were hiking down the road toward Heudicourt, some inquisitive soldier, listening to rumors had found out that the firing was supposed to stop at 11:00 A.M. We just couldn't believe it. We were in what was termed a quiet sector so there was little firing of guns to be heard but we could hear or thought we could hear, the distant rumble of heavy artillery north of Verdun and to the west of us. Anyway, we kept listening and looking at our timepieces. Sure enough, the distant rumble of heavy guns seemed to stop promptly

2. Conflans is actually northwest of Metz.

at the appointed hour, then everything was peaceful and quiet. When we finally got back to the company again, we found them camped in the woods as usual. They had open fires burning too, a most unusual thing. There was also great activity among the men who seemed somewhat excited, so we knew something had happened.

"Welcome home, goldbricks!" says O'Hara, coming out to the road to greet us. "Finne la guerre! Finne la guerre!"

"Ya don't gimme a tell," says Belkin.

"I'm tellink you," answers O'Hara mockingly. "After four long years, Hienie has got his belly full, an we'll all be home by Christmas."

"Oh yeah!" says Brizee. "I heered the 39th wuz all goin' up ter Russia ter fight the Bolshevics."

"What fer?" inquires Stevens.

"Well, according ta rumor," says Brizee, "we're goin' up ta help out Kerensky's White Russian Army, an in-cee-dent-lee, do guard dooty over the British officer's source of likker supply at Archangel. Savey?"[3]

"Kin ya e-magine that?" replies Stevens. "After walkin' all over France, half starved, lousy an sick, now we gotta go up ter Russia just so some gahdamn Britisher can have his whikky 'n sodey."

"Gotta through this-a-war-a hokay. Now we gotta go uppa an fightta the crazy bushwicks. Figlio di puttana! I'm a gonna go A.W.O.L.," says Vinelli. "Ta hella witta de army!"

"Mebbe they'll have free vodka up there," suggests Belkin.

"An plenty of hot mamas' so's we won't freeze to death," says O'Hara.

"In thatta case, I'll sticka to de army," says Vinelli.

As you will see, this rumor was partly true. Next day we broke camp and hiked to Commercy, southwest of St. Mihiel. At Commercy we were to be re-outfitted, but not with the fur lined underwear we had expected. We were the 39th Infantry all right, getting ready for another long trip into a foreign land, but it happened to be the 339th Infantry, 85th Division instead, who were selected and sent to Archangel on the Volga River. Also the 27th and 31st U.S. Infantry was brought direct from the Philippines and sent

3. Alexander Kerensky (1881–1970), the leader of the Russian provisional government in the aftermath of the abdication of Czar Nicholas II, was deposed after Vladimir Lenin and the Bolsheviks seized power in November 1917. He fled Russia before American forces arrived.

to Vladivostok in northern Russia for the same purpose. Therefore, instead of Russia, we are going to march into Germany via Lorraine and Luxembourg, which was much more to our liking.[4]

So on Nov. 15th we hiked from Heudicourt, southwest to Commercy on the Meuse River, via the following,

Mars-la-Tour (et Moselle dep't)
Chambley (meuse)
Dommartin
Jaulny
Thiaucourt
Essey (meuse)
Beaumont
Broussey
Gironville
Vignot

Our stay at Commercy was to be until about Nov. 24th. Hiking directly into town, our company was billeted at once in some old artillery barracks that had at one time been a chateau, and dated back to the 17th century. This historic old building had been used in several previous wars as well, for headquarters and billets, even by some of the old Burgundian princes themselves. It is said that King Stanislaus (Leszczynski) of Poland, after he had lost his kingdom and became Duke of Lorraine and Bar, had once entertained Voltaire here when it was a chateau. All of this legend meant little to us, as we knew nothing of it at the time and cared even less. The chateau-barracks were now unequipped in any way for soldiery. We slept on the hard bare floors in our blankets as usual. An old war battered French rolling kitchen, supplying the needs of a small detachment of French Colonials stationed here, could be seen steaming away in the walled courtyard to the rear of the chateau.

I was still a runner attached to company headquarters. Our captain, now wearing a brand new olive-drab military overcoat, all

4. The American forces sent to Russia were tasked with guarding stockpiled Allied supplies and supporting "White" (anti-Bolshevik) forces. On September 4, 1918, the recently organized 339th Infantry landed in Archangel, North Russia, where the Americans battled mosquitoes, snow, cold and Bolsheviks for several months. After losing 244 men killed in action, or from wounds or disease, the regiment was evacuated in June 1919. In Siberia, the 27th Infantry arrived at Vladivostok from the Philippines on August 16, 1918, followed by the 31st Infantry. Reinforcements from the United States brought the force in Siberia to more than 9,000 men. These troops were finally withdrawn in March 1920 after losses of 170 men to wounds, combat, and disease.

splashed over and curlicued with black braid, wanted me to get a few things for him in Commercy. He needed a new set of captain's bars to go with the coat, money at the Banc de France, as well as other things. So he gave me a written pass that would allow me to be in town long enough to get them for him. After this errand was done, I kept the pass for the use of my friends, whenever they might want to go sightseeing also. That pass was certainly overworked, but not by me. When I wanted to roam around the town, all I had to do was to put a runner's red brassard on my arm and go anywhere unquestioned.

One day, strolling around alone, I found a small store or confeiture just off the beaten path, not as yet discovered by other soldaten.

This little candy store had recently received a large supply of Chocolat Menier. This delicacy was then much in demand by the soldiery, so I entered and purchased as much as they would let me have, about twenty-four large cakes. I took it back with me to the boys in the chateau and sold it at a good profit. My friends were glad to get it at almost any price. I could have sold twice as much easily.

Soldiers found in Commercy also, without half looking, several small estaminets or wine shops located in quite convenient parts of the town. They reported that the mademoiselles around these places could be induced to be very sociable for about deux franc. Vin-blanc and vin-rouge was also very cheap and of fair quality for vins ordinaire, coming at deux sous per glass or "un franc ze botte." Yes mam! We were right at home in Commercy, or any other French town for that matter, as long as our money held out. "Encore le cognac garcon, toot sweet!" The soldats were temporarily on the loose.

"Gimme yer pass tonight, will ya sojer?" requests O'Hara, waylaying me outside the chateau. "I got a date wit a honey."

"Can I come along too?" says I, fully expecting a negative answer.

"Sure," saya O'Hara. "I wants ya ta meet her. She sure is a pip."

"All right. Here's yer pass, then," says I, putting a runner's red brassard on my own arm.

"I gotta real mademoiselle all to meself, all fer me very own," says O'Hara growing confidential.

"I've heard that one before," says I. "Sounds familiar."

"Well, you wait 'n see. I owns the place," confides O'Hara.

"Fer how much?" says I, unconvinced.

After walking down the main street a short distance and passing the Banc de France, we turned in a little side street and shortly entered a bake shop or patisserie. The store was deserted, apparently. A small bell tinkled merrily behind us as we closed the door from the inside. We waited a little, eyeing hungrily the fancy colored cakes and madeleines in the glass cases. Presently a neat looking jeunesse appeared behind the counter coming through the little door at the back. She was smiling prettily at two very uncouth looking soldats.

"Jay voodray bee-en la belle Nanette?" says O'Hara in poor French lingo.

"Oui, une plasir," says mademoiselle beckoning to us. "Venir en arriere."

"Jeeze, I never saw her before!" exclaims O'Hara. "Come on in quick, sojer!"

So we went through the little door back of the counter, entering a snug little sitting room. There was O'Hara's la belle Nanette in the arms of a cuirassier of French cavalry. This gentleman cast us a furtive glance as we entered but Nanette gave him a lovely kiss right in front of O'Hara. Picking up his blue helmet slowly, he bowed to us graciously, opened the door and stepped out.

"La brave homme," says Nanette, waving a fond farewell as he disappeared in the street.

O'Hara's face was scarlet with jealousy and Nanette was slyly watching him out of the corner of her eye. As he was about to explode, she suddenly turned, threw her soft arms around his neck and purred, "Oh babee! Eet wuz moi brozzier. Le brave soldat de France." The musical lilt in her voice was like a canary in full song. O'Hara just stood there hypnotized.

"It was her brother, ya big sap," says I, aiming to bring him back to earth again.

Now O'Hara was all smiles again. "Moi beeg cherie," coos Nanette as she patted his cheek caressingly.

At that moment also, I felt a soft little hand in mine and wondered how it got there. The other jeunesse had pulled me gently down on a seat beside her and I noticed Nanette was on O'Hara's lap, so everyone was happy.

"Let's hear you sing, Nanette," says O'Hara.

"Zing? Oui," answered Nanette, as she began humming the song O'Hara had been teaching her. O'Hara kept time with his foot.

"Mademoiselle from ze Armentiere. She parley-voo.
Mademoiselle from ze Armentiere. Amour mais vous.
She nevaire can addz, an zats a fac,
Mais bien, but ze babee, she can subztrac.
Peenkie weenkie, she par-le-voo."[5]

We all laughed heartily, including Nanette who also blushed prettily.

"Try it over again," says O'Hara.

So Nanette sang it once more for us. This time with appropriate gestures.

Suddenly we heard the tinkle of the little bell on the door of the shop. Nanette jumped up and looked out through the doorway into the store. Probably a customer, we thought.

"Sacre bleuie! Laisser, tout de suite!" exclaims Nanette, pushing us two soldiers frantically out the rear door.

"Well, I'll be gahdamned!" exclaims O'Hara. "An we wuz havin' such a swell time too."

We were so disappointed and disgusted that we just sat down on the ground outside the door and smoked a cigarette in silence. It was now very dark, but as we had no special place to go, we just sat there.

After a few moments of waiting thus, the door was softly opened and a voice of liquid honey whispered, "O'Hara, entrer."

Another voice says, "entrer ma cherie." So we went back in the house once more, intrigued and delighted beyond measure.

Eet wuz ze grandmere, babee. C'est bien, ho-K?" says Nanette, smiling.

"Okay with me," replies O'Hara, thoroughly satisfied with the explanation.

The mademoiselles then drew down the shutters and closed their little shop. They brought us some wine and cakes, and so, far into the night.

5. "Mademoiselle from Armentieres" was perhaps the most famous A.E.F. song of World War I. Former doughboy Melbert B. Cary, Jr. collected approximately 180 verses and published them in two volumes in 1930 and 1935. "Then and Now," *The American Legion Monthly* 8, no. 5 (May 1930): 31. Numerous variations of the song may be found in Edward Arthur Dolph's *"Sound Off!": Soldier Songs From the Revolution to World War II*, published by Farrar and Rinehart in 1942.

Next morning at roll call, the captain made a cursory inspection of the company. Something was wrong, we could see that by the scowl he wore.

"Those two privates who were out last night without permission, front and center!" orders the captain.

A complete silence followed. Nobody stepped forward. Everyone is standing rigidly at attention.

"Private O'Hara! Front and center!" snarls the captain. O'Hara steps forward and the captain looks at me also.

"Company dismissed!" orders the captain.

Seeing O'Hara was caught and I was suspected, I stepped forward also with some misgiving and saluted.

"So you two birds don't care to recognize your superior officer and run out the back way," says the captain with just a ghost of a smile. "I heard you singing last night and wanted to be in on the revelry too."

"Then you saw us through the door, sir?" says O'Hara, sheepishly.

"Yes, certainly! One week on K.P. each of you, for being out of the barracks without permission! Dismissed!" orders the captain, turning on his heel.

"Now look what we got," says O'Hara, crestfallen. "An she said it wuz her grandmother."

"Well, the captain looks like an old woman," says I. "Ya can't blame Nanette fer tryin' ta protect us."

While we were catching our breath, as it were, here in the town of Commercy, other outfits or regiments of the 4th Division were also celebrating the cessation of hostilities in other ways, peculiar to their respective locations in small towns near us.

For example, Co. F, 59th Infantry of General Booth's brigade were located in the town of Apremont, near Lérouville (meuse).[6]

6. Ewing E. Booth (1870–1949), a native of Missouri, served as a captain in the 1st Colorado Infantry during the Spanish-American War and as a captain in the 36th U.S. Volunteer Infantry during the Philippine-American War. He was commissioned a first lieutenant in the Regular Army in 1901, and by the time of America's entry into World War I held the rank of major. Booth was commissioned a lieutenant colonel in the National Army in August 1917, a colonel in February 1918, and a brigadier general in July 1918. He commanded the 8th Infantry Brigade from July 27, 1918 to January 9, 1919. Following the war, he rose to the rank of major general and retired in 1934. He was awarded the Distinguished Service Medal for his leadership of the 8th Infantry Brigade in September and October 1918. U.S. Adjutant General's Office, *American Decorations*, 679; U.S. Adjutant General, *Official Army Register, January 1, 1935* (Washington, D.C.: U.S. Government Printing Office, 1935), 796; Bach and Hall, *The Fourth Division* 282.

There were no estaminets in town and therefore supposedly no drinking. The soldats were apparently enjoying themselves in their spare time with ordinary "crap shootin'." But, somehow, four or five of the company could be noted each day more or less under the influence of intoxicants. The company commander couldn't understand this, as he knew that wine or cognac could not be purchased in the town. Also, not enough of it could be smuggled in, to keep this condition in evidence continuously over a period of several days.

Where could it be coming from? He called in the mess sergeant of the company and inquired if he was bringing in booze with the rations. The mess sergeant was as completely in the dark as was the captain, therefore, both of them checked up the available kitchen supply of lemon and vanilla extract, but found it untouched. It was evident that the boys weren't taking vanilla these days, so it must be something else.

And so, one morning shortly thereafter, two company cooks were reported drunk and in the guard house. On this particular morning, the mess sergeant was forced to prepare the breakfast for over a hundred men, alone and single handed, so you can imagine the frame of mind he was in. He resolved then and there to find out, if possible, where the stuff was coming from.

When one of the cooks, finally, was able to talk legibly and audibly, the mess sergeant began questioning him as to the source of the laughing water.

"Why, I thought you knew, sergeant!" exclaims the cook. "We must have forgotten ta tell you."

"You'll tell me now, goldbrick," says the sergeant, "er I'll quarter yer belly fer tripe, so it won't ever get pickled again."

"Well now, honest sarge, I thought ya knew all the time," says the cook with a sarcastic smirk. "We got it down at the tank, right out of the spigot."

"What tank, you striped jackass?" snaps the sergeant, grabbing the cook's blouse and shaking him. "The water tank holds only chlorinated water, an I knows yer can't git soused on that. Tell me where ya got it, quick, afore I puts yer ta sleep again."

"All right! Let go a me! Git me outta the brig, sarge, an I'll take ya with me tonight and let you'se in on a little secret," answers the cook.

So that evening as arranged, the cook and the mess sergeant went over the hill and down in a gully behind the town of Apremont, thence entering a somewhat ramshackle looking building having one end built into the side of a hill. Once inside, there was a long table in the center with a row of stationary benches along the walls on either side. A large brass spigot emanated from the wall at one end of the room while nearby hung a large copper container or cup of about one gallon capacity. When you turned on the spigot, out would come real foamy beer which was estimated by experts as being about six percent proof. The spigot was connected to a large storage vat or hogshead located under the surface of the hill.

This cache of good old German brew had been left by the Boche when he hurriedly evacuated the St. Mihiel salient and was re-discovered by some of the doughboys of F Company, nosing around for souvenirs. You may well imagine all the "hooks" to "der Kaiser und der Vaterland" that must have been celebrated here. On this particular night, there were probably fifteen privates present, including the cook and the mess sergeant. They were having a grand old time too—a regular "gesellschaft abend."

Two days later, the captain finally learned of the beer cache. He immediately placed a military guard over the same, thereby ending all celebration for the time being, or until he could investigate for himself. This he carried out the following night in company with a few officers and commanders whom he had invited from nearby regiments. The captain and his high ranking guests became gloriously drunk, of course, ending by hugging and kissing the private soldiers and slapping them on the back. Discipline in the company, therefore, was all shot to pieces. He had invited the whole company in for a grand spree. He figured the war was over, so who had a better right to celebrate, especially as the beverage was free and had been so thoughtfully provided by the late enemy. This blow-off was as good as a trip to Paris for officers and men alike. The private who had originally discovered the tank, was promoted to sergeant by the captain on the night of the grand spree, and demoted to private again next day, for being drunk and disorderly. C'est le armee.

The whole affair was unusual, of course, and only represented one of the brief and very infrequent play spells possible in an army where morale and discipline was always of the highest standard.

After all they had been through in previous months, you couldn't blame soldiers for enjoying themselves whenever and wherever possible, so long as it didn't interfere with duty or cast reflection on the U.S. Army.

Now, returning to Commercy once more. Our original company commander of the Marne and Vesle River campaigns, Lieutenant Holstlaw, injured at Étampes-sur-marne, again paid his old command a visit at the old chateau here. Not many of the original company were left who had come over with the outfit from the U.S. The whole company now consisted of only forty men, all that were left of the original one hundred who had entered the Argonne Offensive. The lieutenant would have liked to continue on with his old command, and we would have been pleased to have him, but he was outranked by our present "ninety-day" National Army captain. Anyway, being a Regular Army officer, he was already attached to some other battalion of the 39th Regiment that he had originally organized in the U.S.

At Commercy, we were now completely re-outfitted. New uniforms, new hobnailed shoes, new accoutrement all the way through. Even the cooks had a new chow wagon, salvaged from Paris. We were ready for the trek through Lorraine, Luxembourg and down the beautiful Moselle River valley to Coblenz-au-Rhine, to become a part of the 3d U.S. Army—the Army of Occupation of the Rhineland.[7] Everyone was pleased to know that we were not to be sent to Siberia.

Most of us were seized with the spirit of new adventure that would carry us through the late enemy's country and to the fabled, castled Rhine. Some would rather go home of course but that wasn't to become possible for at least another ten months.

Thanks to the advice of the old war lord Von Hindenburg to his Kaiser to abdicate, and President Wilson's "fourteen points," we were now to bid farewell to the thunder of artillery bombardment,

7. The Third Army initially consisted of the 1st, 2nd, 3rd, and 4th Regular Army divisions, the 32nd and 42nd National Guard divisions, and the 89th and 90th National Army divisions. The 5th (Regular Army) and 33rd (National Guard) divisions were subsequently added. The Armistice terms allowed the Americans to occupy German territory from the Luxembourg border to the Rhine, and a bridgehead thirty kilometers (18 miles) in radius east of the Rhine at Coblenz, with a neutral zone 6 miles in width along the east bank of the Rhine and around each bridgehead, in which neither Allied nor German forces would be maintained. Headquarters of the American Third Army or Army of Occupation was established at Coblenz, a city of about 65,000 inhabitants. In all, the Americans were responsible for a million Germans living in an area of 2,500 square miles.

scarlet night horizons, dark mysterious woods and the panic of the Front lines.[8] Also the nauseous odor of dead men and horses on the battlefield, typewriter staccato of the vicious machine gun and the ever present mud, water and slimy shambles of ruin which was on every side at the front. It was a great relief as it had been a great adventure and we looked to the future with renewed hope and confidence. We had come safely through the devastated ruin and holocaust that was France, whose very existence we had fought to protect and extend, feeling that now at last we would see happier and better days. It is doubtful if the whole people of France or even the U.S. have ever fully appreciated what the A.E.F. did here in 1918.

Every morning from now on the sun will seem to rise with a more cheerful aspect. Packs however, continue to be just as heavy as ever and there is still plenty of rain, but who cares. On the march the soldiers grumble and curse as usual. They wouldn't have been healthy happy soldiery if they didn't. It is their makeup. Grumbles, profanity, wild rumors, fight, exhaustion, always hungry "when do we eat?", asleep standing up on the road but always hearing the command "Forward!" Yes, fini la guerre. Our morale is good and nobody gets over excited. Eyes and ears are awake for grand adventure that lies just ahead. It means new country, new scenes, new customs, new situations without the great distress and hardship of war.

War itself gives nothing important or of lasting value to any individual. It is a hard experience with early disillusionment and to the unfortunate—lasting despair. Still, we are glad to be in "this man's army."

HOME BOYS HOME
"Its home boys, home.
Its home we'd ought to be.
Home boys, home,
In God's count-ter-ree.
We'll nail Old Glory,
To the top of the pole,
And we'll all re-inlist,
In a pig's. . . . . .Oh! Oh!
(Old Army Song)

8. President Woodrow Wilson's "Fourteen Points" address, delivered to Congress on January 8, 1918, stated America's war aims.

Chapter 14

Advance of the 3d American Army (Army of Occupation)

The advance of the A.E.F. to the Rhine was in the majority of cases and with the infantry in particular, just one grand long hike. It was a sight-seeing tour also, if you like, but one that entailed much hardship on the individual soldier.[1]

The first units to enter Germany after the Armistice, were the famous combat divisions of the U.S. Regular Army and two divisions of National Guard troops. They were the 1st, 2d, 3d, & 4th Divisions, U.S. Regulars, the 26th Division (New Eng. Natn'l [National] Guard) and the 42d Division (Rainbow, Natn'l Guard, all states). These units therefore constituted the newly formed 3d U.S. Army, or Army of Occupation. Other units and divisions followed later on, as required, to relieve such divisions as were being sent home.

This army, some 200,000 strong, was under the command of Major General Joseph T. Dickman, an old regular army officer of long service, who could be depended upon for his diplomacy,

1. The "long, tedious, winding march into Germany" allowed the doughboys to pass through "magnificent" scenery, "but the tired doughboy with a pack on his back usually knew more about the height of a hillside than its beauty." Record Group 120, 4th Division Historical, Box 29, Folder: 39th Infantry, Histories, Commendations & Battle Participants, NARA.

Maj, Gen. Mark L. Hersey, commanding 4th Division. Bourcq, Ardennes, France, November 19, 1918. U.S. Army Signal Corps Collection, National Archives, 42084 [3221D8].

judgement and military efficiency in any emergency, as might suddenly occur in an occupied territory under martial law.

We of the 4th Division, now re-outfitted and assembled in and around Commercy, France, ready to move, are under the direct command of Major General Mark L. Hersey, with Major General

C.H. Muir as commander of the IVth Corps, Army of Occupation, of which we will now become an integral part.[2]

On Nov. 24th, 1918 therefore, the battalion "falls in," slings packs, takes rifles, "Forward March!" We are now leaving Commercy, taking a route a little north and directly east toward Germany, passing through the following towns on our way out of France.

Gironville (et Moselle dep't)
Rambucourt
Beaumont
Flirey
Limey
Montauville
Pont-à-Mousson

At Pont-à-Mousson we crossed the Moselle River on a narrow pontoon bridge as the regular bridge at this point had been damaged from past shelling. Crossing the bridge, we then entered Old Lorraine which today is the Muerthe-et-Moselle province or departmente under the flag of France instead of Germany.

For the most part, the towns in Lorraine were apparently deserted in the earlier part of our journey. When we entered Germany proper, later on, towns were passed through in parade formation, with our regimental bands blowing their heads off in one glorious blare of brassy braggadocio. Shutters too, were closed on all the houses but we knew we were being closely watched and appraised by unseen eyes. However, we were prepared for any hostility on the part of German natives, as we carried a sufficient supply of ammunition to meet any emergency.

Passing through Old Lorraine and Luxembourg however, which preceded our entry into Germany, we were received with open arms and hailed as liberators. The natives of these provinces put on

2. Charles Henry Muir (1860–1933), a native of Michigan, graduated from West Point in 1885. Recommended for the Medal of Honor for his actions in Cuba during the Spanish-American War, Muir was awarded the Distinguished Service Cross instead, many years later. After serving as major of the 38th U.S. Volunteer Infantry in the Philippine-American War, Muir returned to Regular Army service and was stationed again in the Philippines. Promoted to colonel in 1916, he was commissioned a brigadier general in the National Army in August 1917 and a major general that November. Muir led the 28th Division through combat in France, and in October 1918 took command of the Fourth Corps. In April 1919 Muir reverted back to command of the 28th Division. Muir retired from the army in 1924 as a major general. *Sixty-fifth Annual Report of the Association of Graduates, June 11, 1934*, 130–35.

Supply train. Thirty-ninth Infantry, passing through Conflans on march to point of occupation. Note decorations by inhabitants to welcome return of French and Allies. Conflans, Meurthe et Moselle, France, November 22, 1918. U.S. Army Signal Corps Collection, National Archives, 37665 [164D8].

their colorful gala attire and exhibited their population profusely. The town mayors even wore their high silk hats for ze grande occasione de entrance of the victorious U.S. Army.

Entering into Germany later on, the natives there made themselves quite scarce at first, but as soon as the news spread ahead of us that we were not taking advantage of the ancient custom of conquering European armies to pillage, burn, etc., they received us with much cordiality and even friendship. We now had an opportunity to study the late enemy in his native habitat. These home loving folk had been for the most part, forced into a war they did not desire, by their statesmen and rulers. On the whole, they were playing the role of unwilling combatants, victims of their Junker military system. They were not hard to get along with, in spite of all war propaganda, when you got to know them better. If you spoke their language, and a goodly number of the A.E.F. did, you were welcome to anything they owned. Some of them in towns where we stopped at first, even thought they had to shine our boots and wait on us, after the arrogant and tyrannical manner of their own soldiery, such as Herr Hauptmanns (captains), who usually made the German peasant grovel in the dust like dogs, if they happened to be passing.

The German people liked the "Americain Soldaten," that we soon found out, but they bitterly hated our Allies, the French—an ancient inherited trait. Hence in our sector at least, the natives considered themselves lucky to have us among them. And to make us doubly desirable, we spent "grosse pfennigs" too, exchanging our French francs for German marks so we could buy anything offered by civilians in the line of eats, such as black bread, Moselle wines, apple butter, etc.

The march through Alsace-Lorraine, Luxembourg and down the beautiful Moselle River valley to Coblenz, Germany now begun, will take from fourteen to twenty days according to the general route followed by each separate battalion. All companies did not follow the same route. We are now taking a direct northeast course advancing through Metz, Thionville and on into Bettembourg, a part of the little principality of Luxembourg, lying between Belgium (belge) and Germany (allemagne) and which we will pass through on our way to Coblenz au Rhine.

Arriving at dusk in Bettembourg on our first day's hike, a few of us picked out a wood-carver's shop in the town square as billets for the night. Inside the shop we spread our blankets on the floor, or in a pile of wood shavings which we considered a great luxury at the time. The shop was also full of hand carvings, exquisitely wrought in various woods and fashioned in various apostolic figures and other church cabinetry.

"This is a swell place, eh sojers?" remarks Stevens, picking out a nice pile of shavings to lay in.

"No smoking in here, men! It's too dangerous," orders Corporal Andrews.

"That's right, Corp.," agrees Stevens. "We don't wanna sacrifice ourselves among all these Saint Peters and Pauls just fer a smoke."

"Saint Mary, bless us," says O'Hara, stroking his rosary beads and gazing enraptured at her wooden replica on the shelf above him.

"Geeze, you'se guys is awful religious all of a sudden," says Brizee. "I'll bet St. Peter up there on the shelf would tell you'se all ta go ta hell, if he could speak his real thoughts."

"That goes fer you, too," replies O'Hara, "I'se got some respect fer them sacred images, even if you hasn't."

"Aw pipe down!" yells Belkin from under a bench in the corner. "The last I ever heard of St. Peter, he wuz in Rome lookin' up the Tiber."

"Eyah. He wuz probably lookin' fer Father Abraham, who wuz hiding behind a crop of long bush whiskers," says O'Hara somewhat heatedly.

"Aw, what's the use of argyfying religion?" says Stevens. "None of you'se guys knows what yer talkin' about anyway."

At that moment, a goat tied to a stake in the rear of the shop, let loose a loud vociferous blah-ha-a. "Blah, blah, black sheep," says O'Hara, falling in a doze along with the rest of the tired soldats.

Much has been written along satirical lines, of the friendly little country of Luxembourg, with its quaint customs and picturesque countryside. But the impression it created on the A.E.F. soldiery was also much in the nature of travesty or burlesque. It gave them something to joke about.

Looking through attic window of house by roadside. Machine Gun Company, 39th Infantry, marching by. Third day of march, Hettange Grande, Lorraine, November 23, 1918. U.S. Army Signal Corps Collection, National Archives, 37679 [178D8].

Advancing through Luxembourg

To enter the Grand Duchy of Luxembourg is like turning Time's forelock and entering old worlds of ancient splendor. A land of old feudal castles and great scenic beauty, on the border of the Latin and Germanic worlds, it is not France, not Belgium, nor Germany, but it has the medieval atmosphere, with its quiet streams, its romantic gorges, lonely forests and old burghs of legend, such as LaRochette and Beaufort which are the two most remarkable remaining specimens. One even imagines he can hear the call of St. Hubert's stag, as he moves in deep, green carpeted forests, as in the legends of the far distant Ardennes.

But everything was not quite so peaceful and serene when we entered the Duchy. The country was full of dark and deadly intrigues, enough for a country ten times its small size of two-hundred square miles.

After the armistice, the secret service and spy systems of all the warring countries remained just as active as during the war. France talked of annexing both Luxembourg and the Rhineland. To General Pershing and President Wilson, this looked quite imperialistic, so therefore they frowned upon it. France decreed also that the Grand Duchess, Marie-Adelheid, the then ruling princess of Luxembourg should go, as they claimed she had been pro-German during the war. This was not true, as her little Duchy was helpless to stop German invasion, so had made the best of it. How could a small army of only four-hundred rifles stop an invader with unlimited resources behind them and no conscience?

The citizens of the Grand Duchy were all agreed on one thing, however. "Mir welle bliew wat wir sin." We want to remain what we are, an independent Grand Duchy of guaranteed neutrality. "If however, France says that the Grand Duchess must go, then to keep our small state independent, we will request her to abdicate in favor of her sister, Princess Charlotte." So spoke the statesmen of the little principality late in 1918.

Luxembourg was directly in the path of the advancing U.S. armies to the Rhine. Marshall Foch had previously announced that he would make Luxembourg City his headquarters and all Americans would be excluded. This, of course, started friction between French and U.S. commands which was most regrettable.

At the request of the Grand Duchess Marie herself and on advice from President Wilson, General Pershing told the advancing Americans (part of them were the 39th & 58th Infantry, 4th Divis[ion]) not to bother about what the French colonel in Luxembourg might have to say, or Marshall Foch either, but to continue on as he (General Pershing) had already guaranteed the independence and neutrality of the little country, so there would be no interference by France or anyone else in its internal affairs.

Later on, Foch officially placed Luxembourg in the American zone of occupation. This showed excellent judgment and was a sportsmanlike gesture. Therefore, thanks to Americans and the U.S. Army, this picturesque little country still stands today an independent state, serene and peaceful in the administration of its own affairs.[3]

When the A.E.F. soldiery entered Luxembourg City and found out about the Duchy's standing army of four-hundred rifles, and saw a few of them on parade around the Grande Place in their circus uniforms, they remarked, "Crimey! Look atta tin soldiers from toyland! Wonder if them gingerbread men gits any pay?" When they found out that the Lux soldiers received only about twelve to fourteen cents per day, they figured there was no use trying to get them in a crap game as they wouldn't have any money, so they bought them a few barrels of red wine just to show they were sociable. Thereafter, every time a detachment of U.S. troops marched by any of them on work detail or guard duty, the Lux soldiery would start shouting "Vive! Vive! Le Americaine!" But the doughboys just couldn't understand this "vive" business at all and therefore classed the Luxembourgers as motion picture soldiers and tried to forget them.

3. Howell may overstate Pershing's role in determining the future of Luxembourg. In his proclamation to the people of Luxembourg in November 1918, Pershing stated that the country's "Government and institutions will nowhere be interfered with. You will be undisturbed in the peaceful pursuit of your lives and occupations." U.S. Army Center of Military History, *United States Army in the World War, 1917–1919*, 18 vols. (Washington, D.C.: U.S. Government Printing Office, 1991), vol. 10, pt. 1: 117–18. In his "Final Report," Pershing wrote that "Upon entering the Duchy of Luxemburg in the advance, a policy of noninterference in the affairs of the Grand Duchy was announced." When the French commander in Luxembourg City was given command of all troops in the Duchy, Pershing ordered that American troops would not be subject to his control. Later, at Pershing's request, Marshal Foch placed the entire Grand Duchy in the American zone. John J. Pershing, *Final Report of Gen. John J. Pershing, Commander-in-Chief, American Expeditionary Forces* (Washington, D.C.: U.S. Government Printing Office, 1920), 57.

But everywhere you went it was "vive!" The citizenry thought a revolution had started and so, therefore, called on the U.S. commander for troops to put down the sudden rebellion of the Lux Army. This was quickly done without bloodshed. The Lux Army then stormily demanded a raise in pay. This was quickly granted by the Grand Chancellor without a quibble. Thus, this pseudo revolution, if you could call it that, was played up, exaggerated and broadcast as important news all over the world, because war correspondents with nothing else to do except to follow the advance of the A.E.F. made a big story of the incident.

It is said that a couple of A.E.F. soldats, actually did enter the palace of the young Grand Duchess unannounced, and interviewed her, posing as correspondents for a large New York Daily. The Grand Duchess was surprised but not at all displeased with them or their brazen effrontery. They brought her a box of bon bons and a bunch of flowers which she accepted graciously, because she was much intrigued by the nervy soldats. This is perhaps the closest the A.E.F. or any of its members, except the generals, ever got to blue-blooded royalty. Anyway it gave them something to write home and brag about.

It is a matter of record however, that there was actually a small revolution in Luxembourg later on in 1919, which resulted disastrously for the ruling Grand Duchess, Marie Adelheid. This young, beautiful and intelligent princess of the old house of Nassau, had ruled the principality since 1912. No matter how beautiful or accomplished she may have been however, she was not at all popular with her people at the time. Now they accused her, as had the French, of being pro-German. It has been stated as fact by several historians, that it was really the Grand Chancellor or Premier of the Duchy who was actually pro-German, instead of Marie.

Accordingly in January 1919, a mob appeared before the doors of her palace and in characteristic European manner, booed and denounced her. This went on for about two days. To still them and prevent widespread disorder and revolution in the little state, Marie appeared early one morning on the balcony of her palace, wearing only a plain schoolgirl's dress. In a clear voice and without visible emotion she announced, that as it was their will, she had abdicated (Jan. 11th, 1919) in favor of her sister, Princess Charlotte.[4] At this moment a company of efficient U.S. infantry rounded a corner and in good old "here come the Marines" style, proceeded to quickly disperse the mob. They were not Marines however, just plain ordinary garden variety doughboys. Shortly afterward, the Ex-Grand Duchess Marie-Adelheid entered an Italian convent with the hope of becoming a nun. This was denied her and she died there of a broken heart in 1924, disillusioned, disappointed and neglected.

The new ruler, Grand Duchess Charlotte was also young, charming and intelligent like her sister Marie, whom she loved. While the peppy, aggressive U.S. doughboys must have certainly intrigued her also, she was already the mother of five charming robust children and had a devoted husband—Prince Felix of Bourbon-Parma. Now that it is all over and too late to rectify a mistake, Princess Marie-Adelheid is today looked upon in the Duchy as their martyred Saint Marie, who sacrificed herself for her people.

The citizens of this little independent state have known of the grim experience called war for over five thousand years back. At one time or another they have been vassals of Holland, Denmark, Austria, Prussia, France and the Holy Roman Empire. The youthful Ex-Grand Duchess Marie, daughter of the Grand Duke William however, saw more excitement in her short reign of six or seven years, than several of her predecessors or antecedents had known in their lifetime. Her small neutral country was invaded by arrogant German armies and milked dry at the start of the World War. Her people, helpless to do anything, suffered under the German yoke from 1914 to 1918, when the Germans again fell back to the Rhine in panic and defeat. The French and Americans then started moving in and her streets and villages were soon being patrolled by U.S. doughboys. Thus, due to the stubborn foresight of General Pershing who included Luxembourg in his zone of advance to the Rhine, the personal request for occupation by Marie herself, defying France, the independence of Luxembourg was save from again being annexed to France, as it had been under Louis XIV and Napoleon.

Therefore throughout the winter of 1918 and early 1919, elements of the 39th Infantry, 4th Division and the 5th and 33d Divisions, A.E.F. led a pleasant existence in this charming, hospitable country.

4. Charlotte, the Grand Duchess of Luxembourg, ruled until her abdication in 1964.

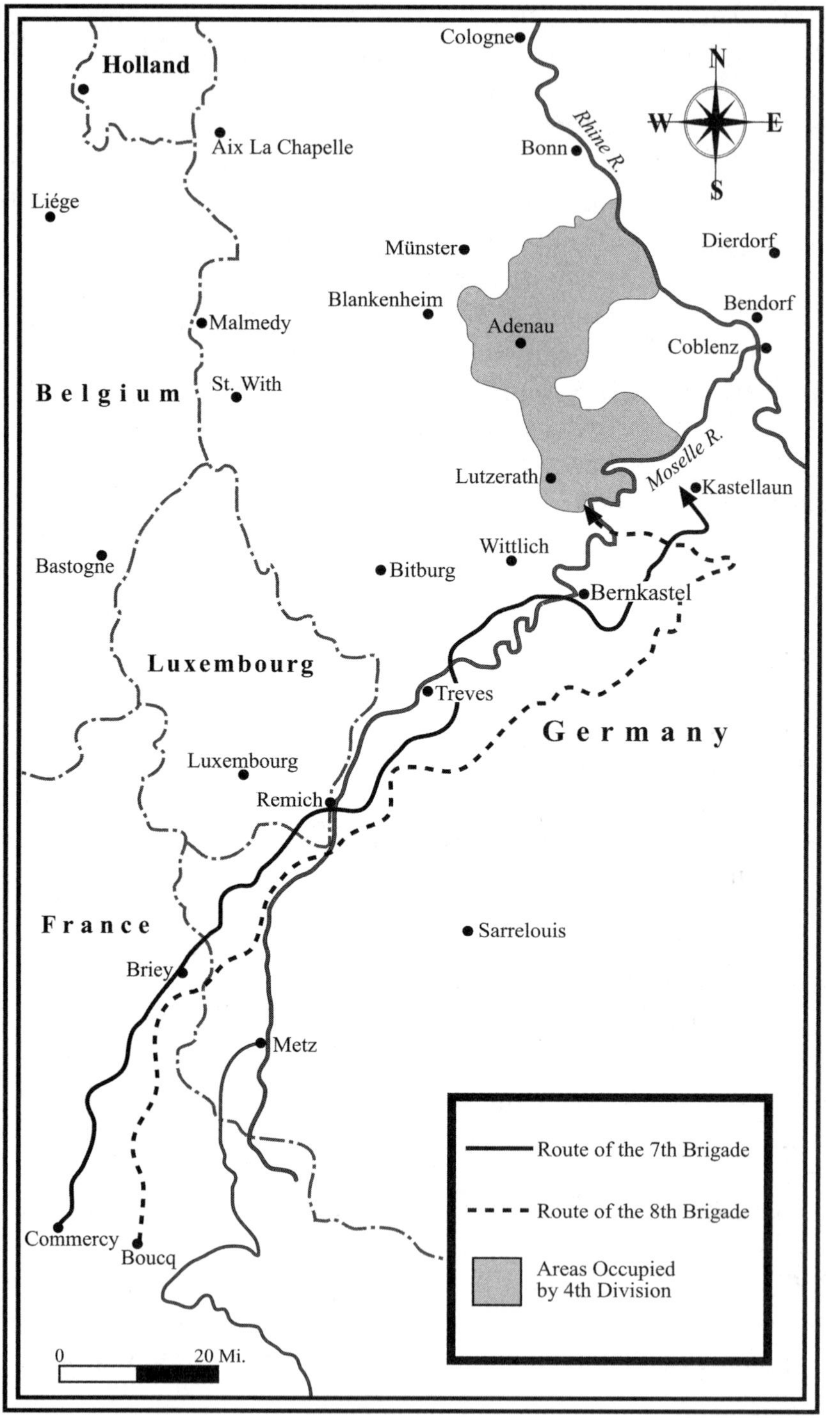

March to Germany

En Route to Germany (First U.S. Troops on the Rhine)

Nov. 26th , found us of B Company, 39th Infantry in the town of Nach Hiediegan [Gross Hettingen] and close to the German-Luxembourg frontier. This was Thanksgiving Day. We stayed in this town several days and were billeted in the local schoolhouse. The company occupied the entire building which had two rooms upstairs and two down. Those of us who couldn't find a place inside the school or cellar, pitched pup tents outside in the yard where our soup-gun was located.

Being Lorraine and a former province of Germany, we saw pictures of the Kaiser and the Crown Prince on the walls. German textbooks were also in evidence. Otherwise the schoolrooms closely resembled those of the U.S.A. There was a rostrum or raised platform for the teacher, the Herr Professor to you, and the usual slant type double desks with their cast-iron inkwell covers so familiar to all of us. The desks were sadly in need of varnish and even a few initials were to be seen carved in the tops. School-boys are much the same the world over. The doughboys however, put the finishing touches on a few desks by standing on them with their destructive hob-nailed shoes. Slate blackboards were on three sides of the room with windows on the remaining side.

Private Brizee, who was somewhat of a cartoonist, drew a picture of Colonel Bolles, commander of our regiment, on the blackboard. This he labeled "Colonel Bowels" because he had a big belly. It would have made the colonel's belly ache, if he had seen this one.

Another private addicted to poetry wrote a verse about the company commander on the blackboard, as follows—

"The captain struts around all day.
He wears his spurs, of course.
But why wear a set of riding irons,
When he can't even ride on a horse?"

Private O'Hara thought of adding another verse, as follows—

"The captain has sure got a lot of pep.
His orders are brim full of starch.
When he knows the company is all fagged out,
His command always is, 'Forward! March!'"

We were privileged to go in the town anytime we desired without a pass if we carried our rifles, probably a needless precaution. Of course we usually went out looking for something to eat or drink. Soldiers can always find both. The local girls, however, were kept discreetly inside the houses out of reach of the amorous soldiery. Some types of soldiers are always successful in "chiseling" their way behind closed doors in search of delicacies to fill their empty stomachs. Such types were O'Hara and Stevens. They always "got in" anywhere.

Therefore, the three of us went about as usual in this town, hunting for eats, same as once before at Andelot. Stevens acted as our self-appointed official spokesman because he was the only one who could "parley-voo," so he said.

"Madam, avez vous le des oeufs?" inquires Stevens at one of the houses.

"Ah, non, non," answers Madam somewhat impatiently and ready to close the door on us.

"Avez vous le des fromage?" continues Stevens unperturbed.

"Ah, non, non," replies Madam with some finality.

Stevens was now non-plussed. He couldn't make out if the madam was French or German and therefore didn't quite know how to approach her.

"Comprenie vous Francais?" inquires Stevens to hold attention.

"Oui, oui, Monsieur," says Madam, interested.

"Sprecken se Deutsch?" continues Stevens.

"Ja, ja," answers Madam, smiling a little.

"Compree eggs, und cheese, und potatoes? Omelettes and vin-blanc?" inquires Stevens, warming up to the subject.

"Oui, oui! Mon cherie! Entrer messieurs," says Madam, smiling and standing aside for us to enter.

So we stepped into the salle-a-manger or dining room, which was also the parlor, kitchen and sleeping room combined. It was quite a large room, having a red tiled floor, with a large fireplace and pot-hook kettle at one end. A little girl sat on the floor in front of the fireplace playing with a rag doll and paid not the slightest attention to us.

Madam soon rejoined us bringing a bottle of white wine and some thin, cool glasses which she sat before us on the table. She then began a long dissertation in French to Stevens which we couldn't understand, except such words as cherie, offizier, amour, la guerre, monsieur and so on.

"What's all the parley-vooin' about?" demands O'Hara. "Don't we git no chow, after all?"

"She says she's a widow an lost her husband in the war and is now very lonely, except for her little girl. She and her husband are French, but he was forced to join the German Army at the point of the bayonet and later was killed," explains Stevens.

"Why, the dirty, rotten bastards!" exclaims O'Hara.

"An she says she has lots of eggs, cheese and potatoes, an will make us a nice omelette. But she says she can't give us much wine because she is afraid of 'ze offizier' who forbids her ta sell wine ta us soldaten," continues Stevens.

"Tell her, we don't give a damn fer officers," answers O'Hara.

"What's that you just said, sojer?" inquires Sergeant Painting, just then entering through the open door.

"I says, we don't give a damn fer non-coms below the rank of sergeant," replies O'Hara with characteristic Irish diplomacy.

"Well now, that's different," says the sergeant. "Give 'em all the vin-rooge they want," turning to Madam.

"Oui, oui! Beaucoup, beaucoup!" answers Madam, lifting the trap door in the floor leading to the cellar, that mysterious compartment of all French houses.

Soon she was back again with an armful of little round cheeses, eggs, potatoes and wine. In short order she made up a very appetizing omelette, served with black bread and apple butter. It was the best feed we'd had in any town. We paid her off in francs and later sent our friends around to patronize her.

At one end of the village street there was a patisserie, or bake shop, which attracted our attention. It displayed several small cakes in the window and one large one, colored with different figures and designs. It closely resembled a large wedding cake. We passed the shop several times and couldn't keep our eyes off from the cake. It sure was a whizbang for looks. Finally, Stevens went in and priced the cake, for which they asked twenty franc, or about $3.20 at the time. That was a lot of money to us, but we couldn't get the cake out of our minds. We told several others in the company about it and finally someone suggested that we take up a collection and buy it. This was done and so the large cake was finally transported back to our room in the schoolhouse. We got ready for a party.

With much ceremony, we cut into the cake. We found, however, that the cake itself was made from egg yolks and dark flour, blowed up or made to rise to its large size by chemicals. Therefore, it was mostly a sponge full of air holes. The frosting encrusted on the outside, was made of egg-whites sweetened with saccharin and flavored with synthetic vanilla. We had simply purchased a table decoration.

The soldats were quite angry and disappointed in their purchase and threatened to go back and raid the bake shop and demand their money back. But we talked over the matter before acting and it was soon realized we had bought the cake solely on its appearance alone without asking questions and therefore we were mostly to blame. It was also realized that these people had no white flour or sugar with which to make up a real cake, as their supplies had been depleted by four years of warfare. The cake, what there was of it, tasted O.K. and was a beautiful replica of the real thing. Can you blame hungry soldiers for wanting to sample the biggest one they had seen in months?

Our Thanksgiving dinner with the army had consisted of fried cornwillie, tomato stew, white bread and black coffee without any sugar. Did I hear you say that you had "turkey with all the fixins'" that day? We went into town afterwards, of course, and had our fill of omelettes, that is, all we could pay for. After several days in this village, we again are on the move. One of the many delights of the army is, that you are always moving somewhere else, and the scene is ever changing.

Dec. 3d finds us crossing the frontier into Germany. This was at the same place that other outfits of the A.E.F. crossed into the Boche homeland, the town of Remich, Luxembourg on the German frontier across the Moselle River. The battalion, after crossing the Moselle bridge, was now arranged in parade formation, the 39th Infantry Band playing and the regimental flag unfurled. This is one of the few times I ever saw the regimental standard during the war or afterward.

The nights are now getting colder and the frost is commencing to appear on the housetops. We haven't as yet had an army issue of winter overcoats or gloves, so it is necessary that we sleep under

Company B, 39th Regiment Infantry, leaving bridge on German side of Moselle. Remich, Luxemburg, at Moselle River bridge. December 3, 1918. U.S. Army Signal Corps Collection, National Archives, 42077 [3214D8].

suitable shelter at night. We are now passing down the picturesque, historic and beautiful Moselle River valley toward Coblenz, famous the world over for its varied and exquisite vintages. We didn't see much of the vintage however, as we never stayed for very long in any one village. Anyway the civilians were not allowed to sell us any.

It was a grueling march. Up steep hills and down into beautiful valleys, battalions of men, bent under the weight of full service packs, dragging themselves along with difficulty over the rolling hills, with an occasional halt for rest. Some of the time our supply wagons and soup cannon were drawn by old fashioned yoke oxen, hired from civilians along the route to augment or replace the limited capacity of the faithful army mule over the hardest, steepest places. This seemed incongruous to me at first, that a glorious conquering army of the machine age, should have to revert to the primitive for its trucking and transportation. Where were all the vast motorized mechanical equipments sent over from the U.S.? Where were all the glittering bandwagons of the 20th Century, calculated to dazzle and impress a defeated, distressed country? The only motors that appeared were the occasional motorcycles of despatch riders or a Red Cross ambulance used to pick up footsore stragglers who dropped out along the march.

Our company seemed to be travelling alone, but we knew there were a small outfits in front of us and hundreds behind us, coming along on the same roads. To see these hundreds of thousands of U.S. troops passing through their towns, day after day, must have made the German people realize what a stupendous feat had been accomplished by the U.S. in placing such a large army in the field in spite of the efficient German war machine who had informed their people that the U.S. could never send troops in effective numbers because of the ruthless submarine policy. Well, here we are and as effective as I have indicated in previous chapters.

The first few days of our long march were taken easily and without undue fatigue. After the spell of adventure wore off, the packs seemed to get heavier every day. When we would come to a long steep hill, we would have a feeling of weariness, as we contemplated the ascent. The heavy packs we carried would cut into our shoulder muscles until it seemed that you must drop out from fatigue, as you couldn't stand it much longer. We were rapidly becoming a stoop shouldered army, bent over from the hardship of continuous hiking with a weight on your back, that killed you by inches. But somehow we stood up under the hardship and the coating of road dust on our backs and in our lungs. The weight of the full pack on your back was increased and accentuated by the ammunition belt, full canteen of water, steel helmet and other impediments that you carried, together with the additional weight of the Springfield rifle. All this which was usually fastened in some manner to the pack harness, made the narrow pack straps seem like bands of steel cutting into shoulder muscles like a dull knife. There was no jaunty marching along the road at a brisk clip, swinging your arms and singing military marching songs with smiles on your faces, such as you occasionally see in some movie or the way they instructed us to hike in training camps in the States. That was all bunk. We just dragged along day after day and all day from seven A.M. to ten P.M. at a pace less than four miles per hour. There was no dashing military music or colors unfurled after the first day of entrance into Germany proper. Instead of singing there was plenty of cursing and grumbling among the men whose feet and legs commenced to give out through weakness or ill-fitting shoes, and in a number of cases, plain bare feet on the road after shoe leather had been burned through.

"Geeza! My backa shes a broke!" complains Vinelli.

"What's the matter, can't ya take it?" asks Sergeant Painting.

"The steepa hill she make a me sicka," says Vinelli.

"Gimme yer pack then, softie," says the sergeant already weary under his own pack.

It was duly transferred and the sergeant struggles along under two packs for some time as he carried no rifle.

"No gotta da shoes either, Sarge" says Vinelli after a little.

"All right" says the sergeant, "Fall out along the road and wait for the ambulance. Here's yer pack, goldbrick, but show up fer roll call tomorrow."

"All a right Sarge. Tank a you. So longa everybody" says Vinelli, dropping wearily out of the column.

"Aw pull in yer neck, goldbrick, an lay down an die" chorused a few nearby hikers. "We'll tell the Kaiser up in Berlin ta send his personal car and chauffeur fer ya as ya sure needs a wet nurse."

"Jesu Cristo! What you tinka? I no can helpa!" replies Vinelli, shaking his head and rolling over on the grass exposing shoe bottoms with toes sticking through.

Every little while some weary soldier would be forced to fall out of the marching column from fatigue and sit alongside the road to wait for the ambulance to give him a lift.[5]

The hike usually started in the cool of the morning around 7.00 A.M. after a warm breakfast. It would continue until around noon, with short rest periods at regular intervals. At noon we would stop long enough to eat a cornwillie sandwich, with some hot black coffee prepared enroute by the cooks walking alongside the soup gun. Then on through the long afternoons. Sometimes we hiked as late as 10.00 P.M. at night, due to the fact that we had to keep going until we found a village or other cover unoccupied

5. Howell's comrade was not alone. During the march to the Rhine, 2,197 men in the 4th Division were admitted to the division Field Hospitals. Only 732 were returned to duty during the march, and 1,097 were evacuated to hospitals in the rear. Foot troubles, influenza and bronchitis were common ailments. Bach and Hall, *The Fourth Division*, 227–28.

by preceding troops, who had taken shortcuts or other roads and reached a town ahead of us. Sometimes there would be an argument with troops "chiseling in" on a town that had been previously reserved and arranged for by our billeting officer, who acted as a sort of advance agent. In this case we would have to continue our hike from seven to ten kilos further, to the next town, in order to secure shelter for the night. Under these conditions the last part of the hike was a hurried, forced affair, with the leaders of the columns speeding up to get to a town because it was late. This worked untold hardship on the men already overfatigued from a long days march.[6] Those that dropped out of the columns on account of feet or shoes going bad, or for other reasons, were picked up by light motor ambulances patrolling the column and given a lift back to their companies. If very bad they would be taken to a base, treated and returned again in a few days.

Often, we went through long, lonely dense forests on a single road for several hours at a stretch, mostly between the Moselle and Saar Rivers. So far we have passed through the towns of Wasserbillig, Trassem, Saarburg and Karthaus, toward the large town of Trier (Treves) on the Moselle.

At dusk on Dec. 7th, we arrived at a nunnery just outside the gates of the ancient, historic Trier. Here we were billeted in a large hall of some description and slept on the hard bare floors. Although unaware of it at the time, this was the Abbey of St. Matthew, containing the tomb of the Sainte and Apostle. The abbess and the nuns were extra watchful to see to it that we didn't smoke or otherwise injure anything in the large hall with our guns and equipment. We thought they were a little too watchful at the time and remarked about it. Next morning after some little delay, we marched through and out of Trier, crossing the Moselle River bridge (built 4th cent.) into Pallien. Col. Bolles, commander of the 39th Regiment and several other "brass hats" stood at the approach of the bridge and

6. The amount of time that the 1st Battalion of the 39th Infantry marched and the distances traveled varied during the period December 2–15, from 39 kilometers in 13 hours on December 6 to 13 kilometers in 8 hours on December 13. The weather was described as "misty," "rainy" or "rain" on eleven days and "good" on three days. The roads were described as "good" on seven days and "fair," "poor," or "muddy" on seven. The health of the men and their campsites were pronounced "good" on all fourteen days. Record Group 120, Records of the American Expeditionary Forces, World War I, Records of Combat Divisions 1917–1919, 4th Division, 4th Division Historical, Box 31, Folder: 39th Infantry, War Diaries 33.5, National Archives and Records Administration, College Park, Maryland.

reviewed us as we crossed. We were the 1st Battalion (Co's A-B-C-D). The 2d Battalion (Co's E-F-G-H) who had been coming along behind us on the same road into Germany are to leave us here and take a short train ride, of which more later.

Trier (Treves) is the oldest city in Germany and was founded 1300 years before Rome. Julius Caesar quartered his troops in this town when he conquered Gaul, 58 years B.C. In 287 A.D. the Roman Emperor Maxiamanus established his residence here. A large number of Roman relics are still in evidence, the most famous being a large Roman amphitheater (3d Cent.) seating 30,000.

"What kind of a gate do ya call that over there on the hill?" inquires O'Hara moping along the road.

"That's the Porta Negri or three storied gate, an old Roman relic," replies Corporal Andrews who was versed in historical subjects.

"Looks like the entrance to the Cub's baseball park ta me," says O'Hara.

"That's all the Irish knows about ancient history anyway," says Stevens.

"Julius Caesar built the gate about the 3d Cent. B.C.," advised Corporal Andrews with impressive authority.

"What's that B.C. stuff mean, Corp.? Does it mean before Cubs beat St. Louis?" asks O'Hara.

"It means, before Knights of Columbus discovered Ireland, ya big harp," sneers Stevens.

"Yeah? Says you. If it means what I think, B.C. means before you an the corporal wuz conscripted in this man's army. Tee Hee," retorts O'Hara.

During the Frankish reign and all through the Thirty Years War of Gustavus Adolphus, Treves was a Forum town. The Archbishop of Treves exerted a powerful and dominating influence in the Moselle and Rhine country during the Middle Ages, his influence extending as far south as Bingen and Coblenz and as far north as Cologne on the Rhine.

The Cathedral of Treves (4th Cent.) also contains one or two renowned relics, such as the skull of the Empress (St.) Helena and the actual coat of Christ, woven without seams. The latter is carefully embalmed in the high altar of the church and is seldom brought out except on an extra special occasion. It is peculiar that a relic as precious as this would be, is not carefully preserved in the

Vatican. How it came to be here in a city older by 1300 years than Rome is probably a story all by itself.

We of the soldiery, of course, knew next to nothing of these things and our historic surroundings. They would have been of little interest to the average doughboy anyway, as his mind was usually on sleep and eats at this period. To the most of us, Trier was no different than any of the other towns we had passed through, except that it was much larger and there was more activity along the Moselle waterfront.

German troops are now rapidly evacuating the large city of Coblenz, which is to be the American bridgehead on the Rhine and General Army Headquarters of the Army of Occupation (3d U.S. Army). This made it necessary therefore to send an advance guard to occupy the city, prevent sabotage, maintain order, etc., until the main army could arrive in the Rhine, which would not be before Dec. 11th to 15th. This guard was therefore needed in a hurry, so the nearest U.S. Army unit and the one easiest available, was selected for this signal honor—the first on the Rhine.

In the A.E.F. it was always troops of the Regular Army that was delegated first. Therefore, on December 8th, 1918, the 2d Battalion, 39th Infantry, 4th Division, left Trier by train for Coblenz, Germany at the junction of the Rhine and Moselle Rivers. They were under the command of Lieutenant Colonel Lockett, leaving at 9.00 a.m. on the above date. Arriving in Coblenz at 2.30 p.m. the same day, they marched directly to the evacuated German artillery barracks on the Falckensteinstrasse and immediately took up guard duty around powder magazines, military police duty, and so on, as required. These troops then, were the first U.S. soldiers to reach the Rhine after the signing of the Armistice on Nov. 11th, 1918.[7]

7. The 2nd Battalion of the 39th was selected because it "had won special commendation for the manner in which it had got its trains over the hills" on the march to Germany. Record Group 120, Records of the American Expeditionary Forces, World War I, Records of Combat Divisions 1917–1919, 4th Division, 4th Division Historical, Box 29, Folder: 39th Infantry, Histories, Commendations & Battle Participants, 4th Division, 204–11.4, Official History of the 39th Regiment of Infantry, 1917–1918, National Archives and Records Administration, College Park, Maryland.

The 2nd Battalion was rushed to Coblenz not only to maintain order, but also to prevent a possible Bolshevik uprising in the city. James McDonald Lockett (1884–1964), a native of New Mexico, attended West Point from July to December 1902, then joined the Regular Army as an enlisted man. Commissioned a second lieutenant in 1907, Lockett held the rank of captain by 1916. Promoted to major (temporary) in December 1917, he became a lieutenant colonel in the National Army in November 1918. Following World War I,

All of the official war correspondents accredited to the U.S. Army, went along with the above troops on the same train, to tell the world the story of the first U.S. troops to set foot on the Rhine and how the doughboys reacted. The above facts are on the authority of Major General Joseph T. Dickman, commander of the Army of Occupation, under whose orders these troops were sent.

Stories that the official war correspondents may have told of the first doughboy troops and their activities are now lost to oblivion, because bungling writers of personal reminiscence and some historians of other divisions also claim this honor, which has no basis in fact. These writers have erroneously stated that the first troops on the Rhine were the 1st Division, 2d Division, 3d Division, 42d Rainbow Division and even the over advertised Marines.

Troops of the 4th Division, U.S. Regular Army, therefore, the first troops to reach and occupy the Rhine bridgehead at Coblenz, also actually administered and policed this district for another eight months or until August 1st 1919, when they were relieved by the 8th U.S. Infantry under Major General Henry T. Allen and the name changed to "American Forces In Germany."[8]

That they have never been given the proper credit due them for their good work here and in the war, is one of the reasons for this volume. Because of the inherent modesty of its officers, no regiment of the division was ever known to brag of its exploits in wartime or afterward, although it was widely known in the army as the "Bull Dog Fourth." Thus, it has remained little known to the average student of American arms and the public, who probably never heard of the 4th Division, the 39th Infantry or the 7th and 8th Brigades.

Lockett remained in the army, and was promoted to colonel in 1936. He retired in 1944. U.S. Adjutant General, *Official Army Register, 1 January 1944* (Washington, D.C.: U.S. Government Printing Office, 1944), 561, 1042.

8. The 8th U.S. Infantry, the last infantry regiment to arrive in France before the end of the war, arrived in Coblenz in July 1919 as part of the new 7,000-man "American Forces in Germany." Alexander Barnes, *In a Strange Land: The American Occupation of Germany, 1918–1923* (Atglen, PA: Schiffer Military History, 2011), 194. Henry Tureman Allen (1859–1930), a native of Kentucky, graduated from West Point in 1882. After service on the frontier, Allen saw combat with his cavalry regiment in Cuba during the Spanish-American War. He then served with a volunteer regiment in the Philippines, and organized the Philippine Constabulary. Promoted to colonel in 1916, he served with General John J. Pershing's "Punitive Expedition" in Mexico in pursuit of bandit Pancho Villa. Promoted to brigadier general in May 1917 and to major general in the National Army in August 1917, Allen trained and organized the 90th Division and led it in combat in France. He took command of American forces in Germany in July 1919, returned to the United States in 1923, and retired as a major general. *Sixty-Second Annual Report of the Association of Graduates, June 10, 1931* (Chicago: The Lakeside Press, 1931), 183–192; U.S. Adjutant General, *Official Army Register, January 1, 1923* (Washington, D.C.: U.S. Government Printing Office, 1923), 2, 1299.

Thirty-ninth Regiment Infantry Band and troops passing through village. Wiltingen, Germany (above Saarburg). December 4, 1918. U.S. Army Signal Corps Collection, National Archives, 42080 [3217D8].

After the departure of the 2d Battalion for Coblenz, we of the 1st Battalion continued forward on our hike to the same town. But we would not arrive at our final destination until several days after the 2d Battalion was actually on duty at the Rhine bridgehead.

Having now passed through the various picturesque old towns along the Moselle River valley, the names of a lot of them has escaped my memory, as I kept no record. I recall, however, being billeted in the front room of a house in a small village, where the hausfrau presented me with several small coins of very ancient vintage, as souvenirs of the Moselle.

In another town, we went up in the attic of a high gabled house to sleep. The attic floor was covered an inch deep with acorns, spread out to dry. We had to brush them up in a pile before we could find a place to lay our heads for the night. I understand that the natives would grind the dried acorns and then mix them with the toasted chaff of other grains, to use for <u>ersatz</u> coffee.

The names of the towns I recall passing through, besides those already mentioned, are Vitte, Mülheim, Cathalan, Pfalz, Berncastel, Milheim, Enkirk, Burgen, Kastellaun and Oberfell. We finally stopped at a small village within about forty kilos of Coblenz. The name has escaped me, and the village was so small as to be of no consequence, anyway. I slept in a chicken-house here and got my head full of hen lice. This pest, in addition to the cooties with which we were all liberally supplied, made the situation quite uncomfortable for me for awhile.

Vinelli had been the hard-luck guy of our company all through the hike from Commercy, France, falling out alongside the road a number of times, only to be returned to us by ambulance. To help him out, Sergeant Painting detailed him and Brizee to ride a motor truck, carrying among other things, the company trunk containing all our war service records. The sergeant told them, "All you birds has ta do, is ta stay with the trunk. An don't let it git outta yer sight fer a single instant, until ya reaches yer destination." So here they were, arrived at a little hamlet ahead of us and just a wee bit tipsy, but no trunk was to be found. They were in for it, and knew it.

Taking in the situation at a glance, Sergeant Painting grabbed Brizee and Vinelli by the blouse and nearly shook the buttons off them.

"Where is that trunk, you two? Answer me!" exclaims the sergeant.

No answer. Both were dumb and speechless.

"Where in the name of St. Garibaldi-de-Humbert did ya drop that trunk, ya linkheaded spaghetti dodger!" raves the sergeant at Vinelli.

"Wah, wah, wah,—" begins Vinelli, shaking in his boots.

"I'll wah-wah you! You wine bibbing son of a cross eyed shoe cobbler," jaws the sergeant, growing red in the face. "I'll have ya both court martialed! I'll have you, Brizee, the truck driver an the whole gahdamn shidderie court-martialed and chased around with bayonets, unless ya finds that trunk an brings it in here ta me at once! Where is it?" —raising his voice—.

"Answer me!"

"Wah-wah—school-a-house. Town-a-two-a-kilos backa," stutters Vinelli.

"Why you coneyac faced, garlic smudger!" raves the sergeant. "Didn't I say fer you ta stay with it until ya got here? Didn't I?

Answer me! But no, you two pink tea rookies couldn't wait ta git by a wine cellar, without stopping to lap up all the vin-rooge in France."

"Wah-wah—" begins Vinelli again, but he is promptly knocked down by the sergeant. Brizee snickered and was promptly knocked down also.

The sergeant then reaches over, picks them both up by the collar and stands them dizzily up in front of him, shaking them violently.

"Now listen, you two birds! You hike back to that town, wherever it is, get the trunk an bring it in here before midnight, er you'll be in the brig ferever! Understant? Ferever!"

"Yes sir!" answers Vinelli.

"Say, sarge," says Brizee, approaching somewhat timidly, "couldn't we both have a little chow, afore we goes?"

"CHOW!" exclaims the sergeant. "Not by a damn sight, ya chiselin' goldbricks. Ya gits that trunk first an ya gits no sleep er chow till ya brings it here ta me. Understand? Git goin! Allay! Beat it! Scram, afore I gits mad an runs ya through with a bayonet!"

Just at that moment an army slat wagon comes to a stop in the center of the road near the sergeant. It was drawn by the most decrepit pair of mules you ever looked at.

"Hey, sergeant!" yells the mule-skinner. "Did ya lose anything?"

"Lose anything? LOSE ANYTHING! Why no, ya big palooka. I ain't been crap shootin' with any horse outfits lately, that I recalls. What yer askin' fer, jawbone?" inquires the sergeant, temporarily forgetting about the lost trunk.

"Oh, nuttin'. Jest thought I'd ast ya," says the mule driver. "Ya see, I gotta green box here, I won off'n two soldats shootin' crap down the road apiece. It's got yer company's name on it. You don't need it. Well, so long, see ya in Hoboken. Gee! Gee! Giddap, ya damn leathernecks!" coaxes the mule driver moving off down the road.

"Hey! Whoa! Wait a minute, ya bellyachin' oat scrounger! Drop that baggage here!" wails the sergeant. "Ya knows damn well its company property."

"Oh, all right, but it'll cost yer twenty franc," answers the mule skinner stopping his wagon abruptly.

"TWENTY FRANCS! I'll see ya in hell first," says the sergeant. "Say! Wait a minute. Hey Vinelli! Front and center!"

Vinelli comes up slowly and sheepishly.

"There's yer trunk up there on that slat wagon, ya big grease ball," says the sergeant. "Now you pays this man twenty franc fer the safe delivery of yer baggage, an a month on K.P. fer ya, besides."

"Oh! All-a righta," sighs Vinelli, limping a little closer to the slat wagon. "Figlio di puttana. Wait-a till I taka offa da shoe."

"Where is Brizee?" inquires the sergeant. "I'll settle his hash, too."

But Brizee was nowhere to be found.

We had been here in the little hamlet about two days, when an order came through to send ten men from the company to Coblenz, for guard duty with the 2d Battalion 39th Infantry, which as I have indicated, was already on duty there since December 8th. They were now billeted across the Moselle River

Company A, 39th Regiment Infantry, 4th Division, passing through streets. Schweich, Rhenish Prussia. December 6, 1918. U.S. Army Signal Corps Collection, National Archives, 40652 [2333D8].

First Battalion, 39th Regiment Infantry, on march through town. Kaisersesch, Rhine Province, Germany, December 14, 1918. U.S. Army Signal Corps Collection, National Archives, 42414 [3977D8].

bridge opposite Coblenz, or at Coblenz-Lutzel, but their duties take them all over Coblenz.

On the expert advice of an old campaigner, Sergeant Painting, who extolled to me the delights and glories for soldiers in cities under military occupation, I, as well as Stevens and several others, now sever connection with Co. B 39th Inf., with whom we had passed through all the vicissitudes of war and transfer to the 2d Battalion 39th, the first troops on the Rhine.[9]

My old company with Belkin, Vinelli, Brizee, Painting, O'Hara and the rest, moved on also and reached Rieden, Germany about Dec. 30th. There they went into permanent winter quarters or billets in private houses. For us who had transferred, a motor-truck

9. Privates Edward W. Munson, Willie Skaggs, John Wengler, James A. Burris, Fred C. Sparks, James G. Morgan, Elvan S. Welliver and William Bricker, along with Howell, were detached from Company B on December 17, 1918, and detailed for service in Coblenz. Morning Reports of Company B, 39th U.S. Infantry for the month of December 1918, National Personnel Records Center, St. Louis, Missouri. By late December 1918, the 39th was divided and billeted in various areas. The regimental headquarters and special units were at Kempenich; the 1st Battalion at Rieden; the 2nd at Coblenz, and the 3rd at Weibern. *History of the 7th Infantry Brigade*, 62. The various companies of the 39th were moved to a number of other stations between March and June 1919.

arrived early the next morning, taking us on a long jaunt beside the Moselle River which lasted until 3.00 p.m. the same afternoon. As we approached the city, the spires and the outline of the old fort at Ehrenbreitstein gave us a thrill of expectancy as we pondered on what this town might hold in store for us. In due time we unloaded before the main entrance of an old artillery barracks, or kaserne, the headquarters of the 2d Battalion of our regiment.

Chapter 15

The Army of Occupation at Coblenz-Au-Rhine

Arriving at the 2d Battalion headquarters in the old artillery barracks on the Falkensteinstrasse in Coblenz, we passed through the gate and were presently met by an officer who inspected our records, and so on. The kaserne, or artillery depot, consisted of two, long, four-story buildings of red rococo brick opposite each other end to end with a gate between, all parallel with the street. Behind these buildings was a large drill field, mess hall, garages and a railroad.

Our identification over, we now move across the large drill field to a building located at the extreme eastern end of the kaserne tract near the railroad. It had formerly been a supply depot. We went inside and found it was full of buttons, millions of them, as well as dress uniforms and other accoutrement of the German Army. There were buttons in boxes, buttons on strings, and large piles of assorted buttons on the floors. Another room contained a quantity of Prussian dress helmets of the sinister, spiked, variety in patent leather, or lacquered black and gold with the Imperial Eagle on the front. These would have made great souvenirs to send back to the home folks, but we were not allowed to take any of them at the time. Later on, you could buy all you wanted, as well as the famous "Gott mit uns" [God with us] belt buckles, at any store in Coblenz for a few pfennigs.

The city of Coblenz proved to be quite an interesting town. It is located directly on the Rhine River, or rather the junction of the Rhine and Moselle, and is a town of 66,000 population.[1] Founded originally by the Romans in 836 A.D., then called Confluents, it is now the center of a large and flourishing wine trade, chiefly Rhine and Mosel. The city has several first class hotels, electric light and trolleys, a municipal theatre, sewage plant, large hospitals and in other ways it is also quite equal to any third class American city. There are many churches also and ancient houses of the nobility, recalling the days of Electoral-Trier glory, the Romans and Carolingians. Medieval architecture too is notable in the Church of St. Florian (12th Cent) and the Liebfrauen Church (church of Our Lady) with its bulbous towers. The oldest structure is the Romanesque church of St. Castor (9th Cent.).[2]

Coblenz was captured by the Swedes after the 30 years war and in 1688 was unsuccessfully bombarded by the French under Marshall Boufflers. Strongly fortified by Prussia in 1815 and down to 1870, it was considered one of the most important military stations on the Rhine. Fort Ehrenbreitstein, directly across the Rhine from Coblenz was occupied by U.S. troops during our stay at this bridgehead and is located on a high promontory, 383 ft. above the Rhine, overlooking the Rhine and Moselle valleys. The U.S. flag was destined to float proudly in the breeze over the old fortress for several years after the Treaty of Versailles was signed. The fort was a part of the area under control of the Army of Occupation, which the French later tried to take away from us, but we kept the flag on the fortress as long as the U.S. forces were on the Rhine.[3] All active

1. Coblenz, from the Latin "confluente," was located at the junction of the Rhine and Moselle Rivers. A large manufacturing plant for uniforms and shoes was located at Coblenz-Luetzel during World War I. *Report of the Military Commander, Coblenz, Germany, From December 8, 1918 to May 22, 1919* (Fort Leavenworth: The General Service Schools Press, 1921), 18, 16.

2. Howell was mistaken about the date of the founding of Coblenz. A Roman fort was established at the site by about 9AD, a bridge across the Rhine was constructed by 49AD, and a stone wall with towers built after 259–60AD. The Romans abandoned the city and the Franks occupied the area by the mid-5th century. Colum P. Hourihane, ed., *The Grove Encyclopedia of Medieval Art and Architecture*, 6 vols. (New York: Oxford University Press, 2012), I: 561.

3. Located across the river from Coblenz, the fortress Ehrenbreitstein, sometimes called the "Gibraltar of the Rhine," was built in 1019 on the site of a Roman fortification. Demolished in 1801 in accordance with the Peace of Lunaville, it was rebuilt between 1816 and 1826.

forts and ammunition caches found in our sector were dismantled as soon as they could get to it by U.S. Army Engineers, rendering them impotent for any further use.

Shortly before dusk the same afternoon of our arrival, four of us, which included Stevens and a new corporal, were detailed and sent at once for guard duty at one of the powder magazines, or kasernes, in northwest Coblenz. It was easily two miles distant and we had to walk, reaching the place in the early evening. We were detailed to relieve the regular guard here for several days. As we had eaten nothing since early morning, when we had left the little village for the ride to Coblenz, we were naturally hungry. I remember though, that our new corporal "noseyed around a bit" and finally came in with a big pot of steaming boiled rice and about two pounds of brown sugar. He had secured it from the kitchen of an army hospital unit located quite near us. It was most welcome.

"Looks like ya found sumpin', corporal," remarks Stevens, hungrily appraising the succulent rice.

"That's right sojer. There's an army hospital unit located close by, an they wuz glad to get rid of it," answers the corporal.

"What's the matter?" says Stevens. "Do them birds get too much ta eat, or ain't they hungry? Looks like good chow ta me."

"Well, according to the cook, they has rice an merlasses fer breakfast, cornmeal, rice an merlasses for lunch, an rice, cornwillie an jam fer dinner, so they's kinda sick of it 'till the regular supplies starts comin.' The cook wuz about to throw it out, so I takes it," explains the corporal.

"Hooray! fer the pill rollers, then!" exclaims Stevens. "I'm a gonna be a good U.S. Chinaman from now on. I betcha I could eat a bushel an come back fer seconds."

"I could eat two bushels," says I, as we all helped ourselves from the big metal pot.

Our guard duty consisted of patrolling the kaserne grounds. The magazine itself was full of powder, which would later be removed and destroyed by U.S. engineers.[4] We had to keep watch to see that

4. Large stocks of German and captured Allied munitions were found in and around Coblenz, including shells, grenades, small arms ammunition, and powder. Gunpowder was either disintegrated in water or burned, although 2,000 tons of German powder was shipped to America for experimental purposes. Philip H. Bagby, *American Representation in Occupied Germany, 1920–21*, 2 vols. (Coblenz, Germany: No publisher, 1922), 2: 200–1.

no one entered the locked magazine or removed anything from the grounds without authority. Our guard was arranged in two-hour shifts. For a three man guard, this made it two hours on and four hours off for each man, with the corporal getting his sleep whenever he could. It was a lonely assignment. We never saw anyone around, except ourselves, from one day to the next. But for the fact that we wore a uniform and carried a rifle, we could have forgotten that we were in the U.S. Army entirely. The corporal continued to bring us our chow from the hospital at regular intervals, so we had enough to eat, anyway.

On Dec. 17th, the four of us were relieved from duty at the kaserne and sent across the Moselle River to Coblenz-Lutzel, a suburb or extension of Coblenz. We were to join Co. G, 39th Infantry, and found them located in some former German barracks of a large horse remount depot, located at the top of a hill and consisting of several large units. This particular kaserne, or barracks, was located directly over an underground powder magazine. It had secret compartments, cleverly concealed, which an old German revealed to the guards one day by removing a few harmless looking bricks at various points, after our army engineers had pronounced the place empty. The Germans could have easily decimated us in our barracks, had they wished to do so, but the war was now over, so they would have nothing to gain by blasting us and the barracks to smithereens. The engineers took weeks to remove and destroy vast quantities of powder and small arms ammunition. When they would explode some of it, we would be reminded once more of shell bursts at the front.

The kaserne buildings however, had their advantages. They were equipped with excellent shower baths, had plenty of hot water available anytime and were now our permanent base. Every day we saw other outfits moving in and locating around Coblenz, as well as other sections along the Rhine. Along with them came all manner of official and pseudo official sightseers from the U.S.A. swarming into the city, such as U.S. senators, Y.M.C.A. people and other welfare units.

Our duties took us all over Coblenz and the surrounding villages. We were closely confined to barracks during the early days of the occupation, when we were not on duty somewhere, as the Army command did not allow us to fraternize with the natives.

This called for some extreme private initiative on our part, and you can lay to that. We felt that we wanted to see some of the sights of the big town and go on the loose. We were as impatient as little boys locked in a closet. We wanted to visit the Y.M.C.A. and the Salvation Army for some of those doughnuts we had heard so much about, but very seldom saw. We wanted to fraternize with the natives too, pretty fräuleins preferred. But all this was strictly "verboten," so it had to be accomplished in such unauthorized ways as we could command. In a short time as they army grew in numbers, more established and the earlier dangers in occupied territory had passed, the restrictions were gradually removed or "winked at."[5]

During the "verboten" period, we would often slide over the brick wall at the rear of the barracks after dark, or else, slip out the front gate when the sentry's back was turned (purposely) against us. Getting back again was another matter. Those were the happy days. Some of the soldiers would get plenty of schnapps on these clandestine expeditions, especially those who could speak German. How I wish O'Hara and Belkin could have been here. They certainly would have enjoyed it.

Taps sounded at 10.30 p.m. but I don't believe any of the soldiers ever stayed out after midnight. If they were noisy when they returned and crabbed the guard at the gate, they landed straight in the guardhouse without further ceremony. Anyway, they figured, "you gotta be in the brig a few times, before you kin call yerself a good sojer," and let it go at that. "The war is over, so what's the difference, anyway?"

Christmas day, I was on guard duty over a lot of interned German war lorries located in a large park just outside Coblenz-Lutzel, on the road to Wallersheim. There were over three thousand of them, and were later sold to a British syndicate. The weather was quite cold, while a thin film of snow covered the ground. If we got tired walking round and round the trucks we would get inside the glass enclosed cabs and amuse ourselves playing with the shift levers.

5. Pershing's anti-fraternization order decreed that American troops and German civilians could only interact when conducting official business. The ban remained in effect until September 1919. Aspects of fraternization are discussed in Erika Kuhlman, "American Doughboys and German Frauleins: Sexuality, Patriarchy, and Privilege in the American-Occupied Rhineland, 1918–23," *The Journal of Military History* 71 (October 2007), 1077–1106.

American soldiers. Fourth Division, cutting wood in German village. Mullenbach, Rhenish Prussia, Germany, December 21, 1918. U.S. Army Signal Corps Collection, National Archives, 44304 [475N9].

Some of the trucks also contained a little benzol and would even run, giving us a chance to start the engines and obtain a little heat from the same. All had wide flat wheels with steel rims but no rubber tires. Rubber had been used by the Germans for more important purposes in the conduct of the war and was very scarce. As I had previously noted, German telephone wires which I saw on the battlefield, was insulated only with tar and cotton fabric, not every efficient electrically.

On Christmas day too, our company or those fortunate enough to be off guard duty and at home in the barracks, had roast pork and sauerkraut for dinner. As those of us on guard around the trucks, were some two miles away from the barracks, our mess sergeant never bothered to send us anything to eat, so we had cold cornwillie out of the can as usual. They sent us a relief guard that night however, so we were back in the barracks by 11.00 p.m. The mess sergeant was now prevailed upon, I mean ordered by the captain, to fix us up some sort of special chow, because we had missed out on the roast pork Christmas dinner. While it hurt the sergeant's dignity somewhat, he turned out some real good frozen steaks which he thawed out and fried for us to the Queen's taste. They were as good as filet mignon, but were served with cole slaw, instead of mushrooms. He also gave us all the raspberry jam we could eat, so things were not so bad after all.

Sometimes we would go on guard duty around the railroad yards in Coblenz-Lutzel, close to our barracks. Then, at other times, it would be in the main railroad yards across the bridge in Coblenz. One day each week, we also acted as a firing squad at military funerals for one of the hospitals. Many of our men were dying as a result of their grueling war experience, or the flu which was prevalent.[6] Many times, these burial ceremonies in the woods on a hillside to the southwest of Coblenz, were witnessed by German civilians. At such funerals, never have I seen a civilian without his head respectfully uncovered, his hat in his hand. In one instance a civilian walked slowly over to a casket and placed a solitary purple flower on the same. The burials were simple—a plain pine box covered with the American flag, a few words read from the Bible and then the firing of the salute into the air by the firing squad.

When we were not on guard duty or other detail, we usually went into Coblenz. It was an endless delight to me and many carefree hours I have passed, roaming the streets of this ancient town, seeing the sights like a country hick. Old buildings, quaint customs and people appealed to me. If I had known as much of French and German history as I do now, my time would have been more profitably spent.

The Y.M.C.A. operated the Festhall (Stadthalle) which was a large building or halle with a casino attached, built for the use of German singing societies and Turnvereins, municipal social center, etc. It contained one of the largest halls in the city equipped with tiered stage seats and a pipe organ for use of the singing societies. The building itself was centrally located at one end of the Schloss Platz and was very ornate. The Y.M.C.A. operated the restaurant of the building at popular prices, mostly for soldiers in the city on leave or furlough. It was also outfitted as a social center for

6. A total of 763 members of the Third Army died between January 1 and April 11, 1919. Sixty deaths were caused by accidents, the rest from influenza and other diseases. Barnes, *In a Strange Land*, 264–65.

the soldiery in and around Coblenz, contained reading and writing rooms with magazines of ancient vintage sent from the U.S. as well as French and English journals. A small library of American books was also available. There was the usual canteen where you could buy French cookies (madeleines) and hot chocolate. Dear, well intentioned, old ladies from the U.S. would stop and carry on a conversation with you in the halls and vestibules. You forgot for a time that you were in Germany, the land of the Hun.[7]

The Festhalle was the largest of similar establishments located in different parts of the city and run by such organizations as the Jewish Welfare Board, Knights of Columbus, Salvation Army, etc., for enlisted men.[8] In addition, the Y.M.C.A. operated the Coblenzerhof, Monopol Hotel, Park Hotel, Engel Hotel and the Bahnhofhaus, the first being for brass hat officers, Rhineland Commissioners and diplomats. The balance was for enlisted men in the area. The officers too, had a private club of their own on a more elaborate scale, where they could "put on the dog" with some invited fräulein or fight the "Battle of Paris" within the club if they cared to do so without undue observation or loss of caste among privates. They had their moments also as we well knew.

On the whole our stay in Coblenz was a pleasant and interesting experience, after the rigors and filth of war in France. Here you must keep shaved, shoes shined, have your uniform spotless, and be on your best military behavior at all times. And you could keep clean too, which was in itself a great comfort. There were no more cooties.

Life in Coblenz therefore, in these early days of the occupation, was for privates, just an endless round of military police and guard duty. There were no polo teams or athletic field such as followed later. We kept the railroad yards, horse depots, old forts, etc., safe for democracy. Every morning at 11.00 A.M. every soldier who was not on guard duty or otherwise assigned, must join with the rest of the company of Coblenz-Lutzel and march across the Moselle Bridge to 2d Battalion Headq[uarters] in Coblenz on

7. The Coblenz Festhalle consisted of one large hall capable of seating fifteen hundred people, two smaller halls that could be opened to extend the large hall, and a large restaurant in the basement.

8. The Knights of Columbus established nearly 150 huts and clubs overseas during World War I, manned by more than 1,000 workers. Ford, *Americans All*, 105. The other relief organizations have been previously identified.

Coblenz, Germany, from Fort Ehrenbreitstein, Rhine. U.S. Army Signal Corps Collection, National Archives, 49403 [1673D8].

the Falkensteinstrasse near the Kaiserin Augusta Ring. After an inspection we joined in formation with the other companies of the 47th, 58th, and 59th Infantry Regiments of the 4th Division. We would then march all over the main sections of Coblenz in parade formation and at attention, with the 39th Inf. Band heading the parade. Day after day after day, this was the daily routine except Sundays. This procedure was not for our own instruction and discipline alone, but also to let the civilians be reminded that the town was occupied by the U.S. Army and under military law.[9] Military Police were constantly on duty as police and traffic officers, giving the town the constant appearance of an American city on fireman's parade day.

Late every afternoon at Retreat (4.00 p.m.), selected men from various regiments would do a guard mount or close formation drill with the band on the Clemensplatz in front of the post office, and facing one end of the Schlossplatz on the Mainzerstrasse.

The Schlossplatz itself was a well-kept parkway fronting the Schlosshaus or Royal Palace. The latter was built by the last Elector of Treves, Clement Wenceslaus, in the 16th Century. This extensive

9. One member of the 39th believed that the morning parade and afternoon guard mount "knocked the eye out of the natives." Record Group 120, 4th Division Historical, Box 29, Folder: 39th Infantry, Histories, Commendations & Battle Participants, NARA.

building, formerly occupied in the spring and autumn by Emperor Wilhelm 1st (war kaiser's father) and the Empress Augusta until her death in 1890, is now the Municipal Museum with many of the Royal rooms and furniture still in place. There were other historic buildings in and around the city, that could be visited with profit and pleasure, had I known their history at the time. I never visited the palace or other places, because soldiers were mostly interested in other things at the moment. Directly back of the Schloss flows the beautiful, winding, romantic Rhine which passes the legendary Lorelie Rock at St. Goar a few miles south of Coblenz.

Being an old Roman town, there is one street still intact, just as it was paved by Caesar's hosts. The paving is solid rock blocks, three to six feet square and of unknown thickness. It is in daily use as one of the city's main back thoroughfares. Old castles and architecture abound in the city, famous since Gustavus Adolphus and his armies overran Germany in the Thirty Years War.

We as soldiers, were too busy looking for handouts from the Y.M.C.A., Salvation Army, K.C., and so on, to take any notice of the cultural or historical monuments of the city. We were more interested in such things as beer, schnapps, chocolat and fräuleins, all of which were now of poor quality after four years of war and neglect. The Salvation Army with its doughnuts, and the K.C. with its canned milk and chocolate, seemed to be giving the best handouts and without cost usually. At the Y they gave free handouts occasionally, and a free picture show was run evenings at one of the theatres they had taken over. However, you usually paid the Y for your Chocolat Menier or Hers[h]ey Bar or the French cookies (madeleines) from Commercy. Hot chocolate was usually free if made from cocoa.

There may have been some reason for the difference in the quality of various soldier welfare and social services connected with the U.S. Army, but I suspect some of it was due to politics within the organizations.

So we would start out of an evening, after chow, and go to town. We would visit the Salvation Army on the Clemenstrasse, get two or three doughnuts and a hot chocolate, thence to the Festhalle to look around and buy some cookies, if we had any money, then to the K.C. officer's canteen where the privates were as welcome as the officers. At the K.C. canteen we would get a

The Royal Palace built by the last elector of Treves, the "Oberprasident." Pvt. Paul E. Yattaw, Company E, 39th Regiment Infantry, in foreground. Coblenz, Germany, January 7, 1919. U.S. Army Signal Corps Collection, National Archives, 51714 [3079N9].

can of evaporated milk or a Hers[h]ey bar if they had it, if not a nice package of madeleines or a razor blade given with a smile. The young priest in charge was usually a regular sort of a fellow, apparently without any exalted ideas about reforming the A.E.F. soldiery. He never forced his religion on you like some of the newly arrived Methodist and Baptist ministers at the Y. After a soldier has been under fire a second time at the front, he has usually come to know his God without any further prompting. Whether he displays it or not, he sometimes has more religion than a lot of the gentry who wear their collars backward.

There was no question though regarding the Y.M.C.A. as being an effective, efficient, organization which functioned throughout the entire occupied area with signal success. No matter what is done for them, some of the men would be sure to grumble anyway, at anything. That is the nature of the civilian soldier, chafing under military restraint and discipline. A soldier from a small village in the occupied area expressed it to us as follows—

"In the village where I am billeted, I sleep in the best room in the best house in town. My hosts, of course, are forced to billet me, but are well paid for it and they treat me with every respect, kindness and consideration. I am even allowed loose with some of the fräuleins of the town."

"I get plenty to eat, but still I am not satisfied. Wish I was back in the good old U.S.A. again."

"What the hell good do I do moping around the small hamlet, drilling in the mud, or carrying in firewood to keep warm? Or forever listening to the lingo of the Germans, and seeing their struggle for existence."

This is how he felt about the situation and there were hundreds of others like him. That is where the Y had their greatest opportunity.

Sometimes while on guard duty in a railroad yard, we would come across a leaking car of Mosel or French wine. When this occurred, we would promptly fill our canteens and make the most of it. In these same yards I have also seen husky young German women climbing telephone poles with leg hooks, acting as regular linemen and repairing the wires. I have seen cars of women's shoes standing wide open with the contents sadly pilfered and scattered. Also carloads of soft coal brickettes, with some of the contents sifting out along the tracks, by the intentional removal of plates or other parts of the car. These were German shipments with which we were not concerned, but we often reported them to the German authorities. Our own shipments and cars usually came through intact from France, as they were accompanied by military escort sergeants or convoys.

As we came into frequent contact with the Escort Sergeants, we thought they had it quite soft and easy. They would usually have one end of a boxcar on their train outfitted for them to live in comfortably enroute, with a small stove to keep them warm. From them, you would get all the news of the back areas of Germany and France and learn of the progress of the Peace Conference, as well as a whole slew of rumors and scandal. Once in a while you would also hear a new naughty story imported direct from the U.S. This sort of kept you up to date. Even if the escorts did live on canned beans and corned willie enroute, they were their own bosses on the train. They had a grand opportunity to secure many little luxuries such as candy and cigarettes, which we had to do without.

These trains coming to Coblenz often contained large supplies of tobacco, milk, jam, candy, molasses, gloves, socks, shoes, underwear, uniforms, etc., for the Army of Occupation. All the Escort Sergeant had to do was to help himself. Sometimes we did the same and for a good reason.

A year or more in the army or navy will teach you many things. You have to be a good "chiseler" and look out for yourself to a certain extent or else go without some of the things you need. But don't get caught at it! So we acted accordingly. In other words, we let ourselves "in" on some of the supplies, sometimes with the cooperation of the convoy sergeant and sometimes not. We could easily learn from him at any time just what the shipment consisted of. As a rule, we kept everyone else out and took only what we actually needed. Of course a carton of cigarettes or a slab of chewing tobacco always came in handy anytime. Very often soldiers would volunteer for disagreeable railroad yard duty when it wasn't expected of them, just to get a whack at something they needed, such as a new pair of gloves, a pair of shoes or pants which the company supply sergeant was unable to supply at the moment. Did we do wrong? If you say "yes," you don't know the army.

Some soldiers were lucky to get detailed on what was termed "detached service," or special duty away from your regular company. I was not fortunate along these lines at first, so more about it later. Men who had been waiters, bartenders, flunkeys, policemen, etc. back in the U.S. would now have a chance to become the same here in Germany, on detached service in such places as the officer's club and elsewhere. Some worked in the Y.M.C.A. hotels or Jewish Welfare Board. Those who had been policemen, became plainclothes men, dressed in mufti and were detectives or investigators for the U.S. Intelligence Dep't. In this capacity, they often mingled with the civilians in Coblenz, or in the small villages in the occupied area, wherever they might be needed. In this way, Army Headquarters kept in constant touch with the persistent undercurrent of political intrigue that was prevalent in Coblenz for a long time after we arrived. A strike of sewage, electric and trolley service employees was averted and rendered impotent in this manner. The new German republic, then just being established at Weimar, was not as yet accepted by all the states of the Reich and was not therefore, very strong. The Rhenish towns where we were located, had even threatened for a time to establish an independent republic of their own.

The U.S. Army, with the French and English battalions along the Rhine, thus kept prepared for further movement into German territory or Berlin if necessary, by being well armed and prepared for any emergency. Heavy artillery and numerous field pieces were brought up in large quantity to the Rhine and made ready for possible action. There were also military outposts all over our sector on the left bank of the Rhine. The Germans, of course, knew all about this and as they did not wish their towns and cities destroyed like those in northern France, they were cautious in their actions. This served as a damper to check Germany until the new republic became stronger and able to hold the various states more firmly together. As we all know now, this lasted only until the demise of the last Reich president, General Paul Von Hindenburg whom most of the nation trusted, but who was deceived and double crossed by the Nazis.

With the death of Von Hindenburg, came the death of the German Republic, as such, in 1933 and the advent of the dictatorial reign of Adolf Hitler with his totalitarian state. He, of course, has been most instrumental in cementing the various states of the Reich with an iron band, returning the Saar Basin to Germany through a successful controlled plebiscite, and the Rhineland through military occupation in defiance of the Treaty of Versailles of 1919 with the sad results to the civilized world, all of which is now history.

France and Germany had been stupid enemies for over 2,000 years back with the Hun mostly on the aggressive. After all that has happened since with the recent occupation of France, they will probably be enemies for centuries to come or as long as European psychology remains as it is. So, perhaps after all, the net effect of all our effort and sacrifice was zero. We succeeded then, in stopping four, weary, long years of holocaust, only to allow a breathing spell for the preparation of a larger, quicker and deadlier world catastrophe. Our greatest mistake was that we didn't go on to Berlin in 1918. All this, of course, is hindsight.

On several occasions I was detailed with a corporal for military police duty in the villages of Neuendorf, Metternich and

Wallersheim. One of our duties as police, was to see that the beer halls and bars were closed at 11.00 p.m. sharp. We never had any trouble with soldiers and the civilians seemed sufficiently wary of the military, to comply with our orders without resistance. On weekends, mostly Sundays, the civilians would get a little noisy, usually by singing in the streets when returning home from a gesellschaft abend.

A German gasthaus is a sociable place to eat and drink, somewhat in the nature of our present day restaurants. They had buxom, often pretty barmaids. The civilians however, usually brought their own food, such as sausages and the like, when they patronized these places along with their entire family. The beer, of course, they purchased in the gasthaus and on weekends, especially Sundays, everyone would seem to be having a harmless sociable afternoon or evening, meeting their friends, all in the manner characteristic of their country. "Zwie bier bitte." "Prosit."

Sometimes when no one was about, the military police on duty in the town, were offered and usually accepted some of the beer at the invitation of the proprietor. We had no strict orders against this, but it was dangerous from a military point of view. It would probably be considered a breach of discipline in the U.S. Army when on duty. Anyway no harm was ever done, that I know of.[10]

While I was in Coblenz, I also had the opportunity one evening through a German acquaintance, to visit a German masonic lodge in session. It was an interesting experience and to me an unexpected privilege. The "work" was about the same as in the States, but of course the language and little idiosyncrasies of the Teuton made the session seem different. The lodge room itself was standard in arrangement and the furnishings were executed in a luxurious manner, which any mason in the world will understand. These lodges have all long since been closed and their properties confiscated by the Nazi decree of dictator Hitler, but they are probably still in session secretly, somewhere else.

In order to counteract the Army decree against fraternization with the civilians, and ease the growing unrest of some of the soldiery, the army officials opened up, as an experiment, a section of the Stegemannstrasse in Coblenz, a high class red

10. Only beer and wine could be sold to American soldiers in the Army of Occupation.

light district of one city block previously closed and under guard to prevent the spread of disease among the soldiery. Of course the officers had been going in right along, guard or no guard. There was also plenty of clandestine fraternization all over town. But on this particular occasion, a contingent of the 42d Rainbow Division who were stationed at Fort Ehrenbreitstein directly across the river from Coblenz, came over and were allowed to visit the street for one evening. One night, that was enough. They became boisterous and uncontrollable, broke window panes, purloined madam's jewelry, ripped off piano tops, paid the girls in cigarette coupons which looked like paper marks and almost completely wrecked the lane of easy diversion. After that episode the street was closed and kept permanently closed under double guard.

About this time, I had some trouble with the top sergeant of my company, a small, large mouthed, la[n]tern jawed individual, currently acting company commander. He found fault with me at inspection and gave me a blast for not being slicked up. Explaining that I had just returned from a three day and night guard assignment, made no difference to him, even when I stated facts.

"Look at those shoes! Look at that belt! Look at that rifle! It's filthy!" raves the sergeant in front of the whole platoon, "Why aren't you cleaned up? Answer me! Guess you don't want to stay with a first class outfit, any longer." All this and he throws my rifle back at me again.

"Who wants to stay in an outfit with a Sears & Roebuck sergeant like you!" says I, talking back carelessly.

This was, of course, a serious breach of military discipline. You are supposed to stand the insults of a superior officer, real or imagined, when standing in formation and say nothing, except perhaps, "yes sir." I had now pricked the ego of the little sergeant and completely ruined his dignity in front of the company, so I expected the worst.

"I'll fix you later on, sojer, an don't you fergit it," was his only reply as he passed on down the line.

His face was as red as the setting sun because the whole platoon, hearing my remarks had burst out laughing. Oh Man! The sergeant pulled himself together and proceeded to bawl out the whole formation to the Nth degree for laughing and soon had them standing at attention again. Thereupon he suddenly dismissed the company, with a dark look in my direction but he said nothing more to me.

Two weeks passed and nothing happened. I thought the incident was forgotten. One fine morning, after chow, I was called to the orderly-room to report to the top sergeant, along with another private named Sparks. He was from "way down thar" in Alabam[a] and didn't give a damn. I really didn't care much either, as I was weary of guard duty and felt a transfer would be welcome at this particular time.

"I've decided that you and Sparks need a change," begins the top sergeant in a voice of rasping fuzz. "You two birds can't stand a regular outfit like this one, so I'm transferring you into a horse-manure brigade where you can scrub harness an be a mule's chambermaid for a change. This ought ta teach ya what the real Army is, if yer ever gits back in it again. Report to Sergeant Dumont, 2d Battalion, 39th Infantry Supply Train in Coblenz. Turn in yer rifle an ammunition." When we got outside the orderly-room, Sparks gave the sergeant a lusty "Bronx cheer." So I asked him what he had done to be transferred.

"I wuz A.W.O.L. fer two weeks back in Trier," said Sparks.

Well now, this wasn't so bad. Not as bad as I had expected anyway. The little sergeant was placing us on detached service with a horse outfit who had probably just made a request for two men. This was the way he would get even by spending the rest of our army service, grooming mules and harness.

As long as it wasn't the "honey wagon" we didn't care much. With the supply company we would get three square meals per day, have less military discipline and sleep in the barracks every night, instead of walking post somewhere in the wet and cold.

It wasn't as dignified as parade or guard duty, I'll admit that, but we were tired of that sort of thing weeks ago. To get a full night's rest each day and have regular chow and hours, was more than we had been able to do while we were with G Co., with its incessant inspections, guard details, morning parades and what not. Also the supply company had a large brick mess hall, with a hotel kitchen and beer bar located at one end of the mess hall, where you could purchase a fair quality potato beer at five pfennigs per glass. The beer concession was run by a civilian, well patronized, but never abused because the beer was only about three percent.

In due time, Sparks and I reported to Sergeant Dumont at the supply company's horsebarns located along a railroad track back of the Kaiserin Augusta Ring. The barracks were close by, also, in the 2d Battalion Headquarters building on the Falkensteinstrasse, our original point of entry to Coblenz in December.

"Do you know anything about horses?" inquired Sergeant Dumont, speaking to Sparks.

"Sure. I wuz brought up with 'em down in Alabam," replied Sparks, very much pleased.

"Very good, Sparks," says the sergeant, smiling, "See that harness over there on the wall? Now snap out of it and get it clean before inspection."

"Yes sir," answers Sparks, as his face fell a mile. But he got busy as there was no other choice.

Now turning to me, the sergeant asked me practically the same question in regard to horses. I replied that I was brought up in the city, didn't like horses and was afraid of them which was more or less true.

"You will damn soon get used to them around here," says the sergeant. "But I may be able to use you on something else. Wait a minute!"

So he finally gave me a job as helper to a corporal on a baggage truck which was a break for me. On the truck job, our duty was to go to the Haupt Bahnhof (R.R. station) each morning around 10.00 a.m. and pick up and deliver Red Cross, Y.M.C.A. and officer's baggage to the required address in Coblenz which is quite a large town. We usually maneuvered this detail so that it took us the greater part of the day. For, if we came into headquarters early, we would then have to go out and haul supplies from the railroad yards over in Coblenz-Lutzel, directly across the Moselle River bridge, a job that wasn't always so easy. Sometimes, however, our baggage delivery was very heavy too, so there would be some hard work attending its distribution. But mostly we took it easy. Anyhow, it got us around the town and gave us an opportunity to see what was going on in all quarters. It took away the dull monotony and often landed us in some queer, even dangerous places about town. Altogether it was a soft army job and I liked it.

On one of these trips, we picked up three newly arrived Y.M.C.A. Canteen girls and their baggage. They were just three weeks out of New York and looked good to us because they were a breath from home. We couldn't date them however. They were for officers. They decided they would ride with us to their destination and we were proud to have them with us. They gave us a dollar tip in good old U.S. currency.

On another trip delivering baggage, we unintentionally intruded on a U.S. officer in the act of kissing a pretty, young fräulein in a room hung heavy with red velvet draperies and tapestry. It was a beautiful room and I recall there was a grand piano. It was not a boudoir-studio. Getting no response to our knock on the door, we had merely stepped through the doorway with the trunk, just as the lieutenant was bending over for a smack from the reclining girl. He was furious, of course, and we fully expected a bawling out for the unthinkable military crime of intruding on the privacy of an officer, unannounced. He must have realized, however, that we were there merely to deliver his baggage and our intrusion was accidental. We had already lugged his trunk up three flights of stairs, so we didn't care much what he thought, anyway. He simply ordered us to "leave it and get out at once!," handing us a five mark tip which suited us.

On our way out, the corporal and I noticed a back stairway and decided to follow it down, just to see where it would lead us. Imagine our surprise when we subsequently arrived in the back kitchen of this four story, city type, residence. Here we found staring at us, three, fair looking young fräuleins dressed in red and blue ruffled aprons or dresses, whom you can well guess were much surprised to see us. They began talking excitedly to each other, all in a jargon we didn't understand, but we knew it concerned us. So we just stood there and grinned at them. We knew however, by their actions, that they had been around U.S. soldiery before, as they were trying to hum a few bars of "Mademoiselle from Armentieres." Finally, after a lot of silly fooling around and giggling, one of the mädchens pointed out 9.00 p.m. on the kitchen clock. We got wise and says, "yah, yah, mine shots" which was all the German lingo we knew at the time. It was really a funny and bizarre situation.

That same evening we went back at the appointed time, armed with chocolate bars and a loaf of white bread we had previously picked up at the ration dump. Nothing could have kept us away. This was new stuff. As per schedule, there were two of the fräuleins awaiting us at one of the rear entrances. With much gesturing, ja-jahing, schones and jawols, they made us understand that we were to remove our hob-nailed shoes, which we did. These were carefully concealed in a nearby kitchen closet and then beckoned us to follow them. But of course we were afraid, got our shoes and went back to the barracks. Yes, we did not. We followed them up the back stairway to a sort of a maid's reception room and sat down with them on a sofa.

To amuse us, as well as themselves, they brought out the family album, or its equivalent, showed us stereoscopic views of "der Vaterland und der Rhine," all the time keeping up a ceaseless chatter among themselves which was all Greek to us. During the evening they also brought us a few good stiff drinks of schnapps and let us kiss them quite a few times.[11] This was right up our alley and we made the most of it while it lasted. We felt right at home and enjoyed ourselves immensely. As you perhaps know, there is nothing quite like strange females to quicken the heavy pulse of soldiers, especially in a foreign country. Could it be possible, that these friendly and amorous girls were once enemies of our country and we killed their fathers and brothers, as their fathers, brothers and cousins had killed us?

In return for all this hospitality, we showed them all the souvenirs, gadgets, new testaments, dog tags, buttons, folding pocket knives, brass rings and other cheap jewelry that a soldier possesses. The corporal showed them his stripes and his sharpshooter's badge which they thought was a medal for bravery like their iron cross. We presented them with the chocolate bars and the loaf of white bread we had brought along. It certainly was a grand evening, making signs and speaking to each other like deaf and dumb mutes, because neither could understand what the other was talking about. It really didn't matter anyhow as long as we could kiss them. I thought of O'Hara and Belkin back in some small village mudhole along the Rhine, and Stevens over in Coblenz-Lutzel doing guard duty. How these three would envy me if they could

11. A soldier in Howell's own 39th Infantry was arrested for fraternization and sentenced to 30 days in the guardhouse for merely kissing a German woman. The offender then escaped and repeated the offense, for which he was sentenced to an additional 60 days. *The Daily Courier* (Connellsville, PA), April 15, 1919.

only see me now. Or would they? We taught our girls some more or less varicolored bars of "Mademoiselle" and split our sides laughing at their crude attempts at pronunciation of the English words. Also we decided that the next time we came to see them we would bring along some Ivory soap that was 99/100ths per cent pure, even if we weren't. They looked a little greasy and soap to them was a luxury. We didn't drive a truck for nothing.

After about two hours of this sort of thing, the fräuleins suddenly jumped up and left us. They returned very soon, bringing us our shoes, telling us something about "raus mit!" and "offizier kaput!" which we understood to mean that we should leave at once or be discovered by the U.S. officer who was billeted in the same house. Phooey on him! But if he was to discover us here after 10.30 p.m., which was our deadline, then there might be trouble. We ordinary privates would be guilty of fraternization with the enemy, etc., which, of course, was more or less forbidden—except for officers. We got out undiscovered, but the next time we called on the mädchens, they were not there, so I don't know what became of them.

How about Sparks? Well, he and I were doing very well for ourselves in the supply company, even though he was still manicuring harness. That is, we were glad that we were away from the grind of guard detail and the petty tyrannies of top sergeants and lieutenants in the infantry. Now, I had noticed lately, that Sparks and several others were becoming regularly absent from the barracks after 9.30 p.m. in the evening and stayed out until after 12.30 p.m. or later. I was curious, or perhaps I felt a little slighted because I was not a party to their racket. So I decided to do a little questioning and see if I could learn anything.

"Hey, Sparks! Where ya goin' tonight?" says I, as I saw him preparing to leave.

"Who wants ta know?" replies Sparks. "I ain't a goin' anywhere in perticular, an if I wuz, I wouldn't tell you. Why?"

"Oh nuthin'," says I. "It's none of my business, only I notices lately that you an several others is always out nights between 9.30 an 12.30 p.m. an if it's a new racket, I'd sorta like ta be in on the know. Of course, bein' we both graduated from the infantry together, I thought ya might put me wise ta what's goin' on. I'm just curious, that's all."

"Say, kin ya keep a secret, sojer?" inquires Sparks.

"Sure I kin," says I. "I kin keep it as long as I kin keep two marks."

"Which ain't very long," observes Sparks. "But you come along with me tonight, an you'll see something. Its down by the horse barns, so above all, don't breathe a word of it to the sergeant, er I'll knock yer damn block off. We has ta be mighty keerful about this, an no foolin.'"

"All right. I promise," says I. "What is it, a Faro game er just plain Black Jack?"

"Neither," says Sparks, "but you'll see sumpin', bein' yer asked fer it."

I begin to wonder what it can all be about, surrounded with so much secrecy.

So about 10.00 p.m. we left the barracks through the front gate. Sparks had previously looked in on the sergeant, who now seemed to be sound asleep and snoring his head off. Even Mike Finnegan, the mule skinner, coming in the barracks with a skin full and throwing mess kits all around, couldn't have wakened him, so we thought. He was a perfect working buzz saw.

Soon we were on our way to the supply company barns which were located in several old gray stone buildings along the railroad tracks not far away, near the center of Coblenz. One building was stables, while another was full of baled hay, and so on. We walked slowly and quietly through the driveway. Sparks never said a word, nor I either, although I was still doing a lot of wondering. From the building containing the baled hay, I thought I heard singing, but I wasn't quite sure. As we approached closer to the same I distinctly heard someone say "duck" and then all was quiet again. Sparks smiled at me as he slowly and cautiously opened the door. It was pitch dark inside, so Sparks lit a match. All I could see was large piles of baled hay, but I noticed there were candles around standing safely in tin boxes, having just recently been snuffed out and still smoking. Sparks now relit one of them and says, "aubdunk-aufdunk," which was the password. Immediately from behind innocent looking bales of hay came several supply company soldiers that I knew, probably eight or ten in all.

"Where's all the fräuleins at?" inquires Sparks.

"Come on out, mädchens. Its O.K.," says someone, and out from behind the bales of hay like the others, came several little black eyed fräuleins looking like schoolgirls, laughing and tittering like so many skylarks, and screaming with pleasure if one so much as tickled them.

It seems that a couple of weeks back, some of the soldiers had flirted with some of these girls sitting in the windows of a girl's school, or gymnasium, located about two blocks away in the center of Coblenz. Soldiers who could speak German, playfully invited them over for a visit to the supply company barns, without any idea, of course, that they would ever come. But come they did and had been coming ever since, uninvited. Of course they were little girls, although quite mature, with a yen for soldiery and some excitement.

Bales of hay were arranged in the barn so as to make a fair stage and on these the mädchens sang folk songs, danced ballet and performed anything else they knew. The boys certainly had a good show whenever one of these dances started. We sang and danced around, and played German parlor games that I can't even remember. This was the best break, we, as soldiers, ever got anywhere in the Army of Occupation. It was clandestine entertainment supreme. It was too good.

But by now this sort of thing had been going on too long and in some way the top-sergeant of the supply company got wise to it. We had left him fast asleep in the barracks, at least we thought so. After Sparks and I had been in the barn for an hour or so, we again heard footsteps on the gravel, outside. Someone with good ears yelled, "duck!," so we all ducked behind the bales of hay after snuffing out the candles. The door was now slowly opened and in walked our sergeant big and important, but he couldn't see a thing.

"Come on out, ya ornery bunch of hay smackers, before I reports ya at headquarters," commands the sergeant. "I knows yer there."

Nobody breathed, but we all knew we were caught, redhanded.

"Come on out! Yer under arrest!" orders the sergeant.

Someone gave the sergeant a muffled "Bronx cheer," so we all started laughing. The girls giggled. We just couldn't keep quiet any longer.

"Well I'll be gahdamned! Playin' hide an seek!" exclaims the sergeant as the girls and everyone else came out from behind the bales of hay and the candles were re-lit.

"Raus mit! Offizier kaput!" yelled the girls and started to leave, but changed their minds.

Instead of leaving, they all clustered around our big shot sergeant, sat on his lap, toyed with his sharpshooter badge and called him "mine grosse brave Marine" which he was not, but it pleased him immensely and made his chest swell out a yard.

"How does ya like our haymow fräuleins, sarge?" says one of the boys.

Oh, schone, schone," replies the sergeant blushing, as one of the little mädchens plants a smacking kiss on his red cheek in front the whole gang.

"Ain't fur'rin women the winnin' things?" says our gruff sergeant, talking like a cissy, he was so embarrassed.

"Oh, fudgie-wudgie!" exclaims Sparks, losing his balance and falling backwards among the bales of hay.

For some time afterwards, our sergeant was quite a regular visitor and concealed our clandestine entertainment from reaching the ears of the lieutenant in command of the supply train. We used to brag among ourselves about our conquests among the schoolgirl fräuleins who were also tight lipped as to our rendezvous.

I have now been in Coblenz since Dec. 17th, 1918. Since about March 1919 I have been on duty with the 2d Battalion Supply Train and having more fun than I ever had with a rifle company where there is more discipline. It is now April 5th, 1919. We had seen the 42d Rainbow Division leave for the U.S.A. late in March and had wished that we were among them as they came through Coblenz from their outposts back of Fort Ehrenbreitstein on the left bank of the Rhine. They came through on the railroad right back of the supply company horse-barns, traveling in big gray American boxcars headed for France and home. They were in high spirits as they sat lounging out of the car doors. The sides of the train were labeled with all manner of signs and insignia of the 42d Division. As they passed by us, some of them shouted good-natured, but ribald and uncomplimentary remarks at us. We replied to their remarks with suitable army lingo which ended with the phrase, "What's the color of the Rainbow?" We then answered our own question by shouting "yellow!" Of course we knew that this famous division was not "yellow" but had an enviable war record, although we never considered it any better than our own, or any greater. However, the slam always got their goat, so everyone was happy. We wondered how long it would be, before we too could travel the same route, pass through the same debarkation camps and be back in God's country once more.

Chapter 16

Along the Rhine

Spring in Coblenz is much the same as anywhere else in the temperate climatic zone. Blossoms heavy with perfume, covering the fruit trees, make their appearance early. Grass shoots, orchid and blue-white penciled crocus's and yellow daffodils peek out at the blue German sky, opening their tiny petals to the morning dew as stolid Teutons start their daily tasks.

The air is balmy and promotes lassitude. Even the army has the Spring fever. But the outposts, and other battalions and companies back in the little hamlets, must still drill in the mud and go on guard details, regardless.

About this time an orderly from Army Headquarters appeared at the 2d Battalion horsebarns. He handed the sergeant an order directing me to report to General Army Headquarters in Coblenz, immediately. The sergeant looked at me sort of funny-like, so I now begin to think about some of the things I may have been doing lately that might be considered unmilitary, if anything. How about that sergeant over at Co. G in Coblenz-Lutzel who had sent me here? Did he report me for fancied insubordination? Did army headquarters know anything about our haymow fräuleins? I felt that I was in for something or other, but I didn't know what. Therefore, I lost no time in reporting to the designated officer at the headquarters building. After a lot of running around, I finally found him tucked away in a tiny office at the far end of a long corridor. I entered nervously, saluted, stood at attention and expected the worst.

"Are you from New England, private?" inquired the officer, a lieutenant.

"Yes, sir. Waterbury, Connecticut, sir," I replied.

"Very good then. Shake. So am I," says the lieutenant, extending his hand.

Of course we were behind closed doors, or he wouldn't have been quite so friendly. Believe me, it took a load off from my mind. It seems that he had a record card I had filled out way back in Camp Devens, Massachusetts, when I entered the army. This card showed my civilian occupation, age, etc., and the officer was inquiring if I knew anything about power-plants, electric motors and wiring. I did luckily, and in talking to him I exaggerated a little because I scented a new job of some kind, and a change would be welcome if on detached service. He dismissed me shortly without giving me any encouragement or information but saying something about a good record, and so on.

I now returned to the horsebarns and was left in suspense for about a week afterward. One day unexpectedly, the same orderly again reappears and handed my sergeant travel orders for me to report to the Depot Quartermaster at Bendorf, a town about ten kilometers down the Rhine from Coblenz. It was one of the main supply depots for the Army of Occupation.

"Well, it's too bad," says the sergeant. "It's too bad ya gotta leave a good outfit an join the quartermaster corps, an soldier with a bunch a pen wipers."

"I'm sorry ta go, sarge," says I, "but I guess you'll get along, if ya don't sleep too much nights."

"I knows somebody else that'll be very sorry also," continues the sergeant. "What'll I tell little Fräulein Johanna?"

"You take care of her 'till I gits back," says I. "An don't be too serious with furrin women, 'cuz ya knows they is dynamite, an T.N.T."

"O.K., sojer," replies the sergeant. "If I can't be good, I'll be careful. Report back to the top-sergeant of G Company at Lutzel, at once, before starting for Bendorf! Good by an good luck ta you."

"So long, sarge. I've had a lot of fun in your outfit an I won't fergit it," says I taking my leave.

This was the first I had known that I was simply on detached service and only loaned to the supply company, instead of being permanently transferred as I had supposed.

When I reported back to my old enemy at Lutzel, he began throwing slurs at me the minute I stepped inside the orderly-room door. Now, I had a chance to get back at him, as I was out of his jurisdiction due to the army travel order.

"So ya had ta come back to the old outfit again, eh?" says the topper, scornfully. "Couldn't even git along in a nice horse-manure brigade. Well now, what's the matter? Did the naughty mules kickee too much?"

"Not so fast! Not so fast, yuh big windbag!" says I. "Just take a squint at this, an pull in yer neck, wiseguy."

He was about to burst open and give me the "works" when I pulled out the army travel order and handed it to him. His face fell a mile and his high-falutin' dignity was all but shattered.

"You win, private," is all he had to say.

He couldn't do anything about it either, except to order the company supply sergeant to outfit me with a new uniform and anything else that was necessary, including the return of my rifle and ammunition. Anyway, at best, he was just plain shanty Irish all puffed up with a little authority like an Irish cop.

On the way out of the barracks, I met Stevens.

"Welcome home, goldbrick," says Stevens, by way of greeting. "Gee! But I'm glad ta see ya back again. What's up?"

"Oh nuthin', except I been transferred to the quartermaster corps," says I.

"Worse an worse!" exclaims Stevens. "From oat scrounger ta slacker. Geeze! I wish't I could git outta this damn outfit! The top-sergeant drives me nuts!"

"Why don't ya do something real bad, then?" says I.

"Do something? Phooey! I've done everything I could think of except go A.W.O.L.!" exclaims Stevens. "The worst I gits fer punishment is a coupla days on K.P. They're short of guards around here, so I can't git transferred, nohow, no matter what I do."

"Keep yer chin up an yer tail down," says I, "'cause mebbe you'll go home in a coupla months from now."

"You been in a horse outfit so song, ya talk horsey," replies Stevens. "If ya meets O'Hara an Belkin in any of yer travels, give 'em my best ree-gards. If they's married any fräuleins, tell 'em ta come ta Coblenz on their honeymoon. Well, so long sojer, an good luck. See ya in Hoboken."

That was the last I ever saw of Co. G 39th, as they were relieved shortly afterward by the 58th Infantry, 4th Divis[ion] and went back to the vicinity of Luxembourg. I received a letter later from Stevens in that locality, and he informed me that the Lux fräuleins, or whatever you call Luxembourger girls, all wanted American husbands and would come down to the barracks anytime at the sound of two short toots on a bugle from the barracks roof.

That must have been interesting for Stevens.

After leaving the barracks at Lutzel, I had to report to the army travel officer at the Haupt Banhof in Coblenz, to find out how to get to Bendorf-au-Rhine. I was told to take a suburban trolley at the Festhalle, cross the Rhine River near the town of Ehrenbreitstein and get off at Bendorf about ten kilos north on the east bank of the Rhine. As my date to report was two days away, I took the opportunity to stay around Coblenz and do as I wished. Finally, I boarded a suburban car and started down the Rhine. It seemed funny to board a car and not have to pay any fare. In fact, most of the commuters on the car were soldiers, anyway. But there were a few civilians who carried large heavy satchels and bundles of sausages and cheese. They were none too friendly with us, either.

Subsequently I reported to the depot quartermaster at Bendorf. He was a gruff old Regular Army colonel, whom I found out later had been reduced from a higher rank for being drunk and disorderly while in command of a motor transport corps, running the trucks ragged somewhere around Nogales, Arizona, while helping Pershing chase Villa in the Mexican campaign.

When I reported to him in person and presented my papers, I clicked heels together and gave him a snappy infantry salute. Well do I remember his facial expression as he looked up at me from under dark bushy eyebrows.

"Don't salute me, private!" says the colonel in a loud irritated voice. "And don't salute any of my officers while you are here, either. This ain't the regular army; this is only the gahdamn quartermaster corps. Yuh understand?"

View of building occupied as headquarters by 4th Division, Hotel Pitz-Kurhotel. Shows American soldiers in front of hotel. Bad Bertrich, Rhine Province, Germany, January 23, 1919. U.S. Army Signal Corps Collection, National Archives, 51895 [357F9].

"Yessir!" I gulped, not knowing what to make of it.

"Tomorrow, you will report to Engineer-Lieutenant Barclay for further instructions," he continued.[1] "While here, you will take charge of the power plant and see that it runs every day for the refrigeration, and every night for lights. If you fall down on the job an it doesn't run, I'll know it an come down an bawl ya out. If anything goes wrong, report to me an nobody else."

"Yessir," says I, forgetting to salute on purpose, and going out.

Now here at last, must be the ideal outfit for goldbrick soldiers. One that would be a pleasure to be connected with. I could hardly believe my eyes, or my ears either. I'd have something to brag about if I ever saw O'Hara or Belkin again.

As I stepped out in the yard, I noticed an old Overland staff limousine painted an olive drab color, the same as other A.E.F. cars. This car was no different from others I had seen, except, that perched on the roof of the car was a large, live Hoot Owl, one leg

1. This officer could not be identified.

dragging a light chain. This queer outfit belonged to a traveling quartermaster lieutenant and was a frequent visitor at Bendorf, where the car and the owl would stand for hours outside of one of the warehouse buildings. The soldiers around here soon found out that if you talked to the owl, he would always answer with the static phrase, "Whoo! Whoo!" This, of course, made him the object of much ribald repartee with the soldaten.

One day a Convoy Sergeant just in with a long train from Le Mans, France, emerged from a boxcar carrying a live, green, talking parrot in a large brass cage. Hanging the parrot and cage temporarily on a large hook, just outside the colonel's office and alongside a broomhandle standing upright just outside the door, he went inside to report to the colonel. Outside and close by also, was the staff car with the hoot owl perched on top as usual, its large round eyes peering out in apparent amazement at the world, but blinded by the daylight. The whole presented a very unmilitary appearance, to say the least, especially in front of a commandant's headquarters. Parrot, broomstick and hoot owl. But all was serene and quiet until the office door was suddenly opened, jarring the broomstick down across the threshold. As the colonel hurriedly stepped forth in a big rush to get somewhere, he tripped on the broomhandle and nearly went headlong as he stumbled out. Completely losing his temper, of course, he started to bawl out the innocent convoy sergeant, who closely followed him.

"What gahdamn blanket blank fool left that blankety blank broomstick in the doorway fer me to stumble over," bellows the colonel. "Answer me! Do you know?," turning to the convoy sergeant.

"Whoo! Whoo!," screams the old hoot owl from his perch on top of the staff car.

"Who? You seventh son of a biscuit shooter," cries the parrot from his cage on the outside of the wall. "Cheese and crackers, colonel."

The colonel, who had not yet noticed the green and red parrot, thought that some concealed soldiery was trying to rib him through mistaken identity. He was livid with rage.

"Come out from behind that car, you men! All of you!" orders the colonel. "And consider yourselves under arrest fer discourtesy, an trying ta dishonor an officer of the U.S. Army. Come out I say!"

But no one appeared.

"Whoo! Whoo!" again screams the hoot owl on the car, while the colonel now turning full around, also discovers the parrot and cage hanging from the wall a few feet from the doorway. The convoy sergeant is standing with mouth agape watching the scene, unable to speak, unable to move. The colonel, therefore, in a blind rage rushes back and grabs the parrot and cage off the wall and starts inside the door again with murder in his heart, the excited convoy sergeant, owner of the bird, close behind.

"I'll fix you, you blankety blank son of a sea cook!" threatens the colonel, rushing in the door and giving the broomhandle a vicious kick aside and dangling the parrot cage.

"Leave go, goldbrick! Leave go! Can't dishonor me! Awk!" screams the parrot wildly, as he flutters around the bottom of the cage. But all three disappear through the doorway and from the inside still come the screams of the scared parrot.

"Call out the guard! Can't dishonor me! Whooie!"

Then there was a loud whack, and all was silence. The hoot owl on the top of the car says "Whoo! Whoo!"

The convoy sergeant soon emerges alone from the colonel's office carrying a much battered bird cage with the parrot cramped down in one corner, feathers all ruffled, but still alive. The sergeant sets the cage down on the ground alongside the staff car, the cage door now having jarred open. Soon the colonel again emerges from his headquarters.

The owl says "Whoo! Whoo!" while the colonel looks up at him in disgust. The angry parrot, now fully recovered and with blood in his eye, flies out of the open cage door headed directly for the colonel's head, knocking off his overseas cap and clinching his long, talon-like claws in the top of the colonel's bald head. The colonel, now in a panic, throws his arms wildly about trying to dislodge the bird.

"I'll fix you, you baldheaded son of a seacook! Awk!" screeches the parrot, but the colonel finally succeeds in dislodging the bird and runs wildly down the road, a very unmilitary sight indeed. The convoy sergeant, looking around the corner of the building as all this occurs, has a smile of pleasure on his face. With the colonel safely out of the way, the sergeant picks up the cage again, places the parrot inside and walks back to his boxcar where both disappear inside—believe it or not.

But I was never bothered in any way by the quartermaster colonel who seldom visited the power plant. One day, however, he received an order to send me back to Coblenz for guard duty, so he came around to ask me about it. The order was probably from my old friend, the top sergeant at Co. G in Coblenz-Lutzel.

"Do you wish to return to Coblenz?" inquired the colonel, sort of anticipating the answer.

"No sir. Not unless my division is moving back to the U.S.A.," I replied.

"Very good then, soldier. I'll show 'em they can't take my men away from me just when I get them used to me an this command," says the colonel. "I'll tell 'em I need you here."

So here I was and here I stayed. The softest job I ever had in this man's army.

My stay at Bendorf-au-Rhine, of several months duration was both pleasant and instructive. I was practically my own boss as you have already noted. The chow was excellent, being a quartermaster unit. Due to the close proximity of our refrigeration plant, we often had frozen chicken from the U.S. and ice-cream made from evaporated milk and cornstarch. This, of course was extreme luxury for an expeditionary force in the field in wartime. If I ever join the army again, which isn't at all probable, I want to be in the quartermaster corps where you get three square meals per day and a cot to sleep on under suitable shelter. Also regular pay. My only drawback at Bendorf was, that I had plenty of time on my hands but no money, because I was away from my regular company. The men in this quartermaster depot were paid regularly and from time to time gave me small sums, or extended favors in various ways. They were real white men, even if they never saw the Argonne woods.

The power plant itself required very little of my attention, except mornings and early evening. If I wanted to leave it for any reason, I could switch our lines on to the German lines with which we were also connected. I therefore spent a lot of time during the day in roaming the countryside.

The population of the town of Bendorf was around 10,000 and is mostly residential. Further north is the town of Mülhofen. I remember it because of a company of Marines who were stationed there. Also there were several large blast furnaces belonging to Krupps, which had the shiniest and most efficient-looking power plants I saw anywhere on the Rhine.[2]

Back of Mulhofen, to the east, is the village of Sayn, which contained the ruined castle of the princess of Sayn, destroyed in 1689 during the Thirty Years War. This old castle still has a heavy oaken door, hung on massive hand-wrought hinges and studded with heavy hand-forged iron bolts. The door is still in place on the second floor of the ruined tower or donjon. The moat and the enormous main hall outline are still visible, but, of course, there is no roof and the crumbling ruins are covered with a growth of heavy moss. Even the atmosphere around this old castle seems charged with hooded knights and halberds. Writing or scratching on the walls of the second floor of the tower, shows that the spot has been visited by untold numbers for centuries back. Some of the marks are curious monograms with long forgotten meanings. The old castle most probably has an interesting and bloody story to tell, if it could only speak.

Farther on to the north, is the town of Engers, population 4,000. Here is located a steel and stone-arch bridge of large proportions, built by the Russian prisoners of war who were billeted here from 1914 to 1917.

My old outfit, Company B, 39th Infantry, vehicle of my war service in France, was stationed at Engers for about two weeks during June and July 1919. After I discovered they were there, I therefore had the opportunity nearly every day to visit with some of my old buddies. However, a lot of the old-timers were missing, or had been transferred to other outfits like myself.

Belkin was on detached service with the Y.M.C.A. at Neuwied. O'Hara had been transferred to the S.O.S. near Paris. Vinelli and Brizee had long since left, Vinelli being transferred to a bakery outfit somewhere in the back areas, while Brizee was with the 59th Infantry Supply Train near Lerouville and Commercy, France. Sergeant Painting had now become a 2d lieutenant of Engineers in charge of barracks construction in the occupied area. Lieutenant Holstlaw, our original wartime company commander, was now again attached to the company, but had

2. The Krupp company started as a German steel foundry in the early nineteenth century, but by World War I was one of the world's largest arms manufacturers. At this time the company was led by Gustav Krupp von Bohlen and his wife Bertha.

Entrance to bridge at Engers, Germany, with bridge in foreground and Rhine River and village of Engers in background. Pvt. W. J. Haglund, Company A, Second Engineers, on guard. January 8, 1919. U.S. Army Signal Corps Collection, National Archives, 51717 [3084N9]. "Built by Russian prisoners of war, 1916–17," according to Howell.

to take second place as he was outranked by Cap't Eberlin.[3] It didn't seem to worry him much. One of the original cooks, Sergeant Unrath, was still with the company making the soup-gun layout look familiar. Corporal Andrews was the only one of

3. Barnard Eberlin (1895–1964) of New York City was commissioned a first lieutenant of infantry on April 29, 1917, promoted to captain on October 18, 1919, and discharged in January 1920. He served overseas with the 39th Infantry likely from the spring of 1919 until August 1919. *New York, Abstracts of World War I Military Service, 1917–1919*, accessed on Ancestry.com on December 31, 2015.

my original squad left with the company, and he expected to leave soon for an A.E.F. school of architecture located at Bonn, Germany. So that is the way my buddies were moved around after the war was over.

Belkin, now on detached service as a truck driver for the Y.M.C.A. at Neuwied, visited the old company one day at Engers. Luckily, I happened to be there also, so we had a pow-wow and talked over old times to our heart's content.

"Makes me cry," says Belkin, "ta come back ta the old outfit again an see hardly anyone I know, except Holstlaw, Andrews an one er two others. Whoever would a thought that Irish O'Hara would land in the S.O.S.? Then Stevens at Luxembourg, and Vinelli an all the other goldbricks all scattered too. But me, a good Hebrew lad, has ta be transferred ta the Yimka."

"What's a Yimka?" I inquired.

"Why the Y.M.C.A., ya big palooka," replied Belkin. "The Young Men's Chiselers Association."

"Well, you must feel right ta home, there," says I, sarcastically.

"You bet!" answers Belkin. "And I'se chiseled me a good Ford truck with plenty a gas, ta take you, Unrath an all the rest of my buddies fer a good ride all over the left bank of the Rhine. How do ya like that?"

"Boy! That's swell!" says I, somewhat doubtfully. "When do we start?"

Soon we were embarked on a long and enjoyable ride over the surrounding countryside which gave me a chance to see places that otherwise I would miss.

"How do ya like Germany, anyway?" I asked Belkin as we glided along.

"Fine. Germany is wonderful, but I'd rather be back in the good old U.S.A. again," answers Belkin.

"Me too," says I. "The big show is all over now, so we oughtta be home with our mamas."

"Don't laugh, an I'll tell ya something," continues Belkin. "With all the rest of you sojers fraternizing with fräuleins, an you with the haymow girls ya tells about, I'se got me a real honest ta goodness Kosher Sheba back in Neuwied, an she's a pip."

"Seems as though I've heard that one before," says I. "Come again."

"Believe it er not," says Belkin.

"The Queen of Sheba wuz one of King Solomon's thousand wives," suggests Corporal Andrews.

"An she wus black as coal," says Sergeant Unrath. "You ain't doin' any fraternizin' with colored folks, is you?"

"They ain't no coons over here on the Rhine," says Belkin. "What Sheba meant ta Solomon, my Sheba means ta me. An besides, her father is in the wholesale fungite business."

"What's a fungite?" inquires Sergeant Unruth.

"Vitamins fer yeast cakes an beer," replies Belkin, stepping on the gas.

"I'll buy the beer, too. Stop at the next gasthaus," says Sergeant Unrath, and we did.

All this reminds me that I owe Belkin twenty-five francs because, as usual, I was broke, not having been paid in five months.

At the town of Neuwied, where Belkin was stationed, the Y.M.C.A. operated the large Municiple Bath House for the benefit of Yanks in this area on leave. It was a magnificent establishment. There was also a large park containing a cycle racing track. The masonic order of Knights Templars also owned and maintained a medieval castle in this vicinity for years. The town itself, 22,000 pop. was founded in 1653 and is near the sight of old Roman camps dating back to 1020 A.D.

Now returning to Bendorf again. Directly opposite, across the Rhine, are the towns of Andernach, Kesselheim, St. Sebastian, Kaltenengers and Urmitz, each with its own ancient romantic history and legend. I could see the towers of most of these towns directly from Bendorf. I never visited any of them, as I was not much interested in feudal history at that time.

This is the Westerwald section of Germany, located between the Lahn and the Sieg Rivers. The locality which is mostly forests, also yields a sort of pumice-stone clay, gray in color, and used extensively by the natives in the manufacture of sundried brick, which you see piled in the back yards of most of the houses. One of these bricks made to standard size looks as heavy as an ordinary red brick, and has great tensile strength, but when held in the hand, it is as light as a piece of cork.

Along about June 25th, I had another visit from the colonel at the power-plant. This time he informed me that I had been transferred to the 58th Infantry, 4th Divis[ion] and now located in Coblenz. Also that the division was making ready to return to the United States.

"I don't suppose you want to leave me this time?" says the colonel with a wry smile.

"Whoopee! You bet!" I exclaimed. "This is the good news I've been waiting eleven months to hear, sir. When do I start?"

"At once. I wish I could go along too," replies the colonel. "Can you recommend anyone around here for your job?"

So I suggested the name of a Swedish boy from Wisconsin who was attached to a gas and oil outfit located here and tired of wrestling oil drums.

"If the Swede is available, you may report to Coblenz tomorrow," says the colonel very much satisfied.

I had to wait about three days longer, however, and during this time I remember there was a baby born on one of the Rhine barges just off the Bendorf wharf. The barge pulled in at Bendorf and asked for an army doctor, who luckily was available. He looked after them promptly and successfully. I had liked Bendorf but I was glad to leave. It meant the first leg of the long journey that would bring me back to the good old U.S.A.

Back to Coblenz

On July 2d therefore, I returned to the city of Coblenz and reported to Co. D, 58th Infantry at the old kaserne on the Falkensteinstrasse, where I had stayed when I was attached to the horse outfit. The horse unit, of course, had long since left with the rest of the 2d Battalion, 39th Inf., moving back to a new location near Luxembourg City. I am to stay around Coblenz until about July 11th, when the 4th Division is scheduled to start its movement back to the U.S. The few intervening days therefore, were spent in doing nothing of any importance, except following our own fancy most of the time, if we could get by with it.

While we were assigned to the 58th Infantry to return to the States, it was already decided by Julius Mannhiemer and myself, that we wouldn't do any unnecessary drilling with the 58th.[4]

4. Possibly Julius Maurice Mannheimer, born in Chicago on May 26, 1894, who served in the army from May 24, 1918, to August 8, 1919, and died May 19, 1982, in Los Angeles, California.

That would go against the grain of two old veterans of the 39th Infantry. Therefore, to drill with another regiment would be a disgrace, or so we made ourselves believe. We were too soft after having been on detached service away from rifle companies and would rather be goldbricks.

When it was time for drill, we would go up to the attic of the barracks and look out through the circular window facing the drill field. When the drilling was nicely under way, we would come down nonchalantly and walk out the front gate, where there was no sentry on duty in the daytime. We tried this a few times and inasmuch as no one seemed to care whether we drilled with the company, or not, why should we worry. We therefore went downtown to Coblenz and stayed all day, doing whatever we wished with our ample time. If anyone in the company wanted us, of course we could always be found right in the barracks at chow time.

One morning, however, we were stopped just as we were about to slip out the front gate of the barracks.

"Hey, you birds! Where ya goin' so nice an early in the morning?" inquires a sergeant of D Company, catching up with us.

We had been getting by so easily, that we were struck just plain dumb and couldn't think up a suitable excuse.

"Come along with me, you two!" orders the sergeant. "I've been lookin' fer a detail ta do a nice easy job, an one you'll like since you were lookin' around fer something to do. Right this way, men," says the sergeant, wisecracking sarcastically.

"We ain't lookin' fer no work," says Mannhiemer. "We got an appointment at the Y.M.C.A. cookin' school."

"Well now, ain't that jest fine ?," says the sergeant. "I've got a swell job fer you two kitchen mechanics right here, so ya won't need ta report ta the Y.M.C.A."

So we followed him over to the mess-hall, where we saw a large pile of newly arrived cordwood, thrown carelessly in the center of the driveway just outside the kitchen.

"I wants that wood piled up neatly inside the kitchen," orders the sergeant. "An when I says neatly, I means neet-ly, 'cause I've got an inspection on at 1.00 p.m. an the wood's gotta be inside. Savey?"

"Yah, yah, Kommandant!" we chorused, as the sergeant gave us a knowing grin and walked away.

So Mannhiemer and I worked like two beavers to get the large pile in the kitchen and properly placed before 1.00 p.m. We just about made it too. It was a swell job, every stick placed evenly just like brickwork and we were proud of it.

Just about the time we had laid the last stick, after working all through the noon hour without any chow, we heard someone shout "Attention!" As we turned to look, in walks a pompous brass-hat officer to inspect the kitchen.

"Who is in charge here?" he bellows importantly, looking all around.

"I am the sergeant in charge, sir," meekly answers our blustering sergeant of the morning, stepping forward and saluting.

The officer got red in the face and froze the sergeant with a glance. He scowled darkly at us too, but we laughed to ourselves at the discomfiture of the sergeant who had given us the job.

"Get that damn woodpile outta here at once and on the outside, where it belongs!" orders the officer. "I won't have an army kitchen looking like a sawmill. You ought to know better than that, sergeant!"

The laugh was on us. We had to drag all the wood out again and pile it up on the outside. Now was that nice, I ask you?

Directly across from our barracks was an apartment house located on a corner. It was about five stories in height and had a high class Bier Stube or Restauration at the street level. One afternoon we noticed two fräuleins seated on a third floor balcony facing our barracks, busily occupied with some kind of sewing. As Mannhiemer had a good pair of army field glasses, we looked the fräuleins over at our leisure. What we saw looked fairly good, so we began by trying to attract their attention. In this we finally succeeded, by reflecting the afternoon sun in their eyes with a mirror. We flirted with them thusly for a couple of days, and soon got up courage enough to go over and call on them, which was probably what they wanted anyway. Entering the apartment house, we had to knock on several doors before we could find the right one. Mannhiemer, who had been on detached service with the Jewish Welfare Board, had a goodly supply of gumdrops and Chocolat Menier, so we armed ourselves with these confections and walked right into home comforts. He could also speak fluent German and we both got along fine right from the start, as he interpreted for me when it was necessary. These girls entertained us much after the manner of the previous experiences I have already enumerated, so naturally we had a very pleasant time.

One afternoon however, the father, who was a railroad accountant, returned home earlier than usual and found us in his apartment alone with the girls. A straight laced old Prussian, with a dark gloomy face and a square head, he was not of the late army, however. He was much surprised and displeased at seeing us, naturally, and began scolding the girls for fraternizing with the Amerikanischer soldaten and having them alone in the house; a very scandalous thing, especially as we were the late enemy and should be properly snubbed. We were about to be thrown out on our ear when Mannhiemer hearing what was said to the girls, spoke to the old Prussian in German. Well now, he just thawed right out and things were fine after that. Nothing was too good for us. He brought us schnapps and more schnapps, while Mannhiemer told him all about a fake uncle living in Chicago and supposed to be engaged in the meat packing business. I just sat back and enjoyed the schnapps while they talked. I nearly laughed outright at Mannhiemer, who occasionally gave me the wink, for I knew that he was filling the old Prussian with all kinds of fake tales. The scene was very amusing to me, although I didn't know a word that was said.

These fräuleins too, were really nice girls, not rowdies. Their family was of the middle class type, much reduced in circumstances due to the long drawn-out war, but still proud and conservative. Later on we were to meet their mother and brother, absent at the time. When this occurred, the brother played classical selections for us on the piano. Their apartment was furnished and equipped like that of any American city, with gas range, electricity, central heating, bath and was in good taste, except for the German tendency to heaviness.

The night before we were to leave Coblenz permanently, these good people invited us over for dinner. This of course, was a welcome treat to soldiers who could always eat. They served us with the best they had to offer, which was meager. As far as they were concerned however, we pretended to enjoy it greatly. Their black bread was heavy and soggy, more like molasses cake than bread and tasting like sawdust. It couldn't have been very digestible either, but we knew it wouldn't affect the cast iron stomachs of soldiers such as we. It was made of potatoes and bran flour.[5] They also served us tea, then very scarce and highly prized by them, together with some sort of oleomargarine for butter, saccharine for sugar, a small amount of a nameless meat sausage fried in patty form, no condiments or pepper. But they had plenty of schnapps to drink and lots of apple-butter to spread on the bread, all of which suited our taste very well. They also presented us with their photographs, so we promised to correspond with them from the U.S.A. when we returned.

Later the same evening, Mannhiemer and I went across the street to our barracks and got a gallon can of gumdrops which Mannhiemer wouldn't be able to carry along to France because of the weight, some French cakes and two loaves of white bread. All this we brought back and presented to our German friends with the compliments of the Jewish Welfare Board and the U.S. Army. And how these girls did like their gumdrops! They told us that they had not tasted sweets of any kind since about 1916 and this was 1919. White bread was just like angel food cake to these people and it made us feel good to present them with a little taste of luxury, that we knew was appreciated.

One of the girls mentioned a short friendship she had enjoyed with an American army officer, whom she had met in some small hamlet back in the rear areas of the Rhineland. She inquired if we knew him, which of course we didn't. She said he was now in Coblenz, billeted in the home of a cousin of hers, a situation with which she was not at all pleased.

Our last days on the Rhine were therefore pleasant, but we could hardly wait for the start back to France and home. Coblenz had treated us well, but we were growing restless and wanted to be on the move.

Among other things set up and designed to amuse and instruct the soldier and keep him occupied and contented while sojourning on the Rhine, was the A.E.F. newspaper, called the "Amaroc News," meaning Army of Occupation. It was usually a four page sheet,

5. Thomas M. Johnson, a *St. Louis Post-Dispatch* special correspondent, reported that German "war bread" was causing illness in Germany, as it consisted of "the coarsest ground wheat, including bits of straw, a little rye and 40 per cent [*sic*] of potatoes." *St. Louis Post-Dispatch*, December 9, 1918.

like a country newspaper, edited, illustrated and printed by U.S. soldiers on German presses. This always welcome little messenger kept us in touch with the doings of the peace plenipotentiaries, then in Paris. Also excerpts from the world's news. It was distributed gratis to soldiers in the Coblenz area and other occupied parts of the Rhine, as well as back in France.[6]

It won't be very long now till we are on our way again, back to God's country and the U.S.A. After we leave, there will be no more Army of Occupation under that particular title. New soldiers fresh from the United States will soon be coming in to carry on. These young boys who know nothing of actual warfare will be called The American Forces in Germany, or the 8th Regiment, U.S. Regular Army. They will be under the direct command of Major General Henry T. Allen, a military diplomat and administrator, formerly commander of the 90th Infantry Division, A.E.F.

6. The daily *Amaroc News* was first printed in April 1919. Subscriptions reached a peak (63,000) in June 1919. The newspaper ceased publication in January 1923. A thorough history of the paper may be found in Alfred E. Cornebise's *The Amaroc News: The Daily Newspaper of the American Forces in Germany, 1919–1923* (Carbondale: Southern Illinois University Press, 1981).

Chapter 17

Back to the U.S. Via France (Demobilization)

Well, today seems to be the big day. At last, we are about to start on that long return junket, stage by stage, that will eventually end in the U.S.A. Early on the morning of July 11th, 1919, therefore, we find the 4th Combat Division saying a last farewell to Coblenz, the Army of Occupation and the Rhine.

Green recruits of the new 8th U.S. Regiment, mostly boys recently shipped in from the States, will now take over the areas occupied by the 4th and other combat divisions, and will keep our flag flying for several years longer at Coblenz and Fort Ehrenbreitstein. Later these boys will have a soft time of it on the Rhine, much better than we had experienced, due to the money exchange rate, when the U.S. dollar would purchase a whole satchelful of paper marks, as at that time the German currency was losing its value rapidly, day by day. These new soldiers even affected valets and housemaids. And still later on, some of them even married German frauliens and eventually brought them back to the United States. The soldiers of this regiment became our best drilled also, better than any that was ever sent to Europe, because that is all they knew; they never had a war background. Their spare time was mostly spent in playing polo and other athletic games and they saluted all the big wigs whose pleasure it was to visit Coblenz. Detachments of this regiment were also sent, as occasion demanded, to Paris, Brussels, Cologne, Bonn, and so on, but few if any ever went to Berlin.

Speaking of paper marks reminds me of a certain sale the army conducted at the remount depot over in Coblenz-Lutzel. A decrepit old mule along with some others, was placed on the auction block and offered to German farmer-civilian buyers. The army auctioneer ran the price up to the possible equivalent of five dollars and it took a small bale of paper marks, a cubic foot square, to pay off on the purchase. The auctioneer might just as well have given them the mules outright, as the value of the German currency was dropping rapidly, even as the sale took place.[1]

Another time, while on guard duty, I was approached by a civilian, who after much gesturing and ja-jahing, made me understand that he would like very much to have me purchase for him, a slab of Standard Navy chewing tobacco, then on sale to soldiers at the Army and Y.M.C.A. canteens. Each long slab of tobacco was divided into five squares, or plugs, to retail at ten cents each, or fifty cents for the whole slab. I could get it for thirty cents at the canteen. To be accommodating therefore, I bought the tobacco as requested, delivered it while on post the next day, collected fifty marks and a French kiss on each cheek for the service. But the German had paid me two dollars at the old exchange rate, for thirty cents worth of tobacco, according to the new exchange rate at that time. He was glad to get it also, at that price. The civilian had formerly worked for a short time as a mechanic in the U.S. and had therefore become acquainted with a good old American custom.

Conditions in Germany about this time were in a bad state. When well-dressed civilians, whom I noticed time and again hanging around our kitchen refuse barrels with little pails, would reach in and fish out small pieces of bacon, or other fat thrown out by the soldiers from their mess tins, things must have been in a sad state. The Armistice, when it came, must have been a welcome relief to these hard pressed civilians. I don't believe they scavenged the bacon so much to eat, as they did for boiling down to make into

1. From March to May 1919, the Americans auctioned off more than 5,500 horses and mules for farm work and nearly 200 for butchering. The German mark's value plummeted from 7.8 to the dollar in 1918 to 109 to the dollar in early 1920. Alexander F. Barnes, "'Representative of a Victorious People': The Doughboy Watch on the Rhine," *Army History*, Issue 77, Fall 2010, 13–14.

soap, or to use the grease for frying purposes with other food. There was practically no animal fat of any kind available to them in 1918 and 1919. Therefore, fats were worth fishing for.

At the quartermaster depot at Bendorf, there were German civilians of both sexes employed for the purpose of sorting over potatoes, carrots, onions, and so on, sent over from the U.S. for the army. In one instance they were engaged in cutting away the mouldy surface of "sow belly" bacon. The refuse therefore was often dumped in a nearby lot and the civilians of the town would come in large groups to get the onion sprouts, half mouldy potatoes and carrots, and bacon rinds to use for soup and soap.

Civilians working for the army however, in the warehouses, on railroads, power plants and elsewhere, received a full army ration each week as part of their pay and therefore were in better circumstance. That is, they received so many pounds of meat, bread, sugar, flour, coffee, milk and salt. Thus, at this early date, we were conducting a sort of Welfare and Work Relief bureau for these distressed, war impoverished people.

Many doughboys could tell you, if they so desired, interesting stories of their contacts and experience with the civilian population around these quartermaster depots and elsewhere—both humorous, spicy and tragic. But haven't I told you enough in this volume for one ex-doughboy?

So finally, after interminable waiting on the morning of the 11th, we boarded a long gray troop train made up of standard size U.S. boxcars, located in the yards of the terminal or back of the Main Bahnhof in Coblenz. These cars, of course, were about two and one-half times larger than the usual German boxcar, or French 40 & 8's, and were filled with straw, making them quite comfortable for the long ride back to Brest, France. The men are not to be packed in now as they would have been in war time, so there was plenty of leg room for each man, which added to our comfort and kept us good natured.

One old German railroad engineer, with whom I used to fraternize while on guard duty in the railroad yards, could never understand how it was, that we were able to get such a large number of U.S. boxcars to France without taking up all the available deck space on ships. I therefore explained, that these units were shipped knockdown in crates and reassembled by special railroad soldier-mechanics in the back areas, brought to France for the purpose. His reaction when I explained such things would be, to solemnly shake his head and say, "Ach! Der Kron Prinz und der Kaiser! Raus mit im! Allemagne kaput! (Away with the Crown Prince and the Kaiser! Germany is ruined!)."

Once the train got under motion, the soldiers were all smiles and exceedingly good natured; they just relaxed and "let 'er roll."

"Join the army an see the world!" brags one private, sitting in the boxcar door.

"Eyah! See the world through a messkit!" answers the chorus from the inside.

"Where do we go from here, boys? Where do we go from here?" hums a quartette.

"Hallelujah! Give us a handout!" shout a few of the wags through the car door at a Salvation Army worker, standing on the station platform.

They liked the Salvation Army, however.

"Who won the war?" someone inquires of a military policeman strutting importantly around a station platform, with a big pistol in his holster.

"The generals and the M.P.'s!" everybody answers in unison and so on during the long ride.[2]

The trip out of Germany and thence back to Brest, France, took about three days and nights and was made by way of Belgium. We passed through the following towns on our way out, along the west bank of the winding, romantic, Rhine.

July 11th, 1919—Niederbreisig (Rhine) Germany
Oberwinter (Rhine) Germany
Bonn (Rhine) Germany
July 12th, 1919—Godesberg (Rhine) Germany
Cologne or Koln (Rhine) Germany
Liege, Belgium
Charleroi, Belgium
Mons, Belgium

2. The editors of *The Skirmisher*, a magazine produced by the 4th Engineer Regiment in Germany from 1918–1919, cautioned members of the 4th Division not to take part in such arguments about "who won the war." "It may seem funny to yell this phrase to the M.P's," the editors argued, "but that M.P. possibly has two service stripes and a wound stripe or two," indicating lengthy service and a battlefield wound. No author, "Editorial—To the Replacements," *The Skirmisher*, May 10, 1919.

Valenciennes, France
Arras, France
July 13th, 1919—Sotteville, France
St. Aubin, France
L'Aigle, France
Sillé-le-Guillaume, France

By July 14th, we had arrived in ancient Brittany again, at the old familiar port of Brest, France. There is now an enormous military camp here, made up of wooden barracks and called Camp Pontanezen. This was on the site of the small tent camp where I stayed for a couple of days in May 1918, when I first arrived in France. It was amazing to see the change that had taken place in a little over a year. I have previously described somewhat, the construction of this camp. As we now see it, this is the largest military establishment in the world, a city in itself and much larger than the town of Brest. It has all the accoutrements of a city also, such as sewage, water and electric plants, laundries, fire dep't, a theater and other features, all necessary for it to function as an independent military city. It was under the direct command of Brigadier General Smedley D. Butler, U.S.M.C. and D.S.C., famous U.S. Soldier.[3]

Our stay here was for about ten days altogether, during which time we were paid, partly in French francs and the balance in U.S. currency of the good old long-green variety. It seemed good to

3. Smedley Darlington Butler (1881–1940) enlisted in the U.S. Marine Corps in 1898. He saw action in the Philippines, China, Nicaragua, Mexico, and Haiti and by 1917 had attained the rank of lieutenant colonel. Promoted to colonel (temporary) and sent to France, Butler longed to serve at the front, but was assigned to command of this camp instead in October 1918. Butler made many improvements to Camp Pontanezen. Promoted to brigadier general (temporary), Butler remained at the camp until July 1919. He received the Distinguished Service Medal for his "ability and energy" displayed in the management of Pontanezen, when "confronted with problems of extraordinary magnitude." Butler served again in China, was promoted to major general, and retired from the Marine Corps in 1931. He was awarded two Medals of Honor for heroism in Mexico and Haiti, but not the Distinguished Service Cross, as Howell indicates. U.S. Adjutant General's Office, *American Decorations*, 684. By the summer of 1919, one source described the camp as "in excellent shape," with good roads and the men "comfortably situated." Bach and Hall, *The Fourth Division*, 254. By the spring of 1919, the camp was used as an embarkation camp and had expanded to 1,000 acres. A number of improvements had been made, including the installation of more roads and "duckboard" footpaths. Some 450 barracks, each accommodating 110 men, and 5,000 floored tents, each accommodating 6 men, were available for use. M.W. Ireland, *The Medical Department of the United States Army in the World War*, 15 vols., 1921–29 (Washington, D.C.: U.S. Government Printing Office, 1927), Administration, American Expeditionary Forces, 2: 465–71. A complete list of the improvements instituted by Butler may be found in Lowell Thomas, *Old Gimlet Eye: The Adventures of Smedley D. Butler* (New York: Farrar & Rinehart, 1933), 254.

be able to handle the latter once more, as by now it had nearly become a stranger to us.

As we are now preparing to embark for the United States of America, there will be no further drilling or heavy discipline. All that we are now required to do, is to keep ourselves and our barracks clean, work in the mess kitchens peeling potatoes and carrots (except when we could get out of it), stand numerous inspections, get deloused (about three times), buy trinkets to take home and walk down the long hill, through Pontanezen to Brest, where special unofficial entertainment could now be found most anytime day or night, especially for foot-loose soldiers. A lot of our money went for vin-rouge too, and a lot more changed hands in good old army crap games.

Everyone was required to spend some time in the kitchens, or we didn't eat. I must have peeled at least a carload of carrots working nights in one of these kitchens, until I got wise to myself. A few of "us chiselers" had found out that the officers kept no record of those sent on kitchen details. Therefore, we took it upon ourselves to disappear to the barracks or elsewhere, after we had our midnight lunch safely stowed away. Some of the others would stay there, peeling and peeling, until early morning and then try to sleep in the barracks all through the daytime racket. It just couldn't be done and anyway, daytime was for other things. Slow motion bohunks could stand this, but others couldn't. Thus the disappearing act practiced by me and several others, was made possible because the officers had no check on us and also because they were too busy themselves fighting the "Battle of Paris" to pay any attention to our movements. As one mess sergeant put it—

"A hunerd an fif-i-ty men reports ta my kitchen, an works until after midnight lunch. By mornin' there's only about twenty left, but I never sees a one of them leave. Damn me, if I kin unnerstand it!"

But everyone had to help out in the kitchens to a certain extent, as long as our outfit was in the camp. This was right and as it should be, or we couldn't eat; so we did our bit part of the night at least. Anyway, we all got fed. They had the system so arranged here, that they could feed several thousand men in about fifteen minutes time, through a system of ganged kitchens and chow lines.

The chow was unusually good too, at least we were always hungry enough to eat it.

We had a grand time at Camp Pontanezen, as we seemed to have plenty of leisure, with a minimum amount of discipline. Nearly every night there was a prizefight staged in the camp arena, between soldiers and sailors from off the various ships anchored in Brest harbor. The *Leviathan*, the U.S. Transport, *Mount Vernon*, the U.S.S. *Manhatta* and a warship or two with destroyers, furnished many entertainers.[4] It was a constant conjecture among us, as to which vessel would be assigned for the return home. We preferred the "Levi-nathan" being the largest ship, but the *Kron Prinzessan Cecelia* (*Mt. Vernon*), a former Hamburg-American liner, looked good also.[5]

On Thursday morning July 24th, we boarded the U.S.S. *Mt. Vernon* after helping to coal her the day before. We found it to be a nice roomy ship, with decorations in the best German style, lavish with gilt, but now partly boarded over and enclosed at some points to prevent damage to its fittings by crowding, mulling, soldiery. This old Hamburg liner was 707 ft. long, 72 ft. wide and had a draft of 32 ft. of water. She was a four stacker with engines of 49,000 h.p. which could attain a speed of 23.5 knots per hour. When the World War broke out in August 1914, this ship was on the high seas between England and the U.S.A. carrying ten million dollars in gold bullion to England. She turned about in mid-ocean and returned to the U.S. where she was interned at Bar Harbor, Maine. When we entered the war against Germany in 1917, her crews mutinied and destroyed part of her engines by secret order of the German government. The United States then seized her, made the necessary repairs and placed her in the Army transport service, under the name of U.S.S. *Mt. Vernon*.

4. Likely the USS *Nopatin*, a transport built in 1913 as the *Manhattan* and acquired by the U.S. Navy in January 1918. *Nopatin* transported men and supplies between England and France.

5. *Leviathan*, formerly the *Vaterland*, Germany's largest passenger liner, was launched in 1913. Seized when the United States entered World War I and renamed *Leviathan*, the troop ship made 10 round trips between America and Europe before the end of the war, carrying a total of more than 100,000 troops. Following the Armistice, *Leviathan* made 9 trips carrying American troops home before being decommissioned in October 1919. The *Mount Vernon*, originally the *Kronprinzesin Cecilie*, was launched in 1906 and was likewise seized in 1917. The ship made 9 trips carrying U.S. troops to Europe, and was torpedoed by a U-Boat in September 1918, but managed to return to port. After repairs, *Mount Vernon* sailed from America for France in February 1919 to return U.S. troops. The ship was decommissioned in September 1919.

On one of her many trips from Brest to New York during the war, she was torpedoed just outside of Brest harbor and had to turn back to France. The shell struck her near the boilers on the left side, so they filled her up with concrete and again started for New York. She still had the concrete in her side when we were aboard, but no one would have known it from her looks or performance as there was no visible listing.

I can remember how sick all of us were, coming over on the *Dante Alighieri* in May 1918, but coming back on the much larger *Mt. Vernon* in August, with smooth seas most of the way, practically none of us were sick. We were as hard as nails anyway.

There was no rotten rabbit on this boat either; the food was good. We were served two good meals per day with a lunch in between, plenty of oranges and grapefruit which tasted mighty good to us after being deprived of these luxuries for over a year. Little luxuries which are more or less blasé in civilian life, were now appreciated to their utmost. We were required to do no work at all coming back, as there was a crew of 600 gobs aboard to care for 6600 doughboys, nurses and auxiliary and about fifty shell-shock victims. The latter were placed in a large cage, very similar to a park monkey cage, built on the stern end of the main deck of the ship. If they should start to rave or become violent, they would therefore hurt no one except themselves. But they were closely guarded day and night so as to stop any such action. All we had to do was to loll around the decks in the sun all day long. The soldiers often shot craps way up on the top deck behind the life boats.

Some misguided upper crust female, a society war worker with a superiority complex, was standing on the bridge deck one day with a half-baked "shavetail" lieutenant. She happened to notice the rough looking doughboys laying around, sunning themselves on the decks below and was very contemptuous of the soldiery. Within earshot of the ship's captain she remarked, "Look at those dirty pigs down there! All of them might better have been killed in France!"

Asked if she really meant it, she replied, "Why, certainly! They're only a riff-raff army, anyway!"

She was immediately arrested and confined under guard for the rest of the voyage. After that I don't know what happened to her.

View of deck of steamship *Mount Vernon*. Brest, France, May 5, 1918. U.S. Army Signal Corps Collection, National Archives, 13446 [1013Y8PA]).

While a lot of us thought we hated the army, we really didn't, but were actually proud of being in it. What we did hate most, was the domineering ego of some individuals who wore the uniform of commissioned officers. Petty disciplinary tactics employed by some of these hombres were a constant pain in the neck. We had left France somewhat reluctantly when it came right down to brass tacks. I, for one, was thankful that I had been fortunate enough to come through the Great Adventure with very little damage, whereas some of those who went across when I did and to whom I had become attached, would now never return. For these, we felt supreme regret, yet, their worldly troubles and worries were all over and we had more to come.

It certainly was a loss to the world, that some of these young men who went over with us, had to be cut down in the flower of their young manhood, but that is the supreme sacrifice of war. Those of us remaining, were full of the prospect of starting life all over again, so our dreams were rosy. Some would return home to certain happiness, some to sorrow, and for others the starting would be hard. We came back only to discover a changed world, a whole lot different than it was when we had left, a year and a half previously. The flag-wavers of the pre-France era had all suddenly disappeared. Returned soldiers were a drug on the market, and even at this writing, still are.

August 1st, we arrived at Jersey City, N.J., disembarked and went immediately in the warehouse, or boat-slip, where the Red Cross took us in charge. Each man was given a sandwich or two, a couple of bars of chocolate, a cup of excellent coffee and a big piece of good old lemon meringue pie. This certainly touched the spot if anything ever did.

Wooden frame dwellings and other houses along the river front, how funny they looked to us, after being so long acquainted with the stone, brick and tiled masonry of the Old World. Our pavements also looked funny, after our experience with the heavy cobblestone and white limestone paves of European hamlet and city.

Some of our pavements in this country are less than a foot in thickness and often but a few months old, while those of the old world have been in almost constant use for centuries. I have seen shell torn roads in France whose foundations were often as deep as ten feet. The cross-section thus disclosed by bursting shells, would be lined and seamed like rock fissures, with new lines or seams for each succeeding generation of soldiers, peasants, royalty or vandals whose feet and conveyances had worn down these same roads in conquest or vassalage, as far back as Attila the Hun, or Julius Caesar when he conquered Gaul.

The first three American girls we noticed around the docks, also looked funny to us, because their style of dress at the time was so much different from that of the old country to which we had grown accustomed. However, the American girls are the best in the world, of course, but as my old friend O'Hara would say, "The old country certain-lee do have some females of good design, after all."

As we had found out, they did have a certain charm of manner and a winsomeness that always captivated and intrigued those lonesome soldats who were fortunate enough to meet up with them.

Actual combat soldiers, however, whatever may be their reputation in the matter, seldom saw women of any description for weeks at a stretch during the progress of the war. Whatever may have been the experience of the soldier over there, he never forgot those near and dear to him back home—but some of them completely forgot him. The old country mademoiselles and fräuleins were expert in the use of cosmetics, when they had any, and practiced their feminine wiles like the maids of any other part of the world, so, even though they were classed as enemies in some cases, we liked them and didn't care who knew it—and I like to think they liked us.

Our stay was short on the docks at Jersey City. As soon as the ship discharged its soldier cargo, we boarded a regular troop train bound for Camp Merritt at Tenafly, N.J., where we stayed for a week, doing nothing in particular.[6] Discipline wasn't even thought of. Here the 4th Division was broken up, one regiment at a time. That is, men who were enlisted for the duration of the war only, were now mustered out. If they belonged to the East, they were sent to Camp Upton at Yaphank, L.I. or other camps close to their point of enlistment. Others went to Camp Dodge, Des Moines, Iowa with the balance of the 4th Division, and other western camps for demobilization.[7] Long term men or re-enlistments and regular officers, were sent to the future 4th Division Headquarters at Fort Dodge (1919) or otherwise assigned.

By 1923, the grand old "Ivy Division," the "Bull Dog" division of the Argonne and Vesle River campaigns and the original occupation troops in Germany, is all but forgotten. After a few years it existed chiefly in historical records and on paper in the war office. It was re-activated and assigned to the U.S. 3d Army under General Patton in World War II, serving in Italy and then making a name for itself when it spearheaded the invasion of France, near Cherbourg, capturing St. Lo and Montebourg (June 12th, 1944) in old

6. Named for Major General Wesley Merritt of Civil and Spanish American War fame, the camp was established in August 1917 as an embarkation camp for troops sailing from Hoboken, New Jersey. Located 15 miles northwest of Jersey City, Camp Merritt consisted of 1,264 buildings in a cantonment of 580 acres. More than 57,200 officers and men passed through the camp in July 1918 on their way overseas. After the armistice, the camp served as a debarkation camp for troops returning from Europe. *Order of Battle of the United States Land Forces in the World War*, vol. 3, pt. 2, 748–52.

7. Camp Upton, named in honor of Civil War Major General Emory Upton, was located five miles northeast of Yaphank, New York. Established in July 1917, the 4,000-acre cantonment contained nearly 1,500 buildings and could accommodate more than 43,000 troops. *Order of Battle of the United States Land Forces in the World War*, vol. 3, pt. II, 796–99. Camp Dodge, named for Civil War Major General Grenville Dodge and located about 12 miles north of Des Moines, Iowa, was established in June 1917. The cantonment area consisted of more than 3,300 acres, more than 1,400 buildings and had a troop capacity of more than 42,000 men. *Order of Battle of the United States Land Forces in the World War*, vol. 3, pt. II, 870–72.

Normandy under direct command of Major General R.O. Barton and Brigadier General Theodore Roosevelt. It helped to liberate Paris and then fought a bitter infantry battle in the Hurtgen Forest. From Dec 20th-26th 1944, tired and worn out, it pushed back the left shoulder of Von Rundstedt's German Army and saved the city of Luxembourg.[8]

The 39th Infantry Regiment of the 7th Brigade (39th & 47th Inf.) whose exploits are chiefly recorded in this volume also existed only in historical memory, and on army records assigned as a unit of the 7th Division, which was a pity and a sacrilege. It should ever remain a part of the glorious 4th, the "forgotten Fourth Division" with which its fame will always be inseparable. In World War II, it was re-activated at Fort Bragg, N.C. as a unit of the 9th Infantry Division and served throughout the war with distinction, upholding a glorious name.

The ceremony of breaking up a regiment can be sad and even old soldiers, hardened to anything, will sometimes display emotion. We all knew this to be the last time we would assemble as a unit. Officers were glum and silent as we stood in ranks in company front formation. Majors, Colonels, lieutenants, captains, even brigadiers, would now return to pre-war army rank, if they stayed in the Regular Army. Some of them had only been sergeants and corporals in the old standing army. Some would return to civilian life and be listed on the officer's reserve (O.R.C.) for a few years to come.

Those of us sent to Camp Upton, way out on the tip of Long Island, were subjected to another series of inspections, etc. This once famous camp of the valiant 27th Division, now contained only a skeleton soldier personnel, one or two Y.M.C.A. canteens and song leaders. The latter seemed to have lost their punch, pep and purpose.

We soldiers, about to be discharged, somehow didn't seem to warm up to the uplift boys any longer. Vast acres of silent barracks, now vacant and bare, which had once resounded to the tramp of marching legions, are now all packed away with their sagas and legends, in mothballs. Wars come and go, armies of young men go forth to fight to the far ends of the earth and return, all inspired by some pet phrase of propaganda. But those that return as well

8. Field Marshal Karl Rudolf Gerd von Rundstedt, Commander-in-Chief West, was overall commander of the German forces involved in the 1944 Ardennes Offensive.

as those left behind are soon forgotten, while nature, the song of the birds and the industrious tattoo of the woodpecker goes on forever, war or peace. What one of us returning to civilian life, ever dreamed that in twenty-five years this same camp would be reactivated for use again, to train troops for World War II.

After the usual army red tape, in which there is an effort to get you to re-enlist, with pay bonus and the usual sob story about home conditions and you're being sure of three squares per day with Uncle Sam, we were finally discharged from "this man's army" and more or less glad of it. After you were re-outfitted with new clothing throughout, and pronounced medically O.K. you were sent to the Long Island R.R. station at Yaphank, where the local station agent issued you a paid ticket to your point of original enlistment, handed you your much coveted honorable discharge papers and fifty dollars in cash. Thus, as we boarded a waiting train, a funny feeling would come over us, but we didn't look back. Here we are at long last, returning to the old pursuits of civilian life, still wearing the uniform of the U.S. Army but knowing that we are no longer a part of it.

Our connection with the army and the old A.E.F., great or small, has now long since passed into history and overshadowed by the newer exploits of the A.E.F. (both Atlantic & Pacific) of World War II. The stories we could tell of our experience, greatly amplified each time we repeat them have already been passed on to our children and grandchildren, who probably wonder at our greatness, if any. Yesterday there was glory for us, when we thought we were making the world safe for democracy, but it was only illusion. Our sons had to go out again, to make the world safe for democracy and rescue world humanity. And so today the glamour and romance of war no long holds any attraction for returning combat soldiers, veterans of World War II, who also are disillusioned.

The Statue of Liberty looked mighty good to us when we steamed into New York harbor (August 1st, 1919) but when we reached the old home town, as small and slow as it was, gave us a feeling a million times better. No matter how far you may stray from Main Street, U.S.A. you will always see the day when you will be glad to get back and view the old familiar scene, even though you may have become a stranger in your old home town.

When I reached home, my old tomcat "Petie" was waiting in the front yard. He greeted me with his usual "meow" as if I had never been away from home. The next instant I was standing with my arms around my old sweetheart—Mother.

The End

"Whatever be the fortunes of America, I accept them for my own. I shall die upon her bosom. She shall know no peril, but it is my peril, no conflict but it is my conflict, no abyss of ruin into which I shall not share her fall."

—Benjamin Morgan Palmer (U.S. Civil War—1860)[9]

9. Although Howell attempted to quote from the Presbyterian theologian's "Thanksgiving Sermon," delivered in New Orleans on November 29, 1860, Palmer actually said, "Whatever be the fortunes of the South, I accept them for my own." Thomas Cary Johnson, *The Life and Letters of Benjamin Morgan Palmer* (Nashville, TN: The Cumberland Press, 1906), 206–219.

Appendix A

Fourth Combat Division A.E.F. Who Were They? World War I & II

World War I

The Fourth Combat Division (Infantry) U.S. Regular Army, A.E.F. was organized at Camp Greene, Charlotte, North Carolina, December 10th, 1917 under the command of Major General George H. Cameron. It was made up of skeleton units taken from the old U.S. Regular Army. The 3d U.S. Regular Division under command of Major General Joseph T. Dickman also occupied the above camp at the same time.

The Fourth or "Ivy Division" consisted of the following regiments and auxiliary:

39th & 47th Infantry Regiments (7th Brigade)
58th & 59th Infantry Regiments (8th Brigade)
10th, 11th 12th , Machine Gun Battalions
13th, 16th, 18th , Field Artillery Regiments and the 4th Trench Mortar Battery (4th Field Artillery Brigade)
4th Regiment of Engineers
4th Field Signal Battalion
4th Ammunition and Supply Train
4th Sanitary Train
19th, 21st, 28th, 33d, Ambulance Companies and Field Hospitals
Original strength of the division was 27,000 men.

The insignia of the 4th Division, is four green, pointed, ivy leaves, grouped equally (N.E.S.W.) forming a sort of a Maltese Cross with stems branching out from a small circle in center, all mounted on an olive drab background so arranged as to form an inverted square or diamond.

Insignia of some description was worn on the left shoulder at the top of the sleeve by all divisions and had a twofold purpose. It was designed to create pride in the division itself, but mainly as a means of identification for the Military Police behind the lines, guns, limbers, caissons, etc. Most all divisions of the A.E.F. had plenty of stragglers at times who went absent without permission as soon as any fighting started in the lines of battle. History records that there were plenty in the Revolutionary and Civil Wars also who straggled or even deserted for various reasons.

The original strength of the 4th Div[ision] was 27,000 men. The total casualties to May 15th, 1919 (killed, wounded, missing) amounted to 14,000 men of whom 400 were officers. Two officers and 68 men were captured by the Germans. An idea of the size and effectiveness of a single U.S. Divis[ion] can better be obtained when it is known that the U.S. Div[ision] was about twice the size of English combat units and three times the size of the French and German first line combat divisions and storm troops.

The 4th U.S. Divis[ion] captured 2,856 prisoners, 44 field pieces and minnewerfers [minenwerfers] and advanced under heavy artillery and machine gun concentration a total of 32 kilometers. It also captured two tanks and many thousands of rounds of ammunition and supplies of all kinds both German and Austrian. It participated in every active engagement of major importance on all American fronts and was brigaded with the French VIth Army (164th & 33d Fr. Divis[ion]) under Degoutte and Gouraud during the Aisne-Marne Defensive (2d Battle of the Marne) north and east of Château Thierry. It received 19,599 replacements of whom parts were from the 76th Divis[ion] (Mass. Nat'nl [National] Army Camp Devens, Ayer, Mass) as well as western divisions. It contained thousands of men from western and southern states and practically every state in the Union.

The 4th Combat Division left Camp Greene, Charlotte, North Carolina April 18th 1918 for Camp Mills, Garden City, L.I.N.Y. It began overseas movement on May 1st 1918 from (secretly) Jersey

City and Hoboken N.J. The majority of the Divis[ion] and auxiliary landed in England and then proceeded across the English Channel to Boulogne and Calais (British sector near Belgium) by June 3d, 1918. The 39th & 58th Infantry Regiments however landed at Brest, France in old Brittany. The 58th was torpedoed by a German submarine just before entering Brest harbor and therefore had an early taste of war before actually landing on French soil. The 4th Field Artillery Brigade proceeded to Camp de Souge, near Bordeaux in southern France for training.

The 4th Division Commanders during the World War were as follows—

1. Major General George H. Cameron (organizer & original commander) (temporary commander Argonne)
1. Brigadier General Benjamin A. Poore (temporary, Aisne-Marne)
2. Major General John L. Hines (1st U.S. Army, St. Mihiel & Argonne)
3. Major General Mark L. Hersey (2d Army before Metz, Lorraine
   3d Army and Army of Occupation
   Headquarters at Nieder-Breisig, Rhine, Ger[many])

The 4th Combat Divis[ion] was engaged in the following major operations,

1. Aisne-Marne Defensive & Offensive (with French) (2d Battle of the Marne, Battle of Vesle River-Soissons), July 18th to August 20th 1918.
2. St. Mihiel Offensive (1st U.S. Army) Sep't 1st to 16th, 1918.
3. Meuse-Argonne Offensive (1st U.S. Army) Sep't 26th to Nov. 1st, 1918.
4. Lorraine Offensive (never fought) attached to 2d U.S. Army under Lieut. General R.L. Bullard before Metz. Nov. 1st to 11th, 1918.
5. Army of Occupation (3d U.S. Army) Nov. 14th 1918 to Aug. 1st 1919.

Units of the 4th Divis[ion] occupied areas in and around Coblenz au Rhine and Luxemburg and were first on the Rhine after the Armistice.

The Fourth Infantry Division, or "Ivy Division," a Regular Army outfit of the 1st U.S. Army under Major General John L. Hines, was placed in the lines west of Verdun and spearheaded the initial attack in the greatest battle ever fought by U.S. troops in this or any other war—the Meuse-Argonne. They advanced under continuous shellfire, day and night for twenty-four consecutive days without relief, warm food or shelter—a record never equaled by any other division. Later they were selected and became the first U.S. troops to reach the Rhine in 1918. From December 1918 to July 1919 they occupied and policed various points on the Rhine and in Luxemburg. They also were the main garrison of the City of Coblenz, or Main Army Headquarters (3d Army). Late in July 1919 they were relieved by the 8th U.S. Infantry and returned to the States.

World War II

The Fourth Infantry Division or "Ivy Division" of World War II was part of Lieutenant General Patton's 3d U.S. Army. They saw some service in Italy and then spearheaded the invasion of France at St. Lo and Montebourg, near Cherbourg, then went on to help liberate Paris. They were under the direct command of Major General R.O. Barton and Brigadier General Theodore Roosevelt. They sustained a heavy infantry attack within the Hurtgen Forest, stark combat in which they were successful. From Dec. 20th to Dec. 26th 1944, tired and worn out, they pushed back the shoulder of Von Rundstedt's German Army and saved the city of Luxemburg.

Appendix B

The 39th Infantry Regiment. Who Were They?

The 39th Infantry Regiment, 4th Division, U.S. Regular Army, A.E.F. consisted of about 3000 men and 100 officers. It was commanded throughout all its battle experience by Colonel Frank C. Bolles, D.S.C. [Distinguished Service Cross] (Argonne-Septsarges). The regiment was originally made up of three battalions of riflemen, or twelve companies of 250 men each with three commissioned officers per company (Co's A-B-C-D-E-F-G-H-I-J-K-L-M) and a captain or lieutenant in command of each company. Besides a Headquarters Co., it also had a Machine Gun Co. (11th) and Ammunition & Supply Train (39th). Two infantry regiments of the 4th Division, the 39th and 47th, constituted the 7th Brigade. This was commanded by Brigadier General Benjamin A. Poore (Croix de Guerre & D.S.C. Argonne) during the Aisne-Marne Defensive, east of Château Thierry and the Vesle River campaign between Soissons and Reims. The 58th & 59th Inf. Regiments, also of the 4th Divis[ion] constituted the 8th Brigade under Col. Booth and distinguished themselves in the Aisne around Priez and Hautevesnes.

The 39th Infantry was organized at the New York State Fairgrounds in Syracuse, N.Y. on June 1st 1917 through regular recruiting channels and from a nucleus of the old 30th Infantry, U.S. Reg. Army. Its original organizer and commander was Lieutenant Harry J. Holstlaw. After its movement to Camp Greene, Charlotte, North Carolina in October 1917 and subsequently north again to Camp Mills, Garden City, L.I. N.Y. in April 1918 with the rest of the 4th Divis[ion], it began overseas movement from Jersey City, N.J. on May 10th, 1918. It landed in Brest, France on May 25th, 1918 after a zigzag course at sea on the Italian liner *Dante Alighieri*, a voyage of 14 days. Two weeks afterward, it joined the rest of the 4th Divis[ion] at Calais, France (English sector, Flanders) on the English Channel about 50 miles from the Belgian border as part of the British reserve and for training. After a period of less than two weeks, the 4th Divis[ion] (less artillery) was rushed to Meaux (French sector 26 mi. from Paris) as a reserve for the 3d and 26th U.S. Divis[ions] then at Château Thierry. The 39th of course went along with them. The 1st Battalion (Co's A-B-C-D) was billeted in the open woods above the 12th century hamlet or village of Acy-en-Multien, between the upper and lower roads. The balance of the 39th Inf. as well as other units of the 4th Combat Divis[ion] were billeted at Trilport, Quincy, La Ferté-sous-Jouarre (near Château Thierry), Rosoy-sur-Ourcq and Lizy-sur-Ourcq (Gen. Cameron's headq[uarters].). All these towns were in the Marne valley.

The 39th Infantry was one of the crack combat units of the 4th Divis[ion] and served with distinction in every major engagement using U.S. Troops. It served with the French 33d Divis[ion] as part of Degoutte's VIth French Army in its earlier experience. The regiment received a citation from General Petain (defender of Verdun) and a Croix de Guerre on its flag for its action in the battles of July 18th–19th 1918 (Aisne-Marne) in a sector four miles from Château Thierry when it took the town of Chouy, 100 prisoners, several batteries of 88's and minenwerfers and destroyed numerous machine gun nests.

It was actively engaged in the Aisne-Marne Defensive and Offensive and the Battles of Vesle River-Soissons, St. Mihiel, and Meuse-Argonne Offensives. It was among the regiments in the first group of divisions selected to enter Germany with the Army of Occupation (3d Army). The 2d Battalion (Co's A-B-C-D) [Co's E-F-G-H] were the first U.S. troops on the Rhine after the signing of the Armistice. The 39th Inf. won distinction around Montfaucon, Brieulles, Nantillois, Romange, etc., in the Argonne. It was in action for twenty-four consecutive days and nights under continuous shellfire and blasting H.E. shells, without relief, no warm food or shelter. The French and English seldom kept regiments in the front lines more than a week.

The 2d Battalion of the 39th Infantry was the first U.S. troops to reach the Rhine in 1918. Units of the 39th occupied the main barracks on the Falkensteinstrasse in the city of Coblenz from early December 1918 until late July 1919 and served as the main military garrison of the town. Other units occupied various areas along the Rhine and in Luxembourg as part of the Army of Occupation (3d Army).

World War II

In the Second World War the 39th Infantry, which had existed only on paper in the war office for 20 years, was re-activated and trained at Fort Bragg, North Carolina. It served with distinction in the second war as a unit of the 9th Infantry Division, upholding a great and glorious reputation.

Appendix C

World War Americana

Mademoiselle from Armentieres*

1. Mademoiselle from Armentieres, parlez-vous,
   Mademoiselle from Armentieres, parlez-vous.
   The doughboy, he had beaucoup jack,
   Till Mademoiselle got on his track,
   Hinky, dinky, parlez-vous.
2. The Mademoiselle, she had no school, parlez-vous,
   The Mademoiselle, she had no school, parlez-vous.
   She couldn't add and that's a fact,
   But how that baby could subtract,
   Hinky, dinky, parlez-vous.
3. Mademoiselle from Armentieres, parlez-vous,
   Mademoiselle from Armentieres, parlez-vous.
   She kissed the Kellys and Cohens too,
   And many a Swede got the Spanish Flu,
   Hinky, dinky, parlez-vous.

*The above represents a full version of the famous song of the A.E.F. and is not usually found in war volumes. It has many more clever verses—spicy, humorous, tragic.

4. The Medical Corps, they held the line, parlez-vous,
   The Medical Corps, they held the line, parlez-vous.
   The Medical Corps, they held the line,
   With C.C. pills and iodine,
   Hinky, dinky, parlez-vous.
5. The "looies" claim they won the war, parlez-vous,
   The "looies" claim they won the war, parlez-vous.
   The old red cow had just one pelt,
   So the lieut. "shot the bull" for a Sam Browne belt,
   Hinky, dinky, parlez-vous.
6. The General got the Croix-de-Guerre, parlez-vous,
   The General got the Croix-de-Guerre, parlez-vous,
   The General got the Croix-de-Guerre,
   But the S.O.B. . . . . . . was never there,
   Hinky, dinky, parlez-vous.

Mademoiselle from Armentieres really began her military career with the English soldiers, as a "daughter fair" with "lily-white skin" and "golden hair," but before the war was over she was appropriated by the Yanks of the A.E.F. for their own particular sweetheart. She hails from every town in France.

"She is round, and soft, and nice,
And she wiggles her hips, like a pair of dice," etc.
Well, you can guess the rest.

Oh! how I hate to get up (In the morning)

"Oh, how I hate to get up in the morning!
Gee, but I'd like to remain in bed!
For the saddest blow of all,
Is to hear the bugle call;
'You've got to get up,
You've got to get up,
You've got to get up in the morning.'
Some day I'm going to murder the bugler!
Some day I'm going to stay in bed.
I'll give my uniform away,
And move to Phil-a-del-phi-ay,
And spend, the rest of my life in bed."

(copyright 1917 by Irving Berlin)

Appendix D

Station List of Company B, 39th Infantry, May–December 1918

On Transport Dante-Alighieri	At Brest France	Arrived France May 23, 18
STATION	Arrived	Left
Brest (Finistere)	May 23, 18	May 26, 18
Calais (Pas de Calais)	May 26, 18	May 28, 18
Samer (Pas de Calais)	May 28, 18	May 30, 18
Doudeauville (Pas de Calais)	May 30, 18	June 10, 18
Meaux (Pas de Calais)	June 12, 18	June 13, 18
Acy (Oise)	June 14, 18	July 15, 18
Noroy (Aisne)	July 15, 18	July 19, 18
Chouy (Aisne)	July 19, 18	July 20, 18
La Ferté Milon (Aisne)	July 20, 18	July 21, 18
Dammard (Aisne)	July 21, 18	July 25, 18
Latilly (Aisne)	July 25, 18	July 29, 18
Forêt de Fère (Aisne)	July 29, 18	August 2, 18
Forêt de Nesles (Aisne)	August 2, 18	August 3, 18
Forèt de Dôle (Aisne)	August 3, 18	August 12, 18
Forêt de Fère (Aisne)	August 12, 18	August 14, 18
Bois de Nogentel (Aisne)	August 15, 18	August 16, 18
Manois (Haute et Marne)	August 20, 18	August 31, 18
Marats-la-Grande (Meuse)	August 31, 18	September 5, 18

Haudainville (Meuse)	September 5, 18	September 11, 18
Septsarges (Meuse)	September 11, 18	October 24, 18
Jouy (Meuse)	October 24, 18	November 8, 18
Commercy (Meuse)	November 13, 18	November 20, 18
Heudicourt (Meuse)	November 20, 18	November 21, 18
Conflans (Meurthe et Moselle)	November 21, 18	November 22, 18
Algringen (Lorraine)	November 22, 18	November 23, 18
Gros Hettingen (Lorraine)	November 23, 18	December 2, 18
Trassen (Luxemburg)	December 3, 18	December 4, 18
Oberkirk [Oberemmel] (Germany)	December 4, 18	December 5, 18
Waldrach (Germany)	December 5, 18	December 6, 18
Lieser (Germany)	December 6, 18	December 7, 18
Kleinich (Germany)	December 7, 18	December 9, 18
Würrich (Germany)	December 9, 18	December 10, 18
Buch (Germany)	December 10, 18	December 13, 18
Illerich (Germany)	December 13, 18	December 14, 18
Mittelbaar (Germany)	December 14, 18	December 15, 18
Insul (Germany)	December 15, 18	December 18, 18
Schuld (Germany)	December 18, 18	December 28, 18
Kempenich (Germany)	December 28, 18	December 29, 18
Rieden (Germany)	December 29, 18	

Bibliography

Newspapers

Abilene Daily (KS) *Reflector*
Alton (IL) *Evening Telegraph*
The Alexandria (IN) *Daily Times-Tribune*
The Alta Vista Journal (Alma, KS)
The Boston (MA) *Herald*
The Bureau County Tribune (Princeton, IL)
The Bloomfield (IN) *News*
Burlington (VT) *Weekly Free Press*
The Cedar Rapids (IA) *Evening Gazette*
The Charlotte (NC) *News*
The Charlotte (NC) *Observer*
The Corydon (IN) *Republican*
The Daily Courier (Connellsville, PA)
Daily Kennebec Journal (Augusta, ME)
The Daily Northwestern (Oskosh, WI)
DuPage County (IL) *Register*
The Evening News (Harrisburg, PA)
Fitchburg (MA) *Daily Sentinel*
The Gaffney (SC) *Ledger*
The Gastonia (NC) *Gazette*
The Hartford (CT) *Courant*

The Holt County (MO) *Sentinel*
The Indianapolis Sunday Star
The Iola (KS) *Register*
The Ithaca (NY) *Journal*
Keowee Courier (Pickens, SC)
Modesto (CA) *Evening News*
The New Castle (PA) *Herald*
New York Times
Oakland (CA) *Tribune*
The Olean (NY) *Evening Herald*
Philadelphia Inquirer
St. Louis Post-Dispatch
The Topeka (KS) *Daily Capital*
The Tyrone (PA) *Daily Herald*
The Waterbury (CT) *Evening Democrat*
The Wilmington (NC) *Morning Star*

Books

American Battle Monuments Commission, *American Armies and Battlefields in Europe*. Washington, D.C.: U.S. Government Printing Office, 1938.

———. *4th Division Summary of Operations in the World War.* Washington, D.C.: U.S. Government Printing Office, 1944.

Bach, Christian A., and Henry Noble Hall. *The Fourth Division: Its Services and Achievements in the World War.* Garden City, NY: Issued by the Division, Country Life Press, 1920.

Bagby, Philip H. *American Representation in Occupied Germany, 1920–21.* 2 vols. Coblenz, Germany: No publisher, 1922.

Barnes, Alexander. *In a Strange Land: The American Occupation of Germany, 1918–1923.* Atglen, PA: Schiffer Military History, 2011.

Berry, Henry. *Make the Kaiser Dance: Living Memories of the Doughboy.* Garden City, NY: Doubleday, 1978.

Booth, Evangeline, and Grace Livingston Hill. *The War Romance of the Salvation Army*. Philadelphia: J.B. Lippincott, 1919.

Bullard, Robert Lee. *American Soldiers Also Fought*. New York: Longmans, Green & Co., 1936.

Canfield, Bruce. *U.S. Infantry Weapons of the First World War.* Lincoln, RI: Andrew Mowbray Co., 2000.

Center of Military History. *Order of Battle of the United States Land Forces in the World War*, 5 vols. Washington, D.C.: U.S. Army Center of Military History, 1988.

Coffman, Edward M. *The Regulars: The American Army, 1898–1941*. Cambridge: Harvard University Press, 2004.

Cole, Robert B., and Barnard Eberlin, eds. *The History of the 39th U.S. Infantry During the World War*. New York: Press of J.D. McGuire, 1919.

Connecticut, State of. *Office of the Adjutant General, Service Records, Connecticut Men and Women in the Armed Forces of the United States during World War, 1917–1920*. Hartford, CT: Office of the Adjutant General, 1941–1970?.

Cornebise, Alfred E. *The Amaroc News: The Daily Newspaper of the American Forces in Germany, 1919–1923*. Carbondale: Southern Illinois University Press, 1981.

Crowell, Benedict. *America's Munitions, 1917–1918*. Washington, D.C.: U.S. Government Printing Office, 1919.

Crowell, Benedict, and Robert Forrest Wilson. *The Road to France, Part II: The Transportation of Troops and Military Supplies, 1917–1918*. New Haven: Yale University Press, 1921.

DeWeerd, Harvey A. *President Wilson Fights His War: World War I and the American Intervention* (New York: The Macmillan Company, 1968.

Faulkner, Richard S. *The School of Hard Knocks: Combat Leadership in the American Expeditionary Forces*. College Station: Texas A&M University Press, 2012.

Ferrell, Robert H. *America's Deadliest Battle: Meuse-Argonne, 1918*. Lawrence: University Press of Kansas, 2007.

Fogarty, Richard S. *Race and War in France: Colonial Subjects in the French Army, 1914–1918*. Baltimore: The Johns Hopkins University Press, 2008.

Ford, Nancy Gentile. *Americans All! Foreign-born Soldiers in World War I*. College Station: Texas A&M University Press, 2001.

Goodhue, M.P., compiler. *Norton & Goodhue's Ithaca City Directory for 1909*. N.p.: M.P. Goodhue, 1909.

———, compiler. *Norton & Goodhue's Ithaca City Directory for 1913–1914*. N.p.: M.P. Goodhue, 1913.

———, M.P., compiler. *Norton & Goodhue's Ithaca City Directory for 1915–1916*. N.p.: M.P. Goodhue, 1915.

———, compiler. *Norton & Goodhue's Ithaca City Directory for 1919–20*. Ithaca, NY: Norton Printing Company, 1919.

Hanford, George, compiler. *Norton & Hanford's Ithaca City Directory for 1907*. N.p.: M.P. Goodhue, 1907.

Harbord, James G. *Leaves from a War Diary*. New York: Dodd, Mead & Company, 1925.

Hazen, Tracy Elliot. *The Hazen Family in America*. New Haven, CT: The Tuttle, Morehouse & Taylor Company, 1947.

Hourihane, Colum P., ed. *The Grove Encyclopedia of Medieval Art and Architecture*, 6 vols. New York: Oxford University Press, 2012.

Hyde, Charles K. *Storied Independent Automakers: Nash, Hudson, and American Motors*. Detroit: Wayne State University Press, 2009.

Ireland, M.W. *The Medical Department of the United States Army in the World War*, 15 vols., 1921–29. Washington, D.C.: U.S. Government Printing Office, 1927.

Jäger, Herbert. *German Artillery of World War One*. Ramsbury, UK: The Crowood Press, Ltd., 2001.

Johnson, Thomas Cary. *The Life and Letters of Benjamin Morgan Palmer*. Nashville, TN: The Cumberland Press, 1906.

Keene, Jennifer D. *Doughboys, the Great War, and the Remaking of America*. Baltimore: The Johns Hopkins University Press, 2001.

Landau, Henry. *Secrets of the White Lady*. New York: G.P. Putnam's Sons, 1935.

Larson, E.J.D. *Memoirs of France and the Eighty-Eighth Division*. Minneapolis, MN: Scott-Mitchell Publishing Co., 1920.

Lengel, Edward G. *Thunder and Flames: Americans in the Cruible of Combat, 1917–1918*. Lawrence: University Press of Kansas, 2015.

———. *To Conquer Hell: The Meuse-Argonne, 1918*. New York: Henry Holt and Company, 2008.

Library of Congress, Copyright Office. *Catalogue of Copyright Entries, Part 3: Musical Compositions, New Series, Volume 7, Part 1*. Washington, D.C.: U.S. Government Printing Office, 1912.

———. *Catalog of Copyright Entries, Part 1, Group 2, 1919, New Series, Volume 16, No. 9*. Washington, D.C.: U.S. Government Printing Office, 1919.

———. *Catalogue of Copyright Entries, Part 1: Books, Group 2, New Series, Volume 18, Part 2*. Washington, D.C.: U.S. Government Printing Office, 1921.

Liggett, Hunter. *A.E.F.: Ten Years Ago in France*. New York: Dodd, Mead and Company, 1928.

Moore, Frederick F. *Siberia To-day*. New York: D. Appleton and Company, 1919.

No author. *History of the Fortieth (Sunshine) Division*. Los Angeles, CA: C.S. Hutson & Co, 1920.

No author. *History of the 7th Infantry Brigade During the World War, 1918*. Cologne, Germany: M. Dumont Schauberg, 1919.

Palmer, Frederick. *John J. Pershing, General of the Armies: A Biography*. Harrisburg, PA: The Military Service Publishing Company, 1948.

Palmer, Frederick. *Our Greatest Battle (The Meuse-Argonne)*. New York: Dodd, Mead and Company, 1919.

Pershing, John J. *Final Report of Gen. John J. Pershing, Commander-in-Chief, American Expeditionary Forces.* Washington, D.C.: U.S. Government Printing Office, 1920.

———. *My Experiences in the World War.* 2 vols. New York: Frederick A. Stokes Company, 1931.

Prince, Justin G. "Artillery in the Meuse-Argonne." In *A Companion to the Meuse-Argonne Campaign*. Edited by Edward Lengel. New York: John Wiley & Sons, Inc., 2014.

Russell, James C., and William E. Moore. *The United States Navy in the World War*. Washington, D.C.: Pictorial Bureau, 1921.

Sampson & Murdock Co. *Rochester Directory.* Rochester, NY: Sampson & Murdock Co., Inc., 1921.

Sixty-Fifth Annual Report of the Association of Graduates of the United States Military Academy at West Point, New York, June 11, 1934. Newburgh, NY: The Moore Printing Company, 1934.

Sixty-Second Annual Report of the Association of Graduates, June 10, 1931. Chicago: The Lakeside Press, 1931.

Skillman, Willis Rowland. *The A.E.F.: Who They Were, What They Did, How They Did It*. Philadelphia: George W. Jacobs and Company, 1920.

Smith, Eugene W. *Trans-Atlantic Passenger Ships, Past and Present.* N.p.: By the author, 1947.

Smythe, Donald. *Pershing: General of the Armies*. Bloomington: Indiana University Press, 1986.

Sprenger, James Albert, and Franklin Spencer Edmonds, eds. *The Leave Areas of the American Expeditionary Forces, 1918–1919*. Philadelphia: The John C. Winston Company, 1928.

Thomas, Lowell. *Old Gimlet Eye: The Adventures of Smedley D. Butler.* New York: Farrar & Rinehart, 1933.

Trask, David F. *The AEF and Coalition Warmaking, 1917–1918*. Lawrence: University Press of Kansas, 1993.

Tucker, Spencer C., ed. *World War I: The Definitive Encyclopedia and Document Collection*, 5 vols. Santa Barbara, CA: ABC-CLIO, 2014.

U.S. Office of the Adjutant General, *American Decorations: A List of Awards of the Congressional Medal of Honor, the Distinguished-Service Cross and the Distinguished-Service Medal Awarded under Authority of the Congress of the United States, 1862–1926.* Washington, D.C.: U.S. Government Printing Office, 1927.

U.S. Adjutant General. *Manual of Interior Guard Duty, U.S. Army, 1914, Corrected to April 15, 1917.* Washington, D.C.: U.S. Government Printing Office, 1917.

U.S. Adjutant General. *Official Army Register, December 1, 1918.* Washington, D.C.: U.S. Government Printing Office, 1918.

———. *Official Army Register, January 1, 1920.* Washington, D.C.: U.S. Government Printing Office, 1920.

———. *Official Army Register, January 1, 1923.* Washington, D.C.: U.S. Government Printing Office, 1923.

———. *Official Army Register, January 1, 1925*. Washington, D.C.: U.S. Government Printing Office, 1925.

———. *Official Army Register, January 1, 1932.* Washington, D.C.: U.S. Government Printing Office, 1932.

———. *Official Army Register, January 1, 1933.* Washington, D.C.: U.S. Government Printing Office, 1933.

———. *Official Army Register, January 1, 1935.* Washington, D.C.: U.S. Government Printing Office, 1935.

———. *Official Army Register, January 1, 1940*. Washington, D.C.: U.S. Government Printing Office, 1940.

———. *Official Army Register, January 1, 1942*. Washington, D.C.: U.S. Government Printing Office, 1942.

———. *Official Army Register, 1 January 1944*. Washington, D.C.: U.S. Government Printing Office, 1944.

———. Official Army *Register 1 January 1945.* Washington, D.C.: U.S. Government Printing Office, 1945.

———. *Official Army and Air Force Register 1 January 1948.* 2 vols. Washington, D.C.: U.S. Government Printing Office, 1948.

U.S. Army Center of Military History. *United States Army in the World War, 1917–1919*, 18 vols. Washington, D.C.: U.S. Government Printing Office, 1991.

U.S. Army Ordnance Department. *Railway Artillery*, 2 vols. Washington, D.C.: U.S. Government Printing Office, 1921.

U.S. Congress, 74th Congress, 2d Session. Senate Report No. 1568, Calendar No. 1633, "Vincent P. Rousseau, Report to Accompany H.R. 4777," 1936.

U.S. Patent Office, *Annual Report of the Commissioner of Patents for the Year 1914.* Washington, D.C.: U.S. Government Printing Office, 1915.

U.S. War Department. *Histories of Two Hundred Fifty-One Division of the German Army which Participated in the War, 1914–1918.* Washington, D.C.: U.S. Government Printing Office, 1920.

Venzon, Anne Cipriano. *The United States in the First World War: An Encyclopedia.* New York: Garland Publishing, Inc., 1995.

Viereck, George Sylvester. *As They Saw Us: Foch, Ludendorff and Other Leaders Write Our War History*. Garden City, NY: Doubleday, Doran and Company, Inc., 1929.

Walker, William T., Jr. "The Chance of a Miracle at Montfaucon." In *A Companion to the Meuse-Argonne Campaign.* Edited by Edward G. Lengel. New York: John Wiley & Sons, Inc., 2014.

Walker, William. *Betrayal at Little Gibraltar: A German Fortress, a Treacherous American General, and the Battle to End World War I.* New York: Scribner, 2016.

West, Nigel. *Historical Dictionary of World War I Intelligence.* Lanham, MD: Rowman & Littlefield, 2014.

Wise, Frederic May and Meigs O. Frost. *A Marine Tells It to You.* New York: J.H. Sears & Company, Inc., 1929.

Yockelson, Mitchell. *Forty-Seven Days: How Pershing's Warriors Came of Age to Defeat the German Army in World War I.* New York: New American Library, 2016.

Manuscripts

U.S. National Archives and Records Administration, College Park, Maryland

Record Group 120, Records of the American Expeditionary Forces, World War I, Records of Combat Divisions 1917–1919, 4th Division, 4th Division Historical Decimal Files, 39th Infantry, Boxes 29–32.

Registers of Enlistments in the United States Army, 1798–1914, M233, National Archives and Records Administration.

Thirteenth Census of the United States, 1910, City of Ithaca, Tompkins County, New York, Ward 3, E.D. 184, T624, Roll 1083

Fourteenth Census of the United States, 1920, City of Ithaca, Tompkins County, New York, Ward 3, E.D. 188, T625, Roll 1265

Fifteenth Census of the United States, 1930, City of Rochester, Monroe County, New York, Ward 6, E.D. 28-22, T626, Roll 1449

Sixteenth Census of the United States, 1940, City of Rochester, Monroe County, New York, Ward 19, E.D. 65-285, T627, Roll 2850

U.S. Army Heritage and Education Center, Carlisle, Pennsylvania:

John A. Barnwell Letters, World War I Service Questionnaires

New York State Department of Health:

Death Certificate of Gerald A. Howell, Monroe County

National Personnel Records Center, St. Louis, Missouri:

Morning Reports of Company B, 39th U.S. Infantry for the month of December 1918

Muster Roll of Company B, 39th U.S. Infantry, April 30-June 30, 1918

Electronic Sources

Eddy, M.S. "Machine Gun Company, 39th Infantry (4th Division) in the Aisne-Marne Offensive," The Infantry School, Advance Course, 1929–30, Maneuver Center of Excellence Libraries, Donovan

Research Library, World War I Student Paper Collection, Fort Benning, Georgia.

Image Patent Database, United States Patent and Trademark Office

New York, Abstracts of World War I Military Service, 1917–1919, ancestry.com

Report of the Military Commander, Coblenz, Germany, From December 8, 1918 to May 22, 1919. Fort Leavenworth: The General Service Schools Press, 1921, U.S. Army Heritage and Education Center.

Smith, Walter B. "Operations of the 1st Battalion 39th Infantry (4th Division), in the Aisne-Marne Offensive, July 18–20, 1918," The Infantry School, Advanced Course, 1931–32, Maneuver Center of Excellence Libraries, Donovan Research Library, World War I Student Paper Collection, Fort Benning, Georgia.

Terrell, Henry. "The Attack of the 39th Infantry (U.S.) as part of the 33rd French Division South of Faverolles, July 18–19, 1918," The Infantry School, Advanced Officers' Course, 1923–1924, Maneuver Center of Excellence Libraries, Donovan Research Library, World War I Student Paper Collection, Fort Benning, Georgia.

World War I Draft Registration Cards, 1917–1918, ancestry.com

Articles

Association of Graduates, United States Military Academy. "Robert Lee Bullard." *Assembly* 7, no. 2 (July 1948): 3–5.

Association of Graduates, United States Military Academy. "Frank Crandall Bolles." *Assembly* 16, no. 3 (Fall 1957): 63–64.

Association of Graduates, United States Military Academy. "Hanson Edward Ely." *Assembly* 18, no. 1 (Spring, 1959): 83–84.

Barnes, Alexander F. "'Representative of a Victorious People': The Doughboy Watch on the Rhine." *Army History* Issue 77 (Fall 2010): 6–19.

Belloc, Hilaire. "America in the Argonne." *The American Legion Monthly* 5, no. 5 (November 1928): 28–46.

Faulkner, Richard S. "Disappearing Doughboys: The American Expeditionary Forces' Straggler Crisis in the Meuse-Argonne." *Army History*, Issue 83, Spring 2012, 6–25.

Kuhlman, Erika. "American Doughboys and German Frauleins: Sexuality, Patriarchy, and Privilege in the American-Occupied Rhineland, 1918–23." *The Journal of Military History* 71 (October 2007): 1077–1106.

Miller, H.W. "The German Long-Range Gun." *Army Ordnance* 4, no. 21 (November-December 1923): 167–76.

No author. "Editorial—To the Replacements." *The Skirmisher*, May 10, 1919.

No author. "Then and Now." *The American Legion Monthly 8*, no. 5 (May 1930): 31.

Index

C